The Electr̄...

The Stories We A

An Essay on Self-Creation

From time to time we all tend to wonder what sort of 'story' our life might comprise: what it means, where it is going, and whether it hangs together as a whole. William Lowell Randall sets out to explore certain implications of the familiar metaphor, 'the story of my life,' and analyses its possible significance with respect to our self-understanding. In *The Stories We Are* he suggests our life's story may be our most important possession.

To examine life-as-story involves the enrichment of the psychological approach we usually take in looking at learning and growth with a poetic approach. Randall explores the links between literature and life and speculates on what may be called 'the range of story-telling styles' according to which people compose their lives, transform the events of their lives into experiences, and seek coherence amid the diversity of the inner world of the self. In doing so, he draws on a variety of fields, including psychology, psychotherapy, theology, philosophy, feminist theory, and literary theory.

Using categories such as plot, character, point of view, and style, Randall plays with the possibility that we each make sense of the events of our lives to the extent that we weave them into our own unfolding novel, simultaneously as its author, narrator, main character, and reader – a novel we are continuously, sometimes consciously, re-storying. As a kind of 'poetics' of everyday life, he inquires into the narrative dimensions of our self-creation and the storied dynamics of our relationships with others, as members of the same family, community, or culture. In the process, he offers us a unique perspective on such features of our day-to-day world as secrecy, self-deception, gossip, prejudice, intimacy, maturity, and the proverbial 'art of living.'

WILLIAM LOWELL RANDALL is an instructor in the School of English Studies, Seneca College.

Diss: p. 7 (VN);

WILLIAM LOWELL RANDALL

The Stories We Are

An Essay on Self-Creation

UNIVERSITY OF TORONTO PRESS

Toronto Buffalo London

© University of Toronto Press Incorporated 1995
Toronto Buffalo London
Printed in Canada

ISBN 0-8020-0564-0 (cloth)
ISBN 0-8020-6986-x (paper)

Printed on acid-free paper

Canadian Cataloguing in Publication Data

Randall, William Lowell, 1950–
The stories we are : an essay on self-creation

Includes bibliographical references and index.
ISBN 0-8020-0564-0 (bound) ISBN 0-8020-6986-X (pbk.)

1. Psychology and Literature.
2. Narration (Rhetoric) – Psychological aspects.
3. Fiction – Psychological aspects.
4. Psychology – Biographical methods.
I. Title.

PN56.P93R35 1995   801'.92   C94-932603-8

University of Toronto Press acknowledges
the financial assistance to its publishing program of
the Canada Council and the Ontario Arts Council.

This book has been published with the help of a grant
from the Social Science Federation of Canada,
using funds provided by the Social Sciences and
Humanities Research Council of Canada.

Contents

Contents

Acknowledgments

This document could not have come together without the insight and input of a large number of people over a long period of time. Foremost are the members of my immediate family for shaping my own life-story in a thousand subtle ways: specifically, Donna for the mountain retreat she and John so generously let me use, Carol for her insistence that I make myself computer-friendly, my father for his love of language and his talents as a raconteur, and, finally, my mother for the stick-to-it-iveness she somehow bequeathed me, along with her longsuffering as a listener.

Next to these good folk are my peers and advisers at the Ontario Institute for Studies in Education – notably Don Brundage, Alan Thomas, and Ian Winchester – all of whom deserve my gratitude for keeping me honest and encouraged. Similarly deserving are Lois Kunkel for helping me 're-story my soul'; the Atkinson clan for keeping my story safe; Bill MacKinnon for the steadiness of his friendship; a parade of former parishioners for the grist from which much of this has been ground; and Don Cupitt of Emmanuel College, Cambridge, for his optimistic observation long ago and far away that 'it isn't until one's forties that one acquires a point of view.'

On the publishing front, I am indebted to Virgil Duff of the University of Toronto Press for his commitment to this project throughout; to Darlene Money for her care in copy-editing the final manuscript; and to Willard Brehaut, Jerome Bruner, Stephen Burns, Diana Denton, Virginia Griffin, John Haddad, Robert Hawkes, Carolyn Nesselroth, Rex Stainton Rogers, and Musa P. Shamuyarira for the stiff reading they each gave to one of its earlier incarnations.

Lastly, I am grateful to Glen Brotherston, Bill Cook, Sydney Dreksler, John Gillis, Jane Haddad, Elayne Harris, Gary Kenyon, Lutia Lausane, Galen McLeish, Bev Scott, Nancy Thompson, Norm Whitney, Carol Wilkinson, and Cristina Zepedeo for the delicious conversation I enjoyed with each of them in probing the themes of the book; to Inez Flemington, Doreen Kissick, Thelma Thompson, and Jack and Winona

Heslip for their moral and material support of its writing; to the family of the late W. Norman McLeod for the scholarship they established in his honour; and to my students and co-workers at Seneca College for the challenges they have placed in my path.

By way of a postscript to this litany, however, I have to express my profound appreciation to Sam Lee of Baker's Dozen Donuts, Toronto; Lynn Eddy of Eddy's Restaurant, Great Valley, New York; and the late Tim Horton of the Toronto Maple Leafs – who, along with their counterparts and patrons in coffee shops wherever, provided the sort of sanctuary – and the stories – that inspired me to write.

The Stories We Are:

An Essay on Self-Creation

PROLOGUE

A man is always a teller of tales;
he lives surrounded by his stories and
the stories of others; he sees everything
that happens to him through them,
and he tries to live his life as
if he were recounting it.

Jean-Paul Sartre, *Nausea*

Most of us, we could agree, like to talk about ourselves. Whether because it gives us a sense of power, makes us feel less lonely, or meets a myriad of needs at once, most of us appear to benefit from telling others – and, in a sense, ourselves – some portion or version of our personal history. Given the right conditions, often with only the hint of an invitation, most of us welcome the opportunity to pour out part or all of what we tend to think of, with a mixture of both affection and resignation, as the overall 'story' of our lives.

But is it true? Is our life a story? Is there such a thing as 'the story of my life'? The phrase is so familiar, it is difficult to keep from exclaiming, 'Of course there is!' But *is* there? Or are we indulging in what is merely a manner of speaking? If we are, then what do we mean, and what are the implications, when we speak in such a manner?

These may seem unusual questions to ponder, but pondering them, I believe, is an important thing to do, and doing so in some detail is what this book is about. This is a book about the relationship we have with our own lives, and about one of the commonest metaphors by which that relationship is conceived. It is about the merits of the metaphor of life-as-*story* – about where it comes from and where it leads us, where it holds up and where it breaks down. It is about the Pandora's box of insights and issues that is opened as soon as we push at such a metaphor, play with it, and peer into it through the lenses of typical story categories like plot and character and point of view. It is also about expanding the metaphor to embrace the possibility that we make sense of the events of our lives to the degree we incorporate them into our own unfolding *novel* – as simultaneously its narrator, protagonist, and reader – making it up as we go, so to speak, even authoring ourselves into being.

This is a book, then, about not only *having* a story but *being* a story as well, and about the complex relationship between the two. It is about self-creation through self-storying; about the literary dimensions of self-understanding; about 'the fictional side of human nature' (Hillman, 1975a, 128); and about the aesthetic aspects of human development as a whole, especially that great, long 'stage' of development we have come to call adulthood. It is about the links between experience and art, between life and literature, and between psychology and poetics. In short, it is about the poetics of self-creation.

In this introduction – this extended prologue to my larger story – I want to offer provisional definitions of some of the book's more pivotal terms. In fact, definition is a task to which I turn repeatedly throughout, given the semantic minefield through which this sort of undertaking requires us to tread. I also want to comment on the responses that might be elicited by the title of the book, as well as to sketch the agenda to which each chapter will attend. Finally, I want to outline the limitations by which the project as a whole is admittedly beset, due to the particular background, to the story, I happen to be bringing to it. Before tackling any of these tasks, however, let me stress the relevance of such an endeavour in the first place.

The Poetics of Self-Creation

Begging the question of definition straight away, few of us have not at some point been intrigued (or troubled) by our own unique 'story' – curious about its direction, concerned about its meaning, amazed at the material it contains: the sheer number of people we have known, places we have been, things we have said and done, thought and felt, suffered and seen. Similarly, few of us have never been touched by or entrusted with the story of someone else. Many of us – as counsellors, therapists, or teachers; partners, parents, or friends – become entrusted, indeed entwined, with others' stories in particularly intentional ways. When we do, what might be said to be happening is that we are helping them to get their story straight, to tell it in the fullest and truest way. Such a process is part and parcel of their development as persons, their drawing out, their e-*duc*-ation. Any discussion of education, however, leads us sooner or later to a discussion of learning, ambiguously though the two topics are linked. In a general way, then, an examination of the metaphor of life-as-story is an examination of the mystery of learning.

Much has been written, and rightly so, on the psychological dimensions of learning, and much again on the sociological ones. Much, too, has been written about the economics and the politics of learning. Very little, however, has been written about the *poetics* of learning. That there is value in such writing seems to me obvious for at least three related reasons.

First, it should be of interest to those – and I count myself among them – whose principal concern is the nature of adult learning. Within adult education and related circles, a number of counselling approaches are currently employed that are rooted in one version or another of the 'story' model. With roots in disciplines as diverse as gerontology, anthropology, and narratology, these include practices associated with labels like life review, guided autobiography, reminiscence therapy, bibliotherapy, oral history, and personal mythology. In addition, two influential movements in present-day adult education, namely feminism and popular education, share the conviction that storytelling is intrinsically empowering: that through the sharing of personal and corporate stories consciousness is raised, knowledge is generated, community is created, and a vision is stimulated that has transformative powers. The current epidemic of storytelling well outside these circles only testifies to the strength of this conviction. The need for evaluating such categories, then, seems to me self-evident – if for no other reason than to minimize the fuzzying effects of the enthusiasm with which talk of story is so often accompanied.

Second, and more specifically, an inquiry into the poetics of learning is called for because of the power of our 'past experience' (Brundage and MacKeracher, 1980, 32f), our 'self-concept,' and our personal 'baggage' (Even, 1987) in determining how, what, and why we adults learn. To the extent, however, that these things are rooted in or related to our story – a story about not only our past, but our present and future as well – the need to consider the construction of that story is unquestionable. The same is true when it comes to the process by which we do research in adult education. The qualitative method commonly employed entails interviewing subjects concerning specific aspects of their personal 'experience,' transcripts from which are then viewed as 'data' for conclusions drawn or theories devised. However, if this data is inseparable from a story – a story of considerable complexity, a story told afresh in the interview itself, and story that afterward the researcher artfully 'smooths' (Spence, 1986) – then the assumptions underlying this process require a particular brand of critical reflection (Mishler, 1986, 67f). By pondering the poetics of self-creation, I believe I am contributing to such reflection and pointing in the direction of a theoretical framework in terms of which it can be carried out more fully.

Third, whether our focus be therapy or practice, a discussion of life-as-story has particular significance in relation – as a sort of footnote – to a much larger debate within psychology as a whole. Giving rise to this debate is a shift from a predominantly psychodynamic view of personality to one that goes under labels like 'constructivist' (Bruner, 1987), 'constructive-developmentalist' (Kegan, 1982), or 'social constructionism' (Berger and Luckmann, 1967; Gergen, 1977; Gergen and Gergen, 1986; Shotter and Gergen, 1989; Shotter, 1993). In broad terms, the psychodynamic view is pre-occupied with drives, instincts, and causes, and, in a real sense, sees us in passive terms – even mechanical terms – as reacting this way and that to forces and factors that operate within us yet are largely beyond our control. In contrast, the constructivist view, while thoroughly appreciating the influence of societal forces on the shaping of our sense of self, opens the way for an appreciation of us as much more active, more protagonist, in the process of our own becoming (White and Epston, 1990, 82). It sees the mind, for example, not as an information processor or as a mediator between stimulus and response but as a 'world creator' (Chafe, 1990; Goodman, 1986). Indeed, it sees the whole 'self-process' (Lifton, 1970, 38) as a complicated hermeneutical enterprise in which we are continually reconstructing our world and our selves through the routine reinterpretation of our experience. Accordingly, it is able to see us as, in significant measure, the designers of our own development. For this reason, I think it fair to say that one of its implicit themes, like that articulated by psychologist Ira Progoff, is that 'each of us can become an artist-in-life with our finest creation being our own Self' (1975, 296).

In this connection, my eagerness to explore such an unusual (and

William Randall, *The Stories We Are: An Essay in Self-Creation*
Toronto: Univ. of Toronto Press, 1995

largely uncharted) area originates in my curiosity about popular usage
not only of 'the story of my life' but also of 'the art of living.' Indeed,
this dual curiosity constitutes a critical subplot threading its way
through the book as a whole. However glibly they get employed, both
expressions suggest subtle and easily missed insights into the mystery
of learning. Moreover, the two are linked. If it is meaningful to speak of
life as a story, it is meaningful to speak of living as an art, for a story is
an art form. Thus, the art of living may have much in common with that
of composing a story. In the tantalizing words of psychologist Jerome
Bruner, 'a life as lived is inseparable from a life as told' (1987, 31).

Start Here:

Some Provisional Definitions

This may help to explain the relevance of my inquiry, but it leaves
unanswered a few key questions. What, for example, does 'the poetics
of self-creation' actually mean? Moreover, what is 'poetics' and what
is 'self-creation,' and how are the two connected? In addition, how is
'self-creation' related to 'learning'?

By poetics, I do not mean merely poetic, which is an adjective obviously and can connote nothing more substantial than pretty or frilly
or nice – though many of the so-called learning experiences in our
lives might, under certain conditions, be accurately described by any
or all such words. *Poetics*, the noun, is in fact a technical term desig-
nating one branch of a broader avenue of philosophical inquiry known
as aesthetics, the central concern of which has traditionally been the
nature, function, and value of art. In its original, classical usage, beginning with Aristotle, poetics had to do with the articulation of rules for
the composition of poetry and drama – tragedy in particular. In modern times, however, its application has expanded to refer to the analysis and evaluation of literature in general, including kinds of literature
as diverse as autobiography and the novel. As one critic writes, poetics
'deals with the question "What is literature?" and with all possible
questions developed from it' (Rimmon-Kenan, 1983, 2). But even with
this broader use of the term, the relation of poetics to learning may
still not be clear.

By learning, I refer to what educator Alan Thomas calls 'a uniquely
human characteristic' (1992, 6). Beyond the 'learning' that animals may
be said to do as they develop the instinctive habits of their kind, learning is what most distinguishes us from other known forms of life. It
is a grand term, one of the grandest there is, yet it is an elusive term

to define. It can be understood variously as an act, an outcome, a possession, or merely the hoped-for result of teaching or education. As I
use the term here, however, it is primarily a process, a grand process.
In the words of philosopher John Dewey, it is 'the continuous reconstruction of experience' ([1916] 1966, 80). In learning, 'the learner opens
up himself, he stretches himself, he reaches out, he incorporates new
experience, he relates it to his previous experience, he reorganizes this
experience, he expresses or unfolds what is latent within him' (Kidd,
1973, 14).

Put another way, learning is that entire active process whereby, consciously or otherwise, we are forever trying to 'make meaning' out of
our existence and 'make something' out of our lives. In short, learning
is 'making': making sense, making a life, making ourselves. To borrow
a term from the poet, John Keats, learning is 'soul-making.' Thus, given
that 'to make' is one of the most basic definitions of 'to create,' learning is a creative process as well, perhaps *the* creative process par
excellence. 'A "new person" is created,' writes Thomas, 'with each act
of learning' (1992, 6); thus, 'we are the total of all we have learned.'
'We are what we learn,' echoes Kate, hero of Doris Lessing's novel *The
Summer before the Dark* (1973, 8). Ultimately, says Roby Kidd, 'the
cathedral that every learner is building is himself' (1973, 124). Such
comments, I believe, give us justification for seeing learning as synonymous with *self*-creation, and for seeing what educators call 'learning
projects' (Tough, 1971) as tied intimately to what others have called
'projects of self-creation' (Glover, 1988, 131ff).

Bringing the two together, the poetics of learning – or the poetics of
self-creation (and I shall use the phrases interchangeably) – looks at
learning from an unusual angle. It is concerned with how we continually organize and reorganize – how we story and re-story – both ourselves
and our world. In this way, it plays with possibilities and explores
problems that treatments of both the psychology of learning and the
politics of learning have a tendency to leave aside. In fact, the poetics of
learning offers a creative *via media* between the two – between the personal and the political. Thus, it offers a way out of the ideological dead-
lock in which advocates of each can so easily get caught.

Clearly, the central issue in this whole project is the definition of
'story' itself, a task to which I shall give greater attention in the second
chapter. For the time being, besides the issues already indicated, a
discussion of the poetics of learning will have to wrestle with such
foundational questions as:

- What *is* a story? What are the different *kinds* of stories? How do stories work? What is the secret of their appeal? How is our attraction to movies and novels – as well as to history and biography, gossip and jokes, ballads and ads – connected to the way in which we experience, and express, our identity as persons?
- What is involved in shifting our focus from *literary* stories to *lived* stories? In what respects is the process of change within a life like that within a story – i.e., with its world gradually expanding from beginning to end, its characters steadily unfolding, its plot 'thickening' chapter by chapter, and each, plot and character, shaping the nature and direction of the other?
- What are the implications of seeing the self as, at once, the main *character* in its own story, the principal *reader* of that story, and the story *teller*: striving, more or less consciously, to weave a coherent, believable, original, or at least interesting story from the events and experiences, the conditions and contingencies, the flotsam and jetsam, which constitute its life? And how do we assess its success in carrying out such an intricate enterprise? Is it possible, for example, to tell poor stories about ourselves, bad stories, untrue stories? By what criteria dare we make such judgments at all? If we *are*, as opposed to merely *have*, our stories, then what are the implications of these judgments for how we evaluate our lives?

These are just a few of the questions that I hope, in what follows, to investigate, integrate, or at the very least, acknowledge. If, in the process, I can demonstrate that they are not at all esoteric questions, nor merely interesting ones, but indeed very vital ones, then I shall count my efforts a success. And if they are very vital questions, if they are truly relevant to our lives in 'the real world,' then I would argue at the outset it is because of a very simple logic: the way we story our lives directly affects the way we understand ourselves; the way we understand ourselves directly affects the way we act; and the way we act directly affects the way the world is.

What's in a Title?

The title of this book – which compelled itself to me long before the contents to which it presumably relates – is *The Stories We Are*. The purpose of any title is of course to focus the imagination, for both readers and writers alike. For writers, it provides a symbol under which to organize their thoughts, as well as a starting-point and goal by which to structure the argument or arrange the plot. For readers, it sets certain questions in their minds and raises, if not great expectations, then at least some of that element of suspense – of that wondering 'what next?' – without which no story can proceed. As I have found from the reactions of countless colleagues, this title, too, sets certain questions in the mind, stirs up a mixture of expectations, and piques the curiosity as to what could or should ensue.

For example, it can stimulate within us the same warm reaction as is usually elicited by *story* itself. That is, in a way more technical terms like *narrative* and *text* cannot, story conjures up some of the joy we tasted in the past in reading our favourite novels or seeing our favourite films, or some of the coziness we felt as children at the mere utterance of that spell-binding phrase, 'once upon a time.' Why is this? Perhaps it is because, as adults, what we would like to be able to do, or at least have the permission to do, is to feel *cozy* with 'the most fascinating of all stories: The Story of My Life' (Le Guin, 1989a, 42). If so, such a title extends that permission.

In its plural form, however, *story* entices us with the sense of possibilities it conveys, the sense of options and alternatives. Not only might we be *a* story, it suggests, but we might be *many* stories as well – of many kinds, on many levels, with many subplots and versions. Also, given its emphasis on the stories that *we* are, it points beyond the individual dimension of our existence to the communal one. It reminds us that, in the end, none of us is an island whose saga can be separated from the story of a particular family, from the stories of colleagues and friends, from the countless larger stories of which our world is constructed, or indeed from history as a whole.

Furthermore, the very concept of story is sufficiently ambiguous that we can see it as synonymous with one of a number of other concepts besides: concepts such as *myth*, for example, which connotes a story that is larger than life, that is ancient and archetypal and deeply rooted in the human condition, yet within which our own individual story is conceivably cradled. Or *script*, which suggests a habitual pattern of behaviour, a configuration of ways of reacting to common life situations (Schank and Abelson, 1977), or a mode of being involved in relationships – whether functionally or dysfunctionally (Berne, 1964; Steiner, 1979). Or *fiction*, which connotes a certain made-up-ness, something that may be true but, if so, then surely not in the sense of *history* – a concept we like to think connotes 'the facts,' the way things *really* were, what actually happened, and not as biased and embellished by the inevitable imperfections of human memory. By the same token, the connection between story and *memory* may, in itself, be the principal reason for the title's attraction, given the extent to which we tend to be both amused and enriched by the activity of reminiscence, and given the ease with which we can usually appreciate the centrality of memory in the formation of our identity. The stories we *are*, moreover, implies that our stories are incomplete: that our lives are adventures still unfolding, mysteries yet unsolved, open books for whose endings we can but wait and see. As well, it can imply that each of us, in our own way and our own time, is legend-ary, fabul-ous, fantas-tic. It can also suggest that we 'are' who we *tell* ourselves we are; that 'we' are on some level story-tellers, free to tell ourselves however we wish; that there is therefore an intrinsically imaginative dimension to being human.

On the other hand, the very features of such a title that may pull us in may also put us off. To suggest that we *are* stories, as opposed to merely *have* or can *tell* stories, may unsettle us with the suggestion that the ground on which we stand is really shifting sand; that, even at our healthiest, our 'identity' is not a single reality but a multiple one; that, at best, we are a 'tangle of tales' (Cupitt, 1991, 10) and, at worst, a pack of lies. In addition, while alluding to the creative role we play in the process of our own becoming, such a title can imply that built into who we are is far more of an element of detachment from our own existence than we might otherwise wish to acknowledge; and that, although some such detachment is inevitable by virtue of self-consciousness itself, we are less active *livers* of our lives than we are passive *readers*, *watchers*, or even *dreamers* of them. It can also suggest that the business of being human can be analysed as a problem of cognition alone, a problem in how we conceptualize ourselves in our minds – and in words – and not also a problem of emotion or movement, music or image, colour or form – dimensions that would clearly be implied if, for instance, my title pointed to some other aesthetic medium instead, such as the dances or paintings or sculptures we are. Of such a suggestion we are correct to be cautious. In the words of one philosopher, 'to imply ... that story is by itself an adequate metaphor for interpreting human experience is to obscure the complexity of life under the rule of an aesthetic form. Life is distinguishable from literature, and the aesthetic categories applicable to storied literature do not exhaust human reality' (Estess, 1974, 433).

Though there are undoubtedly more respects in which my title both makes promises and yet raises problems concerning what ensues, I shall resist cataloguing these here. At some point a piece of writing must become more than a commentary on its own title. At the same time, by engaging in such commentary here, I have not only alluded to the agenda for what follows but also, I trust, set the tone. It is the tone suitable to an exercise in wondering 'what if?' – what if we take life-as-story at face value: an exercise that is admittedly less 'scientific' than it is speculative, less an argument than it is an inquiry, and less a report of research done than a record of the search itself. In all, it is less an assertion than an essay – in the literal sense intended by the French *essai*. It is an attempt to ask after a few of the subtler and perhaps overlooked aspects of the mystery of learning.

The Plan of the Book

What I shall be doing in the first chapter, 'The Aesthetics of Living,' is looking into the concept of *self*-creation, a phenomenon that gets strangely scant attention in our otherwise exuberant treatments of creativity *per se*. In considering some of the main means of self-creation, I shall introduce the role played in it by what philosopher Jonathan Glover calls 'inner story.' Picking up where Glover leaves off, I shall attempt to sort through some of the associations that the expression 'the story of my life' can bring to mind and the different levels on which its meaning can be taken. Finally, I shall begin to consider the means of self-creation and the meaning of 'the story of my life' in relation to the concept of 'the art of living.'

In the second chapter, 'Life and Literature,' I shall look more closely at the concept of story itself, in order to bring a discussion of *literary* story – of its overall dynamic, its essential elements, its basic allure – into some sort of interface with the discussion of *lived* story. What is distinct about this approach, however, is that, while literature is the lens, life is the focus, not the other way around. Rather than looking at the psychology in fiction, which is the usual trend (Hillman, 1989, 80), I shall be looking at the fiction in psychology – at 'the fictional side of human nature.' Such an exercise should help us to identify ways in which story is – and is not – a practicable category with which to view our lives. In the final section, I shall consider how the notion of 'the story of my life' is problematic when understood in the singular, insofar as our lives are constituted, within and without, by a plurality of stories.

In the third chapter, 'The Poetics of Learning,' I shall attempt to integrate insights from the two preceding chapters in order to apply a story perspective to concepts commonly associated with the study of adult learning and development. This leads me to explore what I call the *autobiographical imperative*, the *re-storying* of our souls, and, finally, the *novel-ty* of our lives – a notion suggested by Glover's observation that 'self-creation tends to make a life like a novel by a single author' (1988, 152). Throughout, I shall be trying to appreciate the range of differences between individual learners that pertain to their storying style. In the end, I shall return to the concept of 'the art of living' in light of what we can infer about the art of telling – and living – our personal stories.

Inherent Limitations

Having touched on the tone of the book and outlined its plan, the final matter I want to address is that of the principal limitations by which the project in general is beset. These limitations relate, first, to the writing itself and, second and more briefly, to the subject being written about.

Concerning the writing itself, though this essay is not a story in the normal sense of the word, it still consists of a series of intellectual 'events' arranged in such a way as to elicit certain intellectual and emotional responses in the reader. As such, it draws directly and indirectly upon the events, experiences, and emotions – indeed, the life story – of the writer. (Hence much of it is written not with 'the royal we' but with 'the general I.') Although I am not writing about *my* self-creation, or recounting the story of *my* life, I am working out issues that, while generally human, may be peculiarly mine – issues such as the relationship between continuity and change, appearance and reality, in my own life; between essence and existence, unity and diversity, in my particular personality; between intimacy and individuality, authenticity and author-ity, in my relationships; and between freedom and determinism, chance and destiny, in the world I happen to share with everyone else. Like any piece of writing then, it is ultimately a species of autobiography (Olney, 1980, 5), however thickly veiled. Hence it is bound by a particular range of perspectives.

It is bound, for example, by a perspective that is North American and middle-class. Though storytelling appears to be a universal phenomenon (White, 1980, 1), there may be modes of storytelling peculiar to other cultures and classes that qualify the claims I shall seem to be making here about how 'people in general' go about fashioning the stories of their lives. As well, our North American, middle-class context has tended to be relatively comfortable economically and stable politically; thus, to date at least, it has managed to escape the chronic upheavals – whether wars or famines or floods – that can impact so dramatically upon the life stories of so many in our world.

It is also an English perspective. Thus, though every language surely has its own word for story, my study is constricted by the peculiar set of meanings we associate with it as speakers of English – and of North American, middle-class English at that. Furthermore, the meaning we assign it will be in a particular relationship to the meanings we assign to each of a web of other words besides it, as we have already seen. It will assume a certain understanding of what stories are and of how they are structured, and of the connections between stories in general and the stream of time as a whole – something whose nature itself we can neither express nor explore except through the medium of a particular tongue.

We have become aware, however, that English, like other dominant tongues, is largely 'man-made' (Spender, 1980), a point that leads to a further perspective limiting my project: the male perspective. Though we live in an age when, largely through the vision and efforts of women, a more egalitarian order is being forged between the sexes, the personal stories of men and the personal stories of women may still be as different from each other – in both structure and style – as some would argue are the fictional stories by men from the fictional stories by women. 'The self, self-creation, and self-consciousness,' one critic insists, 'are profoundly different for women' (Friedman, 1988, 34). Though it is just such differences I shall be trying to note, my perspective as noter is male. Thus, what I note, and how I note it, is at best only half of the story.

In addition to being middle-class, North American, and male – not to mention white – the perspective from which I write is problematized still more because for ten years I was a minister of the Christian religion. Compared with other religions, Christianity – or, shall we say, Judaeo-Christianity – is a peculiarly historical tradition. By this I mean not simply that it has a history, but that it is founded on the conviction that reality itself – or at least *human* reality – is inherently storied, that all of the events of all of our lives constitute one grand, unfolding story (Cupitt, 1990, 172). This is *the* story, as it were, of the relationship between the world and its Creator, understood 'as the cosmic artist or story-teller by whom the significance of every event and every life is guaranteed' (Haught, 1984, 104). In a sense, such a historical consciousness undergirds all of Western culture, whether 'religious' or not, in so far as it can claim a Judaeo-Christian heritage. Though true that this heritage has helped bequeath to us our all-consuming sense of progress, as well as our much-maligned 'work ethic,' it has also implanted in us a basic and not necessarily negative conviction that history is somehow purposeful, that it is in that sense 'plotted,' and that each event and each moment in each of our lives is therefore novel, charged actually or potentially with unique significance. In his summary of the Christian view of time, theologian Langdon Gilkey expresses this conviction as follows: 'God, who is eternal, has created time with a beginning and an end. Time is thus finite, giving to each of its moments the possibility of being unique and unrepeatable. Time is, moreover, "going somewhere": from its beginning in creation it moves toward its end or goal, and its moments are meaningful because they lead to this eternal goal' (1965, 302).

Such a conviction has come under fire from several quarters, many of them within Christianity itself (Cupitt, 1991; Taylor, 1984). None the less, having worked and spoken and listened – indeed grown up – in an explicitly Christian context, I have lived much of my thinking life in its shadow. Thus, no matter how honestly I acknowledge it here, it has undoubtedly influenced not only my approach to the questions I wrestle with but also my choice of such questions in the first place.

But my past profession has shaped this project not only philosophically but practically too. Operating in the unique setting of parish ministry – though this could be the case in any setting in which an element of counselling is involved, including an educational one – I found it difficult to avoid the conclusion that the most precious possession each of us can claim is our unique personal 'story,' especially the older we grow, the more we move around, or the more extreme our circumstances due to recessions, depressions, disease, and the like. In the final analysis, our story may be all we have. As what we live *in* and what we see the world *through*, it is simultaneously our greatest resource and our biggest burden, playing in our learning the same dual role of help and hindrance that is assigned to 'past experience'

(Brundage and MacKeracher, 1980, 97–9). Our story is to our existence, that is, as a pearl is to an oyster: both irritant and prize, albatross and achievement. Either way, I found it difficult not to feel that if only we are offered a safe and hospitable space in which we can tell and re-tell our story however we wish, then through the storytelling process itself, we open ourselves to whatever measure of clarification or heal-ing for which we are ready at the time. And even if with such a 'talk-ing cure' we never quite get to the 'true' story of who we are, it seemed to me that there is still value in the exercise of becoming aware of, sifting through, and trying to integrate the various versions of that story that rumble around inside us.

I found it difficult not to conclude, therefore, that the process of self-creation is in significant respects a *poetic* enterprise, because of what can be seen as our concern to tell – and live – our stories as integrally, as individually, or, at the very least, as interestingly as we can. Indeed, the hunch at the heart of this book is that this concern is central to our being *human*, both guiding our interpretations of the events of our own lives and structuring our interactions with the lives of others. And yet, in our analyses of humanness to date we may have focused so much on what makes us alike that we have overlooked what makes us unique. If so, I hope to help right that imbalance.

Finally, the limitations that concern the subject I am writing about have to do with its inevitably interdisciplinary nature. This follows from the nature of both life and story themselves. Life is never 'about' any one thing, or any one subject, nor is a story. It is about many things, many subjects, all at once: psychology and ethics, sociology and medicine, history and art, economics and geography, politics and religion. Accordingly, to investigate how the two of these converge in the notion of life-story, and in the notion that we create ourselves through the ways we story our lives, is to situate ourselves – as educa-tors typically do anyway[1] – at the intersection of a bewildering num-ber of fields. This accounts for the less than straight-arrow manner in which I at times proceed, criss-crossing the same territory, spiralling around the same issues, wrestling with the same questions – albeit from a fresh angle every time. This is unavoidable; with such a topic, it is impossible to think in a straight line. As philosopher Herbert Fingarette has observed, 'the idea that we are constitutive of our own experience crosses philosophy, theology, literary criticism, and psychol-ogy' (Kegan, 1982, 11). To Fingarette's list we must add other fields as well, such as anthropology, sociology, and social psychology, narratology, media studies, and feminist studies – not to mention the 'field' of what professional storytellers, novelists for instance, tend to write about the *process* of storytelling itself. From all such sources I shall in fact be drawing throughout, which means that this is ultimately not a book on any one area.

This is not a book on psychoanalysis, though aspects of current debates within that field will surely be echoed. Nor is it a book on the philosophy of either history, personal identity, or self-deception, though themes from the long-standing discussions in each of these areas will undoubtedly be incorporated. Nor, I must stress, is it a book on literary theory (mercifully, since the world of such theory is presently so much in ferment), though literary categories are definitely invoked and though the literary dimensions to ordinary self-understanding, as well as the overall links between literature and life, fiction and fact, will naturally be central. Nor, strictly speaking, is it a book on either of those two types of literature we automatically think of as 'stories' of people's lives, namely autobiography and biography – though a host of psychoanalytic, philosophical, and literary concerns clearly converge in the analysis of each, and though the range of ways we respond to 'the autobiographical imperative,' not simply in writing but in living as well, is an issue of utmost interest.

Ultimately, this is a book about a particular aspect of 'the mysterious yet mundane character of everyday life' (Harré, 1993, vii). It is about our everyday allusions to 'the *story* of my life.' To the extent this is a subject in the philosophy of history, etc., then so be it; I shall be attentive to what thinkers are saying within each of these fields. To the extent it is a subject in literary theory, then so be it once again; I shall be entertaining what the literary theorists are saying about the structure of story, in both its fictional and non-fictional forms. To the extent it is a psychological subject, a sociological subject, or an anthropological subject, then so be it as well; I shall borrow from thinking within each of these fields, too. My dilemma is that in the final analysis it is a subject within that one peculiar field we know simply as 'life.' Obviously, this poses a problem. But perhaps it presents an opportunity as well. While it may frustrate our academic side, it can also free our artistic side – free us to relax, to wean ourselves from our dependency on discipline-d thought, and to let our imaginations fly. It can free us to play with the fearsome but empowering perspective that we are ultimately not pawns of historical or biological processes but, more than we realize, the composers of our own lives and the tellers of our own tales.

> I <

THE AESTHETICS
OF LIVING

I cannot experience your experience.
You cannot experience my experience.
We are both invisible men. All men
Are invisible to one another. Experience
is man's invisibility to man.
Experience used to be called the Soul.

R.D. Laing, *The Politics of Experience*

Story is to human beings what the pearl
is to the oyster.

Joseph Gold, 'The Function of Fiction'

Introduction

The story of my life: what are the implications – and what are the limitations – of this familiar figure of speech? What insights do we generate
concerning the nature of our everyday lives when we examine it
through the lenses of traditional story categories, such as plot, character, and point of view? What issues do we bring to the surface about
our development as persons, about our relationships, about our self-
consciousness itself, when we extend it to include the possibility that
we are each in the midst of our own unfolding novel, as its
author/narrator, its protagonist, and its reader all at once?

To ask such questions, which are in fact the focus of this work, is
to explore issues that concern what the French philosopher Foucault
calls 'the aesthetics of existence' (1988, 47ff). However, thinking of
existence – thinking of our life – as an aesthetic enterprise may not be
entirely familiar to us, dominated as our age has been by the scientific
one. Yet, over the years, figures of speech from one aesthetic medium

after another have wormed their way into the heart of our everyday speech.

One whole family of these, for example, relates to life-as-theatre, a metaphor intriguingly unpacked by Erving Goffman in an inquiry built as much on aesthetic grounds as on those of the social sciences (1959). Accordingly, we 'act,' we 'set the stage,' we 'make a scene,' or we wonder 'what goes on behind the scenes.' Moreover, when we distrust the 'acts' of others, we describe them as 'a song and dance' or a 'farce.' By the same token, we 'paint a scenario' and we 'picture a scene'; we 'march to the beat of a different drummer' and we 'dance to a different tune.' And so the list goes. Though figures of speech from the realm of computers can nowadays seem as numerous as those from the arts (we 'interface,' we 'network,' we are 'programmed,' etc.), perhaps of *all* the arts, the literary ones – specifically the narrative ones, those of story – have supplied expressions that are most central to the vocabulary with which we negotiate our world. Writer Annie Dillard goes so far as to say that 'since words do indeed refer to all the aspects of the world that we know – nature, culture, feeling, and idea – the literary arts are in a better position to interpret the world in all its breadth than are the other arts' (1982, 146–7).

We speak about such-and-such being, for instance, 'the story of my life,' our voices tinged with pleasure or pride, resignation or regret. Or we see some recurring pattern in our behaviour, our relationships, or the world around us, and we bemoan – or we rationalize – that, alas, it is 'the same old story.' Similarly, we hear the 'sob story' of a friend or we suffer through a neighbour's 'tale of woe.' And we listen to the elderly, as we leaf with them through photos of their past, sighing how they must someday write a book. We describe a particular individual as having a certain 'character,' while someone who is a real 'character' (perhaps also a teller of 'tall tales') we see as comic-al or fabul-ous or fantast-ic, – even legend-ary: 'a legend in his time.' Another person, we speak of as living a lie, the story she is enacting seeming hypocritical, deceptive, false. Another, we see as living in a fantasy world, or leading a story-book life, while still another appears to enjoy such a romantic, exotic existence, so melodramatic, so full of ups and downs, that we say his life 'reads like a soap opera.' On a few delicious occasions, upon hearing of the misadventures of some person we happen not to like, we can find ourselves smirking quietly with each added complication, smacking our lips conspiratorially at their unfolding fate, smiling cattily at how nicely 'the plot thickens.' And how keenly we wish we knew 'the *whole* story' or 'the other *side* of the story'! The adage about not 'judging a book by its cover' also of course implies a story connection, as does the phrase 'reading someone like a book' (Nierenberg and Calero, 1973), or 'reading between the lines' of their actions or words. Furthermore, it is common to conceive of some new venture on which we embark as 'turning over a new leaf' in 'the book of life' or as the beginning of one 'chapter' and the end of another. The word 'venture' itself suggests 'ad-venture,' some sense of which is surely at work in our approach to each new day, given the expectancy, the suspense, or at the very least, the curiosity with which we wonder 'whatever will happen next.'

But where does such language originate and what does it mean? Can we write it off as merely a manner of speaking – for surely most language is metaphorical at base, especially that with which we talk about life as a whole (Kenyon, Birren, and Schroots, 1991), whether as journey or joke, battle or game? Or are we trying to capture with it a crucial component of our existence, a fundamental if elusive feature of our everyday lives? On some deep level, do we indeed perceive ourselves as not only *having* but in fact *being* stories – stories in the very process of unfolding? If so, to what extent do we actually author, or create, these stories, and by what means? Furthermore, how do we assess their success as *creative* products, as *aesthetic* achievements, as *works of art*?

My agenda in this opening chapter is to begin wrestling with such enticing questions by attending to four intertwining tasks. The first and most obvious is to consider the nature of what I call 'self-creation.' I do this by situating the concept of self-creation in relation to the broader concept of creativity *per se*; then, by distinguishing it from more popular self- concepts like self-discovery, self-disclosure, self-acceptance, and, especially, self-actualization. The second task is to consider the principal means by which self-creation occurs: specifically, the material, the behaviourial, and the hermeneutical. The third task is to explore the merits of 'story' as a medium for understanding the hermeneutical dimension in particular. This involves cataloguing the principal levels on which the notion of 'life-story' can be taken, as well as entertaining the theory that we transform the *events* of our lives into *experiences* to the extent we weave them into stories. The fourth and final task is to speculate on the concept of 'the art of living,' to ponder the applicability of categories like *art* and *craft* in evaluating the selves we create, and to make certain observations about the links between

the arts of telling a story and living a life – observations that in ensuing sections I shall obviously seek to extend.

The Question of Creativity

Like truth, time, reality, and other grand concepts of traditional interest to philosophers, including learning, creativity is notoriously difficult to define. Exactly what it is, where it comes from, and how it may
be elicited or instilled have been chronic questions throughout the
history of human thought. Indeed, the most pressing question may be
whether it is even an 'it' at all, or merely a more or less helpful fiction
for an aspect of our existence that we assume, erroneously, to be
distinctive and real.

Despite this uncertainty, our culture appears enamoured with the
word. A tour of our local bookshop reveals how intense is its popularity. The psychology section – or 'self-help' section, as it is increasingly
called – is a case in point. 'Creative' titles are legion: *Creative Visualization, Creative Intimacy, Creative Marriage, Creative Aggression, Creative
Divorce*. Though this particular sequence is of course accidental, the list
goes on. Indeed, in the 1993–4 issue of *Books in Print*, more than a
thousand titles are listed in which the very first word is some variation of *creativity* or *create*. In addition, in the Metropolitan Toronto telephone book for 1994 are more than a hundred entries in which *creative*
is the initial descriptor for the company in question. These run the
gamut from Creative Aquatics to Creative Carpentry, Creative Crepes
to Creative Graphics, and Creative Marketing Services to Creative
Vinyl to, inevitably, Creativity Plus.

Not surprisingly, the popularity of creativity has spawned – though
possibly also been spawned by – a tremendous interest on the part of
academics. Scholarly literature on creativity, however, has tended to
orbit around one or another of three principal focuses: creative products,
creative processes, and creative persons (Torrance, 1967; Rothenberg and
Hausman, 1976; Getzels, 1985; Bailin, 1988).

Products, Processes, and Persons

When the question of creativity is approached in terms of creative products, the central issue is the valuation of individual works of art. For

example, what prompts us to consider this particular statue a 'creative masterpiece'? Or what qualities render this *oeuvre* 'a thing of beauty and a joy forever'? Or what enables this symphony or this painting or this poem to capture the imagination of so many of us with so much power over so many years?

When the question of creativity is approached in terms of creative processes, the central issue is not so much philosophical as it is practical; the questions asked are less 'how come' than 'how to.' In a materialistic society, bent on 'progress' at any price, this should not surprise us. It is less critical to *define* creativity than simply to set it in motion because, whatever they may be, creative processes work. They produce creative products, that is, and not only in the peculiarly aesthetic realm but in the realm of mathematics as well (models and formulae), of science (theories and technologies), of education (programs and pedagogies), and of course of organizations (productivity and profit).

When the question of creativity is approached in terms of creative persons, the central issue is different again. The questions asked concern what it is about towering politicians, ground-breaking scientists, or brilliant musicians that leads us to consider them 'creative.' Is it merely our perception of them? Is it the climate and circumstances of their times that have thrust greatness upon them? Or is it something intrinsic to their character, some collection of innate abilities and acquired qualities that sets them apart from the mob? With such questions impelling it, the study of 'genius' has understandably enjoyed recurring popularity throughout the years. Many studies of creativity in more recent times have continued the same somewhat elitist approach by dividing populations rather arbitrarily into 'creative persons' and 'less creative persons,' taking pains to contrast the exciting attributes of the former with the more dreary ones of the latter. These attributes include their unconventionality; their capacity to stand apart from the crowd; their alertness to timing; their playfulness, childlike innocence, energy, restlessness, and unpredictability; their tolerance for tension, for ambiguity, paradox, and complexity; their courage and willingness to take risks; their high self-esteem; and their self-image as indeed creative persons (Zahn, 1966; Briggs, 1988; Gardner, 1988).

Some Issues Obscured

There is much value in applying what amounts to the scientific method to the creativity question: breaking it down into smaller, more specific, and seemingly more manageable questions. As we have seen, such an approach enables us to list the qualities of creative persons, elaborate the criteria for assessing creative products, and identify the steps to replicate creative processes. However, while helping us to divide and conquer the mystery of creativity, it obscures at least three basic issues.

The first concerns the degree to which the distinctions between products, processes, and persons are, at best, naïve, and at worst, arbitrary. Inevitably, discussion of any one focus relies on assumptions about the nature of the other two. Creative products – whether poems, paintings, or solutions to problems – emerge out of creative processes, which are in turn experienced or instigated by creative persons. Yet creative persons can presumably also be stimulated into creative processes in the course of being exposed to creative products. In dealing with such a complicated subject, therefore, we continually run the risk of being overwhelmed by its many and overlapping dimensions.

The second issue concerns the degree to which, despite the vast body of literature devoted to deciphering it, creativity can probably be defined in ultimately rather simple terms. For instance, in *The Courage to Create*, psychologist-philosopher Rollo May offers us a definition that is a mere eight words in length. For him, creativity is simply 'the process of bringing something new into being' (1976, 37). Provided we accept that the 'newness' involved is not absolute but always relative to the tradition within which the judgment of newness is made (Bailin, 1985), it seems safe to say that the one element common to all under-standings of creativity is indeed novelty, an element we can take in its most basic sense. 'No two experiences are ever identical,' writes Robert Weisberg (1986) in his critique of the 'myths' associated with creativi-ty. 'Human beings,' he says, 'never do the same thing twice ... never produce the same response twice' (147). Thus, Weisberg insists, the usual distinction between 'creative' thinking and 'ordinary' thinking is misleading. 'Novelty, and hence creativity, are the norm,' he says, 'and the thought process involved in producing novelty are always being used.' 'To put it another way, there may be no thinking except creative thinking, since our ordinary functioning involves successful adaptation to novel situations, and thus meets the criteria for creativi-ty' (147).

The third issue concerns the degree to which every one of us is engaged in a kind of creativity that, in Tennyson's terms, is 'closer ... than breathing, and nearer than hands and feet': one that collapses our otherwise neat distinctions between products, processes, and persons (Winchester, 1983). It is *self*-creativity, that one aesthetic endeavour in which, arguably, all of us are unavoidably involved: creating not only paintings, poems, or programs but also, and primarily, our own unique lives. Accordingly, each of us is simultaneously the person, product, and process of creation; at once the agent, action, and achievement of creativity. Simply by being alive, that is, each of us embodies the most complex yet most commonplace expression of 'newness' there is. Not only are no two experiences ever identical but so are no two people. Each of us, more or less consciously, more or less deliberately, for better or worse, is in the process of making something incomparable out of our lives. Each of us is becoming a species unto ourselves. Each of us, whether we accept it or not, is novel.

Having acknowledged some of the ways in which traditional treatments of creativity can be limited, I want now to examine this peculiar notion of *self*-creativity – in particular, the conceptual soil from which it has sprung.

The Concept of Self-Creativity

Despite the intrinsic inexplicability of creativity, many have persisted in categorizing *degrees* of creativity. Silvano Arieti (1976), for example, suggests that there exists a creativity 'spectrum.' At one end, with the Newtons, Picassos, and Bachs of the world, are people of 'extraordinary creativity,' while spread out toward the other, or 'ordinary,' end is everyone else. Although more than a hint of elitism lurks in the background of such a schema, the notion that everybody is fundamentally creative is a rather palatable one. It makes us feel good to think that everyone has his special sphere in which he can be considered creative – whether pursuing a profession, raising a family, building a set of cupboards, or devising new sauces for the Sunday roast. We find it reassuring to conceive of creativity in this essentially democratic manner and not as something reserved for the gifted few. However, it is possible to extend the concept to apply not just to what we are able to *do* but to what we are able to *be*, as well. When we do this, we open the way for the energizing idea that there is ultimately no more creative a process than the mysterious one by which each of us 'creates' our own unique self.

At present, the notion of self-creativity is much in the air. The reasons can be traced to trends emanating from a variety of areas. Besides humanistic psychology, on which I shall elaborate shortly, these include the natural sciences, process philosophy, feminism, and what may be called new-age psychology.

The Natural Sciences

The idea that the universe as a whole is self-creative has been growing in currency since the development of quantum theory in the early decades of this century. Before that, under the sway of the Newtonian paradigm, the dominant view of the universe was as a sort of gigantic clockwork, ticking steadily away with colossal precision. Consequently, scientists were possessed of an implicit confidence that with a computer powerful enough to hold the necessary data, all future events on all possible levels could, in principle, be predicted in advance. Their conviction was that 'the future is already contained in the present; indeed, everything has been fixed in detail since time immemorial' (Davies, 1988, 68). The discovery, however, that at its presumably most basic level – that of molecules and atoms – the universe is in fact not terribly predictable at all has led to a perception of it as much less a grand machine than a vast organism, alive and ever-unfolding, attaining at each stage truly new types of organization and capable of surprising us with configurations that we could not previously have imagined. In the words of Nobel laureate J.B.S. Haldane, 'the universe is not only queerer than we suppose, but queerer than we *can* suppose.' Implicit in this perception is the possibility that in some rudimentary manner the universe is 'intelligent,' aware of what it is doing, cognizant of where it is going and why.

What is being stimulated through such a perspective – which biologist Lynn Margulis calls 'autopoiesis' (1991, 215f) – is a vision of the universe as essentially enchanted, as profoundly mysterious, as a place for genuine wonder: a vision that may have been enjoyed by our ancestors but that a more mechanistic, modern paradigm has beclouded for us. It is a vision of the irreducible uniqueness of each organism *within* the universe as well. In the words of biologist Rupert Sheldrake: 'To some extent, every individual organism and every element of its structure and behaviour represents a creative response to its internal and external conditions. No two organisms of the same kind are exactly identical; they are in different places, in different microenvironments, made up of different atoms and molecules, and subject to chance fluctuations from the quantum levels upwards' (1988, 319).

In *The Unfinished Universe*, ecologist-author Louise Young blends physics and biology with aesthetics. In the process, she gives eloquent articulation to the 'paradigm shift' through which the scientific community is reputed to be going, a change in perspective that is leading us to envision the universe as a vast, creative process. Working with a definition of creativity as 'an uncertain reaching out, a growth, rather than a foreplanned or preconceived activity,' Young says:

> The universe is not a static phenomenon; it is changing and evolving, still in the process of becoming ... [W]e are witnessing – and indeed participating in – a creative act that is taking place throughout time ... The universe is unfinished, not just in the limited sense of an incompletely realized plan but in the much deeper sense of a creation that is a living reality of the present. A masterpiece of artistic unity and integrated Form, infused with meaning, is taking shape as time goes by. But its ultimate nature cannot be visualized, its total significance grasped, until the final lines are written. (1986, 205, 208)

Process Philosophy

The physicist's vision of a self-creative cosmos has much in common with that of the philosophy of process, a speculative meta-physics with which names like Alfred North Whitehead and Teilhard de Chardin are usually associated. In addition to these figures, however, we can include sociologist George Herbert Mead, psychologist William James, educator John Dewey, and philosopher Henri Bergson, each of whom has situated his views within a picture of the cosmos as a self-creative process. In Bergson's words: 'To exist is to change, to change is to mature, to mature is to create oneself endlessly' (Poulet, 1956, 35).

For Whitehead, as for the ancient philosopher Heraclitus, the only constant feature of the universe is that it is constantly changing. To talk about such a universe – a universe in which change is constant, in which 'self-creativity is the ultimate reality' (Harshorne, 1971, 59), and in which Being is replaced by Becoming as the fundamental category – Whitehead, like many fashioners of philosophical systems, has created his own unique terminology. For example, he speaks of the fundamental 'things' of the universe as 'actual entities.' Whether atoms, trees, or persons, all come under the category of 'actual entity.' 'Each entity is a center of spontaneity and self-creation, contributing distinctively to the world' (Barbour, 1990, 223–3). Placed against the background of his dictum that 'the many become one, and are increased by one,' Whitehead, says one interpreter, holds that 'to be actual is to be an instance of creativity, which is to create oneself out of the many actualities which are given, and then to be added to that many as a creative influence out of which the next acts of creative synthesis will arise. To be a unity, an individual, is to be a creative synthesis out of a multiplicity' (Griffin, 1989, 42).

As science historian Ian Barbour stresses, Whitehead's model is essentially theistic. The link between the concept of creativity and the idea of a Creator, though implicit in *any* talk about creativity, is made explicit in his framework. But Whitehead's Creator is neither the mercurial patriarch of the Old Testament tradition, nor the personal Father of the New. Instead, it is a comparatively impersonal divinity with a twofold function in the cosmic scheme, as both 'the primordial ground of order' and 'the ground of novelty.' In other words, 'God elicits the self-creation of individual entities and thereby allows for novelty as well as structure ... God influences the world without determining it ... God never determines the outcome of events or violates the self-creation of each being. Every entity is the joint product of past causes, divine purposes, and the new entity's own activity' (Barbour, 224).

From a process perspective, self-creativity is the heart of the universe; it is 'the universal principle' (Hartshorne, 59). For Teilhard de Chardin, whose views are in several respects compatible with Whitehead's, the self-creativity of the universe and the self-creativity of each individual within it are two sides of the same coin. In his words, 'every man, in the course of his life ... must *build* – starting with the most natural territory of his own self – a work, an *opus*, into which something enters from all the elements of the earth. *He makes his own soul* throughout his earthly days; and at the same time he collaborates in another work, in another *opus*, which infinitely transcends, while at the same time it narrowly determines, the perspectives of his individual achievement: the completing of the world' (Sarton, 1977, 66–7; emphasis Chardin's).

Feminism

The feminist movement has been particularly instrumental in sensitizing our age to the possibility of self-creation. Understanding the dynamics of self-creation has become urgent, it says, because of women's need, both individually and collectively, to forge ways of being that transcend the stereotypical, oppressive patterns prescribed for them by a patriarchal system. Analysed in terms of this system, 'womanhood' is the consequence less of biology than of socialization. Sex is given, that is, while gender is constructed. As Simone de Beauvoir has argued, 'one is not born, but rather becomes a woman' (Eisenstein, 1983, 36). But the way women became women in the past is under fire in the present. Thus, as Jean Baker Miller writes in *Toward a New Psychology of Women*, women today are 'the people struggling to create for themselves a new concept of personhood; they are attempting to restructure the central tenets of their lives ... to create a new kind of person in a much bolder, more thoroughgoing, and conscious way' (1976, 44–5).

Elsewhere in her book, however, Miller calls self-creation a 'universal process.' In this way, she acknowledges that though, as a conscious enterprise, it is central more and more to the experience of women, it theoretically embraces the experience of everyone, regardless of gender. Accordingly, she speaks of 'the intense personal creating that we each must do all through life. Everyone repeatedly has to break through to a new vision if she/he is to keep living' (44). As she puts it, in words reminiscent of Weisberg's, 'personal creativity is a continuous process of bringing forth a changing vision of oneself, and of oneself in relation to the world ... Despite all our commonality, each of us, each day, creates our own particular attempt to put the picture together, as it were. It is never exactly the same as anyone else's, and it is never the same as the one we made yesterday' (111).

New-Age Psychology

Weaving insights from the new physics with the cosmic vision of process philosophy and the emancipating energy of feminism and other liberation movements, many writers, loosely labelled 'New Age,' have extended the concept of self-creativity in intriguing, if unconventional, directions. At the core of their thinking is the belief that we can create in our lives whatever reality we wish. While this may be merely the logical conclusion of our belief in unlimited 'progress' – or, more darkly, the final huddling of the privileged few around the flickering flame of the human candle – a few quotations from representative new-age writings provide a flavour of the enthusiasm, even mysticism, that can accompany this confidence in our potential for self-creation.

In *The Path of Least Resistance*, Robert Fritz writes that 'it is not common for people to think of their own lives as creations. You are not encouraged to have with your own life the kind of relationship a creator has with his or her vision. But your life can be a creation ... Your own life can become a separate entity, and when it does, you can form it, mold it, and change it the way you want' (1989, 131).

In *Higher Creativity*, authors Harman and Rheingold echo Fritz's insight in the form of a provocative rhetorical question: 'If we can solve the problem, answer the question, of how to best lead our lives, and we implement that knowledge as we would the result of any other kind of breakthrough, couldn't we in the highest sense be said to be creating our own lives? Wouldn't this in fact *be* "higher creativity?"' (1984, 111).

In *Creative Visualization* by Shakti Gawain, one of the most popular New-Age writings, the fundamental message is that 'you are the constant creator of your life.' Thus, the ultimate point of the discipline proposed is 'to make every moment of our lives a moment of wondrous creation, in which we are just naturally choosing the best, the most beautiful, the most fulfilling lives we can imagine' (1982, 8).

This brief survey suffices to show that the concept of self-creativity has roots in a wide range of fields. Without claiming that each thinker referred to has neither problems nor detractors, it at least gives us a sense of why self-creativity, as a principle, is presently much in vogue, and of why self-creation, as a phenomenon, has currency enough to bear further consideration. To give it such consideration here, I need now to face some of the problems that are involved in speaking not just of *creating* the self but also of creating the *self*.

The Creation of the Self

Several 'self-' combinations have enjoyed the limelight throughout the history of thought, or at least as long as the 'self' has been something seen worthy of being thought about. The *Oxford English Dictionary* cites more than two hundred formulations. Of course, many of these refer not to the self as such but simply to any action initiated, or process experienced, by some agent operating with its own resources (see Toulmin, 1977, 291ff). Thus, an amoeba can be called 'self-replicating,' a system of government 'self-perpetuating,' or a prophecy 'self-fulfilling.' None the less, even after weeding out such phrases, we are still left with a large number of combinations concerning the self as a distinctively human entity – however indefinable that self remains or however entangled with concepts like 'person' or 'individual' or 'character' (Rorty, 1988, 78ff).

Models of the Self

Among the most popular in this family of 'self-' formulations, and the most central to the lexicon of modern psychology, are terms like self-image, self-concept, and self-esteem; or like self-acceptance, self-discovery, and self-disclosure; or like self-fulfilment, self-realization, and self-actualization.[1] Naturally, the meanings of these formulations overlap; moreover, our use of them can be quite cavalier and fail to appreciate the fine distinctions that prevail between them. In general, though, there is a limited range of models to which I believe we point when we invoke them to answer the one fundamental question: What *is* 'the self'?

The first model, and the most exotic – that is, the least mainstream – is the **spiritual** model, where we assign a small 's' to spiritual and a large one to self. Such a Self is a familiar concept in those approaches to psychology inspired by the work of Carl Jung. For such psychologies, the Self is not so much *within* us as we are within *it*. It is 'the organizing principle of the personality ... the archetype of order, organization, and unification' (Hall and Nordby, 1973, 51). For Marie-Louise von Franz, 'Jung's foremost living successor' (von Franz and Boa, 1988), it is 'that supra-ordinate, inner, unknown, divine centre of the psyche which we have to explore all our lifetime' (33). The Self, she says, 'has a plan for us, a kind of destiny' that it wants to reveal to us, primarily through our dreams. Dreams 'are the letters [most times, laden with stories themselves] which the Self writes to us every night, telling us to do a bit more of this, or to do a bit less of that' (33). This Self – this Higher Self or True Self, as it is sometimes called – is less personal in nature, then, than *trans*-personal (Firman and Vargiu, 1978, 3): something mystical, ineffable, inscrutable, whose intentions and designs partake of the Divine, yet with whom we are wise to remain in harmony (von Franz and Boa, 34, 36).

Next is the **social** model. Here, the self is defined less as an entity unto itself than as a function of – and constructed through – our interactions with others. Thus, I have not one self but many: many ways in which I can present myself in the ever-changing drama of everyday life. As a corollary, I have not one self-image or self-concept but several, more or less integrated or contradictory, depending on the audience before which I am performing or the 'side' of me that a given exchange elicits (Goffman, 1959, 252–3). In the words of one source, 'selves are not independently existing soul-pearls, but artifacts of the social processes that create us, and, like other such artifacts, subject to sudden shifts in status' (Dennett, 1991, 423).

Though philosophically worlds apart, both of these models centre the self-process somewhat *outside* the individual human being: the social model on the frontier between self and others, or between the individual and society; the spiritual model, 'above' the individual or on the boundary between the individual and the cosmos. In the remaining models on which I wish to focus, however, the self and the self-process are centred more *inside* the individual.

The third is the **essential** model. It takes at least two forms. The first implies a self that is simply there, fully formed, once and for all: a core self that needs only to be discovered, disclosed, and accepted. thus, we have such 'self-' formulations as self-discovery, self-disclosure, and self-acceptance. Though these terms suggest a dynamic process, that process concerns the accepting, the discovering, and the disclosing, not the formation of the self itself. In this respect, they imply a different meaning of the self than do terms like self-actualization, self-realization, or self-fulfilment. The latter, though still within the essential model, represent a separate, second form of it. With them, the core self in question is less a fixed entity than a kind of seed, a set of potentials (perhaps locked up within the DNA itself) that await the properly nurturing environment to be brought to fruition. I can put the distinction between these two forms of essentialism in terms of a crude analogy: Columbus *discovered* America; he did not *actualize* it. Though the discovering took time, given the width of the Atlantic and the size of his ships, the land itself (if not the nation and the culture) was already there; he had merely to plant his flag upon it and in that sense 'accept' it.

By contrast, self-actualization – as well as self-creation – suggests not that the self is a finished product needing only to be discovered, accepted, and disclosed but that it involves, requires, or *is* itself a process. Yet despite this commonality, despite self-actualization and self-creation both being processes, there is a critical difference between them. It is the difference between an essential model of the self and a fourth or **existential** one. Elaborating this difference will clarify the peculiar element of activity and agency that is connoted by self-creation.

Self-Actualization and Self-Creation

The name most frequently associated with the concept of self-actualization is Abraham Maslow. In his celebrated 'hierarchy of needs,' self-actualization is the highest level toward which the individual strives to grow. At times, however, he is drawn as much to self-*creation* as to self-*actualization*. A summary of his philosophy will help to illustrate.

Central to Maslow's thesis is the belief that each person has 'an essential inner nature which is instinctoid, intrinsic, given, "natural" [which] shows itself as natural inclinations, propensities or inner bent' (1968, 190). 'This inner nature,' he says, 'rarely disappears or dies.' Instead, 'it persists underground, unconsciously, even though denied and repressed ... it has a dynamic force of its own, pressing always for open, uninhibited expression' (192). The direction of this 'inner bent,' he says, and the direction sought by this 'dynamic force,' is 'toward unity of personality ... toward full individuality and identity, toward seeing the truth rather than being blind ... toward fuller and fuller being' (155).

As noted, however, there is vacillation in Maslow's thought. On the one hand, 'some existential philosophers are stressing the self-making of the self too exclusively. Sartre and others speak of the "self as a project," which is wholly created by the continued (and arbitrary) choices of the person himself, almost as if he could make himself into anything he decided to be' (12–13). On the other hand, 'the Freudians, the existential therapists, the Rogerians, and the personal growth psychologists all talk more about *discovering* the self and of *uncovering* therapy, and perhaps have understressed the factors of will, of decision, and of the ways in which we do make ourselves by our choices' (12–13; emphasis Maslow's). In the end, then, 'this inner core, or self, grows into adulthood only *partly* by (objective or subjective) discovery, uncovering, and acceptance of what is "there" beforehand. Partly it is also a creation of the person himself ... *Every person is, in part, "his own project" and makes himself*' (193; emphasis mine).

Maslow's remarks suggest that self-actualization and self-creation are effectively two poles of a common continuum, yet they obscure an important difference between them. In grand terms, it is a difference in how we understand the universe itself. Put baldly, either the universe is closed and therefore, for the most part, determined in advance, or it is open, its future unpredictable in principle, and thus capable, as are we ourselves, of genuine novelty. Either creativity is a real possibility, as in the creation of systems, situations, or persons that are on some level novel, or there is ultimately nothing new under the sun. Against the background of the trends just noted in the natural sciences, the notion of self-creation assumes an open universe, one in which some degree of novelty is constantly entering in. It also assumes a particular understanding of the relationship between life and time.

Edward Lindaman (1976) offers us an illustration of how self-actualization and self-creation reflect different understandings of time when he uses the image of an acorn to make a point about 'human potential.' In speaking of the marvellous capacity inherent in each acorn to become, eventually, a spreading oak tree, he reminds us that the oak tree is actually only the *futura* of the acorn. By this he means that it is 'the future of the past,' for it is known. A human being has a future as well, of course, but it is not a futura in the same way that the oak tree is the futura of the acorn. Rather, it is *adventus*, 'the future of the future,' for it is essentially unknown. Compared with that of an acorn, that is, our future as human beings is not entirely programmed in advance. We lean into a future that is genuinely open. Human potentialities are not just assigned at the start but also created along life's way. In other words, having experienced X we discover within ourselves that the potential has now developed to go on to experience Y. In turn, going on to experience Y creates within us the potential to experience Z, a level that, while we were still at X, was scarcely even imaginable, let alone possible. To return to the issue under discussion here, in both self-actualization and self-creation the self is incomplete, unfinished. However, to complete it, in the first case, one looks to the past, to that which is given though not-yet-fleshed-out. In the second, one looks to the future, to that which may be, to that which is not-yet-fashioned and, in certain respects, not-yet-even-imaginable.

Such thinking is corroborated by John Dewey, a philosopher who Maslow admits exercised a formative influence upon his views (1968, viii). Without using the term itself, however, Dewey sees self-actualization as running counter to the very notion of 'individuality.' In his view, 'the issue involved is perhaps the most fundamental one in philosophy at the present time.' It concerns the question of whether what happens in time is 'simply a spatial rearrangement of what existed previously or ... involve[s] something qualitatively new' ([1940] 1962, 153). While he believes it necessary to revive the category of potentiality as a characteristic of individuality, such as Maslow has done in our time, he says it must take a different form from its classic Aristotelian formulation. As he sees it, 'the idea that potentialities are inherent and fixed by relation to a predetermined end was a product of a highly restricted state of technology' (154). Against this notion he argues that 'potentialities are not fixed and intrinsic, but are a matter of an indefinite range of interactions in which an individual may engage' (154). Using the example of Abraham Lincoln, Dewey roots this indefinite nature of potentiality in the reality of time itself: 'At critical junctures, his response could not be predicted either from his own past or from the nature of the circumstances, except as a probability. To say this is not arbitrarily to introduce mere chance into the world. It is to say that genuine individuality exists; that individuality is pregnant with new developments; that time is real' (156).

Dewey's emphasis on the reality of time is vital to the model this book is exploring: self-creation through the reworking of personal story. Central to this model is the notion that the nature of our experience of time ultimately requires a narrative form for us to understand and communicate it. Dewey agrees with this notion: 'the human individual is himself a history, a career, and for this reason his biography can be related only as a temporal event' (146). In short, the very concept of individuality assumes temporality, while temporality, in turn, assumes novelty and thus (as Weisberg saw too) creativity. By linking individuality so tightly to both creativity and time, Dewey helps us see self-creation as, in a sense, self-evident. It is a distinctive formulation for capturing the nature of the self-process. 'The self,' as philosopher David Polonoff puts it then, 'is not something one finds oneself constrained to be, but something one makes oneself into. An individual is to some extent free to create the kind of self he will become' (1987, 53).

Given that any of our concepts of the self-process is necessarily enshrouded in fog, let me summarize our thinking so far. First, it is not impossible that there is a Higher Self luring us to live up to it, a larger Self we live within, a Transpersonal Self that is the 'ultimately unknown and unknowable greater centre in our psyche' (von Franz and Boa, 33). At the same time, it is also quite possible that much of our so-called self is really a *complex* of selves, a set of roles we act out, or personas we adopt, in our interactions with others. Furthermore, there may be some sense in which we can *discover* and must *accept* an essential self that is already there. In some circles, for instance, we are enjoined to be our 'best' self or 'real' self; in others (often religious), our 'true' self. A similar essentialism has informed much of psycho-analysis (Bruner, 1990, 100; Schafer, 1992, xvi). In addition, there may be much value in the notion that we possess a seminal self it behoves us to *actualize*, as much humanistic psychology has espoused.[2] However, while the notion of self-*creation* can accommodate many aspects of the self-process to which these various formulations point, it highlights other aspects that they neglect.

It underlines, for example, the role played by our images of the future, by the pull of what we perceive to lie ahead of us compared with the push of what lies latent within. It also points to a conception of the universe as genuinely open. Thus, it allows us to have a sense of ourselves as playing a truly active part in the direction of our own becoming, a process that is forever yielding a degree of genuine novelty and ushering into being what did not exist before. In short, self-creation captures the notion that the self is ultimately not a given but a construction. The approach it assumes is, philosophically and psychologically, 'constructivist' (Bruner, 1987, 11), one that sees the self as something we are continually refashioning, by various means and for better or worse. It sees the self as an 'open system' (see Prigogine, 1984, 334). Thus, it leads us to the view that 'man is not a finished creature like an ant or a bee. His essence is not handed to him as a finished product but assigned to him as a task. Thus he is hidden to himself and constantly in search of his true essence. He is for himself and for his equals an open question, a puzzle, and often a dread ... Man in his mere existence is an experiment' (Moltmann, 1975, 20).

Synonyms for Self-Creation

Having considered some of the basic distinctions between various 'self-' formulations, most important between self-actualization and self-creation, I want to look more closely now at the principal means by which the process of self-creation is carried out. Before I do so, though, I want to consider the meaning of a few additional 'self-' formulations with which self-creation can be either connected or confused.

One of these is **self-construction**. This follows from the fact that we are attaching the term *constructivist* to our approach. Of all the candidates, it is probably the closest to a synonym for self-creation; indeed,

I shall often be treating it as such. None the less, constructing carries connotations that creating does not. To 'construct' something implies the assembly of pre-existing materials according to an established design. Thus, a building is constructed: An architect comes up with the concept for a new skyscraper and translates it into a set of plans. These are taken and interpreted by an engineering firm that orders the necessary concrete, glass, and steel and then directs a team of workers to construct the edifice itself. Of course, the element of planning in constructing something need not always be this strong. We can also 'construct' a perfectly workable outhouse by throwing together whatever tag-end materials are handy and cheap, with little precise idea what form the final object will take. Perhaps we construct a 'self' in a comparable way. We take a cliché here, a slogan there, a partial imitation of this role model and of that, a hodgepodge of habits, a repertoire of routines for thinking and acting borrowed from the people around us or breathed from the culture in which we are based, and a scattering of uncritiqued assumptions about power and truth and love – and then, mostly unwittingly, over time, we patch together a life, a way of being in the world, a self.

Another formulation is **self-invention**. Invention and creation would seem to be the same. But are they? In so far as an inven*tion* requires an inven*tor*, what gets conjured up is the image of a Thomas Edison working in his laboratory, sprockets and wheels and wires all strewn about the floor, struggling by trial and error to produce a more or less preconceived, probably practical, end result, such as a piece of time-saving technology to mass-produce and mass-market. Thus, we *invent* a microwave. A poem, however, we *create*. Though each comes into being by employing particular tools and raw materials, thereafter there is a significant difference, not only in the product but in the process as well.

Put bluntly, the process of invention is mechanical; that of creation, organic. Both invention and creation may begin in an equally inchoate idea, but there is always something contrived about the former and something unconscious about the latter. Thus, I might say of someone (never myself!) that he 'invents' an alibi or excuse to get himself out of a ticklish situation. It does not emerge on its own; he cooks it up. Though this may be splitting hairs, there is a distinction between the two terms. To the extent that self-invention gets invoked in discussions of autobiography (Eakin, 1985; Zinsser, 1987), we need to be alert to the nuances it introduces.

The friends that have it I do wrong
Whenever I remake a song,
Should know what issue is at stake:
It is myself that I remake.

Yeats's use of 'remake' reminds us again of one of the most fundamental meanings of 'to create,' which is 'to make.' To speak about
creating ourselves is to speak about making ourselves. The concept of
man-the-maker is by no means new. Building on the phrase's Latin
equivalent, *homo faber*, Lewis Mumford has coined a further formulation: **self-fabrication** (1951, 40). Not lost on us should be the *double
entendre* such a phrase involves: we are the species who both *make*
ourselves and *make* ourselves *up*. Various uses of 'make' in relation to
our lives can be found in our everyday speech: 'make a living,' 'make
time,' 'make money,' 'make it,' 'make love,' 'make out,' 'make good,'
'make sense,' 'make friends,' 'make mistakes,' 'make the best of things'
(or 'a mess of things'), 'make something out of ourselves' in general,
and even, in French circles, 'make a good death.' But the nuance
represented by 'make *up*,' a nuance accounted for by self-fabrication,
adds a key dimension to our sense of the self-process. Something
made up is something illusory, founded on a lie, not to be trusted,
manufactured as opposed to original, artificial rather than real. A
fabrication is a fiction. Complex though they be, the connections
between fiction and self-creation are therefore impossible to ignore. As
we push more deeply into the *poetics* of self-creation, they become our
central concern.

In connection with self-fabrication, a fourth term comes to mind as
an alternative to self-creation: **self-making**. However, 'self-making' –
at least in its past-tense form, 'self-made' – generates the image of the
self-made man: a self-obsessed Horatio Alger who has clambered the
corporate ladder until, at last, having 'made it,' he sits in the panelled
office at the end of the hall at the top of the heap: triumphant and
tough and alone. To be self-made is to pull myself up by my own
bootstraps – an approach to living all too common in today's competitive world. In keeping with a key criterion of any creative product,
however, self-creation captures the sense that something novel is being
fashioned in the process of living. It may not be *utterly* novel, not *ex
nihilo*, since past influences and factors are doubtless at work, but there
is the emergence, none the less, of something not there before, not
even as a potential: some new feature or force that through me is now

entering the universe, thus (however slightly) changing it forever. Where self-made suggests a finished product, self-creation signals an ongoing process: an unprecedented work of art in the course of being brought into the world; a work-in-progress to which the raw material of my little life can alone give rise, and the peculiar pressure of my experience of myself as 'puzzle' or 'question' can alone elicit.

So then, self-creation is a unique 'self-' formulation. One that fits within an existential model of the self, it sees the self as something we effectively make ourselves. As such, there are other formulations we could substitute for it. However, these are not precise equivalents. To construct, invent, or fabricate the self, even (in a sense) to make it, is not exactly the same as to create it. Compared to self-construction, self-creation is purposeful but not preplanned. Compared to self-invention, the self is composed but not concocted. Compared with self-fabrication, the self that is created is fictional yet not necessarily a lie. At the same time, the process of creating *can* imply a little of each. Moreover, as we shall see by looking at the self-process in terms of life story, the concept of *creating* a self gathers up nuances that are implicit in the other overall models of the self: the essential, the social, even the spiritual. For the time being, I need to ask about the means of self-creation.

The Means of Self-Creation

Analysing the self-process in terms of the language of creativity makes for an intriguing project, but it raises a host of thorny questions: What does it really *mean* to create ourselves? In what sense, for instance, can we manage it on our own, or can we do so only with the help of others, whether parents, neighbours, co-workers, or friends? In reality, is not self-creation always a process of *co*-creation? If so, how is it influenced – how is the very form of our self-creation shaped – by the various cultures in which our lives have been embedded, i.e., those of our family, our community, our class? How does a white, middle-class, male child from the suburbs of North America self-create differently, that is, from a poor, indigenous, female child from the barrios of South America – or indeed from *any* child, rich or poor, from a previous century? In addition, is there not a sort of self-creation 'threshold' that we cross, at least consciously, only at a particular stage in our

our development (though one that may vary from individual to individual)? Furthermore, how can we both *create* our self and, at the same time, *be* the self we create? Though I shall return to such questions in subsequent sections, the fundamental questions facing us here are simply: *Do* we create ourselves? Is it *possible* to create ourselves? *How* do we create ourselves?

Some will immediately say that these questions are silly; that, of course, we do not create ourselves because that *does* imply pulling ourselves up by our own bootstraps (Glover, 1988, 179). Others will say that the question is not so much silly as it is blasphemous, thus dismissing it out of hand. It is arguable, however, that it is neither silly nor blasphemous at all but that, in some real way, we *do* create ourselves, that the process goes on continuously, and that it is central to who we are as human beings. The key, of course, is the phrase 'in some way,' to an exegesis of which I need now to turn.

Material Self-Creation

The fact is that when we ask whether we create ourselves, we do so knowing full well that we do not do so at all. That is, we certainly do not create ourselves in the sense of fashioning (*ex nihilo* or not) the molecules or atoms by which we are currently constituted – although through eating and drinking, and to a lesser extent breathing and exercising, we do contribute to our 'constitution,' supplying the raw material with which the involuntary forces of our bodies can fashion muscles, bones, and blood *from* those molecules and atoms. Nor have we created ourselves in that other very specifiic sense of having impregnated our own mother. Such a concept is, so to speak, inconceivable (Glover, 179). Nor did we design the particular ovum and sperm of whose union we are the happy result. Nor, carrying this as far as we can, did we create the entire universe on whose existence all of these things and activities are dependent in the first place. Strictly speaking, we did or can create ourselves – at least physically or *materially* – in a limited sense alone. It can be argued, however, that there is another sense in which we do, indeed, create ourselves.

Behavioural Self-Creation

As we have seen, it is to the existentialists that we owe the lifting up of this sense in our own age, notably Jean-Paul Sartre. 'Man,' he writes, 'is nothing else but what he makes of himself' (1968, 313). Despite Maslow's objection to Sartre's views, which he considers extreme, surely Sartre has a point: we do indeed *make* ourselves, at least within limits. Within the limits set by our particular genetic inheritance, by our gender and race, by our family and culture of origin, and by the specific place in space and time, in society and history, in which we happen to have found ourselves since birth – all of which, admittedly, are formidable limits – are we not free to make of ourselves whatever and whomever we will? Yes, we are, and we do so *behaviourally*. Through our conduct in relationships, through our reactions to the forces and factors impinging upon us, through our responses to the events that happen to us daily, and through the decisions we make and the actions to which those decisions lead – in all of these ways we determine, more or less, for better or worse, the direction our development takes. By marrying person A rather than B, by choosing profession J rather than K, by moving to X rather than Z, and by opting to do a thousand far less life-altering things in this way rather than that, the overall path of our life unwinds steadily, daily, hourly, along this line rather than that. Though all of this might seem only a limited kind of self-creation, it is self-creation none the less. We may not make ourselves materially – we may not make our basic chemical, emotional, intellectual 'make-up' – but we *do* carve out the shape of our lives behaviourally, in a way that accounts for much. It accounts for what sets us apart. An animal can keep itself alive, that is, but only a human can *make* a living. And it accounts for history as a whole, for that entire intricate process whereby from generation to generation not only does the world create us (as does our family, culture, and class) but also we create the world (Abrams, 1982, 2; Palmer, 1983, 12). Such mutual self-creation we may call 'progress.'

Hermeneutical Self-Creation

Someone who gives 'self-creation' pride of place is Oxford philosopher Jonathan Glover. For him, it occurs *hermeneutically* as well, where 'hermeneutics' refers to the process of interpretation: in this case, *of* ourselves *to* ourselves. In a book devoted to the centuries-old question about the basis of personal identity, Glover insists that 'our identity is not something just given to us, but is, in part, something we ourselves create' (1988, 110). Although he accepts that there are obviously limits placed on our self-creation by both genetic and social determinants, 'the scientific picture of human beings,' he says, 'does not exclude our partly creating ourselves in the light of our own values' (17–18). Indeed, 'our partial creation of ourselves is central to what we are like. Although usually hardly noticed, it is one of the things we most value in life' (18).

Even though 'what people become depends partly on things quite outside themselves,' Glover goes on, 'it is also the product of three internally generated processes.' First, 'there is the genetically programmed cycle of life, which we can hardly alter,' including the size of our nose, the shape of our head, and the colour of our hair – as well as the age at which it begins to fall out! Second, though, there is 'the unself-conscious process of living our lives,' by which he means all the many things about our lives – our choice of job or spouse or place of residence – that have 'unintended self-creative side effects.' Beyond this is, third, the process of 'deliberate self-creation' (138), which is directly influenced by 'the way we think of ourselves, and of our past' (110). What both the second and the third of these have in common, then – what both unintended and deliberate self-creation share – is that they depend ultimately 'on the beliefs we have about what we are now like.' They depend on 'the stories we tell about ourselves' (139). Specifically, they depend on what he calls 'the inner story.' This brings us to the heart of Glover's thesis: 'the interaction between self-creation and the inner story about the past' (141).

Glover's emphasis on the role of our 'inner story' in the construction of ourselves underlines the need for a full-blown inquiry into the poetics of self-creation. It is my hope that our ponderings here will contribute to such an inquiry, and will help to identify the questions within the questions with which it must grapple. For the moment, let me elaborate his view that we create ourselves by the stories that we tell ourselves *about* ourselves.

Self-Telling and Self-Creation

We are forever chatting to ourselves, telling ourselves now this and now that about what we are doing or feeling (or ought to) and what is going on. Whether we call this activity daydreaming or the *modus operandi* of ordinary self-consciousness (Booth, 1988, 296), what we may overlook is that what we tell ourselves is not at all neutral. It affects the way we are in the world.

If I tell myself today, for example, that I am a bright, clever, capable person, then, to the extent I believe myself and do not have direct experiences to belie that message, it is quite conceivable that, at least today, I shall *be* a bright, clever, capable person, and that all of my engagements with others will reflect that same brilliance and ability. I shall *do* better because I shall *see* myself as better. If, on the other hand, I tell myself that I am stupid or incompetent, then the chances are that most of my interactions with the world will come off rather badly. I shall project myself poorly and therefore perform poorly (Glover, 177). Furthermore, if I am in a context where no one has known me before, then the impression I create, through my deeds and words alike, can be quite unfortunate for me, playing a disproportionate role in determining how people respond to me, the decisions they make concerning me, and the limits they place upon my options for the future. Such matters become painfully relevant when today happens to be the day of my interview for a much desired placement or job. In this respect, an interesting sort of 'feedback loop' is at work: what I tell myself about myself affects how I present myself to others; how I present myself to others affects the options they make available to me; and what options they make available to me reinforce or challenge what I tell myself about myself thereafter.

The Norman Vincent Peales of our world have of course long advertised this simple fact of life, 'positively thinking' themselves all the way to the bank because of it: what we tell ourselves about ourselves bears directly on the life we lead.[3] However, telling ourselves about ourselves may be a more complicated process than such people make out, in so far as 'what' we tell ourselves about ourselves is, in reality, a whole host of 'whats.'

To return to the negative thinking situation above – to the bad day, that is – what I tell myself about myself will likely include something about my family as well, or my education, or my looks, or my accumulated saga of failures and faults. Thus, I tell myself not only that I am 'no good' but that my father was no good either, that my schooling was a farce, that my nose has always been too big, and that nothing has ever worked out right for me anyway because, on top of everything else, I started my journey on the wrong side of the tracks and have been jinxed every step of the way. What I tell myself, in other words, is a particular summary or segment of my entire history. In this respect, any given 'self-image' or 'self-concept' is not a static, unchanging entity but thoroughly dynamic, historical, and temporal.

It is in reality a 'self-story,' a connecting of the events of my life according to a distinct kind of plot. On my bad days, when my self-image is 'low,' I tell a different story of myself than I do on my good days – a tragic story, we could say – and this story has the power to affect my entire manner of engaging with the world. It is as if the pieces of my past were so many crystals in the far end of a kaleidoscope. How I shuffle them on the bad days yields a decidedly different pattern than what I get on the good. Although this analogy illustrates how many possible stories I could tell myself about myself today, it leaves out the fact that a number of newer crystals will necessarily be added tomorrow. It also prevents us from realizing that each crystal is tied to all of the others in countless subtle and ever-changing ways. We shall get a greater appreciation for this malleability of 'the story of my life' in the following chapter when we explore how the various versions of that story are continually swirling around inside me, combining, conflicting, and/or competing with each other endlessly, and in seemingly unpredictable ways. In the meantime, there is one critical implication of this line of thinking for our understanding of self-creation.

How Others Story Us

It is clearly not just the stories *I* tell about myself that affect the shape and direction of my self-creation but the stories others tell about me as well. For these stories help to create the social climate in which my life is lived and to determine the range of options and opportunities by which it is bound. For instance, parents and other loved ones tell stories about us right from the beginning, many of which, for better or worse, function as self-fulfilling prophecies in relation to what we might thereafter go on to make (or not make) of our lives. Father's story about 'my daughter who is going to be a doctor,' and Mother's about 'my son, the someday lawyer,' can be powerful stories in young people's lives, shaping their spirits profoundly as they struggle to live them out, breaking them with guilt or shame should they happen to fail. Beyond the charmed circle of family and friends, however, the shape of our lives can be influenced by the stories that anyone tells about us. If the story – that is, the reputation – that precedes me to the meeting is of a successful entrepreneur with an impeccable pedigree and a past of 'taking care of business' in a capable manner, then I am more likely to land the contract my résumé requires and my wallet desires. By the same token, if the story being spread about me around the town is largely a pack of lies – about my past actions, my present involvements, and my future intentions – and calls into question the details not only of my marriage but also of my morality, my heredity, and my integrity in general, then I may find the doors of hospitality and opportunity slammed rather abruptly in my face.

This is the power of gossip. But gossip is a complex phenomenon. In general, the stories others tell about me are of two types: specific stories and generic stories. Specific stories are the stories they tell about me based on their association with or knowledge of me as a particular individual. Generic stories, on the other hand, are the stories they tell about me without really knowing me at all but by seeing me as representative of a particular class or group. In so far as departures from the truth in the specific stories others tell about me come under the category of gossip, errors in the generic stories come under the category of prejudice. Prejudice tells the story not of what I *personally* did or said but of what people 'like me' tend to do or say in general, of what people of my 'type' are known to do or say – people of my class or colour or creed, from my language group or my side of town. When a generic story is superimposed on, or undergirds, a specific story, we have a loaded story indeed. In reality, gossip and prejudice are usually mixed; prejudice gives gossip its punch.

Both prejudice and gossip are negative words, however, suggesting stories that are distinguishable from 'the truth' or 'the facts.' In fact, what distinguishes gossip from gospel may not always be clear. A story about me that is untrue is not automatically gossip; the person who started the story may simply have got things wrong. Whatever damage to my reputation may therefore ensue is the result of misinformation, not of malice. Indeed, just as I never have anything but a version of myself so I never have anything but a version of others, nor do they have anything but a version of me, and those versions, even in the minds of those who know me best, will always be coloured to some degree with gossip and prejudice. In actuality, what distinguishes gossip from gospel has to do less with *con*tent than with *in*tent. It is not a matter of *what* we tell as much as of *how* we tell it, and *why*. The how and the why depend of course upon the generic stories to which we gravitate in telling any specific story, and that we allow to shape that story. The point remains, though, that how I am storied by others – whether through gossip, prejudice, ignorance, or all three – has a direct effect on the range of social, professional, and economic options that are open to me. It has an effect on the people who are drawn to me and the company I come to keep. It has an effect, that is, upon the nature and direction, the scope and shape, of my self-creation. And this in turn, as already hinted, has an effect on how I story myself in the future, the versions of my own story toward which I gravitate in times to come. Thus, to discuss the poetics of self-creation is to discuss the politics as well, for stories have power.

One corollary of this is that giving out my story so that others have something 'on' me to misinterpret and spread is a way of giving away my power. Hence, the more I divulge of my past, present, and future, the less control I may have over how I shall be perceived thereafter: less control over those limits to my present fortunes and future prospects – to my self-creation – that others' stories of me have the power to set. Few of us pursue this idea to its logical conclusion. To do so would be to keep silent about ourselves altogether, giving others the least conceivable leverage with respect to us. Clearly, in certain situations such as a new job, a new relationship, or a critical meeting or interview, we can all be a bit evasive, and we obviously all have – and need – our secrets (Bok, 1984, xv). However, most of us resist the temptation to be secretive about our story entirely. Naturally, there is a trade-off. Where secrecy affords a measure of control over our story and reduces the damage done by gossip and prejudice, revelation purchases us a measure of feedback concerning it, a chance both to have it heard by others and to hear it ourselves, something that can both reinforce and clarify for us what that story really is. Where each of us operates along this spectrum of secrecy-revelation will naturally vary. Nevertheless, probably few of us are willing to go to the extreme of the elusive Don Juan, the Yaqui sorcerer celebrated in the seventies in the writings of anthropologist Carlos Castaneda (1975). Perhaps, says Don Juan, 'it is best to erase all personal history ... because that would make us free from the encumbering thoughts of other people ... When one does not have a personal history ... nothing that one says can be taken for a lie ... If we ... erase personal history, we create a fog around us, a very exciting and mysterious state in which nobody knows where the rabbit will pop out, not even ourselves' (30, 32, 33).

To summarize, I see the means of self-creation in relation to three main realms: the material, the behavioural, and the hermeneutical. Though these realms are by no means discrete, overlapping in countless, complex ways, the broad features of each still stand out.

In the material realm, our agency in constructing ourselves is limited by the fact that our genetic endowment, like our 'choice' of the family, culture, and era into which we have been born, is beyond our control. To the extent we have any control at all over our physical construction, it is very basic, on a par with that of our animal colleagues – though, depending on whether it is eating, breathing, or exercising, it can be more or less voluntary in nature.

As we move into the behavioural realm, however, our agency in the self-process grows greater. The further we mature into full adulthood, the more power we have over the direction of our self-creation – through the decisions we make each day, the people we marry, the jobs we take, and the various creations we produce, whether objects, relationships, policies, or lifestyles. All of these help to create us in turn, both directly and indirectly, in so far as they change the world by which we are continually being acted on and shaped.

In the hermeneutical realm, our own agency, though not necessarily greater than in the second realm, is more subtle, more complex, and more intricate. Here, our self-creation depends 'on the beliefs we have about what we are now like: on the stories we tell about ourselves' (Glover, 1988, 139). To prepare for a more detailed examination of the nature of this connection between self-creation and self-storying, then, let me now consider the range of ways in which 'the story of my life' can be taken.

The Story of My Life

The more we probe the metaphor of life-as-story the more problematic it becomes. It is as complex as it is commonplace. Glover has directed us to part of this complexity by distinguishing between the 'inner story' – the one we tell ourselves about ourselves – and what he calls the 'whole story.' Of the former he says, 'it stretches back as far as we can remember. We think of it as the truth from which other stories may deviate a bit.' However, he points out, 'we simplify when we think of the inner story as the truth. What we tell ourselves is not the whole story, as an objective God might tell it' (1988, 139). But what does Glover really mean by the 'inner story,' and by the 'whole story,' and how might this whole story be related to 'the truth'? Unfortunately, he does not elaborate. He says only that the objective God who might tell it 'would include our unconscious motives, and the story would not have items left out or distorted through forgetting or bias.' In this section, I shall pick up where Glover leaves off by trying to clarify what each of these terms might be taken to mean and what is the relationship between them.

When I refer to 'the story of my life,' I may be making a number of associations in my mind all at once: the events of my life themselves (whether minor or main); my memories of those events (which may be quite a different matter); the autobiography I might eventually write; or the biography I hope (or fear) someone else might write *of* me. Or I may be thinking of certain overall patterns I have remarked in my relationships or my life as a whole. Doubtless, I seldom make any one of these associations exclusively. They are frequently mingled, a phenomenon that both enriches and complicates any discussion of the poetics of self-creation. Be that as it may, it is worth taking the time to try to spell out the differences between them. To do so, I propose that if the concept of story applies to a life at all, then that application is in relation to one or the other, or some combination, of four possible levels: **existence, experience, expression,** and **impression.**

Existence: The Outside Story

The first level, that of existence, is the level of 'what actually happened' in the past. The story of my life on this level is simply the sum total of everything I have ever done, said, thought, or felt, in all the different dimensions of my life: the verbal, the emotional, the intellectual, the interpersonal, the conscious, the unconscious, the behavioural, and the physical, even the biochemical, the molecular, and the atomic. It is what Glover calls the whole story of my life: the story of every saying and every cell, every movement and every molecule, every embrace and every breath. It is 'my life' in the sense of 'the facts.' In so far as 'the story of my life' on this level is to any degree truly a 'story,' it falls into the category of *annal*. For it is literally the entire record of every event and every occurrence by which my existence has been constituted, one after the other, from the instant of my conception to the instant just passed.

Where precisely the whole story of my life begins, then, is a matter of debate, for strictly speaking it is inseparable from the whole story of the cosmos. This is true in several senses at once: temporally, physically, and socio-psychologically. For instance, the *temporal* boundary between my existence and that of my parents is technically quite unclear, in so far as I am flesh of their flesh, blood of their blood, gene of their gene, and quark of their quark – as they were of their parents in turn. As philosopher David Carr says, 'my own story was underway in the minds and bodies of my parents even before my birth' (1986, 84). Ultimately, say the cosmologists, we are constructed of the same material as the stars; we are as old as the universe itself. In the same way, the *physical* boundary between my existence and that of everyone (and everything) else is impossible to delineate. The molecules of my body are being continually reconstituted out of those I consume from my environment – again by eating, drinking, and breathing – then returned to it by exhaling and excreting. Finally, on the *socio-psychological* front, as we shall appreciate repeatedly in what follows, we know instinctively that what Tennyson says is true: 'I am a part of all that I have met.'

In general, the whole story of my life is the uninterpreted, unevaluated, unavailable totality of all the minutiae of my particular existence in time and space – in so far as that can be separated from the existence of everything else – as it might be inscribed in utter detail on some cosmic recording device, whether a colossal computer or the mind of Glover's 'objective God.' In 'objective' terms, it is the *outside* story. It is, technically speaking, the truth of my life. It is not only the whole story but the *'true* story' too (though, as we shall see in later sections, the combination of the two terms is not without its problems.) Nevertheless, even if we concede that this whole story exists, I can neither tell it nor access it because of its vastness and multi-dimensionality, and because I am, after all, entirely *inside* of it, like an infant within a womb. Thus the sense of strangeness that can strike me on seeing myself in a photograph, or hearing my voice on a tape recorder, or catching a fleeting glimpse of how I am viewed by others. 'Is that what I *really* look like, sound like, act like?' I ask myself, bewildered. As philosopher David Polonoff puts it, 'the full story of who I am, where this is understood as the life I have in fact lived, is never available to me in its entirety' (1987, 47). For a good third of it, in fact, I am asleep: unconscious and unaware. Like nature, my existence cannot be grasped as it is in itself. It can only be apprehended – partially, imperfectly, and second-hand – through my theories, my senses, my memory, and my imagination.

Experience: The Inside Story

On the second level, experience, the whole story of my life begins to become accessible to me. It becomes accessible, though, not as that

story in itself but only as it is taken up within me and interpreted by
me. It is 'my life' in the sense suggested by the platitude 'life is what
you make it.' It is 'my life,' not in the literal sense of 'how it is' or
'how it was,' but, as Jerome Bruner says, of 'how it is interpreted and
reinterpreted, told and retold' (1987, 31). It is the realm of what cognitive scientists call autobiographical memory (Rubin, 1986). According
to Ulrich Neisser, such memory 'consists of events that we have personally experienced – or ... of our personal experiences of events'
(1986, 71). It is the level of what Glover calls my inner story. The inner
story is the sum total not of what actually happened but only of my
memories or impressions of it, the total not of events *per se* but only
of events I have personally experienced. 'Experienced' is the key. It
implies that I have subjected those events to some sort of process; that
I have worked on them in some sort of manner, attended to them,
noticed them; that somewhere within me I have filed them away for
future reference; or that, as we say, I have 'learned' from them. It
implies that, in the very least, I have *done* something to them, in what
psychologist Robert Kegan describes as 'that most human of "regions"
between an event and a reaction to it – the place where the event is
privately composed, made sense of, the place where it actually *becomes*
an event for that person' (1982, 2).

Whereas the whole story is the objective or outside story, then, the
inner story is the *inside* story: the story of my life as I have internalized or digested it, the 'real, inmost story' (Sacks, 1985, 105), the subjective story that I alone can tell. The inside story is what I *make* of the
outside story; indeed, it is all I *can* make of the outside story, all I can
know of it. It is based on the outside story – that is, I may (naïvely)
assume it to be a fairly accurate representation of it – but the relationship between the two is problematic. In fact, inside and outside are
often at odds. There is a curious gap between them, yet one from
which spring those very features of our humanness that make us the
fascinating species we are: our secrecy, our self-deception, our hypocrisy, our humour, our irony, our insanity, our feelings and fears, even
our capacity for thought itself. The inside story is to the outside story,
we could say, what science is to nature, or what religion is to God, or
what art is to life. The inside story is *my* creation. It is what *I* make in
my mind and my heart out of the raw material of *my* existence. It is
the product of my imagination – which reconstitutes the raw events
of my life as rememberable experiences. Taking these events-turned-
experiences as a whole, the inside story is simply my 'experience.'

In calling the inside story the realm of experience, though, I am invoking a term that has a long and tortured history in intellectual circles; even in everyday speech, it has more than one meaning. It can mean 'wisdom': something inherently good, an accumulated treasure, the pearl of great price shaped slowly but surely within me out of the gritty realities of the long span of my life. It can mean 'expertise': knowledge and ability I have gradually acquired in a particular topic or field or skill. It can also mean a specific event at which I was especially present and aware; thus, I might say, 'yesterday, I had a fascinating "experience."' It can mean simply the sum total of everything I go through or do, with an emphasis upon the negative; so I might sigh how I have 'learned from experience' or how 'experience has taught me.' At the same time, it can mean the ongoing process of my consciousness itself: 'the flow of feelings, perceptions, memories, and fantasies as these occur from moment to moment' (Jourard, 1971, 59). Though not exclusive of elements in any of these meanings, my use of 'experience' here is most closely akin to that of Aldous Huxley: 'experience is not what happens to you, it's what you do with what happens to you' (Kegan, 1982, 11). Intrinsically neither good nor bad, then, experience is simply everything we have somehow taken inside of us, constructed some meaning from, made something of, and so woven into our world. According to R.D. Laing, it is what 'used to be called the Soul' (1967, 18).

In the spirit of such an understanding, researchers Connelly and Clandinin call experience the total of our 'personal practical knowledge' (1988, 25–6). Its personal and practical aspects mean that my soul – my inside story – is selective. It excludes the story of my molecules, for instance, or my enzymes, or my various involuntary bodily functions. What it includes instead is the story of my feelings, my relationships, my thoughts, my more or less conscious engagements with the world – all that involves my life within that world as this particular person, all that I have 'owned, owned up to, appropriated' (Crites, 1986, 161). Because the inside story of my life is my creation, then, and thus uniquely my possession, it is more easily separable than is the whole story from the story of the cosmos. It is what makes me an individual. ('I cannot experience your experience,' says Laing; 'you cannot experience my experience' (18).) This is because it is 'told' not from some objective, all-knowing, impersonal perspective, according to which reality might be viewed as all of one piece, but from my own perspective. It is centred not out there but in here, in my own self-consciousness. It is the totality of everything I know, think, feel, remember, believe, and hope, about *my* self. In a sense, my inside story amounts to my *self*. 'The self,' argues Stephen Crites, 'is a kind of aesthetic construct, recollected in and with the life of experience in narrative fashion' (1986, 162). More to the point, it is a figment of my imagination, a fabrication of my storytelling talents. The self, says psychoanalyst Roy Schafer, 'is always a narrative construction' (1992, xvi). 'The mysterious thing we call a self,' writes ethicist Stanley Hauerwas, 'is best understood exactly as a story' (1977, 78). Thus, my self-creation is tied to my self-story, which means if I change my inner story, I change me.

For the moment, two questions must be asked. The first concerns just how valid the term *story* really is. Though I shall look into the definition of story in more detail in the following chapter, the issue here concerns how justified we are in seeing our inner world as indeed an inner *story*. When I pause to tune in to the actual contents swirling about within me at any given moment, I am aware at once of a bewildering array of activity, very little of which seems terribly story-like. Literary critic Peter Brooks describes this activity as 'an episodic, sometimes semi-conscious but virtually uninterrupted monologue' (1985, 13). But how much of this monologue – if monologue it be, since voices other than my own can seem to interrupt (of internalized parents, etc.) – possesses a story line that connects it together? There are, for example, scraps of dreams from my afternoon nap, stray telephone numbers or statistics, idle observations about the colour of the bird in the garden outdoors, a verse of some jingle or poem, bits of fallout from the conversation with my neighbour last night, flashbacks to a chat with my teacher in grade two, the sounds of my mother's words from long ago or of my partner's words in tomorrow's long overdue talk, traces of anxiety about my child's future if he fails next Thursday's exam, and vestiges of plans for my upcoming weekend, my holidays next year, or my eventual retirement. And so on. However, in so far as each component of this inner activity – this endless 'chattering,' this seemingly aimless 'blind thinking,' as one psychologist calls it (Field, 1952, 130) – is oriented toward either some remembered past, some rehearsed-for future, or some experienced present, it may be said to assume of its own accord a roughly 'story' form – that is, with beginnings, middles, and ends.

Furthermore, even though not all such activity concerns actual *events* in my own life (whether past, present, or potential) – even though I can and do contemplate abstract *concepts*, and can and do consider real or hypothetical events in others' lives and in the world at large – in all such consideration, I am making reference, explicitly or implicity, to what I myself have actually done, said, thought, felt, suffered, seen, or heard ... or can *imagine* doing, saying, thinking, etc. In this respect, nothing within my inner world is not, in the final analysis, autobiographically based. So it is that what we are dealing with is not merely an inner world but, in some rudimentary manner, an inner world of *stories* – stories of which my 'self' is in some way the teller (Bruner, 1990, 111) – stories, moreover, that are about not just the past but the future as well.

This last point is essential. The inside story is filled with projections into and speculations about the future. Within the privacy of our hearts, we can often expend as much energy playing out scenarios for the future as we do pondering situations from the past; as much of our soul can be focused on rehearsing what will be as on rehashing what has been. Thus, if the inside story is our experience, it is also our expectation; if it takes in our learning, it takes in our yearning as well. It is what we 'make up' about the past and future both. Says one writer, 'the past is partly and the future wholly an invention of the mind' (Campbell, 1989, 369). Even if we insist on thinking of the inside story in terms of memory alone, rare is the individual memory that is entirely about the past; each has its accompanying emotion in the present and its associated reference in the future. Memories of a lost love, a specific picnic or argument, a decision made or avoided: most are inseparable from some element of wondering 'what might have happened if,' some wistful speculation about 'the road not taken,' some regret about not knowing then 'what I know now.'

The second question goes one step further. It asks whether this inner *world* of stories is necessarily the same thing as *one* story. Can one story be construed from the many, or is our life 'no more than a bundle of stories, mostly half-finished' (Cupitt, 1991, 154)? I shall return to this question in later sections, especially in 'The Novel-ty of Our Lives.' In the meantime, the dim outlines of an answer can be discerned when we consider the possibility that if our personal practical knowledge, our self, our experience is an inner story – at least in the sense of an inner *world* of stories – then we are talking about a story-world that is inconceivably complicated. Rather than the simple, short, stylized, seemingly straightforward world of a child's bedtime tale, it is more like the vast, intricate, multi-directional, many-levelled, inherently many-storied world of a full-length novel – a world so complicated in fact, so much in progress, with a plot so unclear, that it is virtually impossible for us to say what kind of story it is, for we are right in its midst. It is also virtually impossible for us to say what it is about, for with each passing moment and each new event to account for and incorporate into it, it becomes 'about' more and more. Accordingly, where it has come from thus far will have to remain as unclear to us, given the various ways we could cast its beginning, as where it might be going, given the multiple endings to it we can either fantasize or fear.

It is this strange situation of being poised in the ever-moving middle of our own unique story, or set of stories, on the brink of a multitude of possible renderings of both our overall beginning and our overall end, that makes the *inside* story, though accessible to us, not terribly tellable at all. It is not tellable because, for one thing, it is far too long to tell, and getting longer by the second. For another, it is too malleable, too much in flux interpretively, too susceptible of too many tellings. It cannot be recounted in its entirety without bias or distortion any more than we can communicate clearly or completely the story of science. Thus, to continue the analogy, if the inside story is to the outside story as science is to nature, then each individual telling of the inside story – in either summary or segment form – is to that inside story itself as a particular scientific theory (as seen by a particular scientist on a particular day!) is to science as a whole.

Expression: The Inside-Out Story

This moves me to third level on which we can take the metaphor of life-as-story, that of expression. If the first level is the outside story, the totality of my existence, and the second is the inside story, the totality of my experience, then the third is the level of each individual version of my inside story that I convey to others, what I choose to call the *inside-out* story. It is 'my life' in the sense of what I present or project to the world. It is my 'life-story' as I communicate it to others (Kaufman, 1987, 21). If my inside story is focused most intensely in my autobiographical memory, then my inside-out story attains its sharpest shape in some form of an actual autobiography – from keeping a journal to writing my memoirs – or in some combination of the many other ways in which, intentionally or not, I express to others what is going on inside of me: from the possessions I own, to the words I speak, to the lines upon my face; indeed, from my day-to-day actions and involvements to the whole spread of my accomplishments and achievements, or lack thereof. All of these 'palpable projections of the impalpable and wholly personal inner experience' (Edel, 1959, 88) constitute my 'fullest autobiography' (Olney, 1972, 3). All of these, literally, tell others a story about me. Says psychoanalyst Roy Schafer, 'there is no hard-and-fast line between telling and showing' (1980, 34; 1983, 222).

At the same time, what I tell or show by one means of expression I may belie by another. How often do I not tell one story with my words and another with my eyes, and still another with my actions or body – while my 'fashion statement' tells a story all its own? Though there are times when these media seem wonderfully 'together,' there are just as many when they are not: when I come across in print more powerfully than in person, when my actions speak louder than my words, or when my words themselves are spoken with forked tongue. In general, my inside-out stories, by any means, bear an ambiguous relationship to what lies inside. Again, there is a gap. How often can I say *exactly* what I mean? Diplomacy enters in, the element of tact, a compromising awareness of the needs and agendas of the others to whom I must relate. Even where these restrictions are reduced, my words themselves are inadequate to the complexity of my feelings or the subtleties of my thoughts. In my most intimate attempts to articulate my inner life, say in keeping a journal, my voice is always in part contrived. Language itself edits my experience – refracts it, distorts it – in the very act of my giving it expression. Rhetoric plays a role; content is affected by form. 'All telling modifies what is being told,' writes Lawrence Langer (1991, 41). No matter how hard I try, whether verbally or not, there can be no direct or complete expression of the soul. In the words of Mark Twain, 'what a wee little part of a person's life are his acts and his words! His real life is led in his head, and is known to none but himself ... His acts and his words are merely the visible, thin crust of his world ... and they are so trifling a part of his bulk! a mere skin enveloping it. The mass of him is hidden ...' (Kaplan, 1986, 72–3).

Just as the events of my life are changed in the experiencing, then, so the experiences of my life are changed in the expressing. At least when expressed in words, they become the most obviously story-like: constructed and conveyed with the most conscious attention to how they will be heard, read, and responded to *as* stories (anecdotes, tid-bits, tales), with the most conscious attention to the conventions and clichés of story construction. Such conventions (over which some souls have greater mastery than others) include, as we shall see in the following chapter, the element of conflict that is set up and resolved, the sense of suspense the story elicits, the overall style or voice in which

it is communicated, and the moral or message – the point or theme –
it is used to put across. In a way, our tendency toward story conventions in our self-telling is inevitable, due to the narrative nature of the
very language we employ. 'The subject-verb-object structure of the
sentence,' says one source, 'is already a simple narrative' (Cupitt, 1990,
180). Language itself is storied. Can our lives, as penetrated by language as they surely are, be any less so?

Since this level is my focus in the following chapter under 'The
Stories of Our Lives,' I shall limit myself here to a few fundamental
points. First, these expressed versions of part or all of our inside
story will vary according to a range of factors, such as form, content,
medium, motivation, and origin. Second, these inside-out stories are
just as problematically related to our inside story as, so we have
seen, our inside story can be to our outside story. Third, they can be
seen as swirling continually about within us, interacting with one
another now in a complementary way and now a competitive way,
their complex relationship to one another giving rise to the humour,
the irony, and the self-deception of which we humans seem peculiarly capable. Fourth, though accessible and tellable, they are innumerable. There are conceivably as many versions of part or all of our
inside story as there are moments in a lifetime – thus, the constant
questioning about our 'identity' that, at some stage or other, can
characterize us all.

Impression: The Outside-In Story

The fourth and final level on which we can understand 'the story of
my life' is one to which I have already alluded. It is the level of impression, the level of the stories that are entertained about me *outside-
in*, that are 'read' into my life by all those who know me or encounter
me in any way. It is 'my life' in the sense of what is *made* of me by
others. It is my 'life-history' in the sense of what is *told* of me by
others (Kaufman, 1987, 21; Runyan, 1984). If the sharpest focus of my
inside-out story is my autobiography, then that of my outside-in story
would be my biography – assuming only one can be written. Short of
my 'official' biography, that is, there can be numerous such renderings
of the story of my life, from the concept of me held by my most casual
acquaintance, to the crisply worded case history compiled on me by
a doctor or social worker, analyst or judge, to the flowery-phrased
eulogy delivered upon my death.

An important if incidental point here, however, is that in our everyday relationships there are times when others appear to read us better than we read ourselves, or at least may try to convince us they can! A therapist, parent, or friend, for instance, can frequently have an outside-in story of us that is far 'truer' (in retrospect anyway) than the inside-out story that we express to them: in the sense that they appear to understand what is happening *inside* of us (if not actually experience it) more profoundly than we do ourselves. Similarly, though the distinction between biography and autobiography is simple enough on the surface, our autobiography *could* – when, say, of the memoir variety – be more of an outside-in story than is our biography. The latter, that is, may be much more *auto*-biographical, in the sense of capturing our *inside* story and of being in touch with the 'feel' of our life more accurately than we are ourselves (see Edel, 1959, 133, 153).

Much more often, however, others' stories of us are a far cry from those we entertain on our own. Their impressions can vary wildly from our experience of ourselves. Yet they are never just static snapshots of who we are in the present; they are also dynamic guesses about where we have come from in the past and where we are going in the future. At the same time, they are usually 'only simplified sketches which leave out the fuzzy edges' (Glover, 1988, 147). Rather than detailed narrative portraits, they are un-filled-in outlines – 'story-o-types,' we might say: like 'stereotypes,' only more historical, more tensed, and more inventive, for they entail reading into our lives not merely a hypothetical present but also a possible future and past. Fuzzy or focused, as we have seen in the case of gossip and prejudice, these 'storyotypes' – whether negative or positive, diminutions of us or idolizations – exercise an unquestionable influence upon our self-creation. They help determine others' treatment of us directly; they set limits on the opportunities they open up to us indirectly; and they give shape – often powerfully – to the story we tell of ourselves. They affect our self-creation in the specific sense that our awareness of others' outside-in story of us – more precisely, our perception of that story, since we have no direct access to it – inevitably influences how we express our inside-out story to them, whether to reflect it or reject it.

The Links between the Levels

In general, if the outside story is what happens to me, then the inside story is what I *make* of what happens to me and what I tell to myself.

The inside-out story is what I tell (and show) to *others* of what I make of what happens to me, while the outside-in story is what others make of me on their own, with or (usually) without my consent. A few analogies, however, might further clarify the links that I see between these levels.

In manufacturing terms, the outside story is the raw material from which I fashion the inside story, while the inside story is the raw material from which I fashion the stories I tell inside-out. Accordingly, not everything that could be used from the outside story on the inside is used. Much is jettisoned as slag. By the same token, not everything that could be used from the inside story is used when I move inside-out. Much remains buried, or is left aside as scrap to be used on a later occasion. Still more of me will usually be scrapped by others in composing the commonly cardboard 'storyotype' through which alone they can deal with me.

In computer terms, the outside story is the hardware of my system. The inside story is both the software and the collection of directories and files that I have assembled with its aid – including the particular file I am into at the moment, a portion of which fills the screen. Finally, the inside-out story is the hard copy I decide to print off for distribution to others, while the outside-in is their interpretation of the text of that copy.

In publishing terms, my outside story corresponds to the actual, physical object of a particular novel. It is the paper, ink, and binding that comprise the thing itself, plus the process by which it is produced. My inside story, however, is the novel as I *experience* it, as I reconstruct it in the reading: its life, its atmosphere, its unfolding in time, its reality within me as an entire story-world. My inside-out story is my summary of part or all of that world for the purpose of communicating about it with others. My outside-in story, then, is the set of versions that these others entertain of the same world, or read into it, on the basis of a review, the notes on the jacket, or the design on the cover.

Twain's line above about the mass of us being hidden evokes still another analogy, that of an iceberg. Reaching down to the bottom, beneath the surface, is the vast, spreading reality of my outside story: untellable, inaccessible, barely imaginable at all but, presumably, 'there,' the objective 'facts' of my existence. At or near the surface is my inside story, the totality of my *experience* of my existence, that abridged version of the whole story that I carry around within me: imaginable and accessible yet still not quite tellable because of its size, its complexity, and its flux. Visible on the horizon – the tip, as it were – is my inside-out story, which means each telling (or showing) of some summary or segment of my inside story to others, on the basis of their perception of which, outside-in, they then form the impressions with which they proceed to relate to me.

The iceberg analogy suggests a set of terms that are part of the dogma of modern psychology: the unconscious, the sub- or semi-conscious, and the conscious realms.[4] The unconscious contains all that I have ever been, done, thought, or felt in my life but that is largely lost to conscious retrieval – which might seem to make it correspond nicely to my outside story. However, since so much of that story includes the involuntary dimension of my existence, as well as the voluntary, this correspondence breaks down. In its turn, the sub- or semi-conscious realm contains all that is *available* to me out of the unconscious realm potentially, but is still not quite communicable to others, though some tiny portion of it will be conscious at any given moment – at least when I am not sleeping. This would seem to correspond to the level of my inside story, but since I am so often conscious on the inside, a neat link between it and the sub- or semi-conscious is not to be had. Neither is there a neat link between the conscious realm and the level of inside-out, for much of what I express to others, not just with my words but with my gestures and actions too, I express unawares – in the process often giving mixed messages to others. Thus, the fit between the levels of life-story and these familiar psychological categories is far from exact.

All the same, while these analogies may clarify the relations between the levels of life-story, they may also obscure the fact that the boundaries between them are anything but precise. Moreover, the processes involved in moving from one to the other are intricately entwined. Hence, in the following diagram, I show the arrows between them pointing in two directions at once. There is no hard-and-fast line, for example, between my outside and inside stories, since within the latter are conceivably a number of levels again, stretching as close as possible toward the domain of the former. There is what I am directly aware of in the present moment; what I could be aware of 'if I put my mind to it'; what surfaces in my dreams from the depths below; what, with either hypnosis or an electrode probing of my temporal lobes, I might be able to recall from the dim, distant details of days gone by; and perhaps even what my body itself, well beneath my conscious awareness, feels, remembers, or knows.

In a similar way, within my inside-out story may be another set of levels again, stretching toward the inside level on one end, and my most delicate, unvarnished attempts at self-disclosure, and, on the other, toward the outside-in level and my most studied, most public and polished, self-presentations to the world. My inside-out stories to others, that is, are shaped with a view to others' outside-in stories of me, either to harmonize with them or to counter them. By the same token, my outside-in stories of them influence my inside story of me, for they are characterizations of them within that story. In short, what I make of others affects what I make of myself. If I construct another person as a villain, then that makes me either a victim or a victor (or both) by comparison.

All four levels are linked in other ways as well. The acts of telling our inside-out stories to others and of hearing their outside-in ones of us are 'events' in our outside story, which in turn can become 'experiences' in our inside story. Furthermore, it is often not until we tell somebody else what we are feeling that we realize that that in fact is what we *are* feeling. Similarly, many of us write in order to find out what we think. It is the act of going inside-out that frequently reveals to us what is going on inside. This, says Sidney Jourard (1971), is the lesson we have learned from psychotherapy: 'no man can come to know himself except as an outcome of disclosing himself to another person' (6). In addition, as we saw in considering the nature of gossip and self-image, both the inside-out and outside-in stories directly influence the unfolding of our outside story: by affecting the range of options and opportunities that are open to us in our everyday lives and relationships.

While the interpenetration of these levels cautions us from making over-bold claims about the nature of any one, it does not undo the value of distinguishing between them, for that distinction remains. First, there are the bare, unevaluated facts of my life, the sum of which, objectively speaking, *is* my story. But there is also, second, what I *make* of those facts (or 'make up' from them) inside myself, subjectively, which can be a whole different story indeed: the story-*within*-the-story, the reality behind the facts. Third, there is the way I take this inner story, abridge it, and package it for others, whether wittingly or not, the countless possible versions of which can vary so very much – both from each other and from the original to which they refer. Finally, there is the interpretation of my life that is conveyed to me (or concealed from me) by others: usually inaccurate and incom-

The Story of My Life

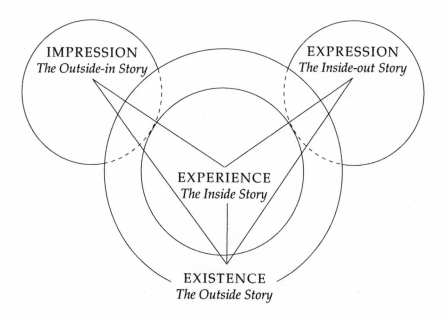

plete, a bare template, a cartoon caricature, a shadow of the real me, yet frequently so influential in the construction of my sense of self. As I hope to show repeatedly, though, it is the continual interplay of these various levels – distinct yet related yet distinct – that constitutes so much of the mystery of my being and the complexity of even the simplest of my involvements with others. Somehow, woven together in one web, swirling about me as one world, all of them *are* 'my life,' all of them *are* 'my self,' and all of them *are* 'my story.'

From Event to Experience: A Closer Look

One of the curious questions raised by this schema concerns just how little of our outside story actually makes it into our inside story, and why. Of 'the near-infinite number of things that *could* be noticed in any given situation' (Berger, 1963, 56), such a tiny fraction *are*. Only a select segment, a particular digest, of our total existence becomes our experience. Correspondingly, how little of our inside story makes it

into our inside-*out* story! We can never say exactly what we think nor
express entirely what we feel. There is always something more behind
our gestures, words, or deeds.

If we wish to, we can feel a sense of loss about this situation. There
seems a wastefulness here, although one that the institutions of therapy and education are presumably committed to combat. A basic goal
of psychotherapy, we could say, is to coax more of the contents of the
first level onto the second, and more of the second onto the third. Put
another way, it is to help us have more of our lives at our disposal,
meaning more of our existence incorporated into our experience and
more of our experience available for expression. In addition, we could
say, a goal of therapy and education alike is to enlighten us sufficiently to critique the stories that others read into our lives outside-in,
rendering them therefore less influential on, and less constricting of,
the form and content of the stories we tell others inside-out.

Since I shall return to these unusual notions in subsequent chapters,
I want to devote the remainder of this section to the inside story – the
most elusive level of 'the story of my life,' though arguably the most
central to my sense of personal identity and my self-creation. It is on
this level that an intriguing kind of *aesthetic* process appears to occur:
the process whereby events are transformed into experiences.

Let us suppose that I undertake to drive from Toronto to New York.
Undoubtedly, many events will happen to me – and within me –
during the ten-hour trip involved: checking road maps, passing vehi-
cles, noticing scenery, stopping for coffee, chatting with my companion, and day-dreaming about my summer vacation, my child's future,
or the state of my world. In addition, I will (I hope) be breathing on
a regular basis, digesting my breakfast, rebuilding muscle tissue, and
'doing' countless other things of a largely involuntary nature. But of
all of these events – conscious and unconscious, voluntary and involuntary – how many will I be able to recall at the end of my journey?
Most will have occurred when I was on 'automatic pilot': that state of
semi-amnesia in which we drive through so frighteningly many miles
and drift through so much of each day, the wide stream of our existence flowing silently by, at the edge of our awareness. Of the involuntary events, I shall likely recall next to none (except perhaps that
one deep, rather guilty breath I drew just before customs!). Of the
other more voluntary events, though all *potentially* memorable, I shall
be able to recount only a tiny percentage, indeed tinier with the passing
of each day. But why? In terms of what has already been suggested, it

is because these events have not become experiences. But how do events become experiences? In the view of psychoanalyst James Hillman, 'an event becomes an experience, moves from outer to inner, is made into soul, when it goes through a psychological process, when it is worked upon by the soul in any of several ways.' (1975a, 149).

Naturally, not every event – certainly not of the involuntary variety – is transformable into an experience. Not every 'real event' is going to become an 'experienced event' (Neisser, 1986, 75). Or is it? For one thing, the very category of 'event' is problematic. From a certain perspective, it is merely an abstraction; one that imposes a degree of discreteness upon a reality that (whether personal, social, or natural) is ultimately indivisible into specific units with clear beginnings, middles, and ends, but is rather one continuous flow of undifferentiated Becoming: a reality in which any given 'event' automatically includes, and is 'nested' within (Neisser, 71f), other events in turn. As such, atomic events are always nested within molecular ones, molecular ones within physiological ones, physiological ones within psychological ones, sociological ones, political ones, cosmic ones, and so on. Any 'event' is on some level, therefore, already an 'experience,' inasmuch as it is worked upon by us, is made part of or taken up into some higher-level, broader, or bigger event.

It could be argued in fact that even the involuntary events of our lives are transformable into experiences, at least more than we might think, which makes the line between voluntary and involuntary a fuzzy one for sure. Our dreams, for example, are commonly considered to be bridges between the two, extending from the known without to the unknown within, where the obscurest details of our daily existence are routinely incorporated into *stories*. 'Each and everyone of us is a great mystery writer,' says one dream researcher. 'Day in and night out we create our stories, filling them with passion and adventure and colorful characters' (Langs, 1988, 3). On this view, if we could only 'decode' them, these stories would show us the nature of our real feelings in the present, the deeper meanings of events in the past, and the direction we ought to be growing in the future. More to the point here, though, there is evidence that these dream-stories even 'have access to happenings within our bodies,' happenings 'unavailable to our conscious waking minds' (12).

So, then, the distinction between event and experience is not exactly sharp, but it is not thereby useless. To return to my trip, there is a difference between my seeing a particular barn between Rochester and

Syracuse and my *recalling* seeing it afterward, if only for a second. The difference lies in the degree to which the seeing penetrates my awareness and makes an experiencable impression upon it, so that I not only *see* it but somehow *know* that I have seen it, however fleeting that knowledge may be (Neisser, 74). Furthermore, the experience of knowingly seeing the barn can itself be an event, which can in turn be experienced – though may not be – to the extent that I not only see the barn and recall seeing it, but also recall the recalling of the seeing. This phenomenon is consistent with what seems an essential dimension of self-consciousness: the capacity to be conscious of ourselves being conscious of ourselves, etc.

Whatever exactly events may be, moving them 'from outer to inner,' from existence to experience, takes time and energy. It requires a measure of reflection, examination, attention: some sort of 'psychological process.' It requires a period of digestion. For different people this will take different forms: keeping a journal, engaging in conversation, going for a meditative walk, or simply taking a few moments at the close of the day to 'collect their thoughts' or 'commit to memory' the main events of their day. Even with these strategies, however, many of us lead relatively unexamined lives, which means we have 'more events than are experienced' (Hillman, 1975a, 150). This makes unavoidable, even normal, a measure of psychic 'indigestion.' Unfortunately, says Hillman, 'what we do not digest is laid out somewhere else, into others, the political world, the dreams, the body's symptoms, becoming literal and outer ... because it is too hard for us, too opaque, to break open and insight' (150). The consequences of this situation are serious, not just for us as individuals but for society in general. As journal-keeper May Sarton puts it, 'in the life of civilizations as in the lives of individuals too much matter that cannot be digested, too much experience that has not been imagined and probed and understood, ends in total rejection of everything – ends in anomie. The structures break down and there is nothing to "hold onto"' (1981, 24–5).

On this rather grand view of things, there is a critical need for us to transform the events of our lives into experiences. Doing so would 'tame appetite' (Hillman, 1975a, 150); it would curb the restlessness by which we feed the consumer*ism* that threatens to consume us all. 'Had we more experiencing,' says Hillman, 'there would be need for fewer events and the quick passage of time would find a stop' (150). The question remains, though, as to what sort of psychological process is at work in making events into 'soul.'

For pastoral psychologist Charles Winquist, there is 'a deep poetic structure in the transformation of events into experience' (1980, 49). 'Poetic' derives from *poiesis*, a term that, as Hillman points out, means 'making' – in his view, 'making by imagination into words' (1975a, 124). Psychoanalysis, he says, is thus 'an activity in the realm of *poesis.*' Indeed, he insists on 'the poetic basis of therapy, of biography, of our very lives' (144). In words that echo those of Glover, he says: 'The way we imagine our lives is the way we are going to go on living our lives. For the manner in which we tell ourselves what is going on is the genre through which events become experiences' (146).

Winquist's reference to poetic structure and Hillman's to 'genre' and 'the poetic basis of our very lives' direct us back to life-as-story. Accordingly, we may be said to remember – to possess within us as experiences – only those incidents in our lives that we are able to assimilate into some sort of story. As Stephen Crites puts it, 'an experience … is an achievement of aesthetic coherence.' Though made out of 'sensory materials, a sight or sound, a taste or touch,' he says, 'the experience does not form until such sensory materials find their aesthetic structure, perhaps a story, or a fully articulated visual image that becomes lodged in memory' (1979, 107).

Cognitive scientist Roger Schank has taken Crites' insight and constructed around it an overall theory of memory, though his distinction between event and experience is less precise than my own. Schank believes that 'if your memory were a collection of every single episode in your entire life, you would never find a damn thing' (1983, 34). For this reason, most of the events of our lives are 'constantly being broken up into their component pieces and are being added to general event memory bit by bit in different places.' Hence, 'no coherent whole remains' (1990, 122). Whether it happens while we are awake or asleep, in the course of our deeds or our dreams, this process of dismantling the events of our lives and storing (or storying) them away for future reference is a necessary aspect of the larger process we think of as 'learning from experience.' 'Whole experiences,' Schank says, 'must be broken up and analysed in order to learn from them and to place the new information that has been learned where it can be found later when needed' (122). For this reason, it is impossible to recall the vast majority of individual events that happen during the course of a ten-hour drive. We can be grateful for this, clearly, since otherwise too much energy would be tied up retaining these events in our conscious awareness. Precious little would be left to devote to other important activities for which long drives afford the luxury, such as day-dreaming, unwinding, and reflecting leisurely on the meaning of life.

When we tell a story about a particular event, however, when we try to recapture or recite it after the fact, we un-do this automatic process of breaking it up into its component pieces. When we tell our spouse or friend about part or all of our journey, what we tell tends, literally, to stick together (to co-here) in our minds. This accords with a general view of story – any story – as a means of bringing order out of chaos. Stories, says Schank, 'are a way of preserving the connectivity of events that would otherwise be dissociated over time' (124). Telling a story 'tends to make a unit of a sequence of events and this unit can be remembered more easily.' Thus, failing to create this unit is … likely to leave its individual pieces in memory disconnected from the preceding and following events' (134). In short, stories 'digest one's experience' (29).

For Schank, 'human beings are collections of stories' or 'repositories of stories' (135, 40). 'They accumulate stories over a lifetime, and when they are given the opportunity, they select an appropriate story and tell it' (135). In fact, says Schank, this is what defines intelligence. Intelligence is the ability to tell the right story at the right time. Correspondingly, the 'knowledge' on which such intelligence draws, 'is really a collection of hundreds of thousands of stories' (63). Indeed, there may be no knowledge at all that is not encoded as stories (12) – a perspective that accords with that of theologian Don Cupitt, who asserts bluntly that '"the mind" is made of stories' (1991, 5). 'What we actually know,' Schank insists, 'is all the stories, experiences, "facts," little epithets, points of view, and so on that we have gathered over the years' (1990, 15). In summary, then, 'story' is central to the definitions of the three terms around which his argument revolves – knowledge, intelligence, and memory: 'Knowledge is experiences and stories, and intelligence is the apt use of experience and the creation and telling of stories. Memory is memory for stories, and the major processes of memory are the creation, storage, and retrieval of stories' (16).

For the purposes of my own argument here, the key consequence of Schank's theory is that these stories constitute our inside story as a whole, our experience. They become, says Schank, 'our own definition of self. We are the stories we like to tell' (137). 'We tell stories to describe ourselves not only so others can understand who we are but also so we can understand ourselves. Telling our stories allows us to compile our personal mythology, and *the collection of stories we have compiled is to some extent who we are'* (44; emphasis mine).

We must bear in mind of course that in trying to understand the process of indexing and retrieving these countless stories, Schank's primary agenda is to better duplicate human intelligence artificially. However, he is also curious about how these stories are woven within us in the first place, for he sees them as being fabricated *by* us and not simply there, ready-made, inherent in events themselves. Though he does not speculate on what might bind the many stories into one – though he is more concerned with the sto*ries* of my life than with the *story* of my life – his insights into story-creation in general deserve further consideration in any fuller treatment we give to self-creation.

For now, working from the hypothesis that our inside story is something we *create* out of our outside story, it is essential to wrestle with a few of the issues we raise when we relate 'the story of my life' to 'the art of living.'

The Art of Living

Paralleling our present fascination with creativity, perhaps propelling it, is our keen interest in the 'art' of one aspect after another of our everyday life. Perhaps it has ever been thus, but, once again, the 1993–4 issue of *Books in Print* lists more than a thousand titles in which Art is the operative word, including *The Art of Loving, The Art of Breathing,* and *The Art of Making Wine.* Using art in such wide-ranging ways betrays an underlying conviction that not only can a particular aspect of life be viewed as aesthetic enterprise but so can life as a whole. Yet the idea of 'the art of *living'* is scarcely a phenomenon of modern times alone. It is traceable to the beginnings of civilization in virtually every culture: wherever there has been a concern for the good life, for the ethical life, for the spiritual life, for life lived to its fullest and highest potential; wherever there has been a searching for 'a better way.' According to Foucault, 'the elaboration of one's life as a personal work of art,' was, in antiquity, 'at the center of moral experience' (1988, 49).

We find the Greeks, for example, much concerned with *arete* (Castle, 1961, 11–12, 101–5), something that at various stages of their culture was understood in terms of qualities like virtue, heroism, honour, and excellence. Similarly, the Romans were concerned with *gravitas*, or earnestness, and with *pietas*, or loyalty to family, the fatherland, and the gods (106f). For the Hebrews, the central concern was with following 'the law,' which meant obedience to the commandments of Yahweh and to the countless elaborations thereon that were worked out by prophets and priests.

For the ancient Chinese, the concern was with living in accordance with 'the Tao,' a term often translated as 'the way' – the way of creative quietude, of active inactivity, of no-mindedness, of balance (Watts, 1957, 15f). However alien the West may have found this 'way' in the past, it is curiously drawn to it in the present. We find 'Tao' being baptized and popularized almost as much as 'Art.' Hence the plethora of books on 'the Tao of' relationships, management, physics, psychology, Pooh, and the like. Such an interest may of course be little more than a passing fad, at a point in Western culture when we are looking longingly at the quick-starter economies of the Orient – notably Japan – in the hopes of implementing whatever philosophical principles may have inspired their success. Viewed less cynically, it may represent our frantic attempt to recover – in an ecologically nightmarish, *post*-modern age – the vision of the simpler, more balanced, more centred life we assume, naïvely and nostalgically, was the lot of our forebears. Viewed less cynically still, however, it may represent a positive step forward from the perception of life's purpose we have inherited from Judaeo-Christianity, in which morality, Foucault says, is understood 'as obedience to a code of rules' (1988, 49). In a post-Christian era, though, such an understanding 'is now disappearing.' Corresponding to 'this absence of morality,' he believes, 'must be the search for an aesthetics of existence' (49).

Throughout this first chapter, I have been developing a perspective on the process of self-creation that roots it in the dynamics of personal story. I believe there is a connection between self-creation and the concept of the art of living. In this section, I shall be focusing on the latter part of that connection: first, by considering the definition of 'art' and its relationship to 'life'; then, by introducing the notion of 'self-culture'; next, by raising the overall issue of the evaluation of the artwork of an individual life; and, finally, by pondering the idea of 'composing' a life and the distinctions it implies between art, craft, and improvisation. I should point out that I see this section merely as an introduction to the larger, less tangible themes that a discussion of the poetics of self-creation tends to raise. In the final section of the final chapter, I shall return to a number of these themes as I reconsider 'the art of living' in light of the more detailed look I shall by then have given to the complexity of life-story.

Art and Life

The first task relates to the definition not of 'a work of art,' nor of 'the arts,' but of 'art' as such. Such a task is neither simple nor concludable. However, we can at least get a sense of the spectrum of possibilities from which there are to choose. That spectrum has to do with the overall relationship between art and life, as well as the basic question of which comes first: art or life? We are able to explore this relationship and ask this question, of course, because however much they may each resist precise definition, art and life are ultimately not the same. Not the same, that is, in the same way that 'experience' and 'existence' are not the same: the former being to the latter what 'the aesthetic object' is to 'the real object' (Chatman, 1978, 26–7). In his discussion of the 'metaphorical relationship' between the two, Richard Shiff (1979) insists that 'art seems to depend upon its distinction from life, and vice versa ...' 'The identity of art and life,' he says, 'is an ideal, not a reality ...' 'Neither an art possessing the immediacy of life's experience nor a life having the fixed formal structure of art would seem to belong to the world as we know it' (116). At the same time, there is no such thing as 'pure art,' any more than there is such a thing as 'pure life.' Instead, he stresses, 'our world lies between the two extremes' (120).

Accordingly, there are theories of art that view its relationship to life as primarily the representation, the mirroring, or the *imitation* of life. Others view art more cynically as an escape from life, an *idealization* of life, or simply the *illusion* of life. Others again view it as but a particular artist's *impression* of life; for some, it is viewed more loftily as the *illumination* of life. For a few even, art is viewed as the *ingestion* of life, a theory implied by Northrop Frye, for example, when he insists that literature neither reflects life nor withdraws from it but in fact swallows it (1963, 33)!

Besides these options, there are theories of art that view it as the creation, the construction, or (for the sake of consistency) the *invention* of life. For novelist John Gardner, for instance, 'invention is central to art.' In his view, 'art does not imitate reality ... but creates a new reality' (1985, 131). Closely related to this perspective is that of John

Dewey's colleague, philosopher Irwin Edman. 'Experience, apart from art and intelligence, is wild and orderless,' he says. 'It is formless matter, aimless movement' (1928, 14–15). By contrast, art is 'that whole process of intelligence by which life, understanding its own conditions, turns them to the most interesting or exquisite account' (12). Art, on this view, is life's way of staving off the chaos to which the second law of thermodynamics otherwise leads (Rifkin, 1989, 47–59). Art, broadly defined, is life's answer to entropy. 'To the extent that life has form,' writes Edman, 'it is an art' (13). 'Wherever materials are given form, wherever movement has direction, wherever life has, as it were, line and composition, there we have intelligence and there we have that transformation of a given chaos into a desired and desirable order that we call Art' (14–15).

Art as imitation, as illumination, as ingestion, and now as invention: obviously, none of these views of art stands entirely on its own. Aspects of one blend imperceptibly with those of the others in any attempt to articulate the nature, function, and value of art as a whole. For example, author Irving Howe speaks of the 'doubled nature' of the novel as both 'mirror and lamp' (1989, 32), both the imitation of life and its illumination. Despite this overlap, surely what is at issue here is the syllable on which the emphasis is placed. In light of my considerations so far, there is value in placing that emphasis, in part, on the theory of art as invention and, in part, on an additional but related theory: art as the *interpretation* of life.

None of us 'interprets the raw world directly,' writes Annie Dillard in *Living by Fiction* (1982, 146). We interpret our world and ourselves *through* the inventions of our imagination, *through* our fictions. 'Humanity has but one product,' she claims, 'and that is fiction.' In fiction, art as invention converges with art as interpretation: 'all mental activity is selective and interpretative; all language is interpretative; all perception is interpretative; all expression and activity is interpretative. And all interpretations miss their mark or invent it, make it up' (148).

In her discussion of 'the fictive roots' of ordinary reality, sociologist Mary Rogers undergirds Dillard's point by detailing the role of the principal institutions that order the world of our everyday life, namely family, work, and government. 'Within those institutions,' she insists, 'fictive understandings let people take much for granted while going about their business with little confusion, apprehension, or even thought' (1991, 209). Of course, the supreme fiction is the institution of 'civilization' as a whole, in any or all of its incarnations, including such specific sub-fictions as science, religion, and art. Indeed, 'the structure of reality,' exclaims the poet Wallace Stevens, is 'an adult make-believe' (Rogers, 210). However, neither reality nor civilization nor any one institution within it *as a work of art* is my focus here. Rather, it is the artwork of an individual life. None the less, the two are related. Their relationship can be understood in terms of the concept of culture.

Self-Culture

In his discussion of human beings as 'self-defining animals,' social psychologist John Shotter insists that 'man must give form to his act of living' (1975, 133). The structures and activities whereby we 'give form' to our living, and thereby define ourselves, come under the category of culture. Culture, he says, is the third term in any equation that tries to relate the two traditionally opposed concepts of man and nature (136). According to this opposition, 'Nature is seen as fully in place and functioning more or less autonomously *before* Culture comes along and builds upon it' (Cupitt, 1991, 16–17). On this view, culture is 'artificial, secondary and inessential' (17). Shotter disagrees, however, with such a tradition, profoundly ingrained though it may be within our thought: 'nowhere is man to be found in a state of nature. Everywhere and at every time he is only to be found in a state of culture, living ways of life that he must have devised for himself in some way – ways of life that his young inherit, not genetically like blue eyes, but in a process of communication which takes place after birth' (130). It is not so much culture that is artificial, then, but the nature-culture dichotomy itself, and its corollary in psychology: nature-nurture. We view the world, Shotter says, and 'deliberate upon how to act in it,' from *within* a culture, and this culture, he insists, 'structures' our consciousness (136). In this respect, art *creates* life.

Culture, however, pertains not only to the corporate level but to the personal level as well. The combination of structures and activities whereby we 'give form' to our living as individuals, and therefore define ourselves, also constitutes a kind of culture – self-culture, as it were. It is from within this self-culture that we view ourselves. It is through this self-culture that our self-consciousness is constructed and our raw world interpreted. It is in terms of this self-culture that we fashion our 'human nature,' something that is less 'a biologically fixed substratum' (Berger and Luckmann, 1967, 49) than something we make ourselves (Shotter, 1993, 3). Clearly, though, self-culture is intertwined with social culture. The latter structures and limits the former. As we shall see in the next chapter, it structures and limits the 'forms of self-telling' (Bruner, 1987, 16). However, it is on the former I wish to focus.

My use of 'self-culture' is in a general sense and not in the specific and pejorative sense in which it might otherwise be taken, as for instance the 'cult' of 'self,' or as what Christopher Lasch calls 'the culture of narcissism' (1978). As such, self-culture may be seen as a synonym for 'the art of living.' It is that dynamic, living, ever-changing, indeed historical, process – like culture in general – in which each of us is involved simply by virtue of being alive, and that we are continually enjoying, exploring, extending, and at times even evaluating. It is that entire aesthetic enterprise in which we are ceaselessly engaged in so far as, consciously or otherwise and for better or worse, we are committed to the task of 'making something' out of our lives – of taking the raw material with which we have to work (genetics, environment, family of origin, and the opportunities and vicissitudes of life in general) and cultivating from it a life that is uniquely ours. Such a life, we may argue, is an artwork, making every one of us thus an artist and, in that sense at least, culture-d. It is an artwork in which, as we saw with self-creation, each of us is automatically involved.

Moreover, it is the most multimedia of all other artforms – simultaneously visible, audible, tangible, and, of course, thoroughly temporal. And it is reflected, directly or indirectly, in countless things about us: from the furniture we own to the mementoes we keep, from the clothes we wear to the company we keep, from the expressions we use to the jokes and anecdotes we carry about, and from the names we drop to the overall 'style' we exude. But it is reflected in perhaps its most complex, most subtle, and most personal form – as is any *social* culture – in the web of stories we tell ourselves (and others) 'to capture our past, sustain our present, and give our future direction' (Aichele, 1985, 27): in the stories by which we carry our beliefs about ourselves and our world, digest the events of our lives and transform them into experiences, and fashion some sort of order from the data of our existence.

Self-culture, self-cultivation, self-creation, lifestyle, the art of living – these concepts converge, then, in the concept of 'the story of my life': a story we not only tell but also show, which we both relate and live. We are 'living stories,' communicated through both our words and our ways. As Alisdair MacIntyre writes, 'stories are lived before they are told' (1981, 196). Or as Paul John Eakin (1985) puts it in his study, the *Fictions in Autobiography*, 'the autobiographical act [is] a mode of self-invention that is always practised first in living and only eventually – sometimes – formalized in writing' (8–9). Linking self-culture with self-creation, and the art of living with the story of my life, moves us even more deeply, then, into the domain of aesthetics. Though the notion of creating ourselves is itself an aesthetic notion, the notion that we create ourselves through the weaving and reworking of our personal story is, because of the concept of story itself, doubly aesthetic. Consequently, it underscores the relevance of inquiring into the *poetics* of self-creation. It leaves outstanding, however, a key question that any discussion of aesthetics must face, that of evaluation.

Evaluating the Art of Living

Are some individuals' lives examples of good art and others' of bad? Is the result of one person's endeavours to make something of himself 'a masterpiece of artistic unity and integrated Form' (Young, 1986, 208), while that of someone else is scarcely more than junk? Are some lives treasures and other lives … trash? These questions may bother us deeply. Who among us is sufficiently uninvolved in (or successful at) the process of life-building ourselves to be in a position to answer them? Moreover, how dare we even ask them when the material, the medium, and the message of each such *oeuvre* is so idiosyncratic? Yet, surely there must be some basis for comparing the artwork of one person's life with that of another. Whether there must be or not, we make such comparisons all the time; in fact, we assume the right, even the necessity, of doing so.

Forming judgments about the beauty, style, or grace – the shape, form, and structure – of one person's life relative to another's is simply part of life. 'Everyone,' writes Virginia Woolf, 'is a judge of character. Indeed it would be impossible to live for a year without disaster unless one practised character-reading and had some skill in the art' (1966, 188). On the positive side, it enables us to wend our way through the world with perception and prudence. On the negative side, though, it can degenerate into judgmentalism, into the most malicious varieties of gossip and prejudice, into slander and discrimination. Either way, aesthetic opinions are impossible to suppress. One poor soul fails to make much of her talents and time and so we tut-tut disapprovingly behind her back as she languishes away in some asylum or slum; while another, at least in view of her circumstances, we consider has done a marvellous job in putting together the package of her life. That is, we see her to have achieved a measure of harmony within herself, fashioned a whole from the particularities of her existence (however negative some of them have been), and worked out a balance between the diverse dimensions of her life that we can acknowledge – through the lenses no doubt of our own priorities, achievements, and regrets – has a genuinely aesthetic appeal.

However, while it is one thing to establish criteria for a work of art – whether a sonnet or sonata – it may be quite another to establish criteria for the artwork of an individual life. What categories can we use to evaluate 'what is the *shape* of my life,' as Anne Morrow Lindbergh asks so poignantly in *Gift from the Sea* (1955, 22)? In a multicultural world, any such categories will inevitably be culture-bound, coloured by the race or gender, class or creed, in which they are conceived. While in one culture the art of living may be defined in terms of the accumulation of high-quality (if unnecessary) material goods, in another it may be defined in terms of sheer survival: survival with dignity and compassion, that is, in the face of conditions too frightful for words.

If a life is inseparable from a story, however, then perhaps there is a set of categories with the potential to cut across cultural boundaries. I propose that there are, and that they are *literary* in nature: for what culture does not tell stories? In fact, all that follows is devoted to using them to analyse the art of living. If 'human life has a determinate form – that of a certain kind of story' (Polkinghorne, 1988, 153), then the question *what makes a good story*? ought to provide clues to what makes a 'good life.'

Composing a Life: Art, Craft, or Improvisation?

As we have seen, Edman views art as the 'transformation of a given chaos into a desired and desirable order.' This insight offers us a way to discuss the connections between art and two related concepts: craft and improvisation.

The interplay between what Edman calls chaos and order can also be seen as the interplay between chance and design, or between the unprecedented and the determined, or between novelty and tradition. Whether we talk about chaos as opposed to order, however, or novelty as opposed to tradition, it is the nature of the peculiar relationship between each of these two elements that the enterprise of art and (in so far as they are connected) creativity may be analysed in terms of.

As Rothenberg and Hausman have observed, for example, in considering 'the irreducible paradox' involved in creativity, 'creations, when they appear, are in some way recognizable and familiar to us and, therefore, they must have something in common with antecedent experiences. However, creations, in the most complete sense, are also radically new and therefore, in some respect, unfamiliar ... Creativity is both determined and undetermined at the same time' (1976, 23).

So, when we speak of self-creation and the art of living, we are raising questions about how we resolve the tension between the determined and undetermined dimensions of our existence. We are raising questions about how we weave the fabric of our lives from the warp of the new and the woof of the old, from both the unprecedented and the preprogrammed, from what is coming into the present from the future and what is receding away from it into the past. This process, as Progoff says, is 'the most important artwork of all.' How each of us carries it out – that is, in what proportions we blend these elements – is one of the things that make us unique.

Some of us, for instance, are creatures of habit, taking few risks, leaning naturally toward the ways we have been or behaved in the past, following established patterns of living to which we have fallen heir by virtue of our gender, culture, or class. In a sense, we live an unoriginal life, a clichéd life, even an unauthentic life, because it is an excessively controlled or planned life. The 'art' of our living is less reflective of 'art properly so-called' (Collingwood, 1958) than of 'craft,' a term I shall come back to in a moment. It is conceivable, however, that others of us are inclined toward what are, even in the context of our own lives, unprecedented ways of doing and being. We feel the need always to 'plough up new ground, to 're-invent the wheel,' to walk 'the road less travelled' – to resist doing anything the same way twice – even if it means our lives are fraught with instability and strife. To express this difference in terms of story, some of us live each day as if it were a brand-new page or chapter, an ever-unfolding adventure, while for others it amounts to the same old story, even the same chapter and verse, repeated over and over. In *The Aims of Education*, Whitehead explores this notion of life as adventure as he affirms the related notion of life as art and the role of education in its stimulation: 'Education is the guidance of the individual towards a comprehension of the art of life; and by the art of life I mean the most complete achievement of varied activity expressing the potentialities of that living creature in the face of its actual environment ... *Each individual embodies an adventure of existence. The art of life is the guidance of this adventure'* ([1929] 1967, 39; emphasis mine).

Another writer to explore the idea of life as art is Mary Catherine Bateson, daughter of Gregory Bateson and Margaret Mead. In her reflections on the experience of herself and five of her women friends in putting their lives together amid the vicissitudes of marriage, family, and career, she coins the phrase 'composing a life.' By this she means 'that act of creation that engages us all – the composition of our lives. Each of us has worked by improvisation, discovering the shape of our creation along the way, rather than pursuing a vision already defined' (1989, 1).

For Bateson, if life is an art, it is 'an improvisatory art,' involving the combination of 'familiar and unfamiliar components in response to new situations, following an underlying grammar and an evolving aesthetic' (3). As a woman, her central question concerns 'whether indeed the model of improvisation might prove more creative and appropriate to the twentieth century than the model of single-track ambition' (15). Because of the dominance of the model of single-track ambition, which she sees as essentially male, woman's 'aesthetic sense, whether in works of art or in lives, has overfocused on the stubborn struggle toward a single goal rather than on the fluid, the protean, the improvisatory' (4). Thus, hand in hand with Bateson's critique of ambition is her praise of ambiguity, something she says is the common lot of women's lives:

> Our lives are full of surprises, for none of us has followed a specific ambition toward a specific goal. Instead, we have learned from interruptions and improvised from the materials that came to hand, reshaping and reinterpreting. As a result, all of us have lived with high levels of ambiguity ... Absolute solutions give way to compromises, but the compromises are organic hybrids able to flourish in a complex ecosystem that spreads more widely and endures longer than we would once have imagined. None of us follows a single vision; instead, our very visions are products of growth and adaptation, not fixed but emergent. (237)

By underscoring the concept of life as 'improvisation' – as something we 'make up' as we go – Bateson underlines the understanding of creativity put forward by Louise Young: 'an uncertain reaching out, a growth, rather than a foreplanned or preconceived activity' (1986, 208). She also offers us an image with which to grasp how all of us, regardless of gender, are constantly seeking to reconcile the inevitable tension between the laid-down structures of our lives as already lived and the element of chaos or chance, the element of the unprecedented that is forever breaking into our world, unsettling our existence, scuttling our plans, and forcing us to 'make do.' She offers us a means of appreciating how our lives can reflect the elements of both art *and* craft.

Bateson's thoughts on the relationship between art, craft, and improvisation help us appreciate further the point raised earlier by John Dewey. In commenting on the difference between self-actualization and what I am calling self-creation, Dewey argues that for the essentialist view of the self-process, which corresponds to self-actualization, potentialities are inherent and connected with a fixed and 'predetermined end.' In contrast, for the existentialist view, which corresponds to self-creation, 'potentialities are not fixed and intrinsic, but are a matter of an indefinite range of interactions in which an individual may engage' (1962, 154). This insight parallels the classic distinction between art and craft. The craftsman, says historian-philosopher R.G. Collingwood, works in terms of a predetermined end. He 'knows what he wants to make before he makes it. This foreknowledge is absolutely indispensable to craft' (1958, 15–16). By contrast, the works produced by the artist 'are not made as means to an end; they are not made according to any preconceived plan ... Yet they are made deliberately and responsibly, by people who know what they are doing, even though they do not know in advance what is going to come of it' (129).

It is possible of course to connect Collingwood's craftsman not with the individual human being carrying out the artwork of her own unique life but with some Divine Craftsman whose creatures we might all conceivably be. But, if the Creator is really a Craftsman – a belief held either implicitly or explicitly by certain theologies – then our lives are the result of craft and not of art; our end is not undetermined nor our destiny open but neatly programmed in advance, needing only to be actualized, realized, and fulfilled. If we were to take this one step further and think of the Divine Craftsman as in fact a Master Story teller, then the parts assigned to us, as the characters, are meticulously scripted from the start, allowing us no opportunity to tell a story that is truly our own. Though this situation is assumed by many to be the case, it is separated by a great chasm from that typical of the author who approaches his work as an art. For such an author – William

Faulkner, for example – 'there is always a point in the book where the characters themselves rise up and take charge and finish the job' (1977, 129).

It is not my place here to be focusing on matters of theology, however much they may hover in the wings. I can only reiterate that while the concept of self-actualization tends to see personal development in terms of craft, where the end is contained in the beginning, that of self-creation sees it in terms of art, where the end, if there be one at all, neither is nor can be in the beginning; therefore, novelty is possible at every stage and improvisation is the name of the game. As one source puts it, 'each person's life is like a diary, in which we mean to write one story and are forced to write another' (Allen, 1978, 79). In the following chapters, I shall delve even more into the nature of the stories we compose about our lives by trying to understand the peculiarly open-ended, creative process whereby many novelists compose their works of fiction. In doing so, I hope to show how through the constantly evolving interplay between our self-plotting and our self-characterization, as through the steady swirl of versions that constitute our inner world, there is a genuine novel-ty about the stories we are.

Summary

In this chapter I have been laying the groundwork for an investigation of the idea that we are continually creating ourselves through the ceaseless reworking of the story of our lives. In one sense, this idea is so simple it requires no elaboration – provided, that is, that we take 'the story of my life' as merely a manner of speaking. In another sense, it is not simple at all but can be taken on one or another of a variety of levels.

The first is that of **existence**: the level of all of the brute events, all the raw, uninterpreted facts, of my being in space and time. It constitutes the outside story of my life. The second level is that of **experience**: the totality of those events of my life that I remember or on which I have some perspective – that I have taken in, digested, and in some manner 'made something' of. It constitutes the inside story of my life. The third level is that of **expression**: the level of the inside story as it comes out in my interaction with others. It constitutes the inside-out story. Finally, the fourth is the level of **impression**: the level of the story, or stories, that are read into part or all of my life by the people and powers around me. It constitutes the outside-in story.

While this schema should increase our appreciation of the storied complexity of everyday life, it points to a tangle of issues that now require close inspection. These issues concern the aspect of *plot* in personal story and the way it makes possible the selection of events and their transformation into experiences. They also concern the aspects of *character* and *point of view*, and the apparent and rather complicated paradox of the self as not only the *teller* of its own story but at the same time the *tellee* as well – and in a sense, as both the telling and the tale.

Wrestling with these issues is my task in the chapter to come. In it and the chapter that follows, I shall be continuing to develop a perspective on a central though unsung dimension of our everyday lives and relationships: the *aesthetic* dimension. By this I mean that dimension whereby 'we are what we imagine,' whereby 'our very existence consists in our imagination of ourselves' (Wiggins, 1975, 1). It is that dimension whereby we are not merely living our lives – passively, as it were – but are actively giving them shape: ceaselessly interpreting and inventing ourselves afresh. It is that dimension whereby we do not receive a life as much as compose a life – as we might compose a story. As we appreciate the extent of this dimension, it becomes impossible to see how *any* aspect of our lives can escape our self-creative touch.

> II <

LIFE AND LITERATURE

Fiction can deal with the world's objects and
ideas together, with the breadth of human experience in time and space; it can deal with
things the limited disciplines of thought either
ignore completely or destroy by methodological
caution, our most pressing concerns: personality,
family, death, love, time, spirit, goodness,
evil, destiny, beauty, will.

Annie Dillard, *Living by Fiction*

I have taken living people and put them into the
situations, tragic or comic, that their characters
suggested. I might well say that they invented
their own stories.

W. Somerset Maugham, *The Summing Up*

Introduction

In an interview once with the *Paris Review*, novelist William Faulkner
(1977) was reflecting on the number of stories by fellow authors he was
in the habit of rereading on a regular basis. 'I've read these books so
often,' he said, 'that I don't always begin at page one and read to the
end. I just read one scene, or about one character, just as you'd meet
and talk to a friend for a few minutes' (136–7). Faulkner's experience
of the virtual reality of fiction is so common we take it for granted. Yet
anyone who has ever got lost in 'a good read,' or binge-read a particular author, or talked vigorously about the outcome of last week's mini-
series – anyone who has ever been carried away by the spell of some
movie and had to view it again and again – has experienced firsthand
how fine is the line between literature and life. Even the child who, as
soon as she has heard the 'happily ever after,' insists on having her

bedtime tale retold, has an instinctive sense of the curious connection between the world of the story and the world of everyday – and this, even when she knows full well both how it will end and that, after all, it is only a story. That it is 'only a story,' however, may not always be obvious. 'When mothers tell fairy tales,' one critic asks, 'do their children experience fictions or "life"? When children watch television for a third to a half each day – much of it purporting to be "true to life" – is that not their life?' (Booth, 1988, 14–15).

In this chapter I shall wrestle with the implications of such unsettling questions – and with the links between life and literature generally – by looking more closely into the concept of story itself. Though, naturally, not every story is written – is literary or literature, that is – the study of literature, especially of the novel, may be said to represent the most advanced and intense attempt within our culture to study the nature of stories and our experience of them. My questions here, however, are rather basic: What really *is* a story? How does it work? What are its main elements, its limits, its allure? In wrestling with these deceptively simple questions, my goal is not to clarify how this or that specific story might be 'true to life' but to get a handle on how a life is *like* a story, particularly on the *inside* level – on what parallels there are, that is, between story in general and life in general, between literary story and lived story, between the art of writing (and reading) a story and the art of living a life. If there are no such parallels, we have no need to proceed. As we shall see, there are many.

In the first section, I want to muse on those features of any story that, *as* story, make it so unfailingly alluring. In the second and central section, I want to consider what insights into our *inside* story we generate when we look at the role played in a story by the three elements of plot, character, and point of view. In the final section, I want to examine more closely the levels of *inside-out* story and *outside-in*, given how much of our everyday interaction occurs where the two of these intersect, thus generating the multiplicity of versions by which we understand ourselves and identify ourselves to others.

The Allure of Story

Stories have a stubborn appeal. How else do we explain our enduring enjoyment of movies, news, and novels; our addiction to jokes and

gossip, ballads and ads; our interminable interest in history and biography, fantasies and dreams? If we are fiction buffs, we long to be
absorbed in a good book; being 'in-between stories' (Berry, 1987, 187)
can be highly unsettling. Moreover, it is frequently the stories – the
anecdotes and illustrations – that we remember the best from the more
droning parts of a lecture or sermon. Throughout our days, we are
drawn to stories again and again, from our first 'once upon a time' to
our last 'happily ever after.' In a culture and era when the oral tradition
seems all but defunct (Benjamin, 1969), when few of us ever sit by the
campfire listening to our elders recount the creation of the world, we
still love a good story. Even a decidedly bad story has the capacity to
sustain our attention and to lure us, despite our better judgment, into
an engagement with it. Witness the distressing number of hours many
of us are said to devote during an average week to sitcoms and series,
shockers and soaps, talk shows and docudramas and unsolved mysteries, no matter how puerile their content or how insulting to what we
fancy is our intelligence. We are bombarded by stories, morning, noon,
and night. It is no wonder we are attracted to story as a metaphor for
our lives since stories figure so centrally in them. Something about their
feel and flow, their structure and style, seems to resonate with the
deepest features of our being. At times, this resonance can reach deaf-
ening proportions – times when, according to one critic writing about
reading, 'everything but the literary work itself slip(s) to the extreme
verge of consciousness.' In such moments, 'the walls of the room fade
or recede, the chair in which the reader is sitting has little tactile substance, and the printed pages of the book itself exist as objects only to
the extent that they offer obstacles to the smooth continuity of the
experience ... The foreground of consciousness, in which the literary
imagination is active, is brilliantly lighted, the background of practical
reality so dim that it hardly has psychological reality ... The boundaries
between personality and the situation melt away' (Shumaker, 1966, 1).

   What is described here may be an extreme experience, yet is it so
uncommon? Who among us has not felt the fuzziness of 'the border
... between life and narrative' (Booth, 1988, 16)? Breathes any of us
with soul so dead that we have never known the power of a story to
simulate life? But in what does such magic lie, in what dimensions
and dynamics of story *per se*?

   These are compelling questions. Before proceeding with them, however, we must divest ourselves of one naïve notion, which is that we
can hope to say everything about the allure of story – let alone about

the links between story and life. The subject of stories is as vast as the number of stories. Besides, story is not a monolithic category. Not only are there different methods of telling a story – literally, orally, dramatically, cinematically – but there are different *species* of story as well. There are fantasy stories and fairy stories, holy stories and horror stories, news stories and novels. There are epics and legends, parables and jokes, mysteries and myths. There are factual stories, such as histories and memoirs, biographies and autobiographies; and there are fictional stories, too, such as historical fiction and science fiction, realistic fiction and surrealistic fiction, detective fiction and metafiction. Each kind of story employs its own conventions, has its own purpose, possesses its peculiar allure, and 'works' in its own way (and in this broad sense constitutes its own 'genre').[1] Yet we seldom focus on *how* it works, seldom speak of the allure of story in general. As one critic has observed, 'Stories are entertaining and this generally suffices as an explanation of the form ... but the form itself is rarely, if ever, considered problematic' (Wright, 1989, 105). This is the difference between literary criticism and literary theory: the former focuses on the content of stories, the latter on their form (Chatman, 1978, 17–18).

My question in this first section, then, concerns those features of the *form* of story as such – wherever a given story may sit on the story continuum, whatever its content, genre, and medium – in which the allure of story lies. In trying to answer this question, we must consider a number of general matters: first, the definition of story, if such can be formed; then, the prevalence of story, the shape of story, and the power of story; next, the storying of others; and, finally, the motive for metaphor.

A Definition of Story

Depending on the context of its use, 'story' has numerous connotations, many of which stretch it well beyond the commonsense meaning we might assume it to have. In an academic context, it can signify a pattern or trend, a theory or theme. In a legal context, it can refer to an argument, an angle, or an alibi. In a 'post-modern' context, it can stand as a substitute for that overwhelming catchword *paradigm*: thus the grand way it is enlisted by biologists Augros and Stanciu (1986) in writing about 'the new story of science,' or by new-age theologian Thomas Berry, in announcing that humankind is 'in-between stories' (1987, 187), or by mythologist Joseph Campbell, in expressing his interest in 'mankind's one great story': our search 'to be in accord with the grand symphony that this world is' (Campbell and Moyers, 1988, 54–5).

Notwithstanding its use in these liberal or unlikely ways, I want to focus here on the word's more customary connotations, as a particular arrangement of events, real or imagined, in the realm of space and time. Much of the current literature on the nature and dynamics of story, however, is written under the heading not of 'story' but of 'narrative.' Yet the two terms are not sharply delineated; their meanings tend to merge. In one dictionary, narrative is 'a story of events, experiences, or the like; narration.' Story, on the other hand, is 'a narrative, either true or fictitious, in prose or verse; tale' (Random House, 1968). There are some – narratologists, for instance – who see narrative, strictly speaking, as *prior* to story in a logical sense. Narrative is the genus of which story is but one species. Accordingly, while all stories are narratives, not all narratives are stories. What this leads to is a kind of narrative continuum, with an annal at one end and a novel at the other. Thus, as historian Hayden White insists, although annals and chronicles are narratives, they fall short of being history or story. The reason, he says, is that they lack the element of plot (1980, 5, 19–21); an annal, particularly, is merely a list of events.

Whether or not an annal lacks the element of plot is a matter for debate. Compared with a work by Dickens or Hardy, its plot may be much less intricate, intentional, or interesting, and may seem to arrange things according to chronology alone, but this does not mean it not exist. A strictly chronological arrangement is still an arrangement, however flat or predictable, and will reflect the peculiar agenda and biases of the annalist. If a narrative with a plot is considered to be a story, therefore, and yet any narrative, even an annal (Bruner, 1987, 12), can be seen to have some element of plot, then an annal is conceivably a story too, and is different from a novel only in degree, not in kind. Thus, the narrative continuum could just as helpfully be called the story continuum. Though confusion can still plague their discussions, most proponents of narrative theory are inclined to use the two terms interchangeably (Polkinghorne, 1988, 13). I take this as permission to stay with *story* here.

But the option of story over narrative is more than a matter of convenience. It is a matter of preference. People do not generally say 'it's the same old narrative' or 'that's the narrative of my life.' In other words, narrative is ultimately a technical term that is attractive to those who wish to develop a respectable science from the study of stories. Though this is a worthy enterprise, I prefer to use story itself, for if it is not prior to narrative logically, it is surely emotionally so. It is the term to which most of us most readily turn in referring to our experience of life as a whole.

Nevertheless, an exact definition of story (as of creativity) is difficult to obtain. Story is so close to us, so much a part of everyday life, that we can scarcely see it. What Augustine has said of time may thus be said of story: 'I know well enough what it is, provided that nobody asks me; but if I am asked what it is and try to explain, I am baffled' (1961, 264). More recently, author Ursula Le Guin makes the same confession: 'through long practice I know how to tell a story,' she says, 'but I'm not sure I know what a story is' (1989a, 37). In the restrained language of a historian, Hayden White agrees, calling story a 'familiar but conceptually elusive entity' (13–14). The simple question 'what is a story?,' writes film critic Thomas Leitch, 'remains the most fundamental in narrative theory, and the most difficult to resolve' (1986, 3).

If 'what is a story?' is such a simple question, then maybe a simple answer will at least get us going. In writing about literary fiction, Northrop Frye says that 'the plot consists of somebody doing something' (1966, 33). Adapting this dictum slightly, it seems reasonable to propose that a story consists basically of 'someone *telling about* somebody doing something.' To qualify as a story, that is, at least three things are required: first, a storyteller, which means a person by whom it is authored and a *point of view* (and thus a voice) through which it is narrated; second, a *character*, or set of characters, which means either real people or fictional creations whose fortunes it concerns; and, third, a *plot*, which means the framework that lays out whatever these characters do, the actions in which they engage, and the situations and conflicts with which they must cope.

No doubt other elements of a story could be considered as well, such as theme or style, setting or atmosphere. A discussion of each, however, can to some extent be incorporated into a discussion of the three I have isolated here. For example, the style and atmosphere of the story are features that relate to the storyteller, functions of the point of view. So also, at the other end of the equation, is the reception and re-creation of the story by an audience or reader: the someone to whom the story is told. This point is emphasized by critic Barbara Herrnstein Smith in her definition of narratives as 'verbal acts consisting of *someone telling someone that something happened*' (Rogers, 1991,

199). In turn, the theme of a story can be seen as the plot in distilled form, the core content of the story, what it is 'about.' And since it can be about many things at once, there can of course be more than one theme. Finally, the setting is the temporal and spatial context within which the characters do whatever the something is that they do. No doubt these elements all play critical roles in the dynamics of any given story, and to many of them I shall in fact refer. However, it is around the larger elements of plot, character, and point of view that I have chosen to organize the central section of this chapter.

The Prevalence of Story

However we define it, a story is a way of structuring our experience of time. As creatures *of* time, who both want and need to communicate our lives *in* time, it seems we can do no other than tell a story. In the words of philosopher Paul Ricoeur (1980), 'narrativity and temporality are closely related'; indeed, there is a 'reciprocity' between the two: Temporality is 'that structure of existence that reaches language in narrativity and narrativity [is] the language structure that has temporality as its ultimate referent' (165–6). In the less off-putting language of Jerome Bruner, 'we seem to have no other way of describing *lived time* save in the form of a narrative' (1987, 12). To illustrate, let us imagine the most mundane exchange between two people:

'Well, Jack, how are you today?'
'Oh, not too bad, I guess, Mack. I was up to the garage earlier this morning to get them to look at my transmission. Then I dropped down here to pick up my mail. This afternoon, I'm supposed to drive into the city with Mary so we can do a little shopping. Enough about *me*, though, what's new with you?'

When Mack meets Jack and asks him how he *is*, Jack does not reply with a list of abstractions or a litany of facts. Obviously he has met with Mack before; perhaps they 'go back a long way.' There are at least a few things about him that Mack already knows, which is why he does not reply with 'I *am* human,' 'I *am* Protestant,' or 'I *am* five foot ten.' He responds with a story instead. Unless he is from Mars, that is, (in which case 'I am human' might be necessary to conceal his true identity), or is particularly pressed for time (in which case a mere 'I am fine' might do), or is especially shy or rude (in which case he might say nothing at all), he responds with a narrative, however primitive its plot (Polkinghorne, 1988, 152). He responds with an organization (of his interpretations) of lived events – past, present, and future. And the more he meets with his friend, the further into each other's past and future their conversations will likely extend. Not only that, but they will inevitably relate the ups and downs of their personal stories to those in the various larger stories within which their lives may be said to be set – of their families, their neighbours, their community, their country, their culture, their race. From the moment they were first introduced to each other, then, their relationship has been inconceivable apart from the exchanging of stories. It is this storytelling dimension of our involvement with one another every day, this ceaseless trading of tales, that enables life as we know it, and society, to proceed.

The reasons we tell stories may go much deeper, however, than the mere need to maintain our relationships. So, at least, runs the thinking of an increasing number of writers in a wide range of fields beyond literary theory itself.

In the field of education, following the lead of John Dewey, whose openness to such thinking we have already seen ([1940] 1962, 146), researchers like John Dixon and Leslie Stratta have proclaimed narrative as a 'primary act of mind' (1986, 103) and narrating as 'an essential way of making sense of human experience,' 'a fundamental human propensity.' Similarly, Laurent Daloz writes that 'the narrative structure is one of the most basic ways we make sense of our experience' (1986, 22). 'The human mind,' insists Jill Sunday Bartoli, 'is a storyteller' (1985, 332). For Michael Connelly and Jean Clandinin, 'humans are storytelling organisms who, individually and socially, lead storied lives' (1990, 2).

In the field of religious studies, such views have had currency for more than twenty years. Stephen Crites argued as early as 1971 that 'the formal quality of experience through time is inherently narrative' (291). In a suggestive chapter on autobiography and story, written about the same time, Michael Novak insisted that religion 'is the telling of a story with one's life,' and that therefore, 'in this weak sense, all men and women are religious' (1971, 45). Conversely, 'not to have any story to live out is to experience nothingness: the primal formlessness of human life below the threshold of narrative structuring' (52). For Charles Winquist, 'the face of the natural self is a story' (1974, 102–3). More recently, George Stroup has insisted that there is just 'something about the nature of human being and the structure of human experience that makes narrative the appropriate and even necessary form for the articulation of personal identity' (1981, 100). In an overview of what is called 'narrative theology,' Lonnie Kliever states simply that 'the original of all storytelling about life is the story-making of life' (1981, 157). One of the most recent theologians to invoke the story model is Don Cupitt of Cambridge. 'Because we use language and live in time,' he says, 'we *must* tell stories' (1991, 79). In *What Is a Story?* he spells out the exciting if unsettling ramifications, belief-wise, of the post-modern premiss that 'a human being is entirely culturally formed, and made of stories all the way through' (67).

In the field of philosophy, besides Glover, whose work we have already encountered, Dennis Dennett has also been drawn to story. In *Consciousness Explained* (1991), he wrestles with the challenge posed to traditional formulations of the so-called 'mind-body problem' by developments in artificial intelligence. In the process, he writes about how, like spiders, 'human beings spin a self' (413). He qualifies this notion, though, by stressing that 'our fundamental tactic of self-protection, self-control, and self-definition is not spinning webs or building dams, but telling stories, and more particularly concocting and controlling the story we tell others – and ourselves – about who we are' (418). Thus, he advances the rather ornate definition of the Self as 'an abstraction defined by the myriads of attributions and interpretations ... that have composed the biography of the living body whose Center of Narrative Gravity it is' (426–7).

In the subfield of the philosophy of history, the story theme is naturally high on the agenda. For Arthur Danto, 'narration exemplifies one of the basic ways in which we represent the world, and the language of beginnings and endings, of turning points and crises and climaxes, is coimplicated with this mode of representation to so great a degree that our image of our own lives must be deeply narrational' (1985, xiii). Hayden White looks at the implications of such an insight for our understanding of the concept of history itself, and of the task of the historian. His question is 'Does the world really present itself to perception in the form of well-made stories ...?' His answer is no. Hence, 'the notion that sequences of real events possess the formal attributes of the stories we tell about imaginary events could only have its origin in wishes, daydreams, reveries' (1980, 23). David Carr, considering the same question (1986), draws a less cynical conclusion. While White and others, like Louis Mink and Paul Ricoeur, stress 'the

discontinuity between "art" and "life," as regards narrative,' Carr
stresses 'the narrative features of everyday experience and action.' For
him, 'historical and fictional narratives' are 'not distortions of, denials
of, or escapes from reality, but extensions and configurations of its
primary features' (16). His views are summarized in the conviction of
literary critic Barbara Hardy that it is 'nature, not art, which makes us
all storytellers' (66).

In the field of psychology, the voices raised in praise of story are
becoming legion. In a collection of articles on 'narrative psychology,'
Theodore Sarbin proposes what he calls 'the narratory principle.'
Seeing *narrative* as 'coterminous with *story*' (1986, 3), he summarizes
this as the principle 'that human beings think, perceive, imagine, and
make moral choices according to narrative structures' (8). Sarbin's
views are reflected in the wide-ranging argument for the narrative
'root metaphor' advanced by Donald Polkinghorne (1988). Narrative,
Polkinghorne states, is 'the primary form by which human experience
is made meaningful' (1). With others already quoted, then, he sees 'the
self as a story' (151). Likewise, neuropsychologist Oliver Sacks sees
story as coterminous with life. 'Each of us,' he writes, '*is* a biography,
a story. Each of us *is* a singular narrative, which is constructed, continually, unconsciously, by, through, and in us' (1985, 110). Jungian
psychoanalyst James Hillman writes boldly about patients being 'in
search of a new story,' his conviction being that it is generally the
patient's story that needs to be doctored and not the patient him- or
herself (1989, 79). Another psychoanalyst to take the story line is the
Freudian Roy Schafer. Avowedly anti-essentialist in his orientation
(1992, xvi), he sees 'psychoanalysis as a form of text interpretation' in
which 'the analyst treats the analysand in the same manner that many
literary critics treat authors' (1989, 198). Together, however, they construct a new self-story. 'Each analysis,' he writes, 'amounts in the end
to retelling a life in the past and present – and as it may be in the
future. A life is re-authored as it is co-authored' (1992, xv).

One of the leading figures in the turn toward story is psychologist
emeritus Jerome Bruner. Determined to undo some of 'the current
fixation on mind as "information processor"' (a project that, ironically,
he shares with Roger Schank), Bruner insists that there are at work in the
mind two fundamentally different 'modes of thought.' There are 'two
ways of ordering experience, of constructing reality ... of organizing
representation in memory and of "filtering the perceptual world."' He
calls these the 'paradigmatic mode' and the 'narrative mode' (1984,

97). The former, he says, 'leads to good theory, tight analysis, logical proof, and empirical discovery guided by reasoned hypothesis.' The latter, and the more central to everyday life, leads 'to good stories, gripping drama, believable historical accounts' (98). Building on this distinction, Bruner advances the thesis, that 'the nature of a life ... is a story, some narrative however incoherently put together' (1987, 33). 'A life as led,' he stresses, 'is inseparable from a life as told' (31). Thus, 'in the end, we *become* the autobiographical narratives by which we "tell about"our lives' (15).

Assessing these claims in detail, evaluating their merits or their compatibility with each other, is beyond the scope of my efforts here. Yet each represents a particular contribution to a debate that has been brewing for some time somewhere on the border between psychology, philosophy, and literary theory – a debate that can demand the subtlest of thinking to follow. Basically, the debate is about which comes first: story or reality. The central questions are these: Do we tell stories about events because the stories are already there, inherent in the events themselves, or do we impose stories upon events in the act of experiencing them? If we impose them, then how deep does our storying instinct go? From a psychological perspective, two obvious corollary questions are whether there is a fundamental 'narrative grammar structure' that develops in all of us, epigenetically, from childhood on (Mancusco, 1986, 99), which thus makes storying our lives and living them impossible to separate? If so, then how does this development occur and how is it affected (enhanced or impeded) by the lifelong diet of stories we feed on from the world around us?

The core issue here, story-or-reality, is nicely focused for us in a fictional work by Jean-Paul Sartre. Entitled *Nausea,* its main character, who is simultaneously its narrator, is a biographer named Roquentin. In the course of researching the life of his subject, a minor figure in nineteenth-century French politics, Roquentin finds himself increasingly subject to bizarre bouts of what he calls 'nausea.' Inspired no doubt by the vertigo that must accompany his task – reconstructing a life in the present out of scraps of information from the past – these bouts involve flashes of unsettling insight into the raw reality, the sheer, uninterpreted existence, of everything around him: that is, shorn of all the categories, the 'fictions,' by which we normally domesticate, 'make sense' of, and construct our world (Rogers, 1991; Dillard, 1982).

For example, at the library one day an acquaintance approaches him to greet him good-morning. Suddenly the familiar becomes the strange. 'It took me ten seconds to recognize him,' says Roquentin, disturbed. 'I saw an unknown face which was barely a face. And then there was his hand, like a fat maggot in my hand. I let go of it straight away and the arm fell back limply' (Sartre, 1965, 14). As the nausea spreads, more and more of Roquentin's everyday routine is rendered less and less routine and more and more unreal. Gradually, he becomes convinced that there is a great chasm between events as they occur and the accounts we compose about them after the fact. 'When you are living, nothing happens. The settings change, people come in and go out, that's all. There are never any beginnings. Days are tacked on to days without rhyme or reason, it is an endless, monotonous addition ... There isn't any end either: ... That's living. But when you tell about life, everything changes; only it's a change nobody notices: the proof of that is that people talk about true stories. As if there could possibly be such things as true stories; events take place one way and we recount them the opposite way' (61–2). The extension of Roquentin's revelation is the distressing discovery that 'there are no adventures' (81–2). As Iris Murdoch writes in her analysis of *Nausea*, 'adventures are stories, and one does not *live* a story. One tells it later, one can only see it from the outside. The meaning of an adventure comes from its conclusion; future passions give colour to the events. But when one is inside an event, one is not thinking of it. One can live or tell; not both at once' (1967, 11–12).

Sartre's position in the story-reality debate is therefore clear. Living precedes telling. Events come first, stories later. 'If we consider our lives from moment to moment we observe,' says Murdoch, 'as Roquentin does, how much of the sense of what we are doing has to be put in afterwards' (16). Indeed, involved in a pile-up on the freeway from Toronto to New York, we are speechless, for seconds, minutes, maybe hours. Words fail us. *It all happened so fast!* we say. *It was too horrible for words!* The words of course will follow, but with them, with the story, the original occurrence is fabricated, fictionalized, falsified – a point that leads Sartre to a particular program for living life: 'We must live forwards,' he says, 'not backwards ... We are not to live with our eye on History or on our biographer' (16–17). In other words, 'if you want to understand something you must face it naked.' Not doing so 'involves us in *mauvaise foi* [bad faith] and destroys the freshness and sincerity of our projects' (17).

The question of how we resolve the story-reality debate is, on some level, academic. Yet, as ought to be obvious from my thinking in the earlier section, 'The Story of My Life,' I have my preference. Stories may or may not be inherent in events themselves – indeed it is hard to know what this would even mean – but *seeing* stories in events is so central an activity of the consciousness through which we *experience* events that, for us humans anyway, it comes down to the same thing. What sort of person can experience events in the raw, without recourse to beginnings and middles and ends? Who can stare wide-eyed, and for how long, at things-as-they-are-in-themselves, in the moment, naked, outside of an interpretive context within which they are constructed, assigned a past, present, and future? Who can endure what writer Michael Crichton longingly labels 'direct experience' (1988, x, 382–90)? Perhaps a newborn baby can; perhaps a 'pure' scientist can; perhaps a person who is insane in a certain way can; perhaps a saint or mystic can, or a master of Zen; perhaps a Sartre can. But can we? I believe not. However good for the soul it may be to bear reality 'in the now,' we are all, technically, living in 'bad faith.'

Putting this more positively, I agree with David Carr (1986). The distinction between living and telling, he argues, is fundamentally false. 'We are constantly striving, with more or less success, to occupy the story-teller's position with respect to our own actions.' Pure unstoried action, pure unstoried existence in the present, is impossible: 'The present is only possible for us if it is framed and set off against a retained past and a potentially envisaged future.' Accordingly, narration is 'intertwined with the course of life.' 'The actions and sufferings of life can be viewed as a process of telling ourselves stories, listening to those stories, and acting or living them through.' Stories, he concludes, 'are told in being lived and lived in being told' (60–2).

This then is the question I shall be pursuing from here on: not *whether* we story but *how* we story, and with *what sort* of story. Given the storying instinct and the inseparability of living and telling, that is, how many different ways can we story the events of our lives? Given (as we shall shortly see) the seemingly endless ways in which stories can be plotted and narrated and received, their characters conceived, and their themes construed, how many ways can we story our lives as a whole?

The Shape of Story

The language we require to talk about our lives in time – to link remembered pasts to experienced presents to anticipated futures – is, inescapably, the language of story. It is the language, as Aristotle first saw, of beginnings and middles and ends (1963, 15). Such a structure arises, says novelist John Gardner, from the simple fact that all of us have the same root experience. 'To put it grimly,' he says, 'we're born, we suffer, we die' (1985, 43). For this reason, story, writes Hayden White, is 'a human universal' (1980, 2). Though this may represent the most profound of all the links between literature and life, we need to flesh it out.

A story has to have a beginning, obviously. That is, the string of events it relates has to start somewhere. The *telling* of the story, though, may have a different beginning than the string of events themselves, as in the case of a narrator sitting in an armchair recalling events long since concluded. This is a story *within* a story: the outer story being that of the narrator sitting and telling, which of course cannot begin at its own end. (As in baseball, so in storytelling: it ain't over till it's over.) In reading many a detective novel, however, we seem to begin not at the beginning but at the end, given that the crime in question is a *fait accompli*. In reality, of course, we are beginning at the beginning of the *detection* process, the end of which still lies ahead. Led by the narrator, we then work our way back to the beginning of the crime itself, and even before it, until we piece together exactly whodunnit and why. The outer story, that of the detective doing the detecting, is simply the *host* for the inner or main story, that of the crime itself. What is host and what is main can be tough to untangle, however, such as when a detective is telling the story of detecting a crime that occurred much earlier in his career. As filmmaker Jean-Luc Godard puts it, then, a story 'should have a beginning, a middle, and an end, but not necessarily in that order' (Marchand, 1991).

In the classic beginning, 'once upon a time,' the narrator can seem so voiceless and invisible, so removed from the events narrated, as not to exist at all; thus, the telling appears to converge with the told. 'Story-time' and 'discourse-time' seem one and the same (Chatman, 1978, 62–3). But the familiar formula is subject to countless variations: In the beginning … In our top story tonight … I'll never forget the time … Did you ever hear the one about the … It was the best of times; it was the worst of times … It was the night before Christmas … It was a dark and stormy night …

What happens at the sound of such words? We are brought under the spell of the story: our curiosity is pricked, our ears perked, our hearts prepared for whatever will happen next. Wondering 'whatever will happen next' is the key: without this expectation in us that a series of meaningfully connected events is going to unfold we shall feel we are following less a story than a shopping list. Part of the allure of story, therefore, and that which our experience of the beginning ignites, relates to the *suspense* that the story sets off, the sense that something significant is going to happen – a sense that tellers of tales are wise to sustain throughout.

But just as any story must have a beginning, so it must have an end, in the sense either that the events it recounts are concluded, or, simply, that the storyteller at some stage stops talking or writing. Whichever way, the end of a story is important because our sense of it affects how we experience the beginning and the middle, and because, in the final analysis, it determines what sort of story the story is – for example, whether tragic or comic (Pearson, 1989, 9). The classic ending, of course, is 'they all lived happily ever after.' Such an ending, Shakespeare would say, ends well. But though it implies that life will continue in some lovely never-never land, the story itself cannot: the tale must eventually be cut.

As with 'once upon a time,' so with 'happily ever after': it has countless variations. What all of them have in common, however, is that they represent attempts to tie together the possibilities and potentials implied by their respective beginnings. In what many might think the ideal ending, the storm will have spent itself, the darkness will have dissipated, and the evil energies their combination released will have been exorcised for good, leaving the reader or hearer with the peaceful smile of a contented child. Naturally, any given ending will be more or less pleasing in this respect, more or less successful in tying up the threads that were loosed in the beginning, but it is the function of endings in general to bring at least some resolution to the problems the story has raised. Part of the allure of story, therefore, and that which the experience of the ending keeps alive, relates to the 'catharsis,' or the sense of *satisfaction*, the story supplies – a sense any storyteller is advised to provide if he would have his efforts be satisfactorily received.

But just as any story must have a beginning and an end, so it must have a middle, a place between the two where whatever the story is about can in fact occur. It might be neater, of course, for the story not to be 'about' anything at all, but simply to have a beginning and an end. In a technological age, obsessed with minimizing the messiness of life, a minimalist middle might be seen as ideal, as depicted in the accompanying cartoon.

Without a middle, however, the story over which this computerized writer is gloating is no story at all, because the middle is where everything happens. It is also where all of us already are. In contrast, the beginning, like the beginning of the universe itself, is an arbitrary point at which time itself begins – story-time, that is – a time that we cannot hope to reach, though we may approach it to a billionth of a second. As soon as 'in the beginning' is announced, we are already immersed 'in the middest.' For even on page one, we encounter a world already underway – maybe not a paradise but at least a world before that particular element of conflict has been introduced that the story has been set up to resolve. What is *before* the beginning, then, is

"Once upon a time, they lived happily
ever after."

Drawing by H. Martin; © 1991 The New Yorker Magazine, Inc.

outside the story. It can concern us no more than what is north of the North Pole. In the same way, the ending, like the ending of the universe, is also beyond our grasp. It hangs like the carrot in front of the proverbial donkey. We never quite get to it, for even at the sight or sound of 'The End' we are still in the middle, guessing what kind of a life it is that they will go on to live so happily ever after. The middle of the story is the now. We can look back to the beginning (though we cannot reach the absolute beginning) and ahead to the end (though we cannot reach the absolute end) but, in following the story through, the middle is where we are.

The middle, as Kenneth Burke says, is where the trouble is (Bruner, 1987, 18). We may hope for a happy end, and assume a happy beginning, but we would have a boring story if we had a happy middle as well. The middle is where we encounter the 'agon' (Novak, 1971, 53), the conflict required to fuel the story along. A story has to have conflict, whether conflict within characters, conflict between characters (*prot*-agonists vs *ant*-agonists), conflict between characters and circumstances, or conflict of many kinds at once. The middle is the arena of continuous tension – tension between limits and possibilities, dangers and dreams, obstacles and goals, the real and the ideal. In particular, it is in the tension – the push and pull – between the exigencies of the plot and the existence of the characters that we find the central engine of the story, what keeps it pumping from chapter to chapter. Indeed, no struggle, no story; no trouble, no tale; no ill, no thrill; no *agon*, no adventure.

The strength of our thirst for adventure, and therefore *agon*, is seen in our hunger for 'the latest,' whether as gossip or, more formally, 'the news.' But not any old news will do. New news is better than old news, and bad news is better than good – travelling faster and farther and with far more effect. Witness our secret thrill in catching wind of the latest axe murder or plane crash or quake (as long as they affect someone else, that is). This is a peculiar, if familiar, phenomenon. It says something intriguing about 'human nature'; about 'the furious itch of novelty' (Tannen, 1990, 111); about our need to be not merely informed but informed *as it happens*, to be in the know, in the now. Nothing moves our adrenalin quite like the newscaster's opening line: 'Here are the stories we are following this hour ...'

For journalist-critic John Carey (1987), who sees 'the advent of mass communication [as] the greatest change in human consciousness ... in recorded history,' this need for 'reportage' is to us in the present what the need for religion was to others in the past. It supplies us 'with a constant and reassuring sense of events going on beyond [our] immediate horizon.' It provides us 'with a release from [our] trivial routines, and a habitual daily illusion of communication with a reality greater than [ourselves].' By feeding us 'endlessly ... with accounts of the deaths of other people,' it 'places [us] continually in the position of a survivor' – like religion, giving us 'a comforting sense of [our] own immortality' (xxxii, xxxv).

An unusual argument, yet enticing. To complete my argument here, it points to a third main aspect of the allure of story. What is elicited by our experience of the middle, besides Carey's crypto-religious sentiment, is the sense of *sympathy*, of compassion, of 'suffering with' the characters (albeit in relative comfort) in the midst of their struggle – a sense any writer does well to uphold if he or she is to maintain 'the vivid and continuous dream' by which the reader is kept enthralled (Gardner, 1985, 97).

The Power of Story

The beginning, end, and middle of a story are the sources, respectively then, of the suspense, satisfaction, and sympathy that engage us with it from first to last. They are the source of its feel of wholeness for us too – more so anyway than is conveyed by a 'narrative' or, certainly, a 'text,' which by definition can go on and on without need of an aesthetically satisfying conclusion. In its imitation of our own birth, death, and suffering, this basic shape of a story thus gives it an allure that will not let us go. In large part, this is because 'any story is about ourselves' (TeSelle, 1975b, 159). For this reason alone, whether it be fictional or factual, a story possesses a peculiar kind of power. It causes things to happen, indeed a number of things at once. To many of these I have already alluded; a number more can be catalogued under the two terms often enlisted to describe what, generally, literature does: it instructs and it delights.

A story delights when it entertains, when it allows us to escape the monotony or pain of our everyday lives. A story delights when it provides the sense of catharsis mentioned above; when it focuses a particular tension and provides a relief for it that is denied us ordinarily, thus releasing 'stuck energy' within us (Polster, 1987, 39). It delights when it activates our fantasies; when it helps us see unexpected possibilities; when it stretches us, takes us outside ourselves, and opens up an alternate world to the one we normally occupy. A story delights by in fact *creating* a world, within which, vicariously at least, we can live and move and have our being. A story delights by drawing us into a community, by letting us feel part of a group of characters, by making us privy to their actions, thoughts, and feelings. A story delights when it makes us feel less alone or unusual (Coles, 1989, 61); when it confirms our own unformed thoughts and unarticulated questions; when it keeps us company (Booth, 1988) – company that can remain in our hearts far into the future, sometimes farther than do the real people who are part of our lives.

A story instructs when it conveys information; when it tells us how to do things; when it passes on lore; when it explains why people behave the way they behave or why things are the way they are (Wiebe, 1970, xv–xvi). A story instructs when it passes on values; when it gives flesh and blood to abstract ideas; when it enables us to engage in relative safety with otherwise delicate or inflammatory themes (Ross, 1992, 79). A story instructs when it recounts what happens; when it confers order on a chaos of circumstances; when it offers us a comprehensible intepretation of complex events or emotions. A story instructs when it 'rein[s] in the elusiveness of experience' (Polster, 28); when it helps us to identify and understand our own personal concerns; when it reflects the irony, complexity, and ambiguity of our everyday lives (Coles, xvii). A story instructs when it provides us with role models to validate our views and guide our conduct; when, by introducing us to characters whose thoughts and struggles we can know more clearly and profoundly than even our own, it stimulates new levels of self-understanding. A story instructs when it contextualizes our personal conflicts; when it helps us make decisions by letting us consult with characters facing similar dilemmas (203). A story also instructs when, like a parable, it 'defamiliarizes' our everyday world-view (Greene, 1990, 257; Crossan, 1975, 56–7), forcing us to reconstruct it in fresh and healthier ways.

To discuss how stories both instruct and delight (and often both at once) is to appreciate two domains in terms of which art can always be assessed: ethics and aesthetics. I believe these domains are closely entwined, but up to now I have been focusing on story's aesthetic aspects. For the remainder of this section, I want to look at its ethical ones.

On a simple level, every story has its 'moral,' however difficult it may be to articulate, just as every joke has its punch-line, every news clip its bottom line, and every movie its message. 'Stories,' says one critic, 'are not innocent' (Rosen, 1986, 236). They always have an agenda behind them. 'Every fully realized story,' writes Hayden White, 'is a kind of allegory, points to a moral, or endows events, whether real or imaginary, with a significance that they do not possess as a mere sequence' (1980, 13). Stories inherently moralize. Narrativity is 'intimately related to, if not a function of, the impulse to moralize reality, that is to identify it with the social system that is the source of any morality that we can imagine' (13–14). To a great extent, for instance, 'history is written by victors,' by those on top politically or, so they assume, morally; those eager to marshall the facts to buttress their views – usually, however diplomatically, in the spirit of 'I told you so' (Plantinga, 1992, 81). But treatments of the ethical dimensions of fiction do not always veer off in such cynical directions. Indeed, ever since Plato wanted to banish the poets from the Republic, one thinker after another has risen to defend the inherent morality – as opposed to moral-izing – of literary art. 'True art is moral,' insists John Gardner, a modern exponent of this view; 'it seeks to improve life, not debase it.' Art, he maintains, 'is essentially serious and beneficial, a game played against chaos and death, against entropy' (1978, 5, 6).

The defence of literature has a long history; the words devoted to it are many and eloquent. Critic Deanne Bogdan, however, reminds us what has been central to it over the years. 'One of the traditional justifications of literature as the core of a liberal education,' she writes, 'has been its positive role in character development' (1983, 5). Two books in which this role is celebrated are *Read for Your Life*, by Joseph Gold, and *The Call of Stories*, by Robert Coles. Both writers are advocates of bibliotherapy.

For Gold, a marriage and family counsellor and a professor of English, literature is a 'life resource,' indeed a 'life support system' (1990, 24). Moreover, it is fundamentally *connected* to life: 'the story that never ends,' he says, 'is the story of life' (31). Novels, in particular, function as 'analogues of our life experience' because 'we're all story-makers' (51). That is, 'we story our worlds, our selves, our friends and family (31). Without the ability to story our life's events, we are confused, overwhelmed. We are 'lost in content,' he claims, 'like the boy inundated with bicycle parts and lacking the key to their relations' (51). 'Fiction,' however, 'helps you to re-story yourself' (4).

Gold's enthusiasm is echoed by Coles. Through his work as a psychiatrist, professor, and mentor to students, Coles has found that books – specifically books of fiction – can bring personal renewal. The power of story, he says, lies in its capacity to stimulate 'the moral imagination' as readers identify with the struggles of the characters amid the constraints and opportunities of the plots in which they are placed. 'Novels and stories are renderings of life; they can not only keep us company, but admonish us, point us in new directions, or give us the courage to stay a given course. They can offer us kinsmen, kinswomen, comrades, advisors – offer us other eyes through which we might see, other ears with which we might make soundings.' (159–60).

Coles's observations about the moral power of stories suggest two things: first, that stories are, in a sense, calling to us, reaching out to us, extending to us their friendship, guidance, and support; second, that we, in turn, are reaching out to stories, in need of their personable language and peculiar logic, to make sense of our otherwise ambiguous lives. A two-way street is thus involved, a reciprocal attraction, a mutual allure. As researchers Mark Tappan and Lyn Brown put it, 'when we make moral choices and decisions in our lives we represent those choices and decisions, and give them meaning, primarily by telling stories about them ... whether they are as mundane as going to the grocery store or as momentous as moral crises that challenge our lives forever' (1989, 187).

With Coles, Gold, and others already cited, Tappan and Brown share the conviction that on a fundamental level we 'story our worlds, ourselves, our family, our friends.' Without such storying, living would be impossible. We need stories, then, because we are such inveterate storytellers ourselves. 'We want to borrow bits from them,' says Cupitt, 'for use in building our own greatest fictional works – our life-stories' (1991, 67). As even Roquentin reluctantly admits, 'a man is always a teller of tales, he lives surrounded by his stories and the stories of others, he sees everything that happens to him through them; and he tries to live his life as if he were recounting it' (Sartre, 1965, 61).

The claim, however, that we see everything that happens to us *through* our stories forces us to face a question that has been rumbling beneath the surface of everything said so far: Do we indeed see, not just ourselves, but both others and reality in general, as inherently 'storied'? If so, what does this mean, how does it happen, and what does it *feel* like on an everyday basis?

How We Story Others

In gazing casually out my window onto the street below, what do I see? I see a mass of pedestrians, a mess of traffic, a maze of buildings: where is the 'story' in this? Within the buildings, however, I know that there are countless individuals, more or less like myself, engaged in a range of predictable activities, such as walking, talking, making decisions, preparing dinners, or changing diapers. In admitting this, though, I have introduced the element of story, for from the awareness of what these nameless neighbours may be doing *now* it requires little effort to guess what they might have been doing *before* or will go on to do *after*. I impute to them a story, that is, that they, like me, are living out, in the midst of which they, like me, are presumably the star. I impute to them possible pasts, presents, and futures: beginnings, middles, and ends.

That woman there, for instance, scurrying down the sidewalk: she looks as if she has been married for some time, perhaps longer than she wishes, and perhaps to a man who has mistreated her. By her appearance, I suspect she works downtown, maybe in an office or shop. Yet the air of determination she has about her suggests certain plans she might have: perhaps to return to university when her children have left home, or to achieve a long-held dream of being a writer or a lawyer, or, more immediately, to meet with a lover ... That man there, however, sitting hunched on a park bench in his tattered coat and boots: he looks so down and out. Possibly he comes from some remote region outside the city, from a hamlet off the beaten track where he has been thrown out of work because of a lay-off, a closure, or a problem with the bottle. Now, however, his future seems unsure: if he does not soon find a job or a handout or a roof over his head he will ... die, forgotten and unknown.

Whenever I try to explain what the lives of others are like, to interpret their behaviour, or to decide how to act in relation to them, I slip sooner or later into the narrative mode. I am overtaken by a kind of *biographical imperative*. 'To understand the actions of others,' write Tappan and Brown, 'we tend to place those actions in a narrative context' (185). One corollary of this is that in order to 'feel' for another person, however much a stranger he might be, I have to 'read' him 'like a book' (Nierenberg and Calero, 1973). To use a term already introduced, I have to 'storyotype' him. I have to be able to guess at a beginning, a middle, and an end to his existence, at the story he could tell me if I gave him half the chance. The novelist John Steinbeck alludes to this kind of guessing in his touching description of a conversation he had once, while camping, with the warden of a particular park. 'After he drove away in his jeep,' Steinbeck sighs, 'I lived his life for him, and it put a mist of despair on me' (1972, 112). Such guessing can remain a game, of course, and nothing more – like the one we play with people who pass by on the sidewalk, as we sit in our car 'putting in time.' At worst, it can be the beginning of unfounded, malicious gossip; at best, the beginning of compassion, the origin of those countless links of caring that can forge a community from a collection of individuals. It can often be the beginning of that peculiar kind of community we call 'intimacy.' Since intimacy, whether friendship or romance, plays so central a role in everyday life, it is important to appreciate the dynamics of its development.

On meeting someone new – someone to whom I am more than passingly attracted, that is – I generally become curious about the story of her life. In the flurry of early passion, I may feel I must know *everything* about it. Naturally, I also want to know about her hobbies and habits, her ideas and idiosyncrasies, her values and beliefs, her 'nature,' her 'baggage'; but, since these are sure to be rooted in her 'experience,' I want to know her story too. Not necessarily, of course: some forms of intimacy (say, with the stranger-on-the-train) seem to succeed best not when we know *much* about each other's story but when we know *little*; when 'deep down there [is] understanding,' says May Sarton, 'not of the facts of our lives so much as of our essential natures' (1977, 15). There is something to be said, in other words, for trying to start a relationship fresh, story-less, to 'erase personal history' and so spare each other the 'encumbering thoughts' with which our connection can otherwise get cluttered. There is also something to be said for mystique, for the element of suspense, for playing hard to get. For not a few of us, in fact, it can be less a *person* with whom we 'fall in love' – or even *want* to fall in love – than it is a *story*, or only part of a story, or only the promise of a story: with the narrative allure, that is, which she spins around herself – or, more accurately perhaps, which I spin *for* her in the depths of my own imagination, as I make her into a 'character' in a story that is ultimately not hers at all, but mine! As I say, though, generally ... After all, her life and her story are intimately (if not simply) linked. Knowing her means knowing her story.

For one thing, I want to know her outside story, the facts of her life; not just those I can see, such as her hair colour and height, but the details of her life since her earliest years, especially those relevant to my current agenda, like her previous relationships. I cannot know these details in their entirety of course, as might Glover's omniscient God, but I can conceivably know enough of them to piece together a working hypothesis as to what her life has involved up until now – at least its principal turning points. Gaining knowledge of such details, however, is easier said than done, for it is knowledge of the past. I can browse through photo albums, suffer through home movies, or stare at class pictures, and thus grab a few flat glimpses of her life on graduation day, the day of her birth, or the day of some picnic on an unknown sandy beach, but ... I can never peek behind the images and be privy to the actual events of her existence up to now.

Apart from my own more or less informed conjecture, then, all I have to inform me about her outside story are the stories told of her by others outside-in, whether by parents, peers, or former partners. No matter how intimate these purport to be ('the inside track,' as it were), or how 'objective' – even if they are government statistics, or doctor's records since day one – all I have are stories still, inevitably biased or embellished because of these persons' own agendas and imaginations, the accumulated history they have shared with her themselves, or the particular axe they may wish to grind against her. For her parents, for example, she will always be seen as a particular character in the family story, which is not the same as seeing her in her own right. Finally, even without others' outside-in stories of her to clutter my perceptions, there is still my own 'storyotyping' tendency to contend with, complicated in her case by the fact that she reminds me of someone else – of a ghost, an episode, an entire poignant period from my past. I can ever only see *her* story, that is, through my own.

With this many limitations on my knowledge of her outside story, why not bypass it altogether and go straight for her inside one instead? Surely that is what matters most: what is in her heart! Not her actions or achievements, but her soul. If the outside is rich, yet the inside poor, what hope is there for us? True, but my task here is hardly less difficult. What can I really expect to know of that vast, wideranging, many-sided story she has fashioned *for herself* in the depths of her heart? Not very much. I could of course ask her what is inside, and she might tell me, but what I would get would still not be the inside story itself, not what it feels like inside her, only what she expresses to me of it inside-out, whether intentionally or not, through her gestures, deeds, and words. Thus, by my own sleuthing, I may piece together something about the events of her life, something about her existence, even if only partially and second-hand, but I can know precious little about her experience.

So, the overall story I read into her life outside-in – never the same as what she reads into it herself and invariably far cruder – is an ever-changing amalgam of a number of stories at once. Besides her outside story (my version of which will always be influenced by others', plus whatever unfinished business I project onto her out of my own past), and her inside story (in so far as I am able to draw any conclusions concerning it), there is at least – is there not? – her inside-out story. True, but this is problematic in turn because it is only ever parcelled out to me piecemeal, in segments and summaries – few of which will come out the same way twice. It is the story of her world, her family, her life, etc., not as it *is* but as she *sees* it, and the way she sees it today may vary significantly from the way she sees it next week.

Furthermore, she may hold things back, as I may too. In fact, this can be part and parcel of the process between us: letting out our stories strategically, one by one; upping the ante of our intimacy ever so cautiously; taking care not to reveal too much too fast lest the other form the wrong impression and pull away; keeping mindful of the control that each of us retains because of the stories we leave untold. Our caution is proportional to our longing for connection, at least for a better one than before. For instance, perhaps she hopes that with me, a new person, she can be a new person herself, that her story can come out differently than it has with others in the past. Her goal then is to relate to me not necessarily an untrue story of her life but at least a better story, a more flattering one, a more interesting one, a story over which she has more control – anything, as long as it is not the *same old* story ... Thus, depending on her reading of *my* story, she may keep secrets; she may background with me what she foregrounded with others; or she may allude to the stories she *could* tell me if only she knew me better: 'I'll have to tell you the story someday of the time I ...' Sometimes, knowingly or not, she may simply lie.

In the midst of this intricate game I shall, of course, like her with respect to me, be sniffing out gaps: gaps between what she reveals to me inside-out and what I read of her outside-in; gaps between one friend's outside-in story of her and another's; gaps between what she tells me with her words and what she shows me with her actions or eyes. If any of these gaps should get too great; if I detect embellishments, inconsistencies, lies; if I suspect I am not getting the whole story, that there are dark secrets that will haunt us later on; then I may have to consider the cost of continuing in the relationship. At some point, I may simply throw up my hands, exasperated, because I 'can't make her out!'

But this is not all. Muddying the waters even more is that other whole story of which both of us are caught in the middle, the larger story inside of which each of us operates: the unfolding story of our relationship itself, mutually constructed (through small talk and every-day involvement) though differently interpreted – and differently experienced, depending on the media by which it develops. Accordingly, we may be one way with each other in person, another way on the phone, and another again on the pages of the letters that we fire back and forth. Each mediates, to each of us, a slightly different relationship. In all though, 'to become a couple is to agree implicitly to live in terms of another person's story' (Bridges, 1980, 71) – and she, I might add, to live in terms of mine. Furthermore, there will be versions of my story elicited and reinforced by living in terms of *her* story that might not be elicited if I were living in terms of someone else's instead. This means that sharing a story with her uniquely influences my self-creation, as sharing a story with me uniquely influences hers. This shared story, even if our respective readings of it are never exactly shared nor equally certain (i.e., 'she loves me, she loves me not'), exercises a powerful force in the interaction between us. It may well be what holds us most together, like a novel into whose ever-thickening plot we have each been drawn, in which we have gotten ourselves progressively more stuck, and out of which, without major upheavals, we are unable to back, having commonly composed it past the point of no return.

With the passage of time, it gets harder to say where my story begins and her story ends. The two become as one; they 'grow together,' for better or worse. The longer the relationship lasts, the blurrier the boundaries get. The harder it is to 'see' each other except through the complex web of the combined story between us, within which – apart from our efforts to keep open to each other's individuality – our respective roles grow increasingly rigid. Our story itself, then, becomes a barrier to greater intimacy between us. It gets in our way. Within it, we settle on 'storyotypes' as to who each other is, was, and will be – albeit roomier and more up-to-date, probably, than those we impose on our acquaintances – which can become more and more difficult to dislodge, thus screening out new information that could significantly change how we experience each other – at least until we can re-story the relationship as a whole. But this larger story in which we are both enmeshed, and through which we each interpret what happens to us, is shaped in turn by – is nested within – countless other stories besides it, not only those of our respective families of origin, but also of the various organizations and communities, of the culture and class, with which we share an affiliation. And so the story goes.

As exciting as it may be then, 'getting to know you' is far from a simple process. It is a poetic process really, involving interpretations more than events, impressions more than realities, fictions more than facts. Moreover, it is a process that leads not to the whole story of my friend's life, nor to the real story, nor to the true story, but at least, I can hope, to a story that is good enough, coherent enough, and flexible enough to fit such 'facts' as, over time, I am able to ascertain. Poetic or not, it is not a process that always proceeds smoothly. Too often, it is subject to repeated frustrations and endless variations, as evidenced by our culture's vast store of love stories and hurtin' songs.

For example, when one of us draws the wrong impression of something the other has done or said, our relationship is apt to enter a painful period, particularly at the beginning, before we have acquired a wide enough sense of the numberless stories that each of us is. In this case, she may read a story into an event in my life that bears little or no relation to the story I read into it myself. It may be a story based on ignorance or gossip or prejudice; or a story that is largely her own, a projection of her own memories and expectations, 'storyotypes' and biases: a variation on a particular version of – or episode in – the story of *her* life rather than mine. To me, the event is innocuous, one I make little of at all. To her, it is made into a story of great significance, the true story, a parable of my entire past, present, and future. To me, it is a molehill; to her, a mountain. Unless we hear each other's *side* of that story, however, and get the story straight, distrust is likely to grow, and the relationship itself unroll rather rockily, if not completely unravel.

In the end, whether we get them out or straight or not, the stories we piece together about each other have a profound influence upon our involvement with each other, and, through that involvement, upon our respective unfolding fortunes and our respective processes of self-creation. Once again, stories are not innocent. Indeed, variations in stories constitute one of the commonest sources of conflict in human affairs on all levels, from individuals in intimate relationship to entire societies. Every side in every conflict is telling a different story. As one journalist observed concerning a controversy between natives and

whites in Oka, Quebec: 'In many ways, it is a struggle between differ-
ing views of Iroquoian history and laws dating back before the European arrival in North America, with each side saying it is following
history, not changing it' (Platiel, 1990).

So, then, storytelling, story-sharing, story-guessing, story-fabricating,
story-fighting, the story model period – all of this sheds a new light
(though it is more like a strobe light) on such familiar features of
everyday life as honesty and understanding, disclosure and discretion,
trust and love. Just possibly, enough light to make us despair of intimacy at all. Conversely, just possibly enough to renew us with wonder
at its intricacy and depth, and at the ever-changing challenge that
nurturing it represents.

Let me move now beyond the question of how we story our fellow
human beings and ask how, and whether, we story our world in general.

The Motive for Metaphor

I see a city. At short range, it is all hustle and bustle, with little obvious rhyme or reason. At a longer range, it is silent, lifeless, dead: a
cold configuration of concrete and glass, brick and board, asphalt and
steel. Where is the 'story' in this? Once more, however, at both short
range and long, only a little imagination is required for me to impute
a story to what I see. What sort of story? It is the story – the still
unfolding story in fact – of a major world centre, a specific metropolis
with a particular past, present, and future, as well as a cast of countless characters, including, most recently, myself. It is a story, too, that
is in turn but one subplot of a series of larger stories still, each nested
inside another: those of a particular province, country, commonwealth,
and civilization. However staid, the buildings, bricks, and bustle are
part of each of these larger stories as well – in a sense, part of its
setting. Moreover, I know that they have not always been there, that
there was a 'before' when they did not exist and will be an 'after'
when they might exist no more.

Granted that we can see stories in the human realm, can we see
them in the non-human realm as well? Shakespeare would insist we
can, that there are 'tongues in trees, books in the running brooks,
sermons in stones.' And is Shakespeare so wrong? Even for each bird

or bee that flies through the city air, do we not tend to infer a story being lived? Do we not tend to assume that Mr Toad and Ms Frog have pasts and projects peculiar to their kind; that they and their furred and feathered friends narrate their doings to one another with much the same passion (though not the same language) as do we ourselves?

The children's books on which many of us have been raised, from *The Wind in the Willows* to *Winnie the Pooh*, have in any case encouraged this tendency, thereby capitalizing on a capacity that seems to be inherent: the capacity to see in human terms aspects of our world with which we cannot possibly have direct experience. Witness also our references to Mother Nature and Father Time, to Brother Sun and Sister Moon. All of these demonstrate our drive to domesticate our environment, to fashion a cozy nest for ourselves in an otherwise indifferent, if not hostile, setting. We call this capacity anthropomorphism, but we could just as easily call it narrativization, for it is the reading of a human *story* into what may have no connection whatsoever with either humanness *or* story.

It is entirely possible that robins and rabbits, skunks and squirrels, trees and stars, lead entirely un-storied existences, that they have no conversations with one another, no personalities of their own, and no characters apart from those we imagine onto them. It is entirely possible that the world as a whole is no more than a 'booming, buzzing, confusion.' None the less, the drive to story that world is second nature, a poetic impulse instinctive to our soul. It is what the poet Stephen Spender calls 'the motive for metaphor' (Frye, 1963, 1ff): the compulsion to envision the wider context of our lives as yet one more story – no doubt of a different order, on a different scale, with a different language in which it is encoded and told, but a story all the same, no different in principle from the stories we read or watch or hear each day, or believe ourselves to live. Naturally, how that compulsion is expressed in one culture – as in one person – will be different from how it is in another. But that some way of storying the world will be carried out is difficult to question. It is the *modus operandi* of the human species, and with respect not only to art but arguably to both science and religion as well.

Analysing the underlying structure of various models of child development, psychologists Kenneth and Mary Gergen have concluded, for example, that 'literary conventions serve to fashion the theories of science' (1986, 22; see also Stainton Rogers and Stainton Rogers, 1992). In other words, theories tell stories: about what the world is like, where it has come from, where it is going, and who we are in its midst. The more aesthetically satisfying the story the theory tells, the better theory it will be deemed, and the more it will be enlisted to explain. Religious doctrines tell stories too. Don Cupitt describes the whole corpus of doctrine within Christianity as a 'great master narrative' (1991, 64), a story of the entire universe from beginning to end, 'the epic of the fulfillment of God's creative and redemptive purpose in each self and in all the world' (63). However, this story-structure is not true of Christianity alone. Every religion, he argues, is 'a set of stories that in the telling produce a society of emotionally-attuned and evaluatively-attuned selves, differentiated from each other, but sharing a family likeness and able to live a common life together' (61). Scientific or religious, such storying may be much of the reason we have raced as briskly as we have down the long, evolutionary trail, what sets us apart from our more plodding plant and animal cousins.

Seeing how extensively we story our lives, our loves, our neighbours, and our world helps us appreciate, then, why story is so alluring and so universal. 'There have been great societies that did not use the wheel,' writes Ursula Le Guin, 'but there have been no societies that did not tell stories' (1989, 27). It is through our stories that we draw our picture of the world and decide how to act in its midst. In fact, it is through our stories that we *create* our world, an insight that takes us to the heart of post-modernism. Though difficult to define precisely, the post-modern perspective is characterized by an explicit appreciation of the thin wall between fact and fiction in all of our attempts to represent 'reality,' whether historically, culturally, or politically (Hutcheon, 1989). It is characterized, says Mary Rogers, by 'a vivid sense of the fictive' (1991, 202), by an awareness of 'the fictive roots' of our everyday world (209), indeed by 'the fictionalization of everything, the transformation of all reality into a literary text' (201). Seen through post-modernist glasses, 'literature thus disappears' (201), and with it, we note, the line between literature and life.

In the section I turn to now, I shift from this general view of story to a more specific one, by examining the elements of story and the links they lead us to see between story and life.

The Links between Story and Life

How is a life like a story? This is the brash question with which this book is attempting to wrestle. Complex as it is, perhaps the glimmer of an answer is coming into view.

A life has a beginning, middle, and end, like a story. A life is about someone doing something, as is a story. A life has a main person in the middle of it, as a story often has. A life can be fraught with conflict, can be seen as manifesting a set of recurring themes, and can even be divided into certain chapters – again, as can a story. A life is a sort of world within itself, as is a story. Finally, a life is never simply given, but always in part composed, constructed, created – as is a story, even a supposedly 'factual' one.

So far so good, if not so profound, for comparably easy parallels could be identified between life and journey, life and game, and so forth. Besides, having identified them, what need is there to proceed? Maybe none, except that leaving the matter here is like bypassing the middle of the story in the interests of achieving a happy conclusion as quickly as we can. Moreover, having laboured some hundred pages, only to be confronted with platitudes, readers get annoyed. Fortunately, there is more to be said, much more, by way of fleshing out the connections between story and life. What I want to say here is arranged around the three elements of story already alluded to: plot, character, and point of view.

These elements, though, are not easy to untangle. At bottom, they are arbitrary concepts. Referring to them as 'elements' – compared to E.M. Forster's term, 'aspects' (1962) – underlines the fact that in using them to flesh out the life-as-story metaphor I am working on an element-ary level. However, 'element' may mislead us into thinking they are what a story can be dissected into in the same way (we used to assume) the world of physical substances can be dissected into hydrogen and oxygen, and, further than that, into electrons and protons, neutrons and quarks. The impetus to dismantle a story into its constituent plot, character, and point of view, as well as its theme, setting, and style – on all of which we were duty-bound to dwell in organizing our 'book reports' long ago – became focused with particular intensity with the advent in literary circles of the New Criticism. A central thrust of this criticism was that the internal structure of a story is more important to study than the intention of its author (Selden, 1989, 78). While valuable in sensitizing us to the complexity of a given text, this movement represented an invasion of the humanities by the scientific method, with its divide-and-conquer assumption that we can truly understand anything only by reducing it to its component parts.

Though trends in what has been hailed as the 'new science' indicate the opposite invasion is now occurring there – of science by the humanities – applying reductionism to story is highly problematic, for a story is a holistic entity from first to last. Not only is it a whole world within itself, but it has the potential to engage our whole being – emotionally, imaginatively, intellectually, and, as we move to the edge of our seats, teary-eyed and tense, physically as well. Furthermore, its whole is always greater than the sum of its parts. Witness how difficult it can be to convey to someone the meaning of a particular novel without eventually insisting that they read it for themselves. Similarly, if a joke has to be explained, though the explanation may capture the insight intended, it is not entirely the meaning of the joke itself. The meaning of the story *is* the story; it is embedded and embodied in it. The point is: we cannot talk about either plot, character, or point of view without eventually talking about the other elements as well, so thoroughly intertwined are the issues we encounter in discussing the internal workings of a story and in criss-crossing the strange frontier between story and life.

Finally, we must remember that we are employing categories usually applied to a specific kind of story, written fiction, and in some ways to a specific kind of written fiction at that: the novel – arguably the narrative form in which both story and storytelling reach their most intensive and extensive expression, and to which sooner or later the life-story metaphor pushes us. I say 'arguably,' but what arguments does the novel actually have in its favour?

Life-as-Novel: Pros and Cons

For the philosopher Glover, 'self-creation tends to make a life like a novel by a single author' (1988, 152). For the novelist Gustave Flaubert, 'everyone's life is worth a novel' (Polster, 1987). For the critic Leon Surmelian, 'a great novel is a unique human document that re-creates a way of life' in a way 'the sociologist, the psychologist, the historian could not do' (1969, 2). Despite these accolades, though, need life-as-story point us exclusively to this particular medium? Given the multisensual dimension of an individual life – as something visible, tangible, and audible, as something enacted and embodied – might not the novel, as something legible by definition (that is, printed, confined to the book), be in fact the least likely narrative form for us to enlist?

A movie or play, for instance, might seem a far more appropriate medium: a movie because of the strong visual component to most of our memories; a play because of the theatrical component of our everyday lives (Goffman, 1959). A life could also be likened to an epic poem, on the scale of an *Iliad* or an *Odyssey*, because of how much it encompasses, the encyclopaedia of personal lore it embraces, and the endless digressions it entails. A life could be compared to a series of short stories as well, presumably all composed by the same author, more or less connected to one another, though maybe or maybe not featuring the same main character and dealing with the same themes. A life could also be seen in terms of a soap opera because of the fact that, whether it is daytime or prime time, it knows no clear conclusion. It just goes on and on. Though it still frames its action for us, as does any story, leaving out all but the most dramatic details, it manages to withhold from us the same sense of closure that can elude us in everyday life. Unlike what happens in a classical tragedy or the average Hollywood movie, or even the weekly situation comedy, little is ever resolved once and for all. As one critic writes, 'no action necessarily entails anything' (Leitch, 1986, 65). Happy marriages can always end in divorce; best-laid plans usually go awry; and the story as a whole – if there is *one* story – 'does not proceed to a determined and determinative end which incarnates the rationale of the whole' (65).

Each of these media reflects an undeniable aspect of everyday life: its drama, its vastness, its disconnectedness, its never-endingness. Taken together, do they not discredit the novel as an extension of life-as-story? Not entirely, as I hope to show; yet there are three additional respects in which the choice of the novel is challenged.

One of these lies in the fact that, like story in general, the novel is not a monolithic category. Not only is there no ideal novel but only an endless array of actual ones – more or less intricate and, as it were, artistic – but there is also a bewildering number of *kinds* of novel. These include detective novels, psychological novels, propaganda novels, historical novels, novels of manners, regional novels, gothic novels, epistolary novels, novels of the soil, stream-of-consciousness novels, and picaresque novels. In addition, there is a variety of 'modes' in terms of which novels have historically been written, each reflective of the styles, literary conventions, and attitudes toward life of their respective novelists' era. These have been identified as realism, romanticism, impressionism, expressionism, and naturalism (Thrall et al, 1960, 324). Obviously, a detailed history of the novel and a full catalogue of its kinds and modes is beyond my mandate here. Besides, 'attempts to classify the novel usually come to logical grief' (323), for there is so much overlap between the distinctions that need to be employed to do so. As well, these distinctions keep changing with each new generation of novelists – some would say so much that it is now fair to announce the *death* of the novel.

This constitutes the second challenge. The philosopher Ted Estess (1974) has expressed it well. 'It is deeply ironic,' he says, 'that while some humanists engage in a concerted effort to resurrect the metaphor of story as a way of understanding the deepest matters of human existence, many literary artists speak of the death of the novel and despair over the story-form itself' (416). Estess' point is well-taken. There is considerable ambivalence toward the novel in current literary circles, even downright suspicion. As early as 1966, Robert Scholes and Robert Kellogg were heralding 'the disintegration of the novel' (15), insisting on the need to do something 'about our veneration of the novel' (5) as the apex of story, about our 'almost hopelessly novel-centered ... view of narrative literature' (p. 8). In short, they wanted 'to put the novel in its place' (3). As the novelist Milan Kundera (1988) puts it, reflecting rather tongue in cheek on the spate of such nay-sayers, 'they saw the novel dropping off the road of progress, yielding to a radically new future and an art bearing no resemblance to what had existed before. The novel was to be buried in the name of historical justice, like poverty, the ruling classes, obsolete cars, or top hats' (13).

The third challenge arises from the possibility that, dead or alive, the novel represents not the zenith of story but its nadir. For philosopher Walter Benjamin, who has argued this view forcefully, 'the rise of the novel at the beginning of modern times' constitutes 'the earliest symptom of a process whose end is the decline of storytelling' (1969, 87). Though his view has been criticized as 'a fully nostalgic and romantic view of storytelling, one we may even judge to be utopian and mystified' (Brooks, 1988, 288), Benjamin argues, like Plato before him, that our preference for written as opposed to oral communication is not a positive development. Rather, it represents a weakening of the fabric of human community. Storytelling, as he sees it, is an intrinsically and eminently sociable situation. While 'in the novel ... the writer and the reader are both solitary individuals' (Brooks, 1988, 289), 'a man listening to a story is in the company of the storyteller' (Benjamin, 1969, 100). Storytelling is 'always the art of repeating stories, and this art is lost when the stories are no longer retained. It is lost because there is no more weaving and spinning going while they are being listened to' (Brooks, 1988, 288). This leads to the loss of 'the ability to exchange experiences' (Benjamin, 1969, 83).

Compared to the first three, then, the fourth challenge is simple. It goes like this: whether the novel is dead or not, whether it is the deterioration of story or not, it is simply not read, at least not the literary novel. To be sure, novel-writing, novel-publishing, and novel-buying are all very much alive; however, as one recent survey of readers reveals, 'the proportion [of Americans] who read serious literature of all forms in the course of a year seems to be about 7 to 12 percent of the adult population' (Zill and Winglee, 1990, viii). Low as it is, even this figure is shaky, 'for people who claim to be regular readers often admit, when pressed for specifics, that they are regular readers not of Saul Bellow and Eudora Welty but of Stephen King and Danielle Steel' (viii). So, to centre my discussion around the novel is problematic when the sort I have in mind – serious, 'literary' fiction, as opposed to the formulaic fiction we call 'pulp' (though the distinction is far from precise) – is far from the people's choice. What most people choose is not reading stories at all, but viewing them, in the five-minute bites of sitcoms and soaps, with thirty-second morality plays interspersing them to extoll the life-changing virtues of batteries and beer, perfumes and panty hose.

That the novel provides a superior analogy for the poetic subtleties of a human life is hardly, then, a foregone conclusion. Despite the power of these arguments against the novel, however, it is not really my place to defend it once and for all. Besides, we are into metaphor here: It is not that a life *is* a novel, but that it is conceivably *like* a novel, as an atom is *like* a solar system. I am defending not the novel *per se*, that is, only the use of the novel – as a form of story – in exploring the poetics of self-creation. Accordingly, I can at least listen to those who have spoken in its favour, those who see it as 'the latest and most highly evolved form of story-making' (Gold, 1988, 252). If there is any validity to their insights, then surely the novel merits its fair share of consideration amid other narrative forms. There are, I believe, a number of good reasons for this.

For one, like most forms of story and like much of life as we know it, a novel is language-dependent – indeed, with a vengeance: most novels are low on pictures and long on words. To dismiss the novel because it is too verbal to reflect the fullness of everyday life is to miss the word-centredness of most human interaction. Like it or not, we are creatures, indeed creations, of language. Yet, despite its basis in language, a novel affects us on more than the verbal plane alone. We do not merely read a novel; we also see and hear and feel the world that it elicits in our imagination. Against the criticism that it is less alive dramatically than a play or movie, the novel, it can be argued, is 'not (primarily) a narrative form with dramatic moments, but a dramatic form within a narrative framework' (Dawson, 1970, 80). As novelist D.H. Lawrence expresses it (not surprisingly), it is 'the one bright book of life.' Even if 'books are not life' but only tremulations on the other,' a novel 'can make the whole man alive tremble' (Lodge, 1988, 134) – something many a movie might fail to do if it were not for the music telling us what to feel. A novel can make the whole man tremble because the verbal leads invariable to the visual and visceral alike.

The novel is also to be acknowledged for its breadth, for the scope of reality it is able to embrace in both time and space. On the one hand, most novels are rather long; moreover, within them, a long time can be covered, sometimes even generations. Besides taking a long time to read, they require us to hold a large amount of material in memory for a considerable length of time if we are to follow the story and understand it. On the other hand, compared to the average stage play, novels can span a great range of scenes and settings, of cultures and countries. Novels move around. As a result, 'the novel comes closer to the scope of a person's actual life than do poems, plays, music, or sculpture. The time span and the variety of places encompassed by the novel provide a broader spectrum than is available in other art forms' (Polster, 1987, 11).

Furthermore, against the criticism that the novel is over-occupied with the vagaries of individual lives is the fact that it can tell us much about society; it can be 'the vehicle of our collective anxieties and their workings-through' (Brooks, 1988, 285). This double dimension is stressed by Mary Rogers in her attempt to articulate 'a phenomeno-logical sociology of literature.' Novels can recreate whole eras, convey the feel of whole cultures, sketch entire worlds, not just the individuals depicted within them. 'More than any body of oral traditions or any other institutions reliant on print,' Rogers writes, 'the novel probes the meaning of individuality, the challenge of human relationships, and the constitution of human worlds' (1991, 82). In this way, 'the novel readily offers insights that are available but less widely accessible in sociology, anthropology, psychology, history, and investigative journalism.' The novel 'illuminates selves as deeply social creatures' (84).

A novel can also do justice to the *chaotic* quality of life. Choppable into chapters, divisible into subplots and themes, the novel, writes literary theorist Mikhail Bakhtin, is 'the one grand literary form ... capable of a kind of justice to the inherent polyphonies of life' (Lodge, 1988, 137). A novel is not neat. Thus, while 'a script is a dialogue spoken in a particular setting' and 'a play moves singlemindedly towards its denouement ... a novel, the sort of novel one could imagine one's life to be, at any rate, seems to meander, with a ragbag of concerns' (Polster, 1987, 1). Yet it does not meander so much that it becomes a mere anthology. Whatever a novel is, its parts are connected, however weakly, by a continuous story-line.

So, then, wordy enough, dramatic enough, broad enough, long enough, social enough, chaotic enough, yet connected enough too: to such a litany we can add *subjective* enough as well. A novel can take us inside the minds and hearts of its characters – even when written in the third person – in a way that movies, plays, or soap operas are constitutionally unable to do (often more than we can with respect to our *own* minds and hearts!). The novel, says Bruner, is suited to 'the changing, increasingly subjective mind of modern man' (1965, 54). In contrast to myth – a narrative form that is 'objective, transcendental, timeless, moved by impulses beyond man to meet inhuman demands' (52) – 'the contemporary novel is subjective, immanent, living in time, animated by human impulses that lead to human actions' (52–3). Thus, it 'reflects the increase in self-consciousness that has been part of the development of our civilization' (52). 'The novel,' adds literary critic Barbara Hardy, 'merely heightens, isolates, and analyzes the narrative motions of human consciousness' (1968, 5). In this respect, the specific mode of self-consciousness we call autobiography 'merges with the novel by a series of insensible gradations' (Frye, 1966, 33). The boundary between the two genres can be difficult to discern. Indeed, 'all serious work must be at bottom autobiographical,' writes novelist Thomas Wolfe (1983, 19) whose own works epitomize the drive to transform autobiography into art – to translate 'fact into what he considered truth' (viii).

In the end, of course, as the novelist François Mauriac reminds us, 'there is no such thing as a novel which genuinely portrays the indetermination of human life as we know it' (Booth, 1961, 22). This point is hard to dispute. At the same time, even if the claims of these thinkers fail to clinch the question of 'Why the novel?' as the crux of our inquiry, they at least encourage us to look more intentionally in the novel's direction. Consequently, though in what follows I stray at times into the territory of story in general – for example, of filmed stories (many of which have novel beginnings) – it is the novel form of story that will be my focus.

The Element of Plot

What is the plot of a story? In his discussion of the elements of Greek tragedy, Aristotle, who first focused our thinking on plot, assigns it primary importance. He calls it 'the first principle, and, as it were, the soul of tragedy' (Fergusson, 1961, 63). By soul, he means 'the formative principle in any live thing whether man, animal, or plant' (15). His conception of plot is thus 'organic,' for he sees it 'as the basic *form* of the play' (14). That is, 'the action which the poet first glimpses is only potentially a tragedy, until his plot-making forms it into an *actual* tragedy' (15).

This description of plot, though intriguing, may seem a bit abstract. As to what plot 'is' in more concrete terms, however, Aristotle identifies it as 'the arrangement of the incidents' (62), a definition simple enough to be applied not just to tragedy but to any story. Carrying on from it, we may make the primitive observation that the plot of a story is what *happens* in the story. It is the something that the somebody, about whom someone is telling, is actually doing. It is, in Frye's words, 'the rationally communicable sense of the story' (Aichele, 1985, 26). It is what enables us to summarize the story and to remember what it is about. It is the logic of a story, its principal argument, its central story-line.

There is more than one way of looking at this story-line, however. We can see it not just as the soul of the story but also in much more static terms, as its 'least variable element' or skeleton (Scholes and Kellogg, 1966, 238). Indeed, in light of the work of French literary critic Jacques Derrida, the English word *plot* is really quite ambiguous, much like the Greek word *pharmakon* for whose 'deconstruction' he is celebrated (Johnson, 1981). As a verb, plot signifies both *direct* (as in 'plot a course') and *deceive* (as in 'plot to kill'); as a noun, it implies both *design* (as in 'plan') and *demise* (as in 'the place one is buried'). The same ambiguity, perhaps even duplicity, applies to story. The plot of a story, as we shall see, excludes as many incidents as (if not far more than) it includes. Thus, it represents simultaneously the story's development *and* its undoing, its soul *and* its skeleton. Taking a less either-or path through this conceptual maze, however, critic Peter Brooks (1985) urges us to see plot as the principle of both 'interconnectedness' and 'intention' (5). It is 'the outline or armature of the story ... that which supports and organizes the rest' (11). It is what lures us to move purposefully through the story, what makes us curious to know what will happen next, and what inspires in us the confidence that we are getting somewhere as we follow it from beginning to end.

To these attempts at defining plot we must add the note that, whether skeleton or soul, the plot of a story will be different things – that is, will be *experienced* differently – from different perspectives. From that of the characters, it is just the way things are, one damned thing after another: in a sense, the flow of 'fate' with which they have little choice but to go. For the narrator, it is more the way things *were*, since most narration is past tense. For the reader, it is the winding path one follows expectantly into the future yet figures out after the fact (Brooks, 1985, 22–3). For the author, it is the plan of where things *ought* to go, more or less flexible depending on how formulaic or emergent is the design. It is on the latter two perspectives, though, those of reader and author, that I shall be concentrating in the sections that follow. Unfortunately, whenever we talk about plot, even in reference to literature alone, all four perspectives are likely to get blurred – a danger that, though we acknowledge it at the outset, does little to decrease the difficulty of the task ahead of us.

From these first forays into the complexities of plot, I believe there emerge three sets of issues, separate yet related, about the links between literature and life. As 'a trope for human experience' (Leitch, 1986, 148), plot raises issues that have to do with time, with aesthetics, and with what, for purposes of this discussion, I shall call theology. In what follows, I shall introduce aspects of plot that relate to each of these areas, first as they apply to literature itself, then, more tentatively, as they may be extrapolated to life.

Time

In relation to issues of time, an analysis of plot unearths at least three key concepts: profluence, causality, and *energeia*.

We have seen the simplicity of the basic story structure, with its beginning, middle, and end. This is not a static structure, however, but a dynamic one, an intentional, forward-moving one. It is because of the plot that in reading a story we are really 'following' it, for it leans, and leads us, steadily into the future. This future-looking, forward movement is central to the magic of a story. It is summed up in novelist John Gardner's word 'profluence.' Profluence is 'our sense, as we read, that we're "getting somewhere"' (1985, 48). It is our sense, which is 'a powerful part of our interest as we read great literature,' he says, 'that we're "onto something"' (49). 'By definition – and of aesthetic necessity – a story contains profluence' (53). Profluence is the pull of the story upon us, the essence of its al-lure. 'The conventional kind of profluence,' Gardner points out, 'is a causally related sequence of events.' In such sequencing lies 'the root interest of all conventional narrative': 'Because he is intellectually and emotionally involved – that is, interested – the reader is led by successive, seemingly inevitable steps, with no false steps, and no necessary steps missing, from an unstable initial situation to its relatively stable outcome' (55).

Prevalent though profluence be, it is a strange force. While leading us forward, it has us looking backward all the while. We read a story one way but understand it the other. Brooks calls this 'the necessary retrospectivity of narrative' (1985, 22). Accordingly, the end of a story has greater importance than either the beginning or the middle; it is 'the logical place to begin an analysis of the narrative transaction' (Leitch, 1986, 43). 'Only the end can finally determine meaning' (Brooks, 1985, 22), and only the end can finally determine feeling. As we say, all's well that *ends* well. The end confers unity on the story; it is 'the pole of attraction of [its] entire development' (Ricoeur, 1981, 170). It is our 'sense of an ending' (Kermode, 1966) that decides how we interpret what we are reading in the present and have read in the past. 'The end writes the beginning and shapes the middle (Brooks, 1985, 22). Accordingly, 'a story with no intelligible ending ... would be no story at all' (Leitch, 1986, 88). Let me explore a few of the implications of this.

As soon as I open a novel, my imagination goes to work trying to guess where the story is going – and how it will end. The end is already in the beginning, casting its long shadow over the very first line. Even though I never know exactly what that end will be, I am silently speculating, page by page, on the meaning of all of the past and present incidents in relation to one theory after another about the final outcome: whether or not the girl will get the boy, the boy will become a man, or the man will win the day. My guesswork will be more or less intense depending on how easy I feel it is to figure the outcome out. Where I feel at home with a particular genre of story and it is clear to me that the story is of *that* genre and not some other, the guesswork is minimized. I am on familiar turf. I know what *kind* of story it is; thus, I know how a story of that kind tends generally to run, even if the exact steps it takes to get to its destination are not known to me in advance. Small wonder, then, that when the end turns out to be drastically different than anticipated I am not merely surprised but on some level annoyed. It is as if I had been hoodwinked. Although satisfied it was something new and not ultimately the same old story, I feel a bit foolish: my hunches about the real reason behind the arrangement of the incidents were apparently mistaken.

Brooks calls this peculiar, forward-backward dynamic of reading 'the anticipation of retrospection.' It is 'our chief tool in making sense of narrative, the master trope of its strange logic' (1985, 23). Accordingly, 'we read in a spirit of confidence, and also a state of dependence, that what remains to be read will restructure the provisional meanings of the already read' (25). This points to one of the most perplexing aspects of plot: that a story written in the past tense is meant to be read as if it were unfolding in the present. Of this feature of a story's strange logic, Brooks says, 'if the past is to be read as present, it is a curious present that we know to be past in relation to a future we know to be already in place, already in wait for us to reach it' (23).

Our anticipation of retrospection suggests, then, a second aspect of plot, one already hinted at. Plot arranges the incidents according not to chronology ultimately but to causality, not to sequence but to *con*sequence. Part of our pleasure in fiction lies in the feeling that 'one thing leads to another,' and, in that sense, makes sense. This is one reason why we expose children to stories so early (not that we have much choice): to teach them the connection between cause and effect. For Forster, causality is what distinguishes plot from 'mere story.' In one of his most celebrated observations, he says: '"The king died, and then the queen died" is a story. "The king died and then the queen died of grief" is a plot.' Considering the death of the queen, 'If it is in a story we say: "And then?"' However, 'If it is in a plot we ask: "Why?"'' (1962, 87).

As we have seen, this distinction between story and plot is naive. No narrative is devoid of plot, of some 'arrangement of the incidents,' however undramatic it be. Yet Forster's insight into the causal component of plot is critical to a discussion of the links between literature and life. 'We explain our actions in terms of plots, and often no other form of explanation can produce sensible statements' (Polkinghorne, 1988, 160). Why is this? In the view of critic Will Wright, it is because 'narratives explain change.' Every event in a story, he says, 'is a beginning, middle, or end of a narrative sequence that explains a significant change ... either [it] has been caused by something, will cause something, or provides the basis for another event to cause something' (1989, 106). In this way, 'not only do stories demonstrate that experience can make sense, they also demonstrate how it makes sense, by showing that one important event causes another and by ignoring the unimportant events' (107). While 'events in life must be interpreted as significant,' Wright continues, 'events in narrative are inherently significant.' While 'in life meaning is problematic, in narrative it is not.' That is, 'by locating an experience in a narrative sequence with other experiences, experiences are given meaning.' Thus, 'in a story, everything is important.' The form of story itself, then, 'is a primer for making sense of experience ... a paradigm for making sense of life' (106–7).

Related to causality is what Aristotle calls *energeia. Energeia* is 'the actualization of the potential which exists in both character and situation' (Gardner, 1985, 47). As the word suggests, it is energy. It is what drives the story forward – in the same way that Maslow, following Aristotle, believes our lives are driven forward: by our 'essential inner nature,' which seeks 'full individuality and identity, unity of personality, spontaneous expressiveness, fuller and fuller being' (1968, 155). In this sense, a story has an essentialist dimension, too, an organic one. It cannot be denied. As we often say, a story 'unfolds.' The greater the *energeia* inherent in its beginning – the more pregnant with possibilities the initial 'germ of the story,' as Henry James calls it (Allen, 1949, 155)[2] – then the more power the story will have for us: 'the power of inexorable process' (Gardner, 1985, 166). The device by which the writer intensifies this *energeia* is, once again, past-tense narration. Such narration 'locates itself in the past ... in order to allow itself forward movement,' as if the story's own future were a vacuum into which it is steadily sucked. 'Only by locating itself in the "other country" of the past is the narrative free to move towards its future, the present,' (Le Guin, 1989a, 38).

We have a situation, then, where the story's *energeia* pushes us from behind while its profluence pulls us from ahead, thereby making us feel we are going, getting, or being guided somewhere. Put differently, it is as if the writer were but one step ahead of us, beckoning us on, inviting us to a place she has already been. This explains a paradoxical yet common feature of following *any* story: our sense that how it unfolds is both unexpected and yet, in retrospect, 'had to be.' At the same time as the plot 'thickens,' it also 'narrows,' until only one of a decreasing range of possible outcomes comes out in the end. With respect to the climax, for example, 'for [it] to be not only persuasive but interesting, it must come about in a way that seems both inevitable and surprising' (Gardner, 1985, 172). This is the peculiar balancing act at work in 'the well-built energeic plot' (166): suspense against revelation, predictability against surprise. Too much weight on either side and the story loses its tension, and with it the at-tention of its reader. The plot is then declared 'weak.'

So, we read a story forward but understand it backward. In reviewing events that were new to us when we first read them, and whose place and purpose eluded us then, we find that they have turned out to possess an increasing necessity. We know now what we could not know at the time: that A had to happen in order for B to happen as well. And so the story goes. But is the story so different in life? Observations about causality in plot, as well as about inevitability and (implicitly) predestination, tempt us to make comparable observations about the way we experience our lives. They also push us to move from issues of time to those that intrude on the territory of theology. I shall peek into that territory eventually, but for the moment, what is the story with life?

Life has its own blunt brand of beginning, middle, and end: we're born, we suffer, we die. Moreover, amid the suffering there are any number of smaller beginnings, middles, and ends as well, in so far as life has its ups and downs, highs and lows, peaks and valleys: in so far as each day we work and play, rise and recline. Despite Roquentin's complaint about how in living 'nothing happens,' truly unrelieved monotony (as well as unrelieved suspense) is as unlikely as it is un-endurable. Change is the constant in life. However, the boundaries between these various beginnings, middles, and ends are admittedly indistinct. An event that represents the beginning of one set of circumstances may represent the end of another, or be in the middle of still another (Bridges, 1980). Expressed differently, in our lives there is no one to write Chapter Four at the top of the page when Chapter Three is complete. In this sense, life and literature are very different.

At the same time, chapters in literary stories do not necessarily possess the neatness we may think. Chapter Three 'ends,' yes, but only because an interim measure of catharsis has been elicited or suspense aroused. As the verbal spotlight shifts silently away from the protagonist, in other words, and he is left by himself to contemplate his plight, we trust that he will still continue to breathe, to feel the breeze on his face, and perhaps eventually to wander off track with his thoughts – as any of us would do as well. In the name of what Henry James calls 'the sublime economy of art' (Allen, 1949, 156), however, the author typically omits these tedious details. Such economy can be achieved because of our remarkable ability to assume that, between one scene and another, the hero's life goes on. Part of us accepts, that is, that the dramatic pitch the author sustains in us from the end of one chapter to the beginning of the next is the result of an artistic trick it is necessary to play on us because it is impossible to convey completely the passage of time between the two – which may involve not just minutes but hours, months, or years. As readers, we fill in the blanks between the chapters. In our imagination, we make into a coherent whole the temporally chopped-up world that, technically, the story describes. We 'fill in gaps with essential or likely events, traits, and objects which for various reasons have gone unmentioned' (Chatman, 1978, 29). Indeed, our 'capacity to supply plausible details is virtually limitless' (29). That it is, is testimony to the strength of the storying instinct.

Whether because we have a limited attention span or simply cannot bear too much reality, we have a need for periodic closures in reading a work of fiction – a need the convention of chapters is marvellously suited to meet. But is the need any less in life? When a signficant relationship comes to an end, the counsellor assures us that 'getting closure' is a prerequisite to picking up the pieces and 'getting on with our lives.' Without a clear sense that 'it's over,' we shall be hindered from growth. We may not always get that sense, of course, but the importance of it is not thereby negated. Thus, though the neat closures of a novel and its constituent chapters may not mirror our experience, they do reflect our need. Even if in our everyday lives we seldom have the sense of satisfaction that can be stimulated by an intricately crafted novel, when all the potential inherent in its beginning has been actualized and all symbolic connections have been tidily made, the yearning for such satisfaction may be no less intense. Why else, we can ask, are so many of us moved to write our autobiographies, and so many more convinced that we *should* write them if only we had the talent or time?

These questions prompt us to probe more deeply the similarities between reading stories and living lives. The obvious place to begin is the beginning. Technically, this is where we begin in reading a novel. As we have seen, however, the fictional world into which we thereby jump has already been unfolding. For any story, a pre-story is implied, a time before the time that is 'once upon'; a world where, before our arrival upon their scene, the characters were living and growing and getting along quite nicely without us. Therefore, as in literature, so in life: we begin in the middle. In Heideggerian terms, as our consciousness awakes, we find we have been 'thrown' into existence, with no choice in the matter; thrust into the midst of a particular family story, world story, universe story; suspended in time between a beginning we cannot recall and an end we cannot envision. This point is elaborated by Donald Polkinghorne (1988). Having argued that our sense of personal identity is achieved 'through the use of the narrative configuration' and that we understand our life 'as an expression of a single unfolding and developing story,' he says that our predicament is that 'we are in the *middle* of our stories and ... are constantly having to revise the plot as new events are added to our lives' (150). We have to do so, however, 'without knowing how the story will end' (69). Obviously, this need to 'revise the plot' keeps us rather busy, for there is no end to the new events that need incorporation into our story. But is this in fact what we do? Do we really concern ourselves with the 'plot' of our lives: where it is in the present, where it has gone in the past, and where it will unfold in the future?

As we have seen, central to our nature is the compulsion to story the world around us, to locate ourselves within it by assigning it a past, a future ... and a present. Yet this is easier said than done, for the present is where we already are. It is right under our noses, too immediate to be seen. Understandable with clearer vision is either where that story has been in the past or where it may go in the future. Were the relevant statistics available, for instance, we would probably discover that the majority of statements we make in telling our lives on an everyday basis are of the 'I did' or 'I will' variety, rather than the 'I am.' We can appreciate this possibility by recalling what happens whenever we drive a car.

Amid this most ordinary of activities, where is it our attention is fixed? It is fixed on the road ahead – though, for safety's sake, we sneak occasional glances in the rearview mirror at the hills and highway receding from our sight. We focus, that is, on either the future or the past, not the present. To try and make our way by concentrating on the present would be the height of folly. To stare to one side or the other of our speeding vehicle – on the blur of pavement or the whiz of poles and passing cars – would be to risk danger too terrifying to contemplate. Unless we are a passenger, then attending to what Ma, in Steinbeck's story *The Grapes of Wrath*, calls 'just the road goin' by' would get us nowhere – save, at best, the ditch and, at worst, our death. We navigate only by going back and forth between where we will be and where we have been. The present is merely the junction point where all the roads that would lead us ahead intersect with those that have brought us thus far. Bringing this insight to bear on our everyday life, the present is less the focus of our practical thinking than the lens through which we peer either forward into the anticipated future or backward into the remembered past. However short-sighted might be our vision in either direction, we are scarcely if ever capable of looking *exactly* at the ever-passing present. Thus, we are back to bad faith. Polkinghorne advances a similar image. 'We lived immersed in narrative,' he says, 'recounting and reassessing the meanings of our past actions, anticipating the outcomes of future projects, situating ourselves at the intersection of several stories not yet completed' (1988, 160).

Let me move now from thinking about the middle of our plots to considering again our relationship to the end. What is our relationship to the end of the story we live? To answer this question, we can draw parallels with our relationship to the end of the story we read.

Polkinghorne says we are 'at the intersection of several stories not yet completed.' A common reflection we can have in living our lives relates to the path not taken, the experience passed up, the opportunity turned down. Few of us have never wondered 'what might have happened if ...': if we knew then what we know now; if only we had married A rather than B, moved to M rather than N, worked at X rather than Y. This familiar phenomenon – felt with a mixture of curiosity, relief, and regret – is the peculiar form taken by our memory due to our freedom each day to make any number of potentially life-altering choices. Such freedom is both the blessing and the bane of our existence, the source of wonder and terror alike, the origin equally of exhilaration and anxiety. The point is: we can always envision our lives being different than they are. And each different life we can envision assumes the form of a story we can see ourselves living, or having lived – in principle, like each of the stories we imagine onto the strangers we see on the street.

These uncompleted life stories can be either long or short. Working at my desk, I can readily imagine two or three different short stories that correspond to the different plans I am toying with for spending my evening, each more or less enjoyable, desirable, and affordable. However, none of these short stories, if lived out, would necessarily have a dramatic impact on the range of longer stories I am toying with as well, for spending the next month, the next year, or the next decade. Sometimes, though, short stories can turn into long stories if, in living them out, something unforeseen presents itself – a person I meet, a date I set, an otherwise innocuous decision I make – that opens up new possibilities for completing my life as a whole: The stranger on the train turns into my wife, or going to the party rather than staying at home leads to a business venture that ends up changing my whole world. Conversely, long stories can suddenly become short. For instance, when my long-standing dream of becoming a politician is confronted with the terrifying experience of chairing my first meeting, the 'me-as-politician story' gets quietly struck from my list.

This play of possible futures within my imagination, both long and short, is virtually endless. 'If I do this,' I say to myself, 'then I shall have to deal with that person as a result, confront that danger, pay that price, or enjoy that pay-off. If I do that, on the other hand, then I shall likely deal with this and this and this.' I tell myself stories, each with its own expected plot, its own trouble, its own tensions and resolutions, and its own cast of characters, imagined or real. The process of making decisions is a matter, again and again, of trying on alternative stories for size, weighing the pros and cons of each. It is the same in reading a novel or watching a movie. When the story is new, when I have no idea how it will end, then in following it along I tell myself a succession of stories to prepare myself for, and not be totally surprised by, the one and only end it can turn out to have.

In living a life as in reading a story, we are constantly leaning into the future, hoping on some level that when we arrive there we shall be able to look back with understanding on the past, able to see how one event after another, in its own way, 'had to be.' This is the backward-forward dynamic we have already considered: the anticipation

of retrospection, our chief tool in making sense not only of a story but
also of a life. T.S. Eliot has captured this insight for us in a comment
made by the son in *The Confidential Clerk*. Reflecting on his father's
behaviour time and again, he realized that 'he could never predict what
his father would do, but after he had done it he understood.' Like the
son, despite our knowledge that in reading our own lives hindsight is
never twenty-twenty, there lies in us a confidence 'that what remains
to be read will re-structure the provisional meanings of the already
read' (Brooks, 1985, 23). Though this confidence will vary from one of
us to another, it is what enables us to go out into each new day, like the
prophet, 'not knowing where [we are] to go' (Hebrews 11: 8). It is what
enables us to keep on living when our failure to make sense of what is
happening in the present could otherwise cripple us with confusion and
fear. As Kierkegaard says, in defiance of Sartre, though life 'must be
lived forwards,' it 'can only be understood backwards.'

In living a life, as in reading a story, we tend to cling to the conviction that we are 'getting somewhere,' that we are 'onto something,'
that the bits of our existence that seem so scattered today will eventually find their place. We are profluenced by the future. However, the
future is never one future but many. And each envisionable future will
profluence us in a unique way, generating within us its own interpretations, or set of interpretations, upon the past. If in one of the futures
I imagine for myself, I shall in five years be president of the company,
then the anticipation of that future will affect not only how I conduct
myself amid the challenges I face today, but also how I interpret the
promotion I was denied five years ago. I may see it as a fortuitous
setback from the trajectory I was on at the time, one that would not
have led to the presidency at all. Thus, the lack of advancement then
can be seen now as a blessing in disguise, for I have learned from it,
gained some 'character' because of it, and acquired, as a result of it,
the business and bureaucratic savvy that will make the presidency five
years hence a far more certain thing. If, however, in another of the
futures I imagine, I have become redundant in five years' time
because of a merger or recession I cannot now foresee, then how I
experience my present and interpret my past will be different again.
In this way, just as planning entails telling myself stories, so does
worrying too.

In the end, it is our sense of an ending that determines our sense of
both our middle and our beginning. The corollary of this, which I shall
return to in the third chapter, would seem to be that our sense of our
story as a whole emerges side by side with our sense of mortality.

Death, observes Walter Benjamin starkly, 'is the sanction of everything that the storyteller can tell' (1969, 94). Every one of our imagined futures, all our uncompleted stories, we know, must eventually end in (or pass through) our death. Moreover, the *kind* of death we envision – whether rich or poor, comfortable or painful, with loved ones or alone – will make a difference in our attitude *toward* our death. For example, we may approach it as 'welcomers,' 'accepters,' 'postponers,' 'disdainers,' 'fearers,' etc. (Birren, 1964, 274). We may also approach it, bad faith though it be to do so, as 'peekers.' In other words, just as some readers cannot seem to enjoy a story unless they skip first to the final page to find out how it ends, so some of us (maybe many) never quite see ourselves save, in part, through the eyes of our imagined biographer (Edel, 1959, 21, 30, 37) – the one entrusted with sifting through the events of our lives, discerning the plot amid the flotsam and jetsam, and interpreting the details of what we were when we started out, and of what we were along the way, in light of what became of us in the end. By the same token, there may be many others among us who have no interest whatever in knowing how the story will end: readers (and livers?) who do not *want* the story to end in fact, and can work themselves into a proper depression when they realize that it must, that the end is near, that they will eventually have to forsake the company of their fictional friends and return to the tedium of 'real life.'

It is impossible to say, of course, which of these is the 'best' relationship to have towards the end, in reading and living alike – the best, that is, as in the healthiest or the most balanced. But by beginning to speculate on the issue here, as on others I have touched on this section, we should be starting to get a sense of the range of 'storying styles' that are at work in how we experience ourselves and compose our lives. In the next chapter, I shall look at these in more detail. I trust we are also appreciating how, perched as we are between our beginning and our end, peering backwards and forwards from one to the other, what we call our 'experience' is a repository as much of the future as it is of the past. As far as learning (or self-creation) is concerned, if we are going to honour the role played by *past* experience we must not ignore the one played by *future* experience as well.

Aesthetics

In relation to issues that concern aesthetics, a consideration of plot leads us to look at the concepts of coherence, selection, and symbolic interconnection.

The plot of a story is what ensures it will have coherence from beginning to end, that it will co-here, will hold together. For instance, it is the plot that coordinates several strands of action and relationship, dialogue and setting, into a system of intertwining subplots. If it did not, the stuff of the story would not constitute *one* story. The coherence that the plot thus accomplishes amounts to a 'built-in immune system' whereby every story resists contamination from or interaction with every other (Bridges, 1980, 71). It is difficult, for example, to imagine the world of *Moll Flanders* mingled with that of *Robinson Crusoe*, or that of *Great Expectations* with *The World according to Garp*. With the exception of certain prime-time soap operas in which characters from one story figure periodically in the plot of another, each story is a world unto itself. It is a 'framed world' (Aichele, 1985, 26). Unless we have spent too much time in a Disney world, that is, most of us tend not to believe in a world somewhere over the rainbow – 'storyland,' say – where, after hours, Friday plays tennis with Moll or Garp goes pubbing with Pip.

As its guarantee of coherence, the plot of a story ensures it will have a degree of wholeness, which means we are able to infer what *kind* of story it is if we enter it midstream. It is the plot that allows us to project backward and forward to piece together what the story is about. It is the plot that provides us with an overriding framework into which the events of that story fit. It is the plot that helps us identify a certain story as indeed 'the same old story' – even if the particulars change, or we cross the frontier from one medium to another: say, from novels to movies to cartoons. It is the plot that enables us to recognize that even if the Newfoundlander has been changed to the man from Maine, or if it is a priest and a rabbi at the Pearly Gates rather than a doctor and a lawyer, it is the same dumb joke. It is the plot that lets us know instinctively that, in moving from a midweek sitcom to a full-length film to a Victorian novel, we are encountering the same basic motif, be it rags-to-riches, saint-slaying-dragon, or love-conquering-all. Thus, the link between plot and its equivalent in Greek, *mythos*, which we translate 'myth' (Frye, 1988, 112). I shall return to this concept in subsequent sections; for now, we need to look at plot as a principle of selection.

According to Paul Ricoeur, plot is 'the intelligible whole that governs a succession of events in any story ... A story is *made out of* events to the extent that plot *makes* events *into* a story' (1980, 167). As we have seen, the very concept of 'event' is problematic. The boundary between one event and another, where one begins and another ends, is woefully far from clear. Furthermore, however delineated, events never speak for themselves. Their meaning is not inherent in them; it is constructed, given to them by plotting them within some story (Hutcheon, 1989, 66). Thus, we can have the same event getting storied in decidedly different ways. A scandal breaks in the world of politics, for example, and the *Globe* constructs it one way, the *Planet* another, and the *Sun* another again, while for the *Star* it is hardly news-ed at all. Same event, different story: a common if confusing feature of everyday life. 'Different people,' writes one researcher, coolly claiming the obvious, 'may supply very different narratives of a physically identical input' (Chafe, 1990, 96).

This phenomenon is true in the writing of history. 'The historian's job,' Collingwood believed, 'is to tell plausible stories' (Hutcheon, 1989, 67) – likely stories, we could call them. Thus, the raw events of the past are carefully culled. While 'all past "events" are potential historical "facts," ... the ones that become facts are those that are chosen to be narrated' (75). When we ask which comes first, then, the past or the present, the answer is the present, for the past is never simply there, unchangeable and complete. It is constructed, composed, by being plotted in the present (72). So, plot may have interconnected and intentional aspects (Brooks, 1985, 5), but it has artificial and arbitrary ones as well.

Nor do events ever speak for themselves in the writing of biography. William Runyan (1982) shows, for example, how the principal dilemma faced by a biographer is the variety of possible stories that could be told to make sense of – to weave into a coherent whole – any one event in the life of his subject. Summarizing the thirteen most celebrated 'psychodynamic explanations for why Van Gogh cut off his ear and gave it to a prostitute' (41), he poses a series of questions that would unsettle even the most confident chroniclers of another's life (or, for that matter, of their own): 'How should we interpret these alternative explanations? Are all of them true, are some true and some false, or, perhaps, are none of them true? Do the various explanations conflict, so that if one is chosen then one or more of the others must be rejected, or do a number of them supplement each other? Is there, perhaps, some other explanation that would replace all of these possibilities?' (42).

Events certainly never speak for themselves in the writing of fiction either. A fictional 'event' is no more certain a category than a factual one. Here again, plot is the principle of selection. In the same way a picture frame keeps certain details in but the rest of the world out, the plot of a story is what governs the inclusion of these incidents and the exclusion of those. 'In a good story ... all the extraneous noise or static is cut out' (Carr, 1986, 57). We are told only what is necessary to 'further the plot ... A selection is made of all the events and actions the characters may engage in, and only a small minority finds its way into the story' (57–8).

Plot selects by imposing a pattern (whether pre-planned or emergent) on otherwise unrelated events. It transforms those events into a story, giving more weight to one event and less to another, deciding which events are major and which minor, which are figure and which ground, which are important and which not. Consequently, if we instruct thirteen different novelists to plot the same collection of hypothetical, isolated events – a cat crossing an alley, an old man crying in a nursing home, a storm breaking in the mountains, and so forth – then, even if the chronological connections are the same, we get thirteen different stories. This is not to deny the difference between the realms of fiction and fact. Clearly, the construction of historical or biographical 'events' is limited in a way that that of fictional ones is not: While the fictional world is closed, the historical one is open. While *War and Peace* is a unique world that only a Tolstoy could compose, the countless storyings of World War II in textbooks and newsreels must all refer to a common world. Not any old story will do. Different accounts of a common set of events are accountable to each other, for there is 'a single universe or framework of reference within which all the action takes place' (Plantinga, 1992, 106). None the less, 'events' in the real world are still composed and not merely reported. The same is true in real life.

Storying is a selective process – whether in the media, history, biography, or fiction – but living is no less so. Though it is true that in life 'everything is left in; all the static is there' (Carr, 1986, 58), in our *experience* of life a great deal is left out. Attention is selective. Consciousness is choosy. We focus on what counts. But what determines 'what counts'? Our context does, for one. If our life is ringed around on a regular basis by anger and violence and social decay, then what counts is what we must be mindful of in order to survive. What counts thus varies. More constant in determining it, though, are such things as our interests, our learning style, our dominant intelligence (Gardner, 1990), our personality type: whatever combination of factors that makes us alert to, attend to, assign value to – that makes us 'experience' – this in our existence but not that. Furthermore, on the level of expression, we are selective all over again, choosing to package this out of our experience and not that, naming these events as major and those as minor, declaring this part of our story as important and that as not.

But what defines 'major'? And what determines 'important'? And what decides the 'central' story-line, with this as the 'main' plot and those as 'minors'? Such adjectives are slippery at best. What was major one month is minor the next: yesterday's horror story becomes today's tragedy becomes tomorrow's adventure becomes next year's farce. The main plot of our life a year ago is a mere subplot now. Smelling the roses turns out to have the same importance in the twilight of our life as did selling the house in its prime. And there are great differences between individuals. Some see most of their lives as flat, with 'major' and 'minor' seeming much the same. For some, 'important' and 'unimportant' are difficult to distinguish, and evaluating their experience is a chronic challenge. Others, as one travel writer has been described, are 'capable of finding a plot in a grocery bag' (Jenkins, 1989). No matter how mundane to the rest of us, every event in their lives is potentially an adventure – or, worse for us perhaps, a melodrama.

Once again, it is the plot that enables us to determine what a particular story is about. This process is probably easiest in relation to a story that is visible and with whose characters and their typical situations we are already familiar – for example, our favourite sitcom or soap. It becomes harder, though, when we are dealing with a full-length movie of an intricately plotted nature, such as a tale of espionage or one that centres on the internal development of a character or relationship. It can be harder still when we are dealing with a full-length novel. In theory, it should be hardest of all when we are dealing with a real person.

The irony, as we have seen, is that soon after meeting a person I can easily assume that I already know what sort of story his story is. Even with someone about whose background (and foreground) I know nothing at all, I feel I can infer all I need to know about him from the flimsiest of clues: a glance here, a slip of the tongue there; a name dropped, an address mentioned, an adjective employed; the cut of the hair, the colour of the tie. These prompt me not only to guess at the company he keeps and the place he lives but also to trace the trajectory of his whole life-plot, past and future, and for better or worse. I may feel I have known him all my life and so embrace him like a long-lost friend, or else I may push him quietly away because he seems to be spinning an alien tale. Either way, on the strength of first impressions, I 'storyotype' him (as he does me). I presume, usually unconsciously, to know the genre his life represents. I *genre*-lize, just as a novelist does. 'I have taken living people,' admits Somerset Maugham, 'and put them into the situations, tragic or comic, that their characters suggested. I might well say that they invented their own stories' (Allen, 1949, 154). Maugham's words raise questions I shall come back to in the following section. For the moment, let me consider the symbolic interconnectedness on which the unfolding of plot may be said to rely.

Reference has been made now to 'our chief tool in making sense of a story,' what Brooks call 'the anticipation of retrospection.' We expect that the events and details we are reading now, however difficult it may be to appreciate their connection both to each other and to what we have already read, will fall into their proper place in due course, and will be imbued with their rightful measures of meaning. We expect that they will be seen to have all worked together, if not for good then at least for that sense of resolution, of completion, that endings are suited to elicit. Thus, we expect that 'the novel's denouement ... is not simply the end of the story but the story's fulfillment' (Gardner, 1985, 194). It is the tying up of the story's loose ends, the answering of 'all legitimate questions raised in the reader's mind' (4). Accordingly, it is axiomatic in writing circles that 'however subtly ... all of a work's elements should fulfill themselves.' Herein lies the novel's power. However large its 'landscape,' however big the world it describes, it contains 'a tight system of relevance; each detail matters in the total picture' (Polster, 1987, 12). One of the worst sins a writer can commit, therefore, is 'when some idea or event is introduced that ought to change the outcome but then is forgotten, or never recognized for what it is' (Gardner, 1985, 4). For example, 'if we are told that a sheriff in a given story has a Ph.D. in philosophy, an expectation is raised that philosophy will somehow help him do his job. If philosophy is never again mentioned in the story, and if the most careful scrutiny of the story reveals no important way in which philosophy has bearing, we feel dissatisfied, annoyed. The story, we say, has loose ends' (4).

Though not all writers will be successful in meeting this obligation to tie up their stories' loose ends, the pressure is still upon them to integrate the implications set off in their readers' minds by the events unfolded along the way, the details introduced, and the quirks worked into characters' lives. The technical process by which the writer tries to bring this integration about – both for himself and for his reader – is the focus of Gardner's concluding suggestions on the craft of writing: 'Read the story over and over, at least a hundred times – literally – watching for subtle meanings, connections, accidental repetitions, psychological significance. Leave nothing – no slightest detail – unexamined; and when you discover implications in some image or event, oonch those implications toward the surface' (194). If such advice is taken seriously, then the novel achieves its 'chief glory,' by which Gardner means 'its resonant close.' It becomes 'like a symphony in that its closing movement echoes and resounds with all that has gone before' (184). What moves us, though, 'is not just that characters, images, and events get some form of recapitulation or recall: We are moved by the increasing connectedness of things, ultimately a connectedness of values' (192). Readers experience fulfilment because, at last, they 'understand everything and everything is symbolic.' In grand terms, 'life becomes, however briefly and unstably, organized; the universe reveals itself, if only for the moment, as inexorably moral; the outcome of the various characters' actions is at last manifest; and we see the responsibility of free will. It is this closing orchestration that the novel exists for' (184).

'Everything that happens in a well-constructed story,' Gardner stresses, 'from major events to the most trifling turn of phrase, is a matter of aesthetic interest' (77). This may not be *exactly* the case in the living of our lives; however, to the extent we are committed to composing our lives as well as we can, perhaps it is *ideally* the case. We want things to 'fit in' aesthetically; we want loose ends to be tied up as much as they can. Writing in her eighties, Jungian analyst Florida Scott-Maxwell expresses the confidence that such integration can indeed take place. 'You need only claim the events of your life to make yourself yours,' she says. 'When you truly possess all you have been and done, which may take some time, you are fierce with reality' (1968, 42). Though the process may truly 'take some time,' surely there is at least a little desire within us all to have our lives become 'a masterpiece of artistic unity and integrated Form, infused with meaning' (Young, 1986, 208).

One of the ways we seek to do this, I submit, is through 'reading' our story over and over – not just the daily segments of it but entire chapters, and the sweep of it as a whole. What does this mean? It means 'watching for subtle meanings, connections, accidental repetitions, psychological significance' (Gardner, 1985, 194). The intensity of such self-reading will naturally vary from individual to individual, and, within each individual, from life stage to life stage. On the eve of a marriage, in the wake of a divorce, or in the face of death itself (Birren, 1964, 274; Tarman, 1988, 187), for instance, the desire to see my life as a whole is apt to be greater than in the throes of getting an education, becoming established in a profession, or coping with the day-to-day duties of marriage and family. It seems fair to assume, though, that on some level within me the process is going on constantly, if not entirely consciously. If this assumption is valid, then it helps explain those subtle, fleeting epiphanies whereby, without setting out to do so, I suddenly make a connection I had never made before. Or the penny drops and I finally understand why some childhood habit insists on repeating itself in my adult relationships. Or the bulb lights up and I see at last the significance of a remark that has been stuck in my mind since who knows when, of a recurring dream that has troubled me from my earliest days, of a line of poetry that has haunted me for years.

Furthermore, in writing, certain 'accidents' beg to be woven into the story (Steinbeck, 1970, 37); indeed, in stories there can *be* no accidents, only incidents, as authors in their providence give purpose to everything. The same drive, though, is arguably at work in living: we strive to incorporate the slings and arrows of our fortune, however outrageous, into a comprehensive, consistent, narrative construction. We struggle to redeem them, to see some meaning in them if we can, to rescue them from the category of 'accident' (which forces us to accept the reality of blind chance) or 'mistake' (which forces us to accept responsibility for our own failure, a potentially more challenging task). To do this, however, we may eventually have to adjust our whole sense of what kind of a story our story really is. This may be easier said than achieved. In the next chapter, I shall look at the challenge of such adjustment when I explore the process of re-storying our lives. In the meantime, it is enough to realize that our self-story is continually changing direction. That is, our best-laid authorial schemes 'gang aft a-gley,' at the very least because of the new events that, every day, our self-story must accommodate.

Simply put, our story has a life of its own. It has its own, slowly unfolding, internal logic, a point that helps to explain why it can be so difficult for us to change it, so hard to restory. 'Each of us resists change,' writes one therapist, 'because a story is a self-coherent world' (Bridges, 1980, 71). Our story is stubborn. Moreover, it does not always neatly coincide with the actual details of our lives. A person can have what appears an easy life yet spout a tragic tale. Conversely, a tragic life in others' eyes can be a hilarious adventure to the one who lives it. 'The development of my life and the development of its plot,' Hillman reminds us, 'are two distinct unfoldings' (1975a, 131). Thus, as novelist John Steinbeck puts it, 'in the light of what happens you have to go back and correct or change so that the two match' (1970, 43). For us, this means that our self-story, our inside story, is never exactly the same, whether two years, two days, or only two hours in a row. Yesterday, in the face of yesterday's events or yesterday's anticipated futures, it seemed that of a loser. Today, because events are taking a different course, or because we are *viewing* them differently, it is the story of a winner. Tomorrow, who can say?

We are editing our life-story continually. Roy Schafer (1980) has analysed the intricacies of this self-editing in terms of the interaction between analyst and analysand. Though his reflections relate to the intense re-storying peculiar to psychoanalysis, they offer insights into that garden variety of self-editing in which all of us may be seen to be immersed:

> interpretively, one is working in a temporal circle. One works backward from what is told about the autobiographical present in order to define, refine, correct, organize, and complete an analytically coherent and useful account of the past, and one works forward from various tellings of the past to constitute that present and that anticipated future which are most important to explain. Under the provisional and dubious assumption that past, present, and future are separable, each segment of time is used to set up a series of questions about the others and to answer the questions addressed to it by the others. And all of these accounts keep changing as the analytic dialogue continues. (49)

But though today's account of my life is different from both yesterday's and tomorrow's, need this mean – any more than it does in a novel – that there is more than one story in the making? The fact that it is 'in the making' may simply mean what we already know: its final form is not yet fixed, its final lines not yet written. When those final lines are written, however, is it not reasonable to think that the story

will still be one story, even if it has many subplots and is vulnerable
to many interpretations on many levels by many readers? Thus, even
when finished, can it not be both one and many?

These questions anticipate ones I shall be asking more intensely in
the final chapter. In the meantime, is it only 'events' for which we
have to make room in fashioning a coherent personal story, or must
we not wrestle with our 'character' as well? Must we not struggle, as
does the novelist, with 'how many events are accidents and how many
are created and forced by the natures of the protagonists' (Steinbeck,
1970, 37)? We shall soon need to shift from plot to character, then, in
our exploration of life-as-story. Before doing so, let me continue pondering plot, specifically the issues it raises of a theological nature.

Theology

Gardner's vision of the universe revealing itself, of the inexorable
morality of the novel, and of the ultimate 'connectedness of values'
pushes us, inexorably, to certain theological issues. When I say 'theological,' however, I do not mean the term in a doctrinal or denomina-
tional sense, nor in reference to a specific theory of the divine. I mean
it in a broad sense as pertaining to matters of meaning, morality, and
metaphysics – that is, the ultimate context within which our lives are
lived. In mediating these matters, the plot of a story plays a pivotal
role.

As regards matters of meaning, we have seen how plot does more
than merely connect the events of the story like so many beads on a
string. Rather, it constructs them. It rescues them from randomness by
conferring on them a relevance – a purposefulness – because of the
role they play in relation both to each other and to the story overall.
Each event 'means' something in terms not of itself, that is, but of its
place within a developing narrative context. As the story 'unfolds' into
its future, then, fresh events possess increased meaning potential over
those preceding them. As we say, the plot 'thickens.' Of course, there
is more than this to the question of how meaning is mediated within
a given story; none the less, it will suffice for now to help us appreciate a broader point about the importance of plot.

Peter Brooks has observed that 'there have been some historical
moments ... in which cultures have seemed to develop an unquench-
able thirst for plots' (1985, 5). From the mid-eighteenth to mid-twenti-
eth century, because of the gradual 'falling-away' from what he calls

'providential plots' or 'revealed plots' – for example, 'the Chosen People, Apocalypse, the Second Coming' – Western societies 'appear to have felt an extraordinary need or desire for plots.' Thus, even though 'with the advent of Modernism came an era of suspicion toward plot,' we still 'cannot do without plots' (7). There is 'no diminishing of our reliance on plotting,' says Linda Hutcheon, 'however ironized or paradied' (1989, 49). What are the reasons, though, for this ambivalence toward plot?

With decades of literary criticism to encourage us, we have come to look down on 'reading for the plot' as a low form of aesthetic activity (Brooks, 1985, 4), one propelled by what C.S. Lewis calls 'sheer narrative lust' (1966, 103). Plot, Brooks says, 'has been disdained as the element of narrative that least sets off and defines high art – indeed, plot is that which especially characterizes popular mass-consumption literature: plot is why we read *Jaws*, but not Henry James' (1985, 4). Hence, there is a new genre fashionable in literary circles in which plot seems all but omitted. Called metafiction, it is fiction that, 'both in style and theme, investigates fiction' (Gardner, 1985, 86). It is 'a story that calls attention to its methods and shows the reader what is happening to him as he reads' (87). In Gardner's view, such fiction fails *as fiction* because of its disruptive effect upon the reader's sense of 'the vivid and continuous fictional dream' (97). As he puts it, 'we are abruptly snapped out of the dream, forced to think of the writer or the writing.' In one extreme form of metafiction, defined as 'fictional super-realism,' the aim is simply 'to get down reality without the slightest modification by the artist.' Thus, 'the conventional division of narrative into organized scenes is scrupulously avoided; if some insight is awakened or emotion stirred, the fact is simply reported, like any other fact' (135).

There is some justification for this unusual approach to writing fiction. 'Life,' says writer Françoise Sagan, 'is amorphous, literature is formal' (1977, 306), an observation she shares, we have seen, with her contemporary and countryman, Sartre. Life for such writers is not inherently storied, and it is a falsifying of it, therefore, to represent it in storied form – even though both have expended considerable energy doing precisely that (most interestingly, Sartre, who chose fiction to convey many of his philosophical insights). However, both miss a critical point, which is that recourse to raw, unstoried existence is impossible. Consciousness itself, like the language by which it is both constructed and conveyed, forbids it. Even if our existence is not storied, our experience (and thus our expression) of it is – and if storied, then plotted. For this reason, as Brooks says, 'we cannot do without plots,' meaning we cannot avoid 'consuming avidly Harlequin romances and television serials and daily comic strips, creating and demanding narrative in the presentation of persons and news events and sports contests' (7). We need plots because they imply meaning, in literature and life alike. Their very existence tells us what we wish desperately to hear, which is that somehow, somewhere, *things make sense*.

In the previous section, reference was made to what has come to be called post-modernism. The post-modern condition, says the French critic J.-F. Lyotard, is 'the state of people for whom all the master narratives have broken down' (Cupitt, 1991, 93). In such a state, 'when one no longer can look to a sacred masterplot that organizes and explains the world ... the plotting of the individual or social or institutional life story takes on new urgency' (Brooks, 1985, 6). Plotting our life-story is how we 'organize and explain' our world, not merely chronologically but causally as well. To plot, Hillman reminds us, 'is to move from asking the question "and then what happened?" to the question "and why did it happen?"' (1975a, 130). Whether in literature or life, that is, 'the plots are our theories. They are the ways in which we put the intentions of human nature together so that we can understand the why between the sequence of events' (130). To read for the plot, and to live *looking* for the plot, is to catch at least a taste of meaningfulness amid a world in which it can no longer be guaranteed by an over-arching creed.

As regards matters of morality, we have already heard Hayden White's concern with the moralizing impulse at work in any 'fully realized story,' certainly in any history, and with how it is rooted in and required by the sociopolitical realities behind that history, by the interests of the culture or class out of which it is written (1980, 13–14). White's insight applies not just to history, however, but to stories in general. They are not innocent – innocuous often, innocent never. They all have a point to make, a message to convey, an agenda to push, a gospel to sell. A story is not only a self-contained universe, that is, but a moral one as well, and it is through its plot that its morality is mediated. Moreover, the causality by which its events are linked assumes a particular stance toward a supposedly eternal struggle: 'the dramatic conflict between good and evil' (Keen, 1988, 47). While it may well be that 'life is not interested in Good and Evil' (Faulkner,

1977, 138), literature, eternally, is.[2] There is always a right to be upheld and a wrong to be put down, a good to be sought and an evil to be eschewed – however obliquely they are each set out or however little resemblance they bear to what is enshrined in the code of a conventional ethic or religion. In this way, the plot mediates the 'meaning' of the story not just in an aesthetic sense but in an ethical one as well. In other words, the conflict it cradles is the crucible of 'character' – the development or 'building' of which may well be what a given story is most centrally about.

Naturally, the exact identity of the good and its corresponding evil will vary from story to story, writer to writer, and reader to reader. None the less, the division between right and wrong, truth and falsehood, morality and immorality, is played out in the plot of even the silliest sitcom, or of the average detective show, horror story, or thriller. Each has its mythology, its morality, its moral, however subtly encoded. Such a moral is also guaranteed by the fact that, by definition, a story must achieve some resolution, some ending, some tying up of its tag ends and tensions. Let me say more, then, about tension as such.

The plot of a story unfolds according to a number of set steps, from an initial, relatively stable situation through some sort of climax to a final denouement, back and forth though the actual recounting of these steps can sometimes be. As we saw in looking at the allure of story, however, running through these steps is one central dynamic: the generation of tension, 'trouble,' or conflict and the struggle to resolve it. Though that conflict can be of many kinds, if there is none to resolve, there is no story to recount. The same applies in our lives: if there is no conflict, then not only can our 'character' not be built but so is there nothing for us to recall. The less our experience conflicts with out expectations, the less we have to remember – and to talk about. 'People tell each other stories,' Schank reminds us, 'based on what sticks out as funny or odd' (1990, 21). Consequently, narratives that entirely fit expectations are not really narratives at all' (Chafe, 1990, 83). But, 'when we face an input that conflicts with our established expectations … we react … with excitement, anger, and aggression'; we 'enter a state where we are prepared to do something about it' (82–3). In this sense, we are 'wired up to cope with inputs that conflict with our expectations … Rejecting the unfamiliar is what we do best' (83). Thus, where familiarity breeds forgetfulness, novelty enables recollection. Far fewer people are murdered than are not, for example, yet it is their deaths that make the news, their stories that stick, and not those of a mass of folk who die of 'natural means.'

However vigorously we may seek it, then, a smoothly ticking life, empty of *agon*, or change, all rule and no exception, can give rise to a boring story (though, admittedly, calm without often camouflages conflict within). With little to remember and even less to say, we have less insight to impart, less experience to share, and less comprehension of and connection with the experience of others – thus less compassion for them. Fortunately, in even the quietest life conflicts can abound, making the contrived ones of the most intricate novel seem tidy by comparison. Indeed, such conflicts may be necessary for our development. As Carl Jung writes, 'the serious problems in life are never fully solved. If ever they should appear to be so it is a sure sign that something has been lost. The meaning and purpose of a problem seem to lie not in its solution but in our working at it incessantly' (Sarton, 1977, 101).

Whether problems or conflicts are necessary or not, certainly few lives seem to be exempt from them – that is, exempt from suffering. This is not to argue that suffering is inherently good; or to insist, stoically, on *no pain, no gain*; or to prescribe it for its own sake; or to acclaim it as automatically 'the great teacher' that 'forces us to think, to make connections, to sort out what is what' (Sarton, 1986, 208). It is merely to acknowledge that, like it or not, suffering is part of life. As the First Noble Truth of Buddhism asserts, the great disease of the world is *dukkha*, the Sanskrit word for suffering – or, more accurately, frustration. Thus, 'birth is *dukkha*, decay is *dukkha*, sickness is *dukkha*, death is *dukkha*, so also are sorrow and grief … To be bound with things which we dislike, and to be parted from things which we like, these also are *dukkha*. Not to get what one desires, this also is *dukkha*' (Watts, 1957, 46).

To continue, 'all plots,' say Scholes and Kellogg, 'depend on tension and resolution' (1966, 212). Indeed, 'not only every episode or incident but every paragraph and every sentence has its beginning, middle, and end.' It is plotted, with 'its own little system of tension and resolution which contributes its bit to the general system' (239). Consequently, 'one of the reasons stories have appealed to man for so long a time lies in their neatness.' That is, 'the reader of a narrative can expect to finish his reading having achieved a state of equilibrium – something approaching calm of mind, all passion spent. Insofar as the reader is left with this feeling by any narrative, that narrative can be said to have plot' (212).

As we have seen already, the post-modern suspicion of plot, whether in history or fiction, is strong. It arises out of a 'strong terror that it is really someone else – rather than we ourselves – who is plotting, ordering, controlling our life for us' (Hutcheon, 1989, 63). It also arises out of a cynicism toward this neat resolution that a plot manages to achieve out of the conflicting elements of life, a suspicion of the closure it imposes on a 'mess of fragmentary and incomplete facts' (67). Some of this suspicion, though, comes from feminist scholars who have focused on the essence of plot as tension-resolution and thus developed what, if it is valid, is a devastating critique of narrative in general. Working from the framework of psychoanalysis, film critic Teresa de Lauretis says, for instance, that tension-resolution is 'inseparable from the psychosexual process of becoming a man.' In her view, 'the thrust toward fulfillment of desire by way of progression from beginning, middle, to a climactic end, wherein the hero's sense of loss is restored by a renewed vision of how things are, is a male paradigm' (Bogdan, 1990, 186). This 'male paradigm' encompasses a number of needs at once: the need to experience gratification and yet delay it; the need to sate yet sustain the suspense, the 'narrative lust'; the need to make events *into* a story, to make something happen, to be 'on the make,' in hot pursuit. It encompasses the need to know how things will turn out, yet somehow not know; the need to be kept on the edge of our seats; the need to be aroused. Thus, says one commentator, 'we read for the thrill of seeing around the next curve; we're back in the cave sitting at the feet of the story-teller, spinning tales that satisfy our primal curiosity to know "What's next?"' (Groen, 1990).

It is possible, though, that women are no more immune than men to the lure of tension-resolution, that they too enjoy the pleasure – the whole cycle of build-up, climax, and relief (of an entire story or an individual sentence) – that literature allows. Whether it is possible or not, perhaps we would do well to wait for the arrival of sentences suitable 'for a woman's use' on which Virginia Woolf once speculated (1977, 73) to see how things might change, how our consciousness in general could be reconstituted, what new breed of stories we could then compose. Perhaps both plot and story would be transcended by something better, something truer to the experience of us all. In any event, the feminist critique raises questions of a fundamental nature.

Bearing them in mind keeps us honest as we relate the complexities of literary stories to those of the ones we live.

Finally, as regards matters of metaphysics, what Sibelius has said of a symphony can be said of a story as well: it must include a whole world. More precisely, it *creates* a whole world. One critic goes so far as to suggest that stories 'are defined in terms of the worlds they project, rather than the plots they develop' (Leitch, 1986, 119). There are two implications of this. The first I shall come back to in the next chapter. It is that each story radiates its own atmosphere, one often reproduced throughout an author's work – like the 'Greeneland' one enters with each new novel by Graham Greene (Lodge, 1988, 131). The second implication is that each story assumes an entire cosmology. It is a world unto itself, from creation to conclusion, from Big Bang to Big Crunch. The more intense the aspect of plot, as in the novel, the more explicit this cosmology will be. 'The novel, as a genre,' says Gardner (1985), 'has a built-in metaphysic' (184). As soon as we begin to engage a given novel, we are of course already 'in the middest,' caught up in the unfolding conflict that is the driving force of its plot. But we also become possessed by the sense of an ending in which that conflict will be resolved, as well as by the sense of a beginning: a time of relative calm – a sort of Paradise – before all of the trouble began. With these two senses in mind – of an ending and a beginning, a final consummation and an initial calm – we can appreciate how 'the framework of all literature,' as Northrop Frye puts it, is the story of 'lost and found': 'the story that's told so often,' he says, 'of how man once lived in a golden age or a garden of Eden or the Hesperides, or a happy island kingdom in the Atlantic, how that world was lost, and how we some day may be able to get it back again' (1963, 21, 20).

Now then, when we consider the links between story and life, these matters of meaning, morality, and metaphysics become rather maddeningly entangled. As before, we begin with the simple admission: like a story, a life is plotted, inasmuch as it has its own blunt brand of beginning and middle and end: we're born, we suffer, we die. In this general way, 'each person's life is a story that is telling itself in the living' (Bridges, 1980, 71). As well, like a story, a life can be divided both longitudinally, into subplots, and latitudinally, into chapters, though these divisions are contingent on starting-point and point of view. What seems a subplot today, that is, may emerge the main plot tomorrow, and the other way around. Apart from these similarities, though, while a story has its incidents arranged intentionally, no such

intention appears in the arrangements of the incidents in an ordinary
life, at least not obviously. Most of life's incidents – most of its
'events,' in the basic sense of 'things that happen' (Shimon-Renan,
1983, 15) – do precisely that: they happen. We do not choose them.
Their appearance in the midst of and as the stuff of our life appears
for the most part accidental – the so-called 'accident of birth' being a
prime example. And yet, we *do* make plans. We do plot our lives in
some fashion. We do arrange our circumstances in such a way that, all
things being equal, they will unfold in this direction and not that, will
lead to that result and not this. There is an intentionality about our
living of life that parallels the intentionality of a story's plot, in kind
if not degree. This plotting concerns not our future alone, however,
but also our past. Just as we plot our futures so we pick our pasts. We
may not choose the incidents themselves nor their arrangement in
existence, but we choose what we 'make' of them in experience, how
we arrange them in memory and imagination.

As we have seen, the feature of a story that most separates it from
a real life is the *intentional* arrangement of its incidents. Because of the
controlling vision of its author, all incidents and details are excluded
unless they advance its plot or subplots. This again is the 'economy'
of art (Surmelian, 1969, 19). As one source expresses it, 'plot brings
order out of life': 'It selects only one or two emotions out of a dozen,
one or two conflicts out of hundreds, only two or three people out of
thousands, and a half-dozen episodes from possible millions. In this
sense it focuses life' (Thrall, Hibbard, and Holman, 1960, 358).

But is this focusing of life in stories so different from what happens
in lives? In the present, we focus on what counts. Of the past, we are
selective as well. We have to be. Apart from it being impossible, it is
also simply unfeasible to remember all the incidents, all the events, all
the situations, in which we have been involved in the course of a
lifetime. Consciously or not, we select some incidents to be included
in our accessible memory – we some to stick in our minds – while, for
all intents and purposes, we consider others inessential. We allow
them to fall away, to recede to the background, to be forgotten. While
a story is only the story it is, a life, therefore, amounts to many stories
in one, because it can be plotted in so many different ways; it possesses no inherent plot but is, so to speak, poly-plottable. Where
'events in narratives are *inherently* significant ... events in life must be
interpreted as significant' (Wright, 1989, 106). Accordingly, not only
thirteen novelists but thirteen normal individuals, provided the same

set of incidents, will produce thirteen different plots. Since no thirteen, however, will ever have to endure the exact same incidents in their lives in exactly the same sequence, there is little chance of them telling exactly the same story. Each of us is unique and, like each story, a world unto ourselves. Though our stories may be genre-lizable, they are never exactly alike.

Unlike a story, however, since no plot appears to be laid on a life from an external, authorial source, we are left to look for one on our own. Though our lives are poly-plottable, though they possess no *inherent* plot by which their incidents are to be logically and causally arranged, this does not stop us from looking for such a plot, consciously or not. Rather than see our lives as just 'one damned thing after another,' that is, many of us persist in the belief that, somewhere, there exists a plot that can organize them, can make their events into a story according to which, in the long range, they 'go somewhere.' Even in the short range we wonder how a particular situation we see ourselves 'in the middle of' will 'turn out.' We want to feel that getting through problem X – whether it be medical, legal, intellectual, or romantic in nature – will 'get us somewhere,' and in that sense have meaning. Consequently, any *telling* of our story inside-out, even if only of one small segment, will reflect the element of plotting. Indeed, its being tellable at all requires that we have achieved a certain resolution of whatever problem or conflict with which we have been wrestling (Plantinga, 1992, 75).

The quest for the plot to the story of our lives as a whole, however, and the corresponding struggle to distinguish central plot from subplot, is carried out with perhaps greatest intensity in the act of composing an autobiography. This, as I have said, is an act on the level of expression. In engaging in it, the autobiographer is faced with a host of thorny questions: who is my audience; what is my point of view; how shall I characterize myself; what themes will I trace, conflicts lay out, and tone adopt, etc. In reality, these are literary questions. 'As anyone who has attempted an autobiography can attest,' writes David Polonoff, 'such an enterprise quickly becomes literary.' The most basic of these questions concerns the choice of plot by which we shall 'arrange the incidents': 'one must choose a starting point, select the significant events whose interconnections are to be traced, replace the detailed interconnections of entire periods with emblematic episodes, represent simultaneity sequentially and sequence teleologically' (1987, 46).

In tackling such a literary enterprise, we are presumably at liberty to impose upon the incidents of our lives whatever plots we wish. But where do these plots come from? Where do we get them: from other people, from parents, from movies and novels, from the 'master stories' of our inherited gender, culture, class, or creed? Why, in the end, do we choose these plots rather than those? Indeed, do we 'choose' them at all, or do they choose us? Wrestling with such questions has been the traditional domain of psychologists, anthropologists, theologians, and the like – all whose concern is with the scripts, patterns, and myths we employ to construct our sense of self. Since the interplay of plots within us is central to my discussions in subsequent sections, I shall not dwell further on it here. In the meantime, there is another theological connection between story and life.

In the study of adult development we are accustomed to the notion that we live life in a series of stages or phases. Phase theories are tied to age and developmental tasks, while stage theories are linked with formal psychological theories concerning ego, cognitive, or moral development (Cross, 1988, 168–85). Helpful as such theories have been in fathoming the dynamics of growth, and as enthusiastically as they have been embraced, they are frequently used in *pre*-scriptive rather than *de*-scriptive ways, as means of slotting people rather than understanding them. They are also taken to mean that later phases or higher stages are intrinsically better than earlier or lower ones; that the older people are, the more mature and more moral they will automatically be. Philosopher Clive Beck cautions us against drawing such conclusions: 'It could be that, on average, adults are slightly morally superior to children and adolescents, by virtue of the cumulative effect of learning by living. And equally it could be that on average children and adolescents are slightly morally superior to adults by virtue of being closer to nature and having a vision and sensitivity less corrupted by society. Historically, great thinkers have maintained both positions' (1989, 184).

Exploring the implications of the life-as-story metaphor, it is difficult not to concur with Beck, nor to share his concern over the 'adult chauvinism' to which developmental theories easily lead. When we toy with the concept that people are living stories, however, different options emerge. Rather than think in terms of stages or phases, why not think in terms of 'chapters' instead? It is surely no more metaphorical a concept than the others, borrowing no less from a poetic model of the world than 'stage' does from an evolutionary one or 'phase' from a seasonal one. Indeed, once we allow that these are essentially fictive constructs anyway (Gergen and Gergen, 1986; Sarbin, 1986) – 'sexist fictions,' one critic insists (Fisher, 1989, 138) – then it becomes difficult to assert the priority of one over another. But if we employ the notion of chapters, what twist do we add to our view of change over a lifetime? We are so surrounded by stories in everyday life, and thus by chapters and episodes, segments and sequels, that it may well be because of that experience itself that we can accept the notion of life as a series of stages or phases. It may be, yet a chapter is a different story.

Most important, it bypasses the deep-seated conviction of much modern psychology that we all develop according to much the same steps. Without denying such development can occur, it allows for the wide range of individual differences of which we are so often aware. This is the theory, for instance, of William Bridges (1980). All through our lives, he argues, and not just at predictable junctures, we are in transition: at either the beginning, the middle, or the end of some venture or period. How we 'know' when one period is winding down and another starting up, however, can be a subtly personal affair, signalled not just by obvious occurrences like the completion of a degree or the birth of a child but by what to others are the obscurest of clues: a new theme in our dreamworld, a shift in the climate of a close friendship, a change in our tastes in music or books. It is precisely because these transitions are so idiosyncratic that no set number can be placed on them, as stage and phase advocates are wont to do. Some of us, for example, can seem to have as few as four or five extended periods throughout our lives while others have a new one every year, sometimes so dramatic, so discontinuous even, that 'chapters' is really less appropriate than 'parts': Part 1, Part 2, Part 3, and the like. I shall return to this possibility when I consider re-storying in the following chapter.

A further selling-point about the notion of chapters, however, is the way it counters the implicit bias toward 'improvement' concealed in the notion of stages of phases. With each new chapter (a kind of story within a story), the story's plot does not necessarily improve. That is to say, chapter 12 is not intrinsically 'better' than chapter 11, any more than it is necessarily longer – though to a particular reader it may be more interesting or better written. Even if the story as a whole seems to get better because of it, it is not in the sense of 'improvement' really. It is rather that, compared with the opening chapters when we may have been unsure whether to keep reading at all, there is more going on in the story for us, more to hold our interest, more in which to 'lose' ourselves. Chapter 12 is not superior to chapter 11, therefore, nor is it more sophisticated than chapter 1, for each of these others has made its indispensable contribution to the whole. Rather, compared to them, it merely *assumes* more because it is farther along on the story-line. It takes in more of what has preceded it. Each new event it injects, each new character it introduces, each new complication it contributes, is thus that much richer in potential meaning because of the accumulated associations it elicits in us from all we have read so far. The world of the story as a whole does not become better, that is, only bigger, wider, deeper, more complexly textured and richly layered. It becomes 'thicker,' like memory itself (Casey, 1987, 262ff) – and the book by which it is conveyed, quite possibly, becomes that much harder to put down. So much so that it may demand a sequel. As novelist Margaret Drabble notes at the start of *A Natural Curiosity*: 'I had not intended to write a sequel [to *The Radiant Way*], but felt that the earlier novel was in some way unfinished, that it had asked questions it had not answered, and introduced people who had hardly been allowed to speak' (1989).

But does this concept not have its counterpart with respect to the story of our lives? How many of us have relinquished the notion entirely that, somewhere, we shall get a second chance: an opportunity to live our lives over, to right a few wrongs, to take a back a few words, to work out some karma, to develop more responsibly our talents and gifts? How many of us do not harbour some form of the belief (inspiring of apathy and passivity as it often can be) that there will be a sequel to our story that takes our plot in this life, as thick and conflicted as it is, and extends it into another – 'Randall II' – for a happy-ever-after ending; into 'the Great Story,' as C.S. Lewis calls it in *The Chronicles of Narnia*, 'which no one on earth has read: which goes on for ever: in which every chapter is better than the one before' (1964, 165)?

Of course, our 'plot in this life' may not always seem terribly plotted to us, certainly not with the clear climaxing typical of literary plots. Here again, however, literary plotting itself is not necessarily climactic, at least not preprogrammed as such by the writer. Novelist Nelson Algren, for example, 'finds his plots simply by writing page after page, night after night' (Cowley, 1977, 9). 'The only way I could finish a book, and get a plot,' he says, 'was just to keep making it longer and longer until something happens' (9). But might this not be the case for many of us in 'real life,' particularly during its bleaker stretches: we keep making it longer until something happens; we keep hanging on in the hope that eventually our story will come together, that a light will shine in the darkness, and the interconnection of its countless incidents at last be clear? For some – the very old, for instance – the hope that something will happen in this life may be let go of in favour of the next. 'This world is not conclusion,' writes Emily Dickinson, echoing their dream, 'a sequel stands beyond.' The point is that, however secular our culture may be, notions of an afterlife (and/or a beforelife) seem to be dying rather hard. Such notions are not inconsequential for our study of human development. Anything we can learn about how people envision the story of their lives – whether it is to be continued in (or has been continued from) some other realm, or must stand on its own, 'living on' merely in the hearts of those they leave behind – can only increase our understanding of the poetics of self-creation.

These, then are a few of the enticing issues that we generate when we look at life through the lens of literary plot. There are certainly many more. To conclude this section, though, let me come back to the concept of chapters.

In literary stories, it is fair to say, there are often different *genres* of chapters. Just as the plot of a story embraces a mixture of summary, setting, and scene, of dialogue and action (Surmelian, 1968, 5–39), all strategically arranged to manage the pace of the story, its expansion and suspense, so some of the story's individual chapters are action-oriented, while others consist almost entirely of dialogue. By the same token, some are retrospective while others are introspective. Others again can be either descriptive of a certain setting or filled with philosophy or information deemed necessary by the writer for the reader to comprehend the story as a whole. But is there a parallel to such variety in a person's life? I believe there is.

Some periods in our lives – in either the living or the telling or both – can surely seem more 'loaded' than others, or perhaps more significant, more meaningful, with respect to what we perceive as the grand scheme of our existence. Some can be filled with unrelieved suspense or unmitigated terror – our war years, for instance. Some are basically all action and no reflection – the first years with the children, for example. Some are heavy on introspection, others on setting the scene, others still on relationship. Some, by the sheer force of their events, drive us through such shifts in consciousness that, emerging at the other end, we feel ourselves to be in a different life-story altogether. This is the case, for example, when we undergo a 'perspective transformation' (Mezirow, 1978), a 'conversion,' or a change in our 'personal myth' (Feinstein, Krippner, and Granger, 1988) – adjustments in our self-understanding I shall be examining in more detail in the next chapter.

Furthermore, from one telling of our life-story to the next, we frequently change our tack. Thus, we often view the divisions of our lives today differently than we did yesterday, depending on what is happening, what challenges we are facing, or what subplot we feel we are in the midst of. Today, for example, I may view my college years as constituting a clear, definite chapter, with an obvious beginning and end: orientation and convocation. Tomorrow, however, I may see the same period not so much as a chapter in its own right but as part of the backdrop to a different chapter altogether – a chapter about my relationship with Sharon, my career as an actor, or my life as a diabetic. It depends on my point of view in doing the telling and on the turning points I do the telling around, the choices of which are determined in part by the culture(s) in which I have been shaped.

Life narratives, says Bruner, always 'reflect the prevailing theories about "possible lives" that are part of one's culture' (1987, 15). Thus, 'self-told narratives may reveal a common formal structure across a wide variety of content' (16–17). If I have grown up male in the culture of upper-class England in the first half of this century and gone on to become a barrister and then a politician, the form of my self-telling is highly predictable. The chapters of my autobiography have their crisp, set titles almost before I write: Infancy, Eton, Oxford, War, Westminster, Whitehall, Downing Street. The plot from pram to power is given; the events of my 'life itself' must accommodate themselves to this structure, and to these chapters, or not be written about at all. In such a social bracket, any other story is worth neither telling nor reading; the story I tell of myself has to fit the repertoire of stories my culture *tells* me I can tell. Thus, the assumption that my life-story divides naturally into a finite number of self-evident chapters – as of stages or phases – stands on shaky ground. How we determine such chapters is both culture-bound and after the fact. We live our lives forward but understand them backward; there is a stubborn gap between living and understanding. As Hillman reminds us, our plots do not unfold side by side with out lives (1975a, 131).

Before pressing on to the element of character, I want to flag a few final questions by way of anticipating my agenda in the next chapter. For example, at what point in our lives do we first become aware, can we first cope with the realization, that we in fact *have* and *are* a story, and that, within limits, we can tell ourselves however we will? Furthermore, how does the way we tell that story – to others and ourselves – tend to change over time? How does it vary with advancing age? Moreover, what might be the *minimum* age at which we become aware that telling that story is something only we are able and authorized to do? Finally, what does that minimum age have to do with 'adulthood,' defined not physically or psychologically but poetically? It is just such enticing questions as these that Bruner has in mind when he says he 'cannot imagine a more important psychological research project than one that addresses itself to the "development of autobiography" – how our way of telling about ourselves changes, and how these accounts come to take control of our ways of life' (1987, 15).

The Element of Character

What is a *character* in a story? How is a fictional character related to a real human being? What does it mean to speak of character in terms of a *life*-story? What is the connection between character in fiction and character in life, that is, between aesthetics and ethics?

These are some of the questions with which I shall be wrestling in this section. In the course of looking at the links between life and story, they are unavoidable, for reasons I have already shown. First of all, whenever I talk to you about myself I automatically cast myself as a character in the middle of whatever anecdote, like Mack, I am relating: 'Yes, sir, I went up to the garage to get them to look at my car, then I came down here to pick up my mail ...' The 'I' whom I tell you about, whose activity I recount, is a different 'I' than the I – unmentioned – who actually does the telling. The latter is a narrator; the former, a character. Even when I talk to myself, when I rattle on in my own mind in words and pictures about what I have experienced in the past or expect to experience in the future, I see myself as an actor amidst the activities I remember or envision. I character-ize myself.

Because of the storying instinct, I read a story not only into my own life but also, outside-in, into the lives of whomever I encounter. I 'storyotype' them. I re-create them in my imagination not as they are in themselves but only as a distillation, more often a distortion, of them: a pared-down version of their whole story, whatever that might be. As the novelist Ivy Compton-Burnett admits, 'we know much less of each other than we think' (Allen, 1949, 204). Thus, 'it would be a great shock to find oneself suddenly behind another person's eyes. The things we think we know about each other, we often imagine and read in' (204). Unjust though it might seem, and as infected by prejudice as it can be, the vast portion of everyday human interaction is possible only because of this process of characterization. People are characters to us in fiction; they are little less so in real life – in proportion, usually, to our distance from them. 'In real life,' one critic reminds us, 'the people we know intimately are more elusive than our acquaintance – we are aware that there is always something more to be discovered' (Bennett, 1964, 20–1). This is the same distinction as gets made between 'main' characters and 'minor' ones. 'Just as, in life, people less intimately known to us are more easily defined, so it is with the minor characters in fiction. As with comparative strangers, so with these background characters, the more distant viewpoint obscures the finely shaded, ever-varying quality of human performance – what is seen is the firm contour, the typical appearance and behaviour' (37). Notwithstanding Sartre's concern about 'bad faith,' then, we cannot deal with existence in the raw, which means we cannot deal with people without 'encumbering thoughts.' That is, we can no more *not* character-ize others (or ourselves, as we have seen) than we can *not* plot events, not assign them a past, present, and future. If plot is 'a trope for human experience,' character is 'a trope for human identity' (Leitch, 1986, 149). But what exactly is it?

At first glance, the concept of character is straightforward, although 'it is remarkable how little has been said about [it] in literary history and criticism' (Chatman, 1978, 107). While much attention has been devoted to the analysis of plot in contemporary poetics, that is, little has been paid to character (Rimmon-Kenan, 1983, 29). What this omission might say about our society – about its priorities and core beliefs – is intriguing and perhaps unsettling to contemplate. Nevertheless, to get us going, surely we can say at least this: a character is a person we encounter in a story. Having said this, we must go on immediately to add that a character is not a *real* person obviously but – in a novel at least – only the *impression* of one. It is the reasonable facsimile of a person formed in the reader's imagination as it is stimulated by the author's words describing a particular set of physical features, thoughts and emotions, relationships and actions. The creation of a fictional character is consequently one of art's greatest mir-

acles, for the number of words the reader has to work with is frequently not many, as in a novel, but few, as in a short story. Witness
the minimum of curt adjectives with which a Hemingway can summon his hero into being for us, using the same amazing 'economy' as
does the impressionist artist in capturing the essence of her subject
with the fewest of brush strokes. Accordingly, character 'is the result
of the storyteller's sleight-of-hand' (Leitch, 1986, 162). But, even when
there are many words, there is far more to a fictional character (as to
a real person) than appears on the page: 'A good fictional character is
like an iceberg; nine-tenths of it is below the surface, in the depths, as
Hemingway once said in an interview. There is no art without economy, and the reader is bored when nothing is left to his imagination'
(Surmelian, 1969, 147).

There are different variables, then, in the creation of character. A
critical one is the imagination of the reader. It is the old 'if a tree falls
in the forest' riddle: a character cannot 'exist' apart from the exchange
between an author and a reader. What goes on in the imagination of
the author (a miracle in itself) we shall look at momentarily. What
goes on in the imagination of the reader is a complex story of its own.

Obviously, while the author had only one character in mind in
writing, each reader will have a different character in reading. With
a thousand readers, a thousand characters can emerge from the same
set of words. Why is this? In part, it is because each reader will have
a different reaction to the same set of words *as words*. 'The volatile
redhead cursed at the constellations in the night sky, enraged at the
infidelity of her lover.' Each key word in this description of a fictional
character – volatile, cursed, constellation, enraged, infidelity – will
hold slightly different meanings, or mis-meanings, for each reader.
Thus, he will also read a different sentence *as a sentence*. Moreover,
each reader will have a different reaction to the same set of words
taken as a whole, based on 'past experience' – both with other fictional redheads and with real ones. Readers bring their entire life-
stories to any fictional stories (Beach, 1990). The more there is in their
life-stories that 'resonates' with or is sparked by the verbal description
of the fictional characters, then the richer, more layered, and more
meaning-laden that character will be for them, and the more intimate
they will feel themselves to be with them – indeed, more intimate
maybe than they are with the real people in their lives, including
themselves.

Characters and Real Persons

This gets at how a real person is created out of a fictional representation of one in the mind of the reader. But it falls short of explaining the opposite process, which is how a fictional representation is created out of a real person in the mind of the author.

In *Aspects of the Novel*, E.M. Forster (1962) introduces us to some basic concepts that may help us understand this curious transformation. For example, though one critic considers it a 'notorious distinction' (17), Forster draws a line between 'flat' characters and 'round' ones. Flat characters are 'simple, two-dimensional, endowed with very few traits, highly predictable in behaviour' (Prince, 1987, 12). We call them 'stock' characters: their character-istics are steady throughout, their natures fixed. However challenging the circumstances in which the story places them, they undergo little in the way of 'development.' This is essentially the classical understanding (Henn, 1956, 17), from which we have inherited the idea that a person's 'character' is the solid core of values and virtues that will be constant throughout her life. Round characters, on the other hand, are 'complex, multi-dimensional, capable of surprising behaviour' (Prince, 12). Their 'character' can change. They develop – emotionally, intellectually, ethically, spiritually – as the plot unfolds. In fact, their development is what much of literary fiction concerns itself with. 'All novels,' Virgina Woolf tells us, 'deal with character.' In fact, 'it is to express character – not to preach doctrines, sing songs, or celebrate the glories of the British Empire, that the form of the novel, so clumsy, verbose, and undramatic, so rich, elastic, and alive, has been evolved' (1966, 193).

Forster also says that, whether round or flat, characters are ultimately 'word-masses' (Forster, 55). Like the plot of the story, like the arrangement of its incidents, these word-masses are the more or less intentional creations of the author, who 'gives them names and sex, assigns them plausible gestures, and causes them to speak by the use of inverted commas, and perhaps to behave consistently.' 'Their nature,' he reminds us, 'is conditioned by what [the author] guesses about other people, and about himself.' Impishly then, Forster distinguishes between two 'allied species': *Homo sapiens* and *Homo fictus*. *Homo fictus*, he says, 'is more elusive than his cousin ... He is generally born off, he is capable of dying on, he wants little food or sleep, he is tirelessly occupied with human relationships. And – most important

– we can know more about him than we can know about any of our
fellow creatures, because his creator and narrator are one' (63–4). None
the less, *Homo fictus* is not as compliant a species as we might think.
Fictional characters – and here we are talking of the round variety –
lead lives of their own. Although they 'arrive when evoked,' they do
so 'full of the spirit of mutiny. For they have these numerous parallels with people like ourselves,' Forster points out; 'they try to live
their own lives and are consequently often engaged in treason
against the main scheme of the book.' By this he means 'they "run
away," they "get out of hand"; they are creations inside a creation,
and often inharmonious towards it; if they are given complete freedom they kick the book to pieces, and if they are kept too sternly
in check they revenge themselves by dying, and destroy it by intesti-
nal decay' (72).

At the same time, however mutinous or round or convincing they
may be, fictional characters are still not real people. Though Hamlet
lives through the years in the hearts of all who have witnessed his
plight upon the stage and page, he is not an actual man. Even if in
Shakespeare's mind he was based on a real man initially, real princes
tend not to get embroiled in the high moral mess that he did, certainly
not with the same sustained intensity or within the time frame of a
five-act play. 'Living human beings,' André Maurois reminds us, 'are
dangerous enigmas' (1986, 4). While a character in a novel may be
complex, 'this complexity is an ordered complexity and we can grasp
it' (4). But even 'the most complex hero of a novel is infinitely less
complex than the most simple of human beings' (6). 'Even of the
persons we know most intimately,' echoes Somerset Maugham, 'we do
not know them enough to transfer them to the pages of a book and
make human beings of them. People are too elusive, too shadowy, to
be copied; and they are also too incoherent and contradictory' (Allen,
1949, 203). Truth, as we say, is stranger than fiction.

For one thing, fictional characters tend not to talk like real people.
Though they are creations within a creation, what they say is generally on topic; it counts for something. Their words are seldom
inconsequential to the unfolding of the story as a whole. For another,
they do not usually have to cope with the same long, relatively boring, undramatic stretches that can and do characterize the lives of the
rest of us. On the contrary, they are forever doing something, discovering something, or contributing in some way to the atmosphere
of the fiction in which they are found or helping to set up or sort out

some (generally resolvable) problem. If not, they are excluded from the story.

Given these differences, what then is the connection between a real person and a fictional one? Few novelists will deny that the latter is often constructed from the former, that is from a person, in part or in whole, whom the novelist knows.[4] Of the countless people he met in his widely travelled life, Louis L'Amour admits frankly, 'every one was a character, and every one had a story' (1989, 82). None the less, any character pales in comparison with a real soul. In the transformation of the latter into the former, so much of the reality of life must be jettisoned. Describing the jettisoning process, Forster confesses the strategy he employs to complete it: 'A useful trick is to look back upon ... a person with half-closed eyes, fully describing certain characteristics. I am left with about two-thirds of a human being and can get to work ... When all goes well, the original material soon disappears, and *a character who belongs to the book and nowhere else emerges*' (1977, 32–3; emphasis mine).

This may explain the *how* of character construction but not the *why*. Why do novelists create characters in the first place? Besides the royalties their efforts will ideally pull in, what is in it for them? What is their motivation? I have been arguing so far that in everyday life we are all character-creators – of ourselves and each other – and thus differ from novelists only in degree, not in kind. But what is it that drives novelists to enter this creation process with the intensity and devotion they do?

It is not enough to answer that they are creative people and that that is what they do. Of course, everyone is a judge of character (Woolf, 1966, 188); we have to be, in order to manoeuvre our way through the world. In this sense, there is a novelist in us all. But real novelists differ from the rest of us 'because they do not cease to be interested in character when they have learnt enough about it for practical purposes. They go a step further; they feel that there is something permanently interesting in character in itself' (189). Thus, 'the study of character becomes to them an absorbing pursuit; to impart character an obsession' (189).

Novelists create characters, then, because they can do no other. 'Men and women write novels,' submits Woolf, 'because they are lured on to create some character which has ... imposed itself upon them' (187). They give birth to fictional human beings as naturally and necessarily as others do to real ones. And after conceiving them, nurturing them, and unleashing them on their readers, they go on, despite themselves, to conceive others – fertilized by God knows what mysterious source or what obscure need within their own soul – or to conceive the same ones in the same situations again and again. Thus, John Updike is hounded down the labyrinthine ways of four long novels by the ghost of Rabbit Angstrom.

The controversial French writer Samuel Beckett has also wrestled with the relationship between characters and real people, not only with the how and why of it but also with the whether: whether it is even possible. Beckett's style and stories represent an extreme form of the scepticism we saw earlier in Sagan and Sartre, an advance example of the post-modern suspicion of plot that we noted before (Leitch, 1986, 148). From the beginning, Beckett's work constituted 'an assault on the genre of the novel and on the form of story' (Estess, 1974, 418). His later fiction, in particular, 'stands as a contemplation of story, only faintly reflecting what has been but can be no longer' (418). Accordingly, 'many of his characters fail to perceive even the possibility for imposing upon or discovering within their experience a coherently integrated structure which we call "plot"' (420). Their dilemma is summarized by comments of the narrator on the final pages of *The Unnameable*: 'you must go on, I can't go on, you must go on, I'll go on, you must say words, as long as there are any, until they find me, until they say me ... perhaps it's done already, perhaps they have said me already, perhaps they have carried me to *the threshold of my story*, before the door that opens on my story, that would surprise me, if it opens, it will be I, it will be the silence' (414; emphasis mine).

How Beckett presents his characters pushes us to confront the gap between literature and life with special starkness. If fictional characters are not the same as real persons, if they belong to the book and nowhere else, if they stand not on 'the threshold of story' but squarely in the household of story, then such distinctions between, for example, good guys and bad guys as some literature can convey – these too have an illusory dimension. 'Life,' says William Faulkner flatly, 'is not interested in good and evil' (1977, 138). Thus, the moral side of any story, though it may appeal to our imagination or to the way we would like the world to be, may not be reflective of the world as it is – particularly when, as we have shown by Hayden White and others, the 'moral' may be in support of a system that fails to reflect the world as it is. Literature, in this view, is simply an illusion. It helps us neither to engage with life nor to see deeply into the heart of it, but only – at best – to be chronically disappointed by it and – at worst – to abandon it.

This is one perspective on the relationship between literature and life, and it is compelling. It appears to drive the final nail in the coffin of the question about the links between the two. But it is not the whole story. Another perspective is captured by Northrop Frye. 'Literature does not reflect life,' he says, 'but it doesn't escape or withdraw from life either: it swallows it' (1963, 33). What does such a comment mean in relation to the concept of 'character' and the stories we are? Simply put, fictional characters often have a larger-than-life quality. They can exist in our hearts long after the book has been put down or the screen has gone blank – and long after their author has died. They take on, they gather around them, they swallow up, all manner of psychological and philosophical possibilities in our minds, such that generation after generation of us feel dwarfed by their presence on the page. They can thus seem more real, more communicative, than many real people. If this is true for us as readers, it is no less true for writers.

Many writers have attested that their control over their stories is by no means airtight, that there is a tension between the elements of inevitability and surprise, between the necessary and the novel, between that which is determined and that which is discovered along the way. As John Gardner puts it, the writer 'is partly in control of and partly controlled by the fictional process. Again and again, in the process of writing, he will find himself forced to make new discoveries' (1985, 67). In essence, good stories write themselves. As Lawrence Durrell confesses concerning the writing of his own stories, there is 'very little deliberate plotting as such.' Instead, he says, 'I am prepared at any moment to throw all the data overboard and let it live its own life' (1977, 280). As James Thurber asserts, 'I don't believe the writer should know too much where he's going' (1977, 87). As Forster admits, 'characters run away with you' (1977, 28). They 'take over,' Annie Dillard announces – adding impishly, 'powerful rascals, what is a god to do?' (1989, 16). It is the comments of John Steinbeck that illustrate perhaps best, however, this peculiar relationship a storyteller can have with his story.

In his daily letters to his publisher during the writing of *East of Eden*, Steinbeck gives vivid expression to an author's struggle to balance his own sense of where the story should be going with that of the story itself. 'This is a very headstrong story,' he says (1970, 43). By this he means the main dilemma he faces in the composition process is discerning 'how many events are accidents and how many are created and forced by the natures of the protagonists.' How he resolves this, he says, is that 'to a large extent I lean toward the latter' (37). Thus, he submits, 'a story has a life of its own. It must be allowed to take its own pace. It can't be pushed too much. If it is, the warp shows through and the story is unnatural and unsafe. And this story of mine,' he says, 'must be safe' (37).

Steinbeck's comments push us to appreciate the intricate interplay between plot and character. On the one hand, certain events in a story, he says, are in fact 'created and forced by the natures of the protagonists.' On the other hand, says Gardner, for whom 'plotting ... must be the first and foremost concern of the writer' (1985, 56), 'plot not only changes but creates character' (46). That is, 'subtle details change characters' lives in ways too complex for the conscious mind to grasp' (46). This give-and-take, this mutual influence, of character and plot is the engine that drives the story on, what keeps it pumping from page to page. The two elements are inseparably linked. Though in any given story one will be emphasized over the other, where one begins and the other ends is delicate to judge. As Henry James asks, 'what is character but the determination of incident? What is incident but the illustration of character?' (Lynch and Rampton, 1992, 8).

In modern times the line between these two elements has become perhaps increasingly difficult to draw in so far as the plots of many novels have less to do with the sequence of the incidents than with the development of the characters. 'At some point,' says Annie Dillard, 'the people in novels stopped galloping all over the countryside and started brooding from chairs. Everything became psychological and interiorized. External conflict became internal tension ... You may search the novels of Virginia Woolf in vain for so much as a single horse' (1982, 46). Dillard's remarks direct us to a comment made by the Woolf scholar, Joan Bennett. After Woolf published *Night and Day*, Bennett says, her novels 'cease to tell stories.' That is, 'the sequence of events no longer leads to a climax and in the final pages no knot is unravelled.' As Bennett puts it, 'if by a story we mean a connected series of events moving towards a conclusion then ... she tells no stories' (1964, 42). Though Woolf 'abandoned the convention of character drawing' as well, her emphasis, in terms of the elements of plot and character, is clearly on the latter. That is, 'the events she notes are not always the immediate causes or consequences of other events in

the book. Their importance depends upon their effect in the consciousness of her creature and not upon their function in a plot' (42–3).

How then does Woolf arrange her incidents and order her scenes?
What is the pattern? The pattern, says Bennett, 'is composed of
sequences rather than consequences' (51). That is, 'the sequence of
scenes is ordered by their emotional relevance to one another rather
than by their logical interrelation' (43). From what we have said about
stories so far and the great importance of plot, Woolf's approach,
while brilliant, is decidedly unconventional. And what is its value? Its
value, affirms Bennett, is that 'the disappearance of "the story" and,
therefore, of the reader's curiosity about "what happened next," allows
for a fuller communication of the rhythmic ebb and flow of love' (60).

Plot and character – of the two, we wonder then, which will prevail
in a given story? It appears the question has been a live one since the
beginning. Homer's *Iliad* had no characters, Gardner points out, at
least in the modern sense of 'rounded, complex human beings,' while
Beowulf and *The Divine Comedy* had no plot, in the Aristotelian sense
of a 'causually related sequence of events' (1985, 82). From one story
to another, indeed from one life to another, the question is: which
element will predominate and why? Bennett's reference to Woolf's
work could lead us to wonder, for instance, if stories by women do
not tend to deal in the development of character (in the case of *life*
stories, of their own character and those of others close to them, such
as partners or children), while those by men tend to emphasize action
and plot. As this may be a sensitive question to be posing, I shall do
no more than mention it for now, though I shall return to it in the
following chapter when I consider the stories we leave untold.

Before moving on to the next section, we need to remember that the
notion of the development of character through plot is a relatively
recent phenomenon. Indeed, it reaches its apex with the modern
novel. The novel has as 'its central concern ... the development of
character through temporal decision' (Teselle, 1975a, 123). Concurring
with this view is Gardner. 'The writer's business,' he says, 'is to make
up convincing human beings and create for them basic situations and
actions by means of which they come to know themselves and reveal
themselves to the reader' (1985, 15). For characters to come to know
themselves, however, they must have not only conflict to contend
with but also a measure of freedom to do so – freedom, at least,
within the story. 'No fiction can have real interest if the central character is not an agent struggling for his or her own goals but a victim,

subject to the will of others' (65). Hence, Gardner concludes that 'the ultimate value of fiction is its morality,' for 'we respond to fictional problems as though they were real: We sympathize, think, and judge. We act out, vicariously, the trials of the characters and learn from the failures and successes of particular modes of action, particular attitudes, opinions, assertions, and beliefs exactly as we learn from life' (31).

Once again, then, story and life converge. What is life about, we have all no doubt wondered, but the continual building of our character out of the incidents of our lives, the regular testing of it in the face of the exigencies of our existence? That our 'character' can be built at all, of course, and is not some given, consistent core: this is the question. Furthermore, we might well ask, what is our 'character' anyway – compared with our 'personality' – but always, in part, a creation of our imagination, a mass of words within our minds, a set of stories we tell and retell both others and ourselves about who we are, where we have come from, and where we are going?

Ourselves as Characters in Our Own Life-Stories

In the preceding section, we gained an appreciation for the authorial role we play in plotting our own lives. Now our question concerns the role we play in characterizing ourselves in the midst of them. Assuming that 'we are in the middle of our stories … constantly having to revise the plot as new events are added to our lives' (Polkinghorne, 1990, 150), 'without knowing how the story will end' (69), then what kind of a character are we? Are we truly the hero? If so, of what sort, and in what sort of relationship both to our circumstances and to whatever other characters may figure in our lives?

We can get at these questions by realizing that while there is no limit to the *number* of stories, there may well be one to the *kind*: a boundary on the range of patterns by which the events of any story can be connected. In the view of Northrop Frye, 'there are a limited number of possible ways of telling a story' (1988, 54). For critical purposes, he sets the limit at five. By distinguishing between these 'fictional modes,' as he calls them, Frye is following the lead of Aristotle (Hamilton, 1990, 61). Accordingly, he argues that stories can be classified 'by the hero's power of action, which may be greater than ours, less, or roughly the same.' Thus,

1. If superior in kind both to other men and to the environment of other men, the hero is a divine being, and the story about him will be a *myth* in the common sense of a story about a god.
2. If superior in degree to other men and to his environment, the hero is the typical hero of *romance*, whose actions are marvellous but who is himself identified as a human being.
3. If superior in degree to other men but not to his natural environment, the hero is a leader ... This is the hero of ... most epic and *tragedy*.
4. If superior neither to other men nor to his environment, the hero is one of us ... This gives us the hero ... of most *comedy* and of realistic fiction.
5. If inferior in power or intelligence to ourselves, so that we have the sense of looking down on a scene of bondage, frustration, or absurdity, the hero belongs to the *ironic* mode. (Frye, 1966, 23–4)

Offering these categories as 'a taxonomy for a new literary history' (Hamilton, 62), Frye believes 'we can see that European fiction, during the last fifteen centuries, has steadily moved its center of gravity down the list' (1966, 24). In particular, 'during the last hundred years, most serious fiction has tended increasingly to be ironic in mode' (25). A variation on this last mode has been identified by James Hillman.

Hillman, we will recall, insists that our experience itself is moded in some manner, is genre-ated – and here we can use the two terms interchangeably. As he puts it, 'the manner in which we tell ourselves what is going on is the genre through which events becomes experiences' (1975a, 146). Hillman feels the need, however, to add a further mode to Frye's five. He calls it the *picaresque*, a blend of both comedy and tragedy that he feels captures the real-life situation of many. 'Its central figure does not develop (or deteriorate), but goes through episodic, discontinuous movements. His narrative ends abruptly without achievement for there is no goal; so the denouement can neither be the resolution of comedy nor the fatal flaw of tragedy ... There are tales within tales that do not further a plot (for there is no plot)' (1975a, 141).

Whether five or six in number, these are of course very broad and very arbitrary distinctions. We are mistaken if we expect to find them always manifested in their pure form (Hamilton, 65). On the contrary, they are commonly combined in any given work of literature – and

surely in any given life. When we relate them to life, however, we face
the same danger as we do when we wield the notion of stages or
phases: that of using them not only clumsily but also *pre-* rather than
*de-*scriptively. As one psychologist confesses, 'this list is a remarkable
psychological heuristic. One can almost begin classifying one's friends'
(Keen, 1986, 175). Yet the explanatory value of such a list cannot easily
be dismissed. In fact, bearing it in mind can assist us in the 'judging'
of character that we shall no doubt be engaging in anyway, enriching
(though not eradicating) the 'storyotyping' that we do of each other
regardless, every day. Given their merits in this respect, then, it is not
surprising that schemas of this sort are much in vogue, especially in
the literature on 'personal growth.' In *The Hero Within*, for example,
Jungian psychologist Carol Pearson (1989) outlines 'the hero's journey'
through a series of archetypal life-patterns – ones it would be fascinating to correlate with the literary patterns identified by Frye. Given that
this journey is 'more circular or spiral than linear,' says Pearson, 'it
begins with the complete trust of the Innocent, moves on to the longing for safety of the Orphan, the self-sacrifice of the martyr, the exploring of the Wanderer, the competition and triumph of the Warrior, and
then the authenticity and wholeness of the Magician' (xxvi).

I shall return to Pearson's model in the next chapter. For the time
being, what can we make of such categories with respect to our *own*
'character'? For instance, do we see ourselves as a *tragic* hero basically,
for whom woe is perpetually us, besieged continually by the powers
that be, seen and unseen – perhaps in paranoid expectation, like many
of a fundamentalist bent, that all shall come to nought (Keen, 1986)?
Or do we see ourselves as a *romantic* adventurer, rising vigorously
above all odds, time after time, to find the Holy Grail or conquer the
world? How about as a *comic* hero, bumbling laughably along from
one silly mix-up to another? As a *picaresque* hero perhaps, whose life-
story is less a full-length, coherent novel than a series of loosely connected short stories, rather like a stock character in a television program whose situations change with each week's instalment but whose
'nature' remains the same? Or, as a *legend* in our time, a *myth* of our
own making, a demigod beholden to no one but ourselves?

Whichever mode we may feel fits us best, there can of course be
discrepancies – 'gaps,' to use a term I have already introduced. Some
people, for example, experience and express their life events – that is,
those they *do* experience and *can* express – according to what seems
the tragic genre. No matter how normal or serene (even how comical)

their life may appear to us, looking outside-in, the tales they tell of it are routinely fraught with conflict, and they are chronically the victim. For others, no matter how painful their actual life by other accounts, both what we hear and presumably what they feel is either a grand adventure or a glorious comedy – as in the case, perhaps, of a 'real character.' The point is that, like development and emplotment, our life and the genre by which we story it – event by event or overall – do not always jibe. Furthermore, sometimes it seems that our self-genre changes, that in the wake of certain crises we are actually re-genre-ated. As we shall see even more when we look into 're-storying' our lives, the permutations and combinations, the blendings of and changes between genres, may be endless. Here, though, I want to stay focused on the broad question not so much of what kind of characters we might be within our life-story but of what it means to be such a character in the first place. In other words, is it correct to speak of ourselves as a 'hero' at all?

'Whether I shall turn out to be the hero of my own life or whether that station will be held by anybody else, these pages must show': thus wonders David Copperfield at the beginning of his personal history. So far, I have tried to avoid the term 'hero' not just because of the male bias behind it (Hook, 1943) but also because, according to Frye at least, it has been possible – for Thackeray and others since – to write a novel without a hero (1966, 24). Admittedly, though, by invoking the term *prot*-agonist I have not entirely escaped the hero notion. Besides, how many of us would willingly refer to ourselves with the opposite term: *villain*? Although we can be adept at villainizing others, making them into the enemies in our life-adventure and thus the reason for our troubles, we seldom place ourselves on the negative side of our own life's conflicts, as the *ant*-agonist. True, there are times when we are, as we say, 'our own worst enemy,' but this is not usually a role that we assign ourselves deliberately. Rather, it is an assessment we make of ourselves after the fact, upon reflection. By the same token, there can be times in our dealings with others when we intentionally play 'the devil's advocate,' but, again, this is usually in the service of some higher good like logic or reason that is obviously invisible to them. Even in feeling ourselves to be the 'victim,' we betray our sense of moral superiority to the 'victor,' whose thumb we have been under. Those most skilled in the art of doing this – putting themselves up while putting themselves down – we call martyrs. In general, we are ingenious at finding ways to make ourselves come out on top, whenever we tell our stories. Explicitly or implicitly, it is after all *our* case we are pleading, *our* way of thinking, perceiving, acting, deciding, feeling, and so on that we are proclaiming as ultimately the *right* way, the one that will be vindicated in the end. At the same time, it is also true that some of us are so riddled with guilt that we see ourselves as quite naturally at fault, in debt to others, failing to live up to whatever standards we feel that we should, thus deserving of their punishment or rejection. We may even secretly *want* to see ourselves this way, to villainize ourselves, which suggests that whether we see ourselves as heroes or villains in a moral sense, we none the less see ourselves as heroes in a dramatic one. That is, we are the character who is, after all, central to *our* life-story.

Further Questions

But are we *always* central to our life-story? Is it possible, for example, that we are – or at least pretend we are – only a supporting character in someone else's story – our spouse's, our children's, our parents,' our company's, our party's, or our God's? Such a possibility was implied once by a colleague in her comment that for the nine years she was married, not she but her husband was the central character in *her* life-story? Indeed, when asked how they are, how many women in comparable circumstances will not respond, perhaps because they have been conditioned or coached to do so, with a litany of activities in which not *they* are centrally involved but rather their children or their men? This is a serious question. For many, it can be disturbingly so: those, for example, who appear to live the bulk of their lives in silence, little more than extras in someone else's drama, ghosts in the background of some other person's saga, footnotes on the pages of another's novel (cf. Belenky et al, 1986).

For religious people, it is often not a spouse or child or any other *human* being who dominates their stories in this way but, apparently, a divine one. In everything they do and decide, that is, their first thought (so they claim) is of God, 'God's Will,' and what God would want or is guiding them to do. It is not their own life-story that is preeminent, therefore, but God's. By those in their circle, they are esteemed as 'committed' or 'humble.' Then again, there are sometimes individuals who have been accused of a crime yet are let off lightly because their counsel is able to convince the court that, during the deed in question, they were simply 'not themselves'; that the devil made them do it; that they were not merely acting 'out of character' but were actually insane – that is, possessed by another entity or being. Legally speaking, what are we to make of such cases? Are we indeed the 'hero' of our own life-story and therefore responsible for our actions, or can we claim ourselves to be the victims of forces outside of us, pawns in the world's cruel game, exploited extras in the drama of the dominant society? Though the insistence that we *are* the heroes of our own life-stories seems foundational to our entire judicial system, how does it really hold up when looked at from a story perspective? We see, then, how the subject of the stories we are raises not just aesthetic questions but ethical and legal ones as well.

We can approach the question of what kind of character(s) we are inside our life-story from other angles still. Are we the main character in some chapters but only a secondary one in others – just as, for example, we can be comic in some and tragic in others? Furthermore, are we 'flat' characters or 'round'? Are we perhaps flat in some subplots of our life-story (as an employee) while round in others (as a lover)? Are we a stock character, that is, as in the trite television scripts it is easy to disdain, or do we possess a measure of originality, of unpredictability? In general, do we live out our lines as prompted by society, as pre-scribed by our station in life, the profession we pursue, the class or culture into which we fit – or do we do it *our* way? Do we tell it as we are told, or 'like it is'?

Reflecting on similar questions, literary critic Wayne Booth (1988) makes the point that though character is an indispensable term for talking about our lives, it is ultimately misleading to think that each of us has only *one* character. On the contrary, he says, we must speak of 'the social psyche' (246) – what another source calls 'a private theater filled with scenes and characters' (Keen and Fox, 1974, 8). 'A kind of play-acting with characters,' Booth says, 'a kind of faking of characters, is one of the main ways that we build what becomes our character.' In this respect, 'my character is the totality of all the roles I can play effectively, good and bad' (1988, 253). More precisely, 'we are characters in process, taking on and playing widely diverse roles' (292). So then, our self is host not to one character, but to many: once more, suspiciously like a good story. Furthermore, and this is critical, 'the turns in my life, embracing and sloughing off successive "characters," produce a life story that is uniquely my "own." I implicitly "tell" that story as I play my various and perhaps contradictory roles. Its uniqueness provides the only individuality that will still interest me:

my story has its own plot line' (289). In Booth's view, therefore, 'it will be the chief and most difficult business of my life to grope my way along dimly lit paths, hoping to build *a life-'plot' that will be in one of the better genres'* (268; emphasis mine).

Exactly what Booth means by a 'better' genre he does not spell out, but, like Frye, he ties his classification of stories to the fortunes of the characters. The difference is that, in his argument, the stories, characters, and plots in question do not belong to fiction as such. They are our own, and they are distinctive. 'Though most of what is "me" will be traceable to previous storytellers,' he says, 'the particular sequence of roles will be mine, all mine' (289). At the same time, 'though our stories are unique,' they will 'bear many resemblances to other life-plots.' Accordingly, again like Frye, 'they fall into "genres" that are obviously not infinite in number' (289). If we doubt this claim, he says, we need only list all 'the life-plot summaries' we can think of. His list runs as follows: 'from high promise to happiness to misery; from beginning misery to happiness to misery; from misery to misery to maximum misery ...; from happiness to happiness to misery; from happiness to happiness to a higher happiness ...; from promise to promise to sudden accidental death' (289).

In straddling the line between literature and life, Booth has noted that using the term 'character' to explore the stories we are is peculiarly complicated because of its application not to written stories only but also to enacted ones. 'All the world's a stage,' we say, easily accepting Goffman's analysis of everyday life as a theatrical affair and ourselves as actors, forever playing a role. Yet the story being acted out on our own individual stage is still being composed, its final lines not yet written, and so the ultimate shape of our particular character is as yet unrevealed by the vicissitudes of our unfolding plot – of which we ourselves are always partial architects. Where story ends and life begins thus continues as an open question. On the one hand, we know that dramatic or fictional characters are ultimately not real people. Using Hamlet once again as an example, he was never a live human being, at least in the dramatic form in which Shakespeare presents him. On the other hand, to the extent he lives on, strutting and fretting his hour upon the stage for each new era of theatre-goers, he has burst the bonds of his story; his story cannot contain him. In much the same way, all great fictional characters 'exist in their own right, apart from the page. They refuse to be banished. They will not be driven back between covers' (Howe, 1989, 32). We have now seen how this can happen in the course of *writing* a story: characters become mutinous. But might it not happen in living one as well?

Just as there are fictional characters who seem to struggle against the constraints of their plot on a trajectory that would thrust them into a life of their own *outside* of the story, is it possible that there are people in 'real life' engaged, on some level, in insinuating themselves *into* a story? For instance, what about the amazing, if sometimes annoying, people who insist on seeing themselves as larger than life, as the mighty, unignorable stars of their own ongoing soap opera, horror story, or morality play? By the same token, might we not all at some point fancy ourselves as a partial embodiment of one fictional persona or another – perhaps a Virginia Slim woman or a Marlboro Man? Such possibilities cannot be discounted. How else can we explain the intensity of the connection we all occasionally feel in an encounter with a character in a novel or a film? How else can we explain the desire of all of us some of the time, and perhaps some of us all of the time, to emulate someone whose 'life' is confined to the pages of a book? How else can we explain the frenetic fascination with heroes that we have all probably experienced somewhere during our childhood or adolescence, stages of life in which the trying on of personae is generally acceptable and frequently encouraged? How else can we fathom our need at the time to ape those heroes' mannerisms, expressions, fashions, or 'style'? And what can we say about ageing here? Does this need automatically diminish the older we grow? That is, do we lean less on fictional people as we advance in years simply because of an increasing (if unsayable) sense that real ones are ultimately more complex and more interesting, however unknowable they remain? Reversing this, are we more apt to be taken in by fictional people the less intimate we are with real ones?

Story or life: which is stranger? Which is more real? The questions run away on us, but they are not therefore silly. Indeed, we have already had a taste of them in considering the power of story in the previous section. Comedian Woody Allen has taken them up vigorously, in fact, and made them the central motif of his film *The Purple Rose of Cairo*. A summary of it will lend an amusing twist to our thinking so far, for it is a parable not just of Forster's point about characters who 'run away' and 'kick the story to pieces' but also, on a broader level, of the curious interpenetration of story and reality.

Cecilia is the mistreated young wife of an unemployed labourer during the grey days of the Great Depression. A waitress in a corner café of a backwater New Jersey town, she spends every available moment at the local cinema, watching and rewatching each movie that comes along. Afterward, starry-eyed, she recounts to her sister ad nauseam how wonderful, how desirable, and how real she finds the world of each story to be, certainly how preferable to the dreary real world to which she is consigned. One day, while she is watching 'The Purple Rose of Cairo,' the lead actor notices her sitting in the audience. As can happen only in the movies, 'Tom Baxter of the Chicago Baxters' calls out to her from his two-dimensional, black-and-white world and asks her if she has not in fact been present at every showing since the film first arrived in town. Dumbfounded, Cecilia stammers that, yes, she has, at which point he strides off the screen, strolls down the aisle, and starts up with her the most comical of affairs.

Naturally, many people try to persuade the two to end their ill-fated liaison and return to their respective stations in life: Tom to his silver screen, Cecilia to her greasy spoon. Among them are both the other cast members, stalled confusedly in the midst of their plot, and the movie moguls themselves, naturally worried because of the peculiar press their film is receiving nationwide. (It seems Cecilia's is not the only town in which Tom has walked out of his story.) Totally frustrated, one of them throws up his hands in complaint: 'the fictional ones want their lives real,' he cries, 'and the real ones want their lives fictional!' Terrified his career will be ruined, Gil Shephard, the actor who plays Tom, travels to New Jersey to find out for himself what is happening. When he, too, appears to fall in love with Cecilia, the plot thickens all the more. Eventually, Tom is persuaded to return to the screen, Gil flies back to Hollywood, and Cecilia, alas, is left to settle for the pallid pleasures of Coffee Row.

However much they resist systematic presentation, I believe that the issues we have considered in this section underscore the fine line between literature and life, between *Homo fictus* and *Homo sapiens*, between art and reality, between aesthetics and ethics. If literature imitates life, surely the opposite is true as well (Bruner, 1987, 13). Yet, as sensible as this insight seems, has it been sufficiently mined for what it can tell us about how we see ourselves in the midst of our own lives? If we have benefited from studies of 'personality types,' would the study of 'character types' by any less helpful? We have seen the directions in which such a study might lead. For now, I turn to point of view.

The Element of Point of View

What is the point of view of a story? If a story is 'someone telling (to someone) about somebody doing something,' then the point of view concerns the someone who is doing the telling. This point must not be missed: stories do not come from nowhere; they are always told *by* someone. And whoever tells the story has power with respect to it. If a narrative is 'distinguished by two characteristics: the presence of a story and a story-teller' (Scholes and Kellogg, 1966, 4), then the issue around point of view concerns the relationship between the storyteller and the story. A discussion of it is highly relevant to the study of the stories we are, once we accept that there is always a gap between living and telling, and that, perhaps to manage that gap, 'we are constantly striving ... to occupy the story-teller's position with respect to our own actions' (Carr, 1986, 61). To speak of the storyteller, though, is to imply both the authorship of a story and its narration. Yet we seldom consider this distinction.

Authorship and Narration

Authorship and narration are intimately related, but at bottom they are two different functions, two different processes. They occur within two different time-frames and two different worlds. The world of the author is the world of a particular study, a particular writing desk, a particular pad and pen: a world in which there is the freedom to interrupt the process of writing at any time and, between one word and the next, to take off an hour, a week, or a year. In contrast, the world of the narrator is confined to the words themselves, and endures only as long as it takes the reader to read them. Similarly, while the author is free (at least within the confines of her chosen plot) to make up the incidents of her story however she wills, the narrator has no such choice, but must work with whatever events the author supplies. At the same time, despite her greater freedom, she is dependent on the narrator for her story to have a life at all. She may be the source of the story and, in that sense, tells the story, but she can do so only *through* a narrator, a storyteller, a particular point of view. We can theorize all we like about the links between her life and her literature, but it is the narrator through which/whom her story is channelled.

For Wayne Booth, a pioneer in the study of 'the rhetoric of fiction,' there is an 'embarrassing inadequacy,' however, about our usual ways of classifying point of view (1966, 273). The range of rhetorical devices by which narrators narrate their stories is in reality, he says, extremely complicated. The variables at stake relate to more than the obvious matter of person (first, third, and very occasionally second), but concern several matters of degree as well, such as degree of dramatization, self-consciousness, distance, reliability, and omniscience.

Regarding dramatization, Booth distinguishes between three principal approaches to narration. The first is that of 'the implied author,' an approach that gives the reader 'an implicit picture of an author who stands behind the scenes, whether as stage manager, as puppeteer, or as an indifferent God, silently paring his fingernails' (275). This implied author, Booth stresses, is never the same as the actual author – with his human qualities and his understandable needs, while writing, to fix himself a coffee, use the bathroom, or let out the cat – nor even as that 'superior version of himself, a "second self,"' he says, which the actual author creates in the course of his work. In considering the issue of point of view in the stories of our lives, this further distinction 'between real authors and the selves they create as they write' (275) is of special importance. Booth's caution about the 'subtleties that underlie the seemingly simple relations' between the two needs bearing in mind. The second approach in this category is that of 'undramatized' narration, whereby the tale passes through the consciousness of a teller who does not himself enter the action of the story. As readers, however, we must not make the mistake of thinking that because this undramatized narrator 'is given no personal characteristics' (276) the story comes to us unmediated. The third approach, then, is the 'dramatized' narrator. Such narrators, says Booth, become 'characters who are as vivid as those they tell us about' (276).

Regarding self-consciousness, Booth distinguishes between narrators who are very aware of themselves as conveyors of the story and those 'who rarely if ever discuss their writing chores,' who seem unaware that they are writing, thinking, or speaking at all. Regarding distance, Booth distinguishes between narrators who 'may be more or less distant' from the characters in the story, from the reader, and from the implied author. Similarly, the implied author may be more or less distant from the reader and from the characters. Related to the degree of distance, then, is that of reliability. Here Booth distinguishes between 'reliable' narrators and 'unreliable' ones. The reliable narrator 'speaks for an action in accordance with the norms of his writer'; the unreliable narrator does not. The unreliable narrator is not necessarily lying, Booth points out, but is 'mistaken,' or 'believes himself to have qualities which the author denies *him*' (283). For example, in *Huckleberry Finn*, 'the narrator claims to be naturally wicked while the author silently praises his virtues behind his back.' Ultimately, of course, concludes critic Frank Kermode, '*all* narrators are unreliable,' though 'some are more expressly so than others' (1980, 84–5).

Regarding degree of omniscience, or what can be called 'privilege,' Booth says that narrators, 'whether self-conscious or not, reliable or not, commenting or silent ... can be either privileged to know what could not be learned by strictly natural means or limited to realistic vision and inference' (284). Complete privilege, he says, is 'what we usually call omniscience'; it is the kind of narration whereby, as reader, we are taken far more deeply into the inner world of a given character than we are normally able to go even into our own.

As helpful as it is, Booth's analysis is confined largely to the relationship of the story*teller* to the story. There are other points of view in relation to a story, however, besides that of the storyteller. In contemplating the story of my life, it is this more complicated situation we need to ponder.

Self as Protagonist, Narrator, and Reader

'Broadly speaking,' say Scholes and Kellogg, there are three points of view at work 'in any example of narrative art ... those of the characters, the narrator, and the audience' (1966, 240). If there is merit in the metaphor of life-as-story all three will be at work in the narrative art that is involved in self-creation. As we have seen, in narrating my life I am simultaneously narrator and protagonist, in so far as the 'I' who does the telling is also the 'I' about whom I tell. This 'double subjectivity,' says Sidonie Smith (1987, 17), is the central complication faced by the autobiographer. However, there is in fact a *triple* subjectivity at work, to the extent that in listening to myself narrating myself, I am the audience, or reader, of my story as well. 'My life,' writes educator Carol Witherell, 'is the sort of "story" in which I am character, storyteller, and audience all at once' (1991, 75).

Thinking of my self as simultaneously the narrator, protagonist, *and* reader of my own life-story, while intriguing to do, injects curious complications into our usual conception of self-consciousness. (The concept of self-as-*author* injects complications of, indeed, a metaphysical nature, ones I shall look into under 'The Autobiographical Imperative' in the next chapter.) It raises questions about what really is the point of view I have on the story of my own life? For instance, how does the 'reader' point of view I have on my story differ from the 'narrator' or 'protagonist' point of view? Does each of us gravitate toward one point of view more than another? If so, how consistently am I apt to sustain that point of view throughout my life? What sort of factors might initiate a change? To take such questions seriously is to entertain the possibility that through each of these functions – reader, narrator, or protagonist – I enjoy a unique relationship to, knowledge of, and angle on the unfolding story I am. It suggests that by means of each I may be more or less immersed in my story, more or less detached from it, and more or less conscious of where it has been, where it is, and where it might go. Moreover, it implies that through each of these functions, I may be dealing with what is in effect a different story. We began to see this possibility when we considered plot. Though I shall return to it when I consider 'storying styles' in the next chapter, let me take a quick look at it here.

As protagonist, I am basically *inside* my story, acting and reacting in the present, unable to see the whole story or even *any* story. Indeed, in the protagonist mode the very idea of 'the story of my life' may be difficult for me to grasp. Amid my own unfolding novel (though I have trouble seeing it as such) I have little sense of where things have been before, or of where they are going to, because I am caught up in the situation – the action, the *agon* – at hand. Operating by reflex, I make decisions on the fly. Committed to 'getting on with things,' I do and say things with minimal opportunity, perhaps even need, to get the larger picture of the plot of my life. For all intents and purposes, my life *is* the plot. I am as close to raw existence as one can get – at least as a *human* can get, for I am still conscious of my existence, thus still choosy. That is, I still focus on 'what counts.'

As narrator, however, the relation I have to my story is different. Compared to the protagonist mode, I am more outside it in (psychological) time and space, more detached from it, more able to talk about it to others. In this sense, I have greater control over its construction *as* a story – with a past, present, and future. Living more on the level of inside-out, I tend to talk about myself more, casting my character in accordance with whatever genre suits my fancy, my needs, or my audience. Better at storytelling generally, I am more adept at seeing patterns in my past and making plans for my future. The kind of person 'who documents himself' (Blythe, 1980, 152), I live more in bad faith, with one eye ever on my biography.

As reader, I am outside my life-story even more, not controlling it so much as critiquing it, evaluating it, following it. I am regularly trying to figure out what sort it is and what it is about; reading into it now this meaning and now that; analysing what plot it might have and what character I might be in its midst; comparing the sort of story it seems to me to be in the present with each of the different kinds of story I recall having perceived it to be in the past my various hunches about the story it may go on to become in the future. As reader, however, I am in a position to become in turn both protagonist and narrator of a larger story still: the story that includes within it the fact of my critiquing, evaluating, and following 'the story of my life.' Roy Schafer argues that to say the self tells a story to itself implies another story in turn: that there is a self – as audience – to tell that story to (1983, 218). There are levels of self-reading, that is: an insight that is reflected in the distinction made by literary theorists not just between authors and narrators but also between readers and narratees (Rimmon-Kenan, 1989, 86). As soon as I realize that I have been critiquing, evaluating, and following the narration of my experience, then that act of critiquing and evaluating and following becomes one more event to incorporate into my story. On a moment-by-moment basis, this may be what the process of personal storytelling involves: each moment is a moment of self-transcendence in which I advance from one story to another. Thus, the story of my life is one I am continually outgrowing, as I am ever moving, automatically, to a larger and more inclusive story still.

In his analysis of our movement from one stage of our lives to the next – that is, 'imperial' to 'interpersonal' to 'institutional' – psychologist Robert Kegan says that whereas at one stage we *are* our emotions, relationships, etc., at the next stage we are dis-identified from them sufficiently that, instead, we *have* them (1982). In the same way, from one telling to the next, we *have* the *old* story and *are* the *new*. The obvious point in this is that as we move through life, our view of our lives is constantly changing. We are present to ourselves in different ways at different times. As artist Anne Truitt suggests, from one stage of life to the next we 'hold' ourselves in our consciousness differently (1987, 160); we see ourselves differently, and, by implication, read our story differently. Our story is thus never the same from one stage to another, from one chapter to another, not only because it is theoretically longer the more recently in time we tell it, but also because our overall point of view toward it is changing as well. Such constant outgrowing of the stories of our lives conjure up the image of the chambered nautilus immortalized by the poet. This exotic creature, whose self-transcendence is so obvious because so visible, mirrors the hermeneutical process at work in the lives of us all, as our souls build themselves ever 'more stately mansions.' It mirrors 'the true character of learning' whereby 'as one identity is slowly shed, sometimes painfully, another, always elusive, is created' (Thomas, 1985, 96).

No doubt more can be said concerning the subtleties of point of view in relation to 'the story of my life.' As I say, to many I shall return in the next section. However, since I see the purpose of this book as primarily introducing the poetics of self-creation rather than exhausting the issues to which it points, I want to confine myself here to a few of the questions that such considerations raise for us with respect to two things: *tense* and *irony*.

Tense

Discussions of point of view concern not just the person in which the story is told (first or third) but also the tense. The usual choice is between the present and the past, which is more commonly the case, or occasionally the past *within* the past, a popular device in telling a story. Narration in the future, while common in life, is rare in literature, except for predictive writings like parts of the Bible (Rimmon-Kenan, 1983, 90). Though we have already touched on the tense question in examining plot (especially the backward-forward dynamic involved in following one), it bears further reflection here, given our attempts to link the complexities of literary stories to those of lived ones.

Frieda Forman insists, for instance, that people display fundamental differences in the way they orient themselves in time, differences that depend primarily on gender. In commenting on the views of time entrenched in the male-dominated traditions of Western philosophy, she says that 'a critical component of masculine time consciousness' is the 'awareness of death' (1989, 6). This is not, however, women's experience. For women, she argues, 'the *giving* of time, i.e., birth, is prior to and takes both ontological and temporal priority over the *taking away* of time, i.e., death' (7; emphasis mine). The implications of Forman's argument are profound: just as people's stories can be genrelized so perhaps they can be gender-ized as well – at least with respect to the direction they lean toward in time. However, in an article on 'the psychotypology of time,' which anticipates more recent and more popular work on 'personality types' (e.g., Myers-Briggs), researchers Mann, Siegler, and Osmond (1972) imply that temporal orientation is gender-independent.

The core of their work is a schema for categorizing people according to the tense toward which they are most naturally oriented in living their lives, experiencing themselves, and seeing their place in the world. Using the four basic types first set forth by Carl Jung – feeling, thinking, sensing, and intuiting – their schema is as follows:

Feeling

For this type, 'the present may be perceived as deriving from the past.' Thus, they are 'great collectors of memories.' Their major concerns are 'reminiscences, diaries, folklore, heritage, traditions.' They 'do not see the new as being novel, unique, emergent, but attempt, often unsuccessfully, to relate it to the known, the previously experienced and familiar ... They are very likely to say: "Oh, yes, this reminds me of ..."' They evaluate things 'in terms of what place they will take in the past rather than in terms of what effect they have in the present, or where they might lead in the future.' Because 'they value the recollection of emotion ... things are never simply what they are. They are already colored by their long-sustained echoes in the vaults of memory.' In the end, 'the greatest tragedy which life can present to a feeling type' is 'the inability to see continuity between the experiences of youth and the realities of adulthood' (148–55).

Thinking

For this type, 'no particular dimension [of time] is of central importance.' Instead, time is 'a long carpet which is continually unrolled at a precise rate.' His concern is with 'the continuity of the process.' He wants 'to see the process through to completion, and to extend the line as far into the past as possible, and as far into the future as he can project.' Consequently, for this type 'the past ... is not the personal past of feeling' but 'the detached, historical past.' In other words, 'everything has a history, everything came from some unknown (or unknowable) root, and everything exists only insofar as it is heading

in a specific direction.' Predictably, 'the extent of their joy is directly
proportional to the scope of past, present, and future that can be
glimpsed in any set of events.' It is for this reason that thinking types
are especially able 'to frame hypotheses, to draw conclusions, and to
make predictions, in short, to be scientific.' Overall, they tend 'to live
according to principles,' to be concerned with process rather than with
episode, and to be 'the greatest planners in the world' (155–62).

Sensing

Sensing types 'do not experience time as flowing'; rather 'their inner
experience' is 'of a present which is rich, full, deep, and always there.'
Unlike feeling types, 'linkage with the past is weak' and 'there is no
future.' Accordingly, 'events are met in terms of their existential reality, with little concern for how they got to be that way. Life is a happening; where it comes from and where it is going is of minor importance.' Events that 'take priority' are 'events which take place now,
which are tangible, concrete, visible, and sensual.' For this reason, the
sensing type has a 'constant desire to experience new situations'; he is
also 'known through his actions rather than through his words.' In
general, sensing types are 'geared to the present'; thus, they can 'read
the depth of the present' and can 'see much more' in it 'than any other
type.' For them, 'the present is all of life' (162–9).

Intuiting

For people of this type, 'that which will happen is more real than that
which is happening.' They are 'more at home with "will be" than with
"is" or "was."' In this respect, their discontinuity is not unlike that of
the sensing type: 'a failure to integrate the past into the present.' As
a result, 'in their experiential world ... the actual direction of time's
flow is ... backward.' That is, 'it is precisely the future which is first
perceived'; thus, 'to get the current moment,' they go 'backward from
the vision of the future into the other, lesser reality of the present.'
Intuitives 'generally have a great deal of difficulty learning time.' They
find 'painful and bothersome' having 'to be aware of time, to be constrained to be punctual, to have to keep a schedule.' For this reason,
they 'appear to others to be flighty, impractical, and unrealistic.' This
is because 'the intuitive spends his life in the race toward the next

beyond.' The positive side of this is that 'intuitives inspire others with a vision of the future.' Indeed, 'herein lies their greatest talent and the source of their personal happiness' (169–75).

This research is extremely relevant to the poetics of self-creation. One of its main implications is that, 'while common sense and conventional wisdom tell us that we all see the same event,' in fact 'the "same" event occurring at the same time for different people is ... a different event for each one of them' (176). Feeling types experience the event in terms of a story tilted toward the past; sensing types, one tilted toward the present; intuitive types, toward the future; and thinking types, somehow, toward all three tenses at once. This point can be put another way. Just as in chess some players are more talented with respect to the beginning-game, others to the middle- or end-game, and others to the game as a whole – who have the capacity to see it as something complete, already played out from beginning to end, as Mozart saw his symphonies (1955, 45) – so there are people who think of and live their life-stories largely in the past, feeding off memories, harking back continually to the ways thing used to be. On the other hand, some are more focused on 'the road goin' by'; for them, the present is all there is. Others again instinctively believe that the best (or worst) of their story is yet to come; that the next chapter will be more significant than the ones thus far; that 'the road up ahead' is preferable to and more powerful than the race already run. For others, however, who experience their stories primarily as thinkers, what comes most naturally will be a more detached, analytical sense of the sweep of their story as a whole.

Besides this feeling-intuiting schema, there are other ways of categorizing individuals according to their temporal orientations. For psychologist Herbert Rappoport, 'temporal orientation must be viewed as an important personality trait in its own right and must be understood as a primary element in the development and maintenance of psychological disorders' (1990, 143). In his study of such disorders, he has looked at three groups: people who are depressed, people who are addicted, and people he describes as 'Type-A,' 'workaholic,' or 'yuppie.' The first group, he argues, are 'clearly past-oriented' and find 'the future to be without hope' (91–2); the second tend to live very close to the present, 'one day at a time' (87); and the third is 'clearly future-oriented ... harassed by what feels like the compression of time ... highly goal-oriented and ambitious' (91–2).

In his classic analysis of the psychology of mass movements, Eric Hoffer takes yet another tack in detailing individual differences in temporal orientation. For example, 'the true believer' of a reactionary persuasion (whether political or religious) deprecates the present in favour of the past: 'if a stable and health society is to be established, it must be patterned after the proven models of the past' (1955, 71). Radicals, on the other hand, deprecate the present in favour of the future. In between, zealots in the liberal camp see the present 'as the legitimate offspring of the past and as constantly growing and developing toward an improved future: to damage the present is to maim the future' (71). As to which comes first in these matters, psychology or politics, temperament or theology, Hoffer does not answer. However, in so far as a self-story, as we shall see in the next section, is also a world-story – and a world-story thus a self-story – his insights into the question are important to ponder.

Overall, it would seem many of these individual differences in temporal orientation could be accounted for on the basis of age alone. For the young, for example, we would expect the future of their story to be the most critical, since the vast portion of their life is yet to come. Indeed, 'future-oriented words always precede past-oriented words in the child's temporal development' (Rifkin, 1987, 56). For the middle-aged, though, we would expect the present to be more central, as they are caught up in the day-to-day struggle to stay in the race. As for the elderly, with the end in sight, we would expect them to live more in the past, since the larger portion of their life is over (though the task of interpreting it may have only begun). But this breakdown is simplistic. As Mann et al would argue, it is not age or stage but 'type' that is the pivotal variable. Stage-dependent views of human development, they would say, are to be questioned. In his own questioning of such views, William Bridges agrees. 'The path of aging,' he maintains, 'is a unique journey for everyone who takes it' (1980, 53). As he puts it, 'we are like stories that are slowly unfolding according to our own inner theme and plot' (73). Thus, cookie-cutter schemas are to be eschewed, especially those that sell the view that we can all expect to peak at thirty, begin life at forty, or climax at fifty, etc. Rather, Bridges says, quoting Schopenhauer, 'each man's character seems best suited to one particular stage of life; so that he appears at his best in that stage of life.' Indeed, 'although ours is a youth-oriented culture, many of us do not come into our own until our lives are half- or three-quarters over' (53). Such comments open a window on yet another variable affecting our temporal orientation in the midst of our life-stories – the cultural one.

Just as different individuals have different orientations to time, so perhaps do different cultures, *as* cultures: differences that will obviously influence the orientation of the individuals within them. Anthropologist Edward Hall is one among a growing body of scholars preoccupied with the broad differences in our experience of time.[5] Comparing American-European (AE) culture to the culture of the Hopi Indians in the southwestern United States, he criticizes 'our warped and inadequate view of the past and the future,' which condemns the past 'to death as the tomb of irrationality and celebrate(s) the future as the promise of perfectability' (1984, 201–2). In his examination of the contrasts between these cultures – one 'developed,' the other 'primitive' – and of the role of language in perpetuating them, he illustrates with a sharpness invisible in everyday life the range of orientation of which we humans are capable. 'All AE languages, including English, treat time as a continuum divided into past, present, and future. Somehow we have manged to objectify or externalize our imagery of the passage of time, which makes it possible for us to feel that we can manage time, control it, spend it, save it, or waste it ... The Hopi language does *not* do this. No past, present, or future exists as verb tenses in their language. Hopis have no tenses' (36). Thus, 'the Hopi ... feels that time is not a harsh taskmaster nor is it equated with money and progress as it is with AE peoples. For AE peoples, it does have that characteristic of adding up, of never letting them forget. This can be burdensome. To the Hopi, the experience of time must be more natural – like breathing, a rhythmic part of life. Also, the Hopi ... have never become preoccupied with philosophizing about the "experience" of time, or the nature of time' (37).

A discussion of cultural differences in temporal orientation elicits a discussion of class differences as well (133). How does the work we perform, it can be asked, or the worrying we do over money and survival, or the leisure we enjoy to reflect on 'the meaning of life' – all of which can be intimately related to our class – how do these affect not only the time we have to think about 'the story of my life' but also the time toward which we tend in doing so? Putting it crudely, are the poor (at least the working poor) generally more tied to the present, to the challenge of getting the next paycheck or meal; the middle class more focused on the future and on 'getting ahead'; and the rich, with more time on their hands, more free to muse on the meaning of the past – or to pay for the therapy to play with the shape of their story as a whole?

Obviously, detailing cultural and class differences in temporal orientation, and their impact on individual differences, is a vast task, one well beyond the scope of my efforts here. However, it is just such differences (as well as those due to gender, stage, and type) that a consideration of our point of view on the stories of our lives needs to both accommodate and coordinate. Once we accept that 'the sort of temporal unity created by human consciousness varies from one person to another and from one circumstance to another' (Campbell, 1986, 366), then the matter of time has profound implications for our sense of how we compose – and thus live – our lives. In the meantime, another matter is raised by a discussion of point of view. It concerns the concept of irony.

Irony

'The narrative situation,' write Scholes and Kellogg, is 'ineluctably ironical' due to the 'disparity of understanding' between what the narrator, the characters, and the audience each know about the story (1966). In a typical instance of irony, the audience (or reader), the narrator, and perhaps one of the characters, know something that another of the characters does not. Relating this to our experience of the story of our life, what is the potential for irony inherent in the multidimensional nature of our own self-consciousness? Why is it, for example, that some individuals seem to have more of an air of irony about them than do others, to be more aware of themselves than are others, or, as the case may be, more aware of themselves being aware of themselves? Is it that such people are more comfortable in the reader mode *vis-à-vis* their life story than in the narrator or protagonist mode? Or, *as* readers, are they more aware of their unreliability as narrators (of the limits to their own omniscience), or of their unbelievability as protagonists – i.e., the unconvincing aspects of their own projected characters (Goffman, 1959, 17–18)?

From the perspective of one model of the self known as Psychosynthesis, for example, is the greater air of irony some individuals have about them due perhaps to their greater ability to occupy the 'omniscient narrator' point of view, to be centered in their 'I,' more disidentified from and able to moderate between the various 'sub-personalities' by which their inner world – their cast of internal characters – is constituted (Vargiu, 1978)? Moreover, what is the relationship between irony and humour – the self-deprecating humour, that is – of which some are especially capable? In turn, what is the relationship between self-deprecation and self-deception? Among the many mysteries of self-consciousness, is there a sense in which what we *know* about our story, in an ironic way, is tied to what we do *not* know? Do we know some things about our story – and its overall meaning – from the point of view of the narrator or reader of it to which, from the point of view of its protagonist, we remain blind? It we do, then how do we go about reconciling these gaps in our knowledge of ourselves?

These questions around irony merely scratch the surface of the issues involved. Though I shall return to some of them later, I want to offer now an illustration of the complex triple subjectivity we have *vis-à-vis* our personal story, one amusingly conveyed by a peculiar variety of children's literature. I refer to a series of stories known as 'Choose-Your-Own Adventures' in which, essentially, we get to choose our own plot. Indeed, plot is all there *is* to choose, for each book offers little besides pure, unfolding plot. Except for one thing: at each stage of the story's development, I, the reader – a unisex reader-cum-author who is simultaneously the central character as well, playing out my part (fairly 'flatly') not in the past tense but the present – have the power to decide on which of a given number of directions its plot will develop in next. Plot may reign, but in how it reigns, within certain limits, I have considerable say; in this respect, I am the narrator as well. For example, if on page seven I am brought face-to-face with the Black Knight or the Wicked Witch of the West, and I opt to stand and do valiant battle with him/her, then I can turn immediately to page twelve and take up the plot from there. If, on the other hand, I opt to run in the opposite direction and to scurry cowardly up a tree, then I must go to page fourteen instead. And so the story goes ... Ultimately, and this is the series' great selling point, I have the option – at least in one case (Packard, 1982) – to 'choose from 27 possible endings'! Given that in the second edition of *The Magus*, novelist John Fowles offers me only two possible endings, it is difficult not to count myself lucky.

A thoroughly modern read, this is then, even a *post*-modern read, with its multiple endings, its playing with plot, and its clear conferral of power upon the reader. Naturally, it is not serious metafiction, let alone fiction. In fact, it is scarcely more than a 'read.' Yet the genre itself, subliterary though it be, is a parable of the paradox we have been pondering thus far: whereby, while reading the story, we are both authoring it (though we are limited to a set range of possible plots) and acting in it as its central character. Such a paradox raises the issue of control.

Do we control the story – as author/narrator or reader – or does the story control us – as character? Indeed, do we have any control at all, or is our authority only a pseudo-authority, that of a creator within a creation, a storyteller within a story: a story we have not ultimately composed and in which we have 'choices' with respect only to which path we take to reach the end, not to the steps down which each path itself will lead us? It may be around this question of control, and of author-ity, that the differences between literature and life are most sharply focused. As Polkinghorne reminds us, 'in literature and history, the narrator has control of the story and decides what to include or exclude' (1988, 69). However, 'in the life narrative, the self is the narrator of its own story. Unlike authors of fictional narratives, however, the self has to integrate the materials that are at hand' (69). Yet, he insists, 'even with these differences ... there is not a sharp division but a continuity between life – the world of our practical, everyday experience – and the artistic formation of literary and historical narrative' (69).

It is possible, though, that the control question is more complex than Polkinghorne sees it. For Dennis Dennett, 'our fundamental tactic of self-protection, self-control, and self-definition is telling stories, and more particularly concocting and controlling the story we tell others – and ourselves – about who we are' (1991, 418). However, unlike professional storytellers, we 'do not consciously and deliberately figure out what narratives to tell and how to tell them. Our tales are spun,' says Dennett, 'but for the most part we don't spin them; they spin us, Our human consciousness, and our narrative selfhood, is their product, not their source' (418). Thus, it is a live question: which comes first, and which controls which, us or our story?

As we see, 'the story of my life' grows curiouser and curiouser. In the ensuing section, I shall explore how different points of view on it lead automatically to different versions.

The Stories of Our Lives

Most of us have a lot going on inside of us, often all the more so the older we get. Novelist Alex Haley has a moving image for just how much. 'When an old person dies,' he says, 'it's like a library has burned down' (Polster, 1987, 96). In everyone's library there are, of course, several sections: cooking and accounting; humour and home repair; genealogy and general knowledge; theology and philosophy. But the largest section of all may be fiction. That is, we have a lot of stories inside us, too – stories about our own lives, whether short or long, general or specific, public or private. Indeed, we are 'repositories of stories' (Schank, 1990, 40). Witness the incessant narrating we do inside our heads, or the course of our most casual conversation. Get two of us together and what comes out? Not facts or philosophies or statistics so much as … stories. We may discuss the weather or dissect the world or 'talk shop,' but at the base of our talk are stories – accounts, anecdotes, tales, however prosaically told, of what we have done, where we have been, and where we are going next: 'That reminds me of the time' … or 'That's like what happened to me' … or 'That's what I hope to do someday.' These constitute the vast storehouse that each of us carries about, the rich array of stories (of our past, present, and future) by which we store our life inside us – though some of us seem to have better access to it, and more skill in telling it, than others. As obvious (and delicious) as this insight is, however, it has an unsettling side.

From time to time, we find ourselves taking stock of the ways we present ourselves to the people we deal with in the course of a day. For some, such stock-taking is a regular occurrence; for others, rare. For some it is undertaken only with great courage and effort; for others, as naturally as thinking or breathing. Naturally or not, it can stimulate a strange brand of disorientation, indeed embarrassment, because it brings us face-to-face with the protean – even chameleon – nature of our 'self.' What we realize in such experiences (when we ask for 'the real me to please stand up') is that our story refuses to come out quite the same way twice. As was the case for Citizen Kane of movie fame, it is susceptible to a variety of versions. Our life, it turns out, is not one story but many, a plethora of stories in fact, both stories within us and stories we are, in turn, within. As we proceed to explore this multiplicity, we need to be clear about the question that is at stake between the lines: Are these numberless stories swirling about within us just so many variations on the same basic story, or are they the sign that our soul is in fact 'split'? Is such variety the exception, in other words, or the rule? When sociologist Peter Berger says 'we have as many lives as we have points of view' (1963, 57), ought we to be alarmed or accept the situation as an inevitable, indeed normal, fact of life? Where does the spice of life end and pathology begin?

A version and a point of view are inseparable. A version, says Webster, is 'an account or description from a particular point of view, especially as contrasted with another account.' Matthew's version of the story of Jesus is thus rooted in Matthew's point of view, Mark's in Mark's point of view, and so on. Indeed, we can never know anything of the historical Jesus but a version – a fact that, though obvious, has caused the spilling of considerable ink, not to mention blood. In the same way, though, 'we can never know anything but a version of ourselves' (Polonoff, 1987, 47). Sometimes these versions collude with each other; sometimes they collide. Sometimes they complement each other; sometimes they compete. Some versions will cover other versions; some will contradict them. Furthermore, versions can be either official or unofficial, sanitized or sensational, overrated, underrated, or X-rated. Undoubtedly many variables are at work in determining which version, or combination of versions, will hold sway in the telling of a given summary or segment of our story, whether to ourselves or others. These can be grouped according to the following categories: form and content, context and medium, motivation and origin. In the remainder of this section I shall be considering what each category entails, looking at the first four briefly and the last two in greater depth. Though much of what I say applies to the level of expression or to the storying we do inside-out, toward the end I shall try to illustrate how it applies to the level of experience as well, to how these variables and versions interact in the *inner* storying in which we are continually involved.

Form and Content, Context and Medium

Form

Each version reflects its unique way of plotting me, of selecting and sequencing the events of my life, and of tracing my path from a re-membered past through an experienced present to an anticipated future. As we saw in looking at the difference between 'good days' and 'bad days,' each is a particular perception of what has been and projection of what might be. It represents a judgment concerning what is the main plot of my life and what are merely subplots, concerning what is the whole story and what are merely chapters. Each gives a clue to the total story-world that I am. Each has its way of characterizing me, of casting me in the middle of my story, and of depicting my development from beginning to end. Each includes in it, or features the roles played by, a particular range of characters besides myself, such as lovers, friends, colleagues, and children. Certain versions of my life story are untellable, that is, without telling the story of my mother, my mentor, or my closest friend.

Also, each version brings out its unique set of themes (Csikszentmihalyi and Beattie, 1979; Kaufman, 1987), features its own kind of coherence, and possesses its own immune system preventing it from contamination by other versions. Hence, we would expect a measure of competition between them, especially when we include genre in our list of variables. In other words, some versions of part or all of my life-story may be essentially in the tragic genre, others in the comic genre, and so forth. 'While one part of me knows the soul goes to death in tragedy,' Hillman writes, 'another is living a picaresque fantasy, and a third engaged in the heroic comedy of improvement' (1989, 81). Finally, each version is an embodied activity and not a cerebral one only. It is shown and not merely told (Schafer, 1980, 34), lived and not merely relayed. It is fleshed out in countless aspects of my engagement with the world – my decisions, mannerisms, associations, vocabulary – and reflected in a particular configuration of people, possessions, and pastimes with which I fill my world, including clothes, cars, clubs, colours, objets d'art, hobbies, and the like.

Content

Each version I tell will vary according to the scope of the events I select to include within it. It could be a version of my past primarily or of my future: a version of what I have done or would like to do, or some mixture of both. It could be a summary of my life-story as a whole, or only a segment thereof: a short story or long. It could be a version of one particular chapter, such as my college years, my first marriage, or my brief career as a New York cabbie. Or it could be of one ongoing subplot, such as the ups and downs of my life as an allergy sufferer, a cyclist, a blond, or a man. Or it could be of merely one isolated episode, like the time I was mistakenly arrested for shoplifting, or the time I outran my best friend in the hundred-metre dash. Indeed, I have as many such episodes as there are categories to catalogue them by or topics to file them by. For example, I have a collection of 'car breakdown' stories, of 'being stopped by the police' stories, of 'strange things that happened to me in hospitals' stories, and so on. The degree the versions of these episodes vary from one telling to the next will naturally depend, in part at least, on how much I have polished or 'doctored' them over the years. This in turn may depend on how central the episodes seem to be to my self-understanding. The more central, and the more I like or need to tell them – the more they are 'signature' stories, we might say – then the more consistent my rendering of them may be and the less negotiable they are in both form and content.

Context

Each version I tell will vary according to the setting I find myself in. The issue of context is related to that of audience; it has to do with the culture or climate in which my storytelling is done. Some contexts elicit some of my stories more than they do others. That is to say, some stories have more currency in some contexts than they do in others. Thus I tend to reserve my war stories for the lads at the Legion, my hockey stories for the locker room, my college stories for the annual reunion, and my religious stories for the folks at the church. But there is another side to this.

Around the water cooler at the office, I package the anecdotes that I choose to relate in ways – and with words – that honour the fact that I am, after all, at work, and that my listeners, though 'friends,' are fellow employees. Thus, if I am too personal to the wrong ears, then 'word could get around' and my position within the organization, without my realizing it, could become less favourable than before. In other words, different contexts both elicit *and inhibit* the telling of different stories, or of the same stories in different ways. This amounts to a 'natural selection' of storytelling, though the selection involved is no less innocent than are stories in general. The proportion of stories I can tell to those I must keep to myself determines profoundly the scope and direction of my self-creation. Context impacts on the stories I am.

In a closely knit community, for example, where 'everyone knows everyone's business,' I learn to be alert in my self-telling to the impressions people have formed of who I am – past, present, and future. I learn to be wary of the 'storyotypes' they are imposing upon me, my friends, and my family, for they know me both well and *too* well. As I discover that they have thus storied me into a corner, so tightly in fact that my self-creation is curtailed, I may feel that 'I just can't wait to get away' – away to a context where, story-wise, I can start afresh. The exploration of such a possibility represents, of course, an entire agenda for research in social psychology. It would require research into the differences between urban, suburban, and rural societies – or between familiar contexts and foreign ones generally – with respect to the role of mobility and anonymity in the reconstruction of ourselves and our relationships: research regarding the poetics of both self-creation and social interaction.

Medium

We have known for some time that oral communication can be significantly different from literal communication in both content and form (cf. Olson and Torrance, 1991). Naturally, therefore, writing some segment or summary of my life-story can be expected to lead to a different version than will speaking it. Similarly, writing it for myself in a diary will issue in a different version than will submitting it to a professor as part of an assignment. Publishing it for all and sundry to read in a formal autobiography will issue in another version again. This brings us back to the question of context, and of audience. In so far as the medium is the message, these differences are vital. Though I shall return to them in the following chapter, further research into the life-as-story metaphor needs to weigh them carefully. Ultimately, such research is beyond my mandate here, which I see less as detailing every implication of the metaphor than simply as giving it a formal introduction into the discussion of learning.

Motivation

That versions vary with respect to audience is one of a number of variables concerning motivation. By what motivates us to recount a certain version – I mean, what triggers that version to come forward on a given occasion? This variable is more difficult to identify than the others I have just covered because the process whereby one version is triggered as opposed to another has a basis in not only the conscious realm but presumably the unconscious as well – though tracing what transpires on the boundary between the two is in part what this book is about. Under motivation, I want to talk about the following: agenda, audience, mood, and the influence of other stories.

Agenda

Clearly, I have as many versions of my story to tell as I have agendas
for telling it. We got a good sense of this in reviewing the ways in
which story in general both instructs and delights. For instance, I tell
my stories to introduce myself to others and to inform them about who
I am, where I have come from, and where I am going. I tell my stories
to impress others as well, to puff myself up, or to portray myself as
more interesting, intelligent, or respectable than I might otherwise see
myself. I may even be said to tell my stories in order to 'negotiate a lifetime,' as Virginia Tarman puts it in her analysis of the 'yarning' at
which the elderly are often skilled as they vie for status in each other's
eyes (1988). Indeed, so powerful can this agenda sometimes be that I
may find myself engaging in certain activities not so much because they
are enjoyable or meaningful in themselves as because of the story
potential I hope to derive from them after the fact. Thus, I may take up
sky-diving or travel around the world or even go off to war, less out of
interest or altruism than so that I can have something amazing with
which to delight my grandchildren, regale my colleagues, impress my
friends, or, in my golden years, amuse myself.

Much of our everyday storytelling, that is, comes under the category
of the subtle art of 'impression management,' (Goffman, 1959, 208f).
This is evident in social situations – say, parties – where I find myself
trotting out that peculiar stable of time-worn tales from which, across
the years, I have managed to get much mileage; stories that, time and
again, have 'worked' for me; that, I like to think, set me apart; that
give me currency in the economy of casual chat, increasing my stock
in others' eyes and providing me some means of controlling the stories
they are sure to read into me from outside-in. From time to time, of
course, I tell these same stories with no apparent point at all except to
fill up the time.

I can also tell my stories in order to teach or encourage, to persuade
or inspire, or, as a parent or teacher, to pass on my heritage, my
culture, or my particular family's lore. I can tell them to disclose
myself, to develop relationships, and to tighten the ties that bind me
to others. I can tell them to pro-fess and to con-fess, to plead and to
please, to sort myself out and to hear my own voice, thereby to feel I
have some power, some substance, some author-ity over my life. I tell
them to brag, to proselytize, to sell, or simply to set the record
straight. I tell my stories to fish for information, in the hope that by

revealing this tidbit I shall get that in return, or to test the waters to see if more of my story will be safe to tell later on. I tell them both to open discussion up and to shut it down, both to draw others close to me and to keep them at bay, both to gain their trust and to throw them off track, both to achieve intimacy and to assert my individuality. I can also tell them to deceive – both others and, on occasion, myself. Indeed, in telling some summary or segment of my personal story, I may be trying, consciously or not, to accomplish an array of agendas at once: to justify myself, to mystify others, or to defy the powers that be; to conceal or to reveal; to break down walls or to build them up; to vent my fears, to air my frustrations, or to give myself hope.

Audience

Just as no novelist can afford to ignore the tastes of her potential readership in planning the content and tone of her tale, so is how I tell myself always determined in part by the someone to whom I do my telling. The more sensitive I am to my audience – to their vocabulary, interests, attention span, and mood – the better the storyteller I am apt to be. Gauging my audience is as important in everyday interaction as it is in formal communication, whether it be an audience outside myself or one I have internalized within, i.e., my inner or 'true' self, my father, or some larger generalized 'other,' such as society or God, which I fancy to be the silent auditor of all my inner chatter. My story changes (however slightly) with each person before whom I find myself on stage, whether fellow party-ers, gentle therapists, admiring students, ascended saints, or strangers on trains. The degree of intimacy already established between us, of shared story we enjoy, of common background: my awareness of all this affects the tone with which I pitch my words, the choice of those words themselves, the themes I stress, the conflicts I emphasize, and the events and information I include or withhold. For instance, if I am seated before an interview board in the course of applying for a job, then I shall probably tell my story so as to convince my listeners that having this position is the culmination of all my dreams, and that every aspect of my life thus far has been preparing me admirably for it. If I am wooing a potential lover, then I shall portray my story as that of the poet, the jock, or the rogue – whichever I believe will achieve my heart's desire. If I am lecturing my children on the importance of being obedient, then I shall be careful to recite the tale of my life 'when *I* was your age' in such a way as to emphasize only those episodes that will support my case. And so the story goes.

Mood

The version I relate of any given summary or segment of my life-story, the plot-line I employ, and the way I characterize myself, depends in part on my mood at the time. Mood, however, is an obscure sort of trigger. No doubt the roots of moods are largely biochemical, based on fluctuations within a total system whose balance is affected by digestion or disease and is tied to time of day, time of month, or time of life (adolescence, menopause, senescence). But the roots of our moods may be partly poetic as well.[6] Thus, I submit, not only may versions be prompted by moods but so may moods be prompted by versions.

Most of us have experienced being in a wonderful mood one minute, only to find ourselves sliding into another, less happy mood the next. What is the reason for the change? Perhaps it is prompted by a comment made by my partner in casual conversation, by the receipt of disturbing information, by an otherwise innocuous event, or by a stray thought that flits through my mind: anything that triggers another overall version of the story of my life than was in place a moment ago. Where before I had a sense of my story as, say, that of a winner, quite another version is triggered the instant I catch a glimpse of a crucifix around the neck of a fellow subway traveller. Instead of the story of a winner, it is that of a sinner, one that stimulates a corresponding sequencing of my life's events to stream rapidly past my mind's eye (corners cut, white lies told, good deeds undone) and a particular characterization of myself to hold sway (as backslidden, apostate, damned). We can only guess what version might be triggered by such delicate events as the sight of a flock of birds bursting up from a field, the glimpse of a yellowed photograph, the faint sound of a familiar tune, the mere mention of a long forgotten name, the smell of rotting leaves, or, as Proust discovered, the taste of a particular biscuit. Anything, at any time, can resurrect a particular period of my past or recall some poignant, prior chapter from the story of my life. I never know down what memory lane I shall suddenly be sent. But versions can be triggered by the larger and longer-lasting of my life's events as well: by an engagement, a promotion, a divorce – events powerful enough to keep uppermost in my heart, for quite some time, a particular version of who I am and what my story is about.

Other Stories

A change in the version of my own life-story can be triggered by that of someone else, whether mediated by the person himself – say, in conversation – or by a movie, newscast, or novel. Stories without elicit stories within, which leads to a familiar phenomenon: identifying with, getting drawn into – in a sense fitting myself into – another person's story. This takes us to the core of the connection between literature and life, close to the allure of story and to the ties that bind us together. It is as if the plot and characterization of that other person's story had an energy field around it that activates sympathetic vibrations with a comparable story-line within me. Or it could be the other way around. Though pure speculation, it is difficult to resist seeing the inner world of myself in terms of the inner world of an atom: rather than a fixed number of 'official' versions of 'the story of my life' (corresponding to the fixed 'things' we used to think electrons, protons, and neutrons were), perhaps I have within me an infinite array of 'virtual' versions of it – traces of it – that can come fleetingly into existence at any given time, only to return to the trembling chaos from which they first emerged.

Origin

With respect to origin, the version of my life-story that I entertain or tell can be expected to vary according to which of at least five different domains it originates in: the intrapersonal, the interpersonal, the impersonal, the institutional, and the ideological. Though the boundaries between these domains are far from fixed, I see the first three to be in a sub-group of their own because they pertain largely to my inner world. The last two, on the other hand, pertain more to my involvement in the outer world – that is, in the various *larger stories* within which my personal one can be seen to be embedded and which embrace it in a generally concentric fashion. For, to be sure, I do not story my life in a narrative vacuum. To one example of such stories I have already alluded: the couple story in terms of which two people inevitably 'characterize' and 'read' each other. Other examples are the family or clan story, the community story, the company or culture story. In thinking about any of these larger stories, though, it is important to bear in mind that they have at work in them their respective version of the same elements at work in personal ones – like plot, conflict, character, theme, point of view, and style – and can be analysed (though not without difficulty) in terms of the same range of levels as well: outside, inside, inside-out, and outside-in.

Intrapersonal Versions

These versions of my personal story originate principally *within* me. It is possible to have little sense of the range of points of view that dance around inside me but to operate on the assumption that my internal world is somehow indivisible. With maturity, however, and a greater capacity for self-awareness, I become more conscious of my several 'sides.' I recognize 'the grump' within me, for example, the one who can say nothing good about anyone – including myself – who sees the glass of life as half-empty at best, and whose day is perpetually the bad day we talked about in the previous chapter. Or I recognize 'the martyr,' whose version of the story of my life is one long tale of woe, of unending but unrequited service to others, of facing a world that does not care about me yet expects me to be at its beck and call. Or I see 'the fool,' whose version of my life is of a comedy of errors, a series of slip-ups, a gigantic joke, a song and dance full of sound and fury and signifying nothing. And so the list goes, including 'the saint,' 'the tyrant,' the scholar,' 'the good little boy,' 'the weirdo,' and so forth.

In the context of the theory of Psychosynthesis, each of these sides is a specific sub-personality with its own developmental history, its own emotional agenda, its own way of characterizing me and of storying, (sub)plotting, interpreting, and living my life as a whole. Each sub is 'attempting to fulfill its own aims, sometimes cooperating, but more often isolated or in a state of conflict' (Vargiu, 1978, 2). Whenever I talk to myself, the resulting cacophony of voices can be heard as a kind of conferencing among this cast of characters inside me. In the context of the theory of Transactional Analysis, the sides are split according to a different model again: 'parent,' 'adult,' and 'child.' Each of these is internalized within me and interacts with the other two – as well as with the parent, adult, and child in other people – according to a range of possible 'scripts' (Steiner, 1979). To the extent

I have been exposed to more celebrated theories still, such as those of Freud, Jung, or Adler, the version I choose to relate of the story of my life will reflect the particular way of plotting a life that these theories – these 'master narratives' – advocate (Schafer, 1992, 147ff; Hillman, 1975a, 130ff). Clearly, each has its version of my beginning, middle, and end: of how I have come to be the way I am, of where I am likely to go, and of what my story is and means.

Interpersonal Versions

These versions operate principally within me yet they have their roots in my relationships with others, whether parents, children, lovers, spouses, co-workers, acquaintances, or friends. That is, I always see myself, in part, through others' eyes. Each of the people whom I know, or who know me, hold a particular version of who I am – one of which I am never entirely unaware and which calls forth a special aspect of my personality. Part of how I see myself and thus how I act is bound up with how I think my mother sees me, for example, or my brother, my cousin, or my cat. Admittedly, though, all I ever really have is my version of their version of my life-story, only my perception of their perception, and never that version or perception itself. Moreover, part of how I see myself, how I read my own story, is tied to what I perceive is the version of it held not by mother or brother individually, but by my family as a whole. I may have internalized the belief, that is, that the official version my family has had of me over the years is that of the troublemaker, the peacemaker, the *wunderkind,* or the dunce, and so the story I tell about myself always reflects that version. Of course, it may not be the version my family has of me at all (if my family, collectively, has any version of *any* of its members), but that does not matter. It is a matter of perspective. If a particular version is the official version I *think* my family has of my story – or that any group of people to whom I am connected has of it – then that version will shape how I tell the story myself. It will be in the mix of versions with which my inner world is filled and by which the shape of my outer life is influenced.

Impersonal Versions

These are related to interpersonal versions, yet considering them moves us closer to the 'fictive roots' of everyday life (Rogers, 1991,

209). An impersonal version of my story originates in one or another of the many generalized roles that I enact in my life, depending on my engagements, associations, and activities. These include student, tourist, friend, doctor, lawyer, citizen, or consumer. Central to each is a particular version of my life-story, some special way of plotting my life and characterizing myself of which on some level I am always mindful. There is, for example, the version of my story that is related to my role as someone's employee. This version will be elicited at professional development conferences, or while reading a news article on labour legislation, or in talking with a counsellor at the employment office. Many impersonal versions are not so much elicited by specific situations, however, as they are sustained by myself on a steady basis. If my primary professional role is that of counsellor, then in plotting my life and characterizing myself, to both myself and others, it is possible that I will regularly relay – and hold most centrally in my self-consciousness – that version of the story of my life entitled 'Me, The Counsellor.' No matter who my audience, I will tell my story in such a way as to emphasize those childhood experiences that demonstrate my obvious early talent for this important work, and to single out those features of my previous work, education, and relationships that have helped prepare me for serving others. In the extreme, I may be said to be operating with not merely a counsellor *version* but a counsellor *complex*. If, after being fired from my position and banned from my profession, I persist in telling the counsellor version when asked to identify myself, then I am clearly overidentifying, investing unwarranted energy into propping up a version of my life-story that no longer applies to my actual situation.

Institutional Versions

Throughout my life I am connected with, conditioned by, indeed *created* by, a wide range of institutions. Foremost among these, of course, is the particular family in which I have been brought up. Whatever else it may be, my family is a story. More specifically, it is a *collection* of stories – however differently compiled and told by different family members – through which each of us sees ourselves, interprets others, and makes sense of our world. It is a repertoire of 'forms of self-telling' by which we each transform our existence into experience. 'When we talk about family,' writes author Thomas Moore, 'we are talking about the characters and themes that have woven together to form our identities.' The family, 'which seems so concrete,' he says (in his plea for 'an application of poetics to everyday life'), 'is always an imaginal entity' (1992, xix, 29, 32).

Beyond my family, I am also created by the communities I have lived in, the companies I have worked for, the schools I have attended, and the various organizations with which I have been affiliated – whether professional or recreational, political or religious. Each of these institutions, or structures, has not only its own 'culture,' as it is fashionable now to call it, but also, like my family, its own story – with a beginning (the past), a middle (the present), and an end (the future). Whatever my actual job, for example, I am a character in the *company* story: if I play my part well I can expect a gold watch when I reach 'the end.' As sociologist David Flynn argues in his analysis of the concept of community, though, 'community-as-story is more than the culture of the community. The story orders the culture, draws it together, wraps it in meaning' (1991, 24). Naturally, the story of the community I live in (the neighbourhood, town, or city) is a far larger story than my personal one, yet, like my personal one, it is peopled with characters, loaded with subplots, riddled with conflicts, informed by themes, and possessed of a certain atmosphere and a particular view of time – knowledge of all of which is essential for my successful membership in it (Zemke, 1990; Owen, 1987, 11–41). After all, 'those who do not know our narratives do not participate in the same world we do' (McGuire, 1990, 222). Having said this, however, it is perfectly possible (deflating though it be to my ego to admit it) that the story of that community – or indeed of any institution I am involved in (except my family) – can be recounted with no reference to my personal story at all. For I may be at most only a minor character within it and my personal fortunes only the most inconsequential of subplots.

We can think of all such structures and their stories as being nested inside of one another in a roughly concentric manner: the family story within the clan story within the city story within the nation story, and so on. How each one of them unfolds, therefore, is bound to affect the unfolding of the others, and ultimately of my own. For example, a certain event in the national story, like an earthquake or depression, revolution or drought, is likely to have a huge impact on my personal one, determining not just which events will most stand out in the middle of it and but what I actually *make* of them too – that is, in terms of what genres, themes, conflicts, and morality I interpret or construct them. Accordingly, my situation may be similar to that

described by historian Ronald Blythe regarding the life of one of the
seniors whose reminiscences he took pains to record. 'The War,' he
writes of this man, 'remains the moral pivot of all his experience,
attitudes and dreams, and the older he gets, the more the trenches call'
(1980, 132). Put another way, how the national story unfolds (within,
of course, the story of civilization as a whole) determines how the
stories of countless smaller institutions within it unfold as well – bu-
reaucratically, financially, and so on. However, that the plot development of lesser institutions is dependent on that of larger ones can
occasionally have an odd twist.

In times of 'national emergency,' for example, particularly when my
nation is of superpower status, its fate can be intimately yet uncom-
fortably connected to whatever its leader happens to decide in relation
to another leader: to invade or not to invade, to bomb or not to bomb.
Thus, how each of these leaders' *personal* stories unfolds powerfully
determines how their *national* stories unfold as well – as well as does
how the story of the relationship between them unfolds, or, more to
the point, how they each perceive that story to have unfolded in the
past and to need to unfold in the future. It determines the possibilities
that are open for the self-creation both of the institutions and, ultimately, the individuals within them, not to mention of countless other
institutions and individuals well beyond their respective borders. In
this manner, my own life-story is disturbingly contingent on and lived
within the life-story of my leader, just as a child's story is contingent
on and lived (as a subplot) within its parents.'[7] If, during the drive to
work, for instance, the Minister of Finance happens to hear a tune on
the radio that reminds him of the loose ends of his painful first marriage, then the unusually impassioned speech he thus goes on to
deliver to his fellow parliamentarians, as well as the vote eventually
taken and the policy thus put in place, may result in economic misery
for me and millions of my fellow taxpayers, throwing us all into a
tragic new chapter in the story of our land. Similarly, a trigger-happy
President dabbling in brinkmanship on a bad hair day could have a
rather explosive impact on our collective self-creation. We are all at
her mercy, her sanity.

Once again then, where my story begins and others' end is scarcely
clear. The central point, though, is that in so far as I am a character
within any institution, great or small, then its story will inevitably
stimulate a particular version of my own – my life as a Randall, my
life with IBM, my life in Toronto, my life as an alumnus of Acme

University, my life as a Buddhist, and so on. However, institutions do not exist unto themselves. Not only are they nested within larger institutions in turn, but they are each the vehicle of various ideologies, which leads to the last family of versions of 'the story of my life.'

Ideological Versions

These versions of my story are the ways I plot my life and characterize myself because of my exposure or commitment to particular ideologies. Ideology, one scholar reminds us, 'permeates the very core of personhood' (Sampson, 1989, 13). How it does this is intriguing to trace.

An ideology can be defined as 'the body of doctrine, myth, symbol, etc., of a social movement, institution, class, or large group' (*Random House Dictionary*). Naturally, each ideology also has a story of its own in so far as it is embodied in various institutions, each with its own unique history, its own remembered beginning, experienced middle, and projected end, as chronicled by its various exponents. But an ideology has a story in a deeper sense as well, in so far as it implies an interpretation of history as a whole – of 'the world's story' (Hall, 1982). Obvious examples are capitalism, communism, Christianity, Hinduism, and other of the world's major creeds, including, as it were, science-ism. As we have seen, both science and religion are inherently storying movements. They situate me within the world by telling me stories about what kind of world it is, where it has come from, and what will happen to it: *once upon a time there was ...* a Garden, a void, a singularity, or a Big Bang. But ideologies come in more diffuse varieties as well, less easily identified in terms of the specific institutions in which they might be incarnated. Here we can think of atheism or humanism, chauvinism, sexism, or militarism. Indeed, any philosophy or class or culture, any gender or race even, certainly any political party, conveys an ideology, however difficult to identify, inasmuch as it carries with it its own point of view on 'life, the universe, and everything': its own implicit doctrines and myths, symbols, traditions, and stories.

In turn, these doctrines and stories construct the specific stories that are media-ted to us by 'The News,' with different ideologies influencing how different media construct for us the events of the day; how they decide what is 'important,' what 'makes' the news, and what is screened out. Thus, the *Globe* follows this news in this way; the *Sun* follows that news in that; while the *Star* fails to follow either – and the tabloids are simply on another planet! In the same way, item by item, CBS tells us one world-story, CBC another, and CNN another still – a point that leads us to wonder what happens to items that are *not* told, not followed, that make no news whatsoever, that get into no world-story at all. 'What is "the news"?,' asks one writer, and 'what are "real events"? How is it that the story of the plane hijacked in Costa Rica is news, but the one about Johnny [bringing home] the frog is not?' Perhaps, he muses, 'we have been deluded as to what the "real dramas of history" are' (Berman, 1986, 270). The 'real dramas of history,' we may take from this, are ideologically determined.

It is possible, of course, that I can be exposed or committed to a number of ideologies at once, some more explicit and more aggressive than others in their prescription of guidelines – 'master narratives' – for how to plot my life and my world, to character-ize myself in the midst of that world, and to identify and interpret the key conflicts being fought out within it. For example, I might be a Marxist Christian with strong feminist leanings. If so, we would expect such a complex perspective to be reflected in an equally complex version of my life-story – depending, of course, on my audience. By virtue of the Marxist aspect of that version, I shall relate my story as that of someone born a member of the bourgeoisie into a world embroiled in a struggle between the classes, yet who awaits the dawn of a classless society. In telling my story, I shall emphasize those experiences in my life that illustrate the process of progressive political enlightenment that Marxism prescribes. By virtue of the Christian aspect of that version, I shall relate my story as that of someone born a sinner into a world torn by the struggle between Good and Evil, yet who is actively seeking God's promised Kingdom of Peace and Shalom. In telling my story, I shall emphasize those experiences that prove my pilgrimage from darkness to light in the manner Christianity admonishes. In turn, by virtue of the feminist aspect of that version, I shall relate my story as that of someone born privileged, and male, into a world oppressed by a patriarchal system, yet who is participating in the fashioning of a new age in which women and men share power equitably in a climate of mutual respect. In telling my story, I shall emphasize those experiences that reveal my long, slow struggle to have my consciousness raised until it trembles at last with the passion for justice that feminism espouses.

The three versions of my life-story that these ideologies inspire do not of course have to compete with each other in a violent way. However, each ideology by itself obviously contains a spectrum of perspectives – from reactionary to liberal to radical – that may make rather rare the kind of compatibility I have envisioned here. For instance, armed with a fundamentalist Christian viewpoint (which impels me to manipulate each person I meet into storying the world my way and my way alone), I may have a distinct bias in favour only of white Anglo-Saxon Protestant males, and so find myself in sharp conflict with a militant feminist viewpoint – which in turn may deem all males as enemies by definition, including even Marxist ones, and all present social and economic institutions, because of their patriarchal construction, as beyond redemption. The point is that within any given ideology there will naturally be a variety of sub-stories at work, stories of the world as a whole, according to which I shall be led to plot my life and characterize myself in particular and not necessarily complementary ways.

In short, each ideology I subscribe to carries with it an accompanying self-concept. Each world-view or world-story is an implicit self-story, while each self-story is an implicit world-story in turn. Simply put, somewhere in the story I tell myself about who I am (past, present, and future) must be an account of what my world is as well. More than this, how I play the part I see myself to have within the world-story helps determine how *its* plot goes as well: what twists it takes, what themes it traces, whether it unrolls with business as usual or is kicked to pieces. In this rudimentary manner, the personal is always the political; individual change is necessarily social change.

The Variety of Versions Interacting Inside

I want now to use the foregoing to continue probing the complexity of 'the story of my life.' I do this, however, not by considering all of the variables catalogued above (form, content, etc.) but by concentrating on origin. I want to speculate on how a variety of versions of my life-story – from different domains – might actually interact with one another to produce the peculiar blend of story-lines that constitute my identity as a person and thus 'load' the process of my self-creation in a particular direction.

Most of the time, I am inclined to think that who I am is simply who I am. Unless I am troubled by a particular situation or relationship, that is, there will seem to me to be little of the inner narrative complexity we have been hypothesizing so keenly so far. I am simply

me, I like to think – end of story. But this 'me-story' is not as straightforward an entity as it appears. It is possible to see it as nested within
a set of larger stories still.

Let us imagine a situation in which the me-story is tied to the bigger
story of a particular profession – for the sake of argument, one of
which I happen to be a member: the ministry. Although probable that
as a minister I am going to be a key character in the (institutional)
story of a particular congregation, let us focus on the role (impersonal)
of ministers in general. Ministers in general are seen as a certain sort
of people. Much lore has accumulated around them, as a group, concerning numerous aspects of their lives: the vows they are thought to
take, the training they are supposed to receive, the paragon of virtue
they are expected to be, the heritage of piety and power in which they
are seen to be rooted, the proximity to the Divine mystery and the
insight into the Divine mind they are perceived to enjoy, the habits
and opinions they are deemed to hold, the lives they are reckoned to
live, the people they are considered likely to marry, the clothes they
are thought to prefer, the platitudes they are assumed to intone, the
sensitivity and availability they are considered to demonstrate, upon
demand, in the face of human need. And so the story goes. There is
an overall 'minister-story,' that is, which can be told without reference
to the me-story at all: a 'storyotype' of the highest order. Rightly or
wrongly, 'everybody knows' what this minister story involves; hence
the popularity of clergy as stock characters in movies, novels, and
jokes, as well as in commercial advertisements, where they are usually
characterized 'flatly' as gentle, nice, and kind, but for the most part
insipid, ineffectual, and irrelevant. Not only will this minister-story
shape and mis-shape – in short, plot – other people's telling of the me-
story (should they care to deal with that story at all) but it will conceivably affect my own telling of the me-story too. It will result in a
'minister's version' of the me-story within my own self-concept. In
either case, in others' tellings or my own, *how* the minister story
shapes the me-story will certainly vary; *that* it will, is without question.

In addition to being a member of a particular profession, however,
I am also a male. Just as there is a minister-story floating in the air of
the culture, so there is a 'male-story.' However, given the number of
men in the culture compared to the number of ministers, the male-
story is not only much larger than the minister-story but also much
more powerful and pervasive, and for that reason more difficult to

articulate. It is the story of what men are and of what men do, of where men have come from and why they are here and where they are going. It is the story of what is involved and required in becoming and 'being' a man. It is the story, among other things, of relating to women, of wrestling with power, and of reconciling ourselves to death. Told from the point of a radical political consciousness, it has typically been a story more about war than peace, toughness than tenderness, control than compromise, individualism and competition and aggression than relationship and cooperation and compassion. It is an old, old story, of course, enshrined for better or worse, in one form of another, in every culture and age. People's sense of this male-story, however, will shape, mis-shape, structure – indeed plot – their telling both of the me-story and, in interesting ways, of the minister-story. How it will do this depends upon their actual encounters both with men and with ministers. Women's encounters with men will, by and large, be different from men's encounters with men. In any case, *how* the male-story shapes the me-story – as well as the minister story – will certainly vary; *that* it will shape it, is unquestionable.

So, the story of my life will be viewed both by others *and by me* not strictly on its own terms – not solely with respect to the specifics of my life, that is – but through the respective lenses of a number of other stories besides it. Such stories are bigger than the me-story on its own; they are the more general stories by which the me-story is encompassed and in which it is embedded. As such, they amount to the 'forms of self-telling' that 'reflect the prevailing theories about "possible lives" that are part of one's culture' (Bruner, 1987, 15–16). They include the story, therefore, not only of ministers or of men but also of Maritimers, say, or of the middle class, or of the entire human race – depending on the extent we want to go and the combinations we care to make in identifying 'one's culture.' If one's culture is the church, for instance, the form of one's self-telling will be affected in a distinctive way. And in a problematic way as well, in so far as in the church the story of ministers and the story of men have traditionally been combined: ministers, that is, are somehow not 'real men,' nor do real men become ministers (Dittes, 1985).

All of this serves to illustrate only how the various versions of the me-story are shaped by stories that are essentially outside of me. It does not illustrate how they are shaped by another series of stories that are inside of me as well, such as 'the mother's son–story,' which is an *inter*personal verstion told in terms of a relationship I have been

involved in since my birth, or the 'martyr-story,' which is an *intra*personal version told from the point of view of a particular sub-personality within me. Naturally, these outside and inside versions can be
expected to combine in countless ways. For example, given a particular
situation, we can envision aspects of the martyr version at the intra-
personal level converging with and being energized by the mother's
son version at the interpersonal level and the counsellor version at the
impersonal one, as well as the Christian version at the ideological level.
Or, 'the spoiled child' intrapersonal version may resonate with and gain
power from 'the consumer' impersonal version, with the 'capitalist'
ideological version, and so on. Indeed, the *blends* of versions would
seem as many as the *number*, and this whether these blends be complementary in nature, as I have depicted here, or competitive, as the case
can often be. The resulting permutations and combinations are probably
endless, which means, once more, that the story of my life is susceptible
to an endless number of tellings. It also means that, somehow, *all*
stories ultimately meet within me, that like anyone else I am the centre
of the literary universe. Within some corner of me, I can be drawn to
and identify with any story there is. As theologian Sallie TeSelle puts
it, 'any story is about ourselves' (1975b, 159).

As I have hinted, there are other variables that can be cited as
determinative of the version of my life-story that I trot out at a given
time. Besides obvious ones like the time of day I relate it, the state of
my digestion in doing so, my mood, or the developmental stage
through which I happen to be moving in my life as a whole, there is
also the intensity of my desire overall to communicate the 'real story'
of who I am. What is becoming quite clear, though, is that this 'real
story' is stubbornly elusive, that there may be no one 'authorized
version' of my story at all, no 'true story' of my life that is capable of
identification apart from one limited version of it after another. For
most of us, perhaps, one particular combination of these various
versions will stamp our overriding perspective on ourselves. We
could call this our 'dominant version.' How a dominant version gets
formed, how it is blended together from a convergence – or conversion – of the possible versions swarming about inside us, and how
one dominant version comes to be replaced by another: such questions psychologists and psychoanalysts are presumably best qualified
to wrestle with. I am not in a position to do so definitively here. After
all, it is the 'poetics' of the self more than the 'psychologics' (Kegan,
1982, 114) on which I am concentrated. In the next chapter, though,

I shall try to offer insight into the nature of this process of 're-story-ing our souls.'

Summary

Looking at life-story through the lenses of plot, character, and point of view leads us to an unusual but suggestive image. It is an image of ourselves as simultaneously narrator, protagonist, and reader of our own unfolding novel, poised in its middle, page by page, continually plotting ourselves and characterizing ourselves, telling and reading ourselves, as we manoeuvre our way through, and try to make sense of, the unending stream of the events of our lives. It is an image that tries to capture what transpires on the second and particularly the third levels of life-story: the levels of experience and expression. At its centre is the insight that our life does not merely happen to us but that, in part, we continually 'make it up,' 'make it into' something that is distinctively ours, 'make out of it' our own unique story. It is therefore a creative process, an aesthetic process, indeed a *poetic* process. In the next chapter I shall explore how this image can illuminate the poetics of learning in general.

But entertaining such an image, fascinating though it is to do, tends to stir up more questions than can be managed. Looking into the links between life and literature does this inevitably. Many issues are still outstanding, as we shall see in the next chapter. Besides the issue I have just considered, that of the multiple versions of my story swirling about within me, perhaps the central issue at this point concerns just how accurate is 'story' in the first place as a metaphor for an individual life.

Story can imply a single, complete unit, something bound neatly between two covers, a transportable tale that can be read or aired or told at any time. But if our life *is* a story, then it is many stories in one; moreover, this side of death, it is an unfinished story, an unfolding story, a story still in the composing, a work-in-progress concerning whose ultimate direction and kind we are hard-pressed to comment. As its narrator, protagonist, and reader all at once, we are squarely 'in the middest'; making it up as we go; living forward yet understanding backward; ceaselessly adjusting our sense of what sort of story it is, of where it is going, and where it has been; weaving now this 'accident' or 'mistake' and now that into what we think is the plot; playing now with this anticipated future or remembered past and now with that; trying to see now this causal connection between events and now that – wondering not only 'what next?', that is, but also 'why?' ... And all the while, our 'character' is being revealed and re-created by the exigencies of an unfolding 'plot' of which we ourselves are partly the author – a plot that, in turn, is continually being shaped by those of the many larger stories in which it is set.

Perhaps, then, it is the metaphor not of *story* that does justice to our experience as much as it is that of story-*ing*: not the noun as much as the verb, not the product as much as the process. Though it is difficult to imagine any of us not interested in how the plot of our story will turn out, nor undesirous to keep that story 'safe,' the bottom line is that we never know fully what that story is. The kind of story it is, is an ongoing mystery to us; discerning it, an adventure in itself. As Beckett says, we are poised on the 'threshold' of our story, never quite grasping its shape as a whole because so much of it is still untold. Furthermore, what *is* told can be retold in a virtual infinity of versions – which may be why we are drawn to stories in the first place. 'We read books,' writes Ursula Le Guin, 'to find out who we are.' Thus, 'a person who had never listened to nor read a tale or myth or parable or story, would remain ignorant of his own emotional and spiritual heights and depths, would not know quite fully what it is to be human' (1989b).

> III <

THE POETICS
OF LEARNING

No novelist or biographer can ever show us
such fine shades of feeling as those which
we could distinguish if we could contemplate
our own loves, our own ambition, our own
jealousy, our own happiness.

André Maurois, 'Biography as a Work of Art'

Story is living and dynamic. Stories exist
to be exchanged. They are the currency of
human growth.

Jean Houston, *The Search for the Beloved*

Introduction

Carl Jung once said that he viewed his psychiatric patients as 'separated from their stories.' On some level, perhaps we are all in the same situation: separated from our stories, disconnected from our own experience, in search of a soul. If so, then I submit that helping undo this dilemma, for both ourselves and others, is a challenge to which all of us are called. This makes all of us 'educators,' charged with the task of e-ducing each other more fully: with more of our existence assimilated as experience, more of our experience available for expression, and more awareness of the sources and powers of the impressions imposed on us by others.

Those of us who are also educators in a conventional sense deal in stories all the time. We use stories to instruct and stories to delight; we work within, are constrained by, and contribute to the unfolding stories of particular disciplines and institutions, courses and classes; and, intentionally or not, as motivators and mentors, we are involved in enabling individual learners to tell and retell the stories of their own lives (Connelly and Clandinin, 1990, 2). This means that besides being intellectual, political, and ethical, our vocation as educators – in either the conventional or general sense – is *poetic* in nature as well. The purpose of this final chapter, then, is to take the ideas I have been exploring about the poetics of learning and to push them as much as possible in a practical direction.

In the first section, 'The Autobiographical Imperative,' I consider the relationship between story and personal identity in light of the concept of autobiographical memory. I also view the boundary between childhood and adulthood in terms of Beckett's notion of the 'threshold' of story. In addition, in a sub-section entitled 'The Author- ity of Our Stories,' I raise the question of the relationship between self-creation and self-authoring, ponder why we so often squander the authorship of our lives, and point to what might empower us to take such authorship more fully into our hands.

In the second section, 'The Re-storying of Our Souls,' I consider the uniqueness of the stories of our lives; the novel as a genre appropriate to the complexity of those stories; and the question of how within a life, as within a novel, the one and the many converge. In the third section, 'The Novel-ty of Our Lives,' I place the spotlight on the dynamics involved in those turning-points in our personal development when we seem to undergo a dramatic transformation in the fundamental story by which we plot the events of our lives.

In the fourth section, 'The Stories We Leave Untold,' I consider the significance for the poetics of self-creation of such concepts as secrecy, forgetfulness, and self-deception. In the fifth section, 'The Range of Storying Styles,' I sketch the rough outlines of a theoretical schema that could account for the differences and similarities in the ways we story our lives. In the sixth and final section, I return to discussions in the first chapter and review the relationship between the idea of 'the story of my life' and that of 'the art of living.'

As I trust we have come to expect, the issues with which we are wrestling here are intricately intertwined. Trying to separate them puts a strain not only on the logic we bring to the task but on the language as well; hence the hyphenation in many of the titles used in this chapter, such as author-ity, re-storying, and novel-ty. There is a reason for this beyond what might be inferred, which is the desire to be catchy or cute. The central agenda of this book is the exploration of the links between literature and life. Such an exploration has few precedents.

Although we are accustomed to the use of psychological categories in analysing literature, it is not yet natural to reverse the process and use literary categories in analysing psychology and its inevitable subject: life (Hillman, 1975a, 140). To do so, a new vocabulary may be required, one whose words are double enough in meaning to do justice to the two contexts that beg to be bridged.

The Autobiographical Imperative

Throughout this book, I have advanced the view that in our dealings with others we 'read' into them, outside-in, a plausible story about their lives overall: past, present, and future. Close though they be to us, we 'storyotype' them (as they do us), however unconsciously and however wildly, and with them, if tacitly, their family, their background, their roots. This process is central to 'understanding' them. Without it, we have no working hypothesis with which to read their actions and reactions, divine their 'nature,' judge their 'character,' or make sense of their words, ideas, and emotions in an intelligible (if always theoretical) context. The mark of our maturity, interpersonally speaking, is of course our openness to the continual revision of this initial impression of them – this story – in light of new information about them or from them, new observed behaviours, new insights into their various 'sides,' and, indeed, new insights into our own life-story and its apparent similarities to or differences from theirs. None the less, though our story of them so expands and deepens, representing them ever more broadly or accurately, it always remains an outside-in story, never the *whole* story nor the *inside* story not, to be certain, the *true* story.

In one place I called this impulse 'the biographical imperative.' In doing so, I was playing on a phrase first coined by Immanuel Kant. Kant talks about the 'categorical imperative' that impels all of us to adhere to a moral code, to a sense of right and wrong, no matter how widely our respective codes and senses may vary. If moral life is impossible without the categorical imperative, then social life is impossible without the biographical imperative. In this section, and effectively in this entire chapter, I shall be exploring how personal life – how our relationship with ourselves – is impossible (not to mention, inconceivable) without 'the *auto*-biographical imperative' (Eakin, 1985, 277).

The Basis of Personal Identity: Body, Memory, or Story?

With the thesis that I create myself through the continual reworking of the story of my life – that is, the complex web of interactions between its outside, inside, inside-out, and outside-in levels – I am assuming that, ultimately, my life is 'a biographic and not a biological datum' (Weintraub, 1975, 829). I am assuming 'a new way of defining personality and psychology,' in which 'to be a person is to have a story to tell' (Keen and Fox, 1973, 8–9), in which 'the self is always a narrative construction' (Schafer, 1992, xxvi). Thus, I am assuming a particular perspective on – though by no means a solution to – the traditional philosophical question of personal identity. This assumption is given expression by neuro-psychologist Oliver Sacks. 'We have, each of us,' he says, 'a life-story, an inner narrative – whose continuity, whose sense, is our lives. ... If we wish to know about a man, we ask "what is his story – his real, inmost story?" – for each of us *is* a biography, a story' (1985, 105).

The question of personal identity is one we rarely ask in everyday life, however much our involvements with each other presuppose an answer. Yet it is a valid question to ask. First, it is valid in cases of a legal nature, such as when person A is an impostor trying to pass himself off as person B; or, as we saw earlier, when person C claims he was 'not himself' in the course of committing a crime. Second, it is valid in cases of a medical-ethical nature, such as when person D is afflicted with Alzheimer's disease; or when person E is bumped on the head and becomes amnesiac with respect to all but her earliest or most practical memories; or when person F is a victim of multiple personality disorder; or when person G is technically dead for fifteen minutes on the operating table, only to be revived intact. Third, it has for centuries been a valid question in cases of a theological nature as well, such as when person H is resurrected on 'the other side' – not of the operation but of the funeral – and his whole life becomes the object of divine review. These examples may seem unusual, yet they are all possible cases in which we have to determine the criteria by which a particular person can be identified from one time to the next as indeed the *same* person he purports or is proposed to be.

As commonly constructed, says Terence Penelhum (1967), the question of personal identity receives one of two competing answers: one that sees the identity of a person as the identity of his body; and the other, as 'the set of memories which he has' (95). Penelhum himself resists the route of either-or. Instead, he insists on 'the irreducibly psychophysical nature of persons,' considering it 'absurd' for memory to be seen as 'the sole necessary or sufficient of identity.' In his view, 'both the bodily criterion and the memory criterion are ineluctable components of our concept of a person.' Thus, though he considers 'the bodily criterion ... more fundamental,' he insists that 'the memory criterion is, in its own way, indispensable because of the basic epistemological status of memory itself' (106).

Penelhum's reference to 'the basic epistemological status of memory itself' is echoed by Sidney Shoemaker (1975). Taking memory in its broadest sense, such that 'a man can be said to remember anything he knows,' Shoemaker concludes that 'if we have any knowledge at all, we have memory knowledge, unless knowledge is never retained' (273). Memory, for him, is thus the basis of knowledge. But if memory is the basis of knowledge, it is the basis of self-knowledge as well (Glover, 1988, 141). Thus, we can expect our sense of self to be impaired with any impairment of our memory. 'Life without memory,' writes Oliver Sacks, 'is no life at all' (1985, 23). Minus memory, we are 'stuck in a constantly changing meaningless moment,' he says in his discussion of Korsakov's Syndrome, 'reduced to a "Humean" being ... nothing but a bundle ... of different sensations, which succeed each other with an inconceivable rapidity' (30). Memories constitute 'the very basis of our personalities' (Benjamin, 1964, 171). As Ronald Blythe observes concerning memory loss and aging, 'not to be able to recall is in some instances not to be. Time has plucked from the brain ... the great codification of one's essential experiences' (1980, 137).

My own contribution to the question of personal identity is in sympathy with that of Penelhum, yet, with Sacks, Glover, and others, goes one step further. Beyond both my body and my memory is my story. I am who I am from one point in time to another because I have, or can tell, or can be said to live within, one continuous life-story. My story lives within, yet radiates around, my body. It is not confined to my body any more than a literary story is confined to the book in which we encounter it. We are caught up – both by it and in it: we are inside the story. It is larger than our life. Of my own unique world, it is the atmosphere, the air, the allure that I exude, and that can linger with others long after I go – like the 'morphic field' within which, according to scientist Rupert Sheldrake, each of us lives (1989, 197–8). In the words of one biographer, 'we all move through the world surrounded by an atmosphere that is unique to us and by which we

may be recognized as clearly as by our faces' (Malcolm, 1993, 94). My
story-world, with its unique atmosphere, is thus more than my body.
It both is embodied by and yet envelops my body. By the same token,
it is more than my memory, too, for it accommodates not merely my
sense of the past but also my anticipation of the future, not just my
'ruminescences' (Casey, 1987, 156–7) of what has been, but my fantasies (and fears) of what may be.

To play with the implications of this insight, let me consider a
question that a modern metaphysician might have to entertain: Could
a computer, as humanoid as we can imagine, ever be deemed, ever be
identified, as a 'person'? Asked such a question, I answer 'no.' Why?
Because a person is something who is, has, and can tell us her own
life-story. No story, no person. No matter how person-like a computer
is constructed, it cannot tell us its story, its unique *life*-story – at least
in the way a *real* person can tell it.

Borrowing from the story-world of *Star Trek*, let me christen our
hypothetical humanoid 'Data.' There is no question that Data has a
body, perfect though it be on the outside compared with a human one,
and flawless though it be, mechanically, on the inside. In the same
way, Data has a mind; that is, the ability to 'think,' in the basic sense
of analyse data, process information, solve problems, and evaluate
solutions – which processes s/he/it carries out impressively no doubt,
and which require the faculty of memory. Data has a memory as well.
He has the capacity to remember, in the basic sense of being able to
receive, sort, store, and retrieve information, to summon up pre-pro-
grammed rules for solving problems concerning it, and to evaluate
solutions to those problems by running a check on similar solutions in
the past. But there is more to memory than these complex, yet pro-
grammable, functions. Before we deal further with Data's status as a
person, then, let us look at the category of memory as such.

Autobiographical Memory

Memory. As advanced as we are in our study of human psychology,
we understand astonishingly little about so big a feature of everyday
life. The astonishingly brief list of *specific* (not general) things that most
of us can readily recall doing, saying, seeing, etc., from as recently as
a day ago drives home how mysterious the remembering process is.
As cognitive scientist Ulrich Neisser confesses, 'we have almost no
systematic knowledge about memory as it occurs in the course of

ordinary life' (Casey, 1987, ix). 'In short, the nature and structure of memory remains at the frontiers of research' (Schank, 1990, 119).

If we are to consider memory as the basis of personal identity, whether Data's or ours, then a few distinctions need forging between various kinds of memory, for memory is arguably far from one piece. We have memory for faces and names, for places and times; memory for facts and figures and the meanings of words; memory for a broad range of habitual tasks, social rituals, and private routines. Even our bodies have memory of a sort, retaining a knowledge, we are told, of traumas otherwise long forgotten, as well as of how to do things, often intentionally trained into them by sheer repetition – knowledge without which the lion's share of daily activities would be impossible to carry out. Hockey hero and author Ken Dryden calls this 'muscle memory.' Without a few crude distinctions, therefore, a tour of the mysterious house of memory might easily go astray. Fortunately, such distinctions abound.

One of the most common is between short-term memory and long-term memory. This distinction, however, concerns not so much kind of memory as it does degree, for any given kind of memory can be retained for either a short or long period. More helpful for our purposes here, perhaps, are distinctions such as Bertrand Russell has made between 'habit memory' and 'true memory,' or as Norman Malcolm has made between 'factual memory' and 'personal memory' (Shoemaker, 1967, 266). One of the most frequently cited distinctions in discussions of the topic has been advanced by Endel Tulving. It is between 'semantic memory' and 'episodic memory' (Campbell, 1986, 304ff). Through the former, which can be compared with Schank's 'general event memory' (1990, 122), we remember facts and figures, rules of thumb, various sorts of information: items learned at a particular point in the past but which, in order to recall in the present, it is not essential, and often not possible, to recall the actual events surrounding their initial learning. Episodic memory, however, 'is organized around a person's knowledge of his own identity' (Campbell, 1986, 303). Emerging 'in its rich, fully fledged form' only in adulthood, it is tied directly to events. Around those events it constructs what memory theorist Edward Casey (1987) calls 'a quasi-narrative structure.' Such memories, he says, 'seem to constitute a story or part of a story. A tale of sorts is told.' They 'have an identifiable beginning point; a certain development of motifs or themes then takes place; and there may even be a decisive conclusion' (43).

Things remembered episodically, then, cannot be recalled in the abstract, only by retelling their story. Remembering that red, orange, and yellow are the first three colours of the rainbow (semantic memory) does not entail recalling the particular day I was taught about ROY G BIV by Miss Prindle in third grade. Yet, remembering the haunting mix of red, orange, and yellow in that specific summer sky the evening I first made love (not, alas, in the third grade) ... that, ah, I remember it well. And what a story it makes.

Some episodic memories are thus more 'charged' than others (Glover, 1988, 142), both positively and negatively. Some, as we have seen, are more marketable than others, more tellable, and can be trotted out with great effect each time: 'signature stories' with which we tend (and like) to present ourselves to the world. Some, however, are hardly marketable at all. They are so painful or so impervious to interpretation that we have sealed them into the dark vault of the things we leave untold, from which, unexamined, they leak their peculiar poison into our system, silently sabotaging any efforts to fit them into the dominant story by which we understand our lives. Some episodic memories, of course, are more malleable than others, their form – and even content – more negotiable. They can be pitched and plotted however we like (within reason), depending on our audience, our agenda, and so forth. Some are more reliable than others, stubbornly durable in composition each time they are told, while others, we can one day find, are patently false: illusions under which we have laboured long but wrong; anecdotes we have invented holus-bolus, wittingly or (more often) not; memories we have borrowed from others but have been convinced are ours.

The line between semantic memory and episodic memory is in reality less sharp than Tulving's schema suggests. Episodic memories do not sit neatly on the shelves of our memory bank, like clean-edged nuggets of single past events. Very often, as Neisser (1986) argues, there is a transition from the latter to the former: 'The more airplane trips we take, the more we know about flying in general and the less we remember about any particular journey. Sometimes we actually forget all the separate occasions and retain only the invariant properties. More often, however, a few individual events remain accessible' (79). Such memories, however, 'do not fit comfortably on either side of Tulving's dichotomy: They are not purely episodic, but they seem to be.' So, between semantic memories and episodic memories, Neisser inserts a class of memories called *repisodic*. We can think of such memories as memories not of 'the thing I did' but of 'the *kind* of thing I *used* to do.' This means that 'they could equally well be called "representative" or "symbolic" memories. Freud's concept of "screen memory" is also relevant here: A screen memory seems to describe only a single and unimportant childhood episode but really represents something deeper. ... "flashbulb memories" are also repisodic in this sense: We remember the moment when we first heard that Kennedy had been shot because it links us to a historic occasion' (69).

A repisodic memory is to an episodic memory, then, as a summary section in a novel is to the individual scene that it introduces. Or as the 'once upon a time' of a story is to the 'one day' that hones in on the particular incident with which the story proper commences. Or as the 'I used to ...' is to the 'I recall the one time I ...' in everyday reminiscence. In each case, the former refers to the general, the habitual, the rule; the latter to the specific, the anomalous, the exception. I recall not so much the hundreds of 'uneventful' times I milked Old Bessie, that is, as the one weird time she kicked me in the teeth and took off loose down the lane – though telling about the latter loses a lot if the sense of all the normal milkings are not 'there' in the background, lending poignancy to my tale.

Echoing Neisser here is Schank (1983), for whom the memories that are retrievable tend to be only of those episodes in which we have been *failed* by our 'scripts' – not our life-scripts (Steiner, 1979) but our 'dentist's office script' and our 'restaurant script,' etc. Thus, as we have seen, 'the easiest things to remember are the unexpected' (1983, editor's note, 30). The more unusual, the more they conflict with the norm, the more we must tell them. Witness the fierceness with which we go about enlisting a listener, even a total stranger, to hear us out on the heels of some incredible event: 'You'll never guess what just happened to me! I have to tell you!' We remember, and must story, what we cannot forget.

Malcolm's concept of 'personal memory,' Tulving's of 'episodic memory,' and now Neisser's of 'repisodic memory' bring us to a kind of memory that is the focus of a growing circle of memory theorists: autobiographical memory. Autobiographical memory is a kind of super-memory. It is not one more specific kind of memory, added to the others on the list, but inclusive of *all* our memories. It is 'memory for a whole lifetime' (Rubin, 1986, 69). Furthermore, even our memories for ordinary skills, impersonal statistics, or general information are, after all, *our* memories, meaning that autobiographical memory is 'the sum of [our] knowledge of [our] own lives and as such is the basis for a concept of self' (69). Behind our every word or idea (no matter how abstract), behind our every emotion or act, behind our every gesture or facial expression, is the whole of our accumulated memories. And the older we grow, and the more complex our life-story becomes, then the *thicker* this mass of memories gets – 'possessing a depth not easily penetrable by the direct light of consciousness ... sedimented in layers ... and having historical depth' (Casey, 1987, 262ff).

Unfortunately, autobiographical memory 'is one of the least well-developed areas in the study of human memory' (Rubin, 1986, 25), presenting problems 'that memory theorists trying to explain most phenomena can often safely ignore' (69). Because it is memory for a whole lifetime, 'memories have much longer times than usual to change, distort, and be reconstructed.' Moreover, 'this long passage of time is confounded with the development of the rememberer, so that a college sophomore may be asked to recall an event encoded by a six-year-old' (69) – a point that forces us to consider autobiographical memory's peculiarly fictional dimension.

The Autobiographical Act: From Fact to Artifact

As we appreciate the strength of the links between self-knowledge and autobiographical memory (a large part, though not the whole, of the *inside* story), we can understand why literary critic Paul John Eakin speaks about 'the autobiographical *imperative*' (1985, 277). It is essential to our sense of self. Where for any reason our autobiographical memory is impaired, our personhood is impaired as well. We *need* an inner story, Glover says, (1988, 152), and we need to fit into that story as many of our actions and engagements, as many of our experiences and episodes, as we can. Indeed, 'the need to make our life coherent, to make a story out of it, is probably so basic that we are unaware of its importance' (Mancusco, 1986, 101).

This does not mean that we must actually *write* our story, in the sense of compose a formal autobiography. Few among us have the time or the talent – perhaps the temerity – to undertake such writing in an explicit form. Yet 'the autobiographical act,' Eakin argues, is universal. On paper or not, we are constantly composing ourselves, constantly reciting and rehearsing to ourselves who we are, where we have come from, where we might be going. This ongoing act is 'a mode of self-invention that is always practiced first in living and only eventually – sometimes – formalized in writing' (9). Thus, 'when it occurs,' it is 'a third and culminating phase in a history of self-consciousness that begins with the moment of language in early childhood and subsequently deepens in a second-level order of experience in childhood and adolescence in which the individual achieves a distinct and explicit consciousness of himself or herself as a self' (8).

When the autobiographical act *is* formalized, of course, its artificial aspect is all the more apparent. As we have seen, all manner of decisions must be made as to what to keep and what to cull, and how to construct what is kept. The result is a piece of literature. It is not 'the life' it may have set out to capture, but only, at best, a parable of it (TeSelle, 1975a, 145). As David Polonoff puts it, 'through the very process of exposition, the full story is subjected to narrative constraints, becoming something other than the stream of events that constitute the life as lived' (1987, 46). Of this process of poetic selection, scientist Lewis Thomas offers a whimsical description in his musings on the challenges he expects he would face in composing his own autobiography, understood as 'a linear account of one thing after another':

> In my own case this would run to over seventy years, one after the other, discounting maybe twenty-five of the seventy spent sleeping, leaving around forty-five to be dealt with. Even so, a lot of time to be covered if all the events were to be recalled and laid out.
>
> But discount again the portion of those 16,500 days, 264,000 waking hours, spent doing not much of anything – reading the papers, staring at blank sheets of paper, walking from one room to the next, speaking a great deal of small talk and listening to still more, waiting around for the next thing to happen, whatever. Delete all this as irrelevant, then line up what's left in the proper linear order without fudging. There you are with an autobiography, now relieved of an easy three-fourths of the time lived, leaving only eleven years, or 4,000 days, or 64,000 hours. Not much to remember, but still too much to write down.
>
> But now take out all the blurred memories, all the recollections you suspect may have been dressed up by your mind in your favor, leaving only the events you can't keep out of your head, the notions that keep leaping to the top of your mind, the ideas you're stuck with, the images that won't come unstuck, including the ones you'd just as soon do without. Edit these down sharply enough to reduce 64,000 hours to around thirty minutes, and there's your memoir. (1987, 127–8)

Eakin's views, buttressed by Thomas's, then, depart from the traditional treatment of memory as 'a convenient repository in which the past is preserved inviolate, ready for the inspection of retrospect at any future date' (5). This treatment of memory can be called *passivism* – 'in which remembering is reduced to a passive process of registering and storing incoming impressions' (Casey, 1987, 15). Such a view *seems* to be presupposed by the ground-breaking work of Wilder Penfield.

In the course of performing brain surgery, Penfield used an electrode to activate 'the sequential record of consciousness, a record that had been laid down during the patient's earlier experiences. The patient "re-lived" all that he had been aware of in that earlier period of time as in a moving-picture "flashback"' (Talbot, 1992, 12). Penfield thus concluded 'that everything we have ever experienced is recorded in our brain, from every stranger's face we have glanced at in a crowd to every spider web we gazed at as a child.' It is all there: 'our memory is a complete record of even the most mundane of our day-to-day experiences' (12).

That terms like 'consciousness' and 'aware of ' are used here, that 'experiences' is used and not 'events,' is critical. It means that Penfield's perspective on memory is not as passivist as it appears. He is telling us not about our outside story but about our inside story, in all its vastness. What is stimulatable is not the totality of the 'real events' of our existence – noticed or not, within our field of vision or without – but only of '*experienced* events' (Neisser, 1986, 75). The former is to the latter, after all, as 'real object' is to 'aesthetic object' (Chatman, 1978, 26–7); as 'empirical facts' are to 'artifacts' (Renza, 1980, 269). The views espoused by an Eakin lead us in the direction, then, of a more *activist* perception of memory, 'according to which memory involves the creative transformation of experience rather than its internalized reduplication in images or traces construed as copies' (Casey, 1987, 15). Where passivism is a representational theory of memory, activism is a constructivist one. In the former, individual memories are conceived as photographs; in the latter, as fictions.

Memory, that is, is not a recording of our *outside* story, but the pearl (however in the rough) that we fashion from our past on the *inside*. It is not about existence but about experience. It is a collection not of events but of stories (Schank, 1990, 16). We never simply take raw events and tuck them untouched inside our sense of self. We take only those events that, for whatever reason, we have attended to, that have caught our eye or ear, mind or heart, and that we have in that sense 'selected.' We then transform them according to some combination of plotting, characterization, and genre-ation, and so make them into experiences. Thus, we 'make them up.' This, says Eakin, quoting autobiographer William Maxwell, makes the faculty of memory 'really a form of story-telling that goes on continually in the mind and often changes with the telling' (1985, 6).

As André Maurois reminds us, memory 'is a great artist' (1956, 157). It is less a passive repository of the past than an active process in the present, an aesthetic, indeed poetic process. At its heart is the 'drive toward narration of the self' (Eakin, 1985, 6), the need and the desire to fashion a plausible story from the stuff of our lives. The autobiographical act, whether or not it ever results in an actual written product, is a *fictive* process, 'in that the autobiographer constantly tells "a" story rather than "the" story, and tells it "this" way rather than "that"' (Smith, 1987, 46). Thus, it is not just an act but an art: 'both an art of memory and an art of the imagination' (Eakin, 1985, 5–6). This 'fiction-making process' is 'a central constituent of the truth of any life as it is lived' (5).

The autobiographical imperative drives us not just in adulthood, though, but, however diffusely, from childhood on – just as the need to follow where a given novel is going comes upon us in our tentative reading of even its first few lines. 'To learn to speak,' says Ursula Le Guin, 'is to learn to tell a story' (1989a, 39). 'A human being is always already busy constructing life as a story' (Cupitt, 1991, 67). A curious yet powerful example of this is related by Sacks (1987) about a patient of his named Mr Thompson, a sufferer from Korsakov's Syndrome. Each day, Thompson would greet Sacks on the ward with a different story of who he was, and the story would change, pathetically, each time they met, even when only minutes had elapsed. The impairment of autobiographical memory in such a patient is so severe, Sacks concludes, that he 'must literally make himself (and his world) up every moment' (110). 'Deprived of continuity, of a quiet, continuous, inner narrative, he is driven to a sort of narrational frenzy – hence his ceaseless tales, his confabulations, his mythomania' (111). But in considering the stories we are, we can see that Thompson's compulsive fictionalizing is, once again, different from our own only in degree, not in kind. Indeed, we are all a bit like Scheherazade of *Thousand and One Nights* fame, 'who told tales to keep her life going' (Cupitt,. 1990, 67). There is an urgency behind our self-storying since nothing is for sure: 'the stories we can tell about our own lives ... are constantly threatening to break down or become incoherent. We have to keep on improvising, stitching and patching, amending our histories' (67).

I have one further thought on the fictional art-act of autobiographical memory. If memory is indispensable to *self*-knowledge, then it is not in a straightforward memory-of-fact manner, such as passivist theories suppose. Rather, I propose, it is in the same manner as it is indispensable to *story*-knowledge. Poised in the middle of a story (as we are poised in the middle of a life), our sense of the story as a whole – its themes, its conflicts, its characters and their fortunes, its atmosphere, its symbolic interconnectedness, its coherence, its meaning – is possible only because of our capacity to 'keep it all straight in our minds.' We can 'follow' it only because of our ability to grasp the significance of past developments in its plot in relation to both present ones and our projected anticipations of future ones as well (Forster, 1962, 88–9). Indeed, our 'journey through the book is a continuous process of such adjustments. We hold in our minds certain expectations, based on our memory of characters and events, but the expectations are continually modified, and the memories transformed as we pass through the text' (Selden, 1989, 120). This process and this transformation have their counterparts in the way we read our own lives. In the phrase of Edward Casey, 'the past develops'; like plot, it 'thickens' (1987, 275, 262–3).

Reading in general, no less than writing, is a demanding task, taxing not only our imagination but our memory as well. Yet it is entailed in understanding even the simplest narrative. Moreover, we do not always get it right. Failures of memory, as of imagination, account for widely varied readings of the same story by different readers. They also account for much *under*-reading of stories (Kermode, 1980, 84), and no doubt for much *mis*-reading as well, though there is seldom a downright wrong reading of a story any more than an utterly right one. Self-reading is much the same, which raises the question of 'truth' in self-understanding, a question I shall return to in subsequent sections. Before I return to the android Data, though, let me look at the variations in self-reading that may correspond to age.

The Threshold of Story

Children, we can acknowledge, are no less delighted by stories than adults are, and often much more so. As young as two years, at the dawn of 'the moment of language,' they 'appear to retrieve narrative structure in their efforts to comprehend all textual input' (Mancusco, 1986, 102). They are instructed by stories as well, learning about not only 'morals' but also the supposed connection between cause and effect that, as adults, we assume it essential to see. In her study of stories in thus facilitating a child's growth, researcher Gail Tompkins implies that the concern with 'the story of my life' overall may be continuous from a tender age on: 'A story, when a child is able to make symbolic use of it, can be a step toward personal discovery and mastery, the beginning of *that search for identity that continues in more sophisticated forms as children grow older*' (1982, 720; emphasis mine).

At a certain point in the 'search for identity,' however, many of us are driven to wrestle with the question of who we are on an especially conscious level – as if aware, in Cartesian terms, that *raccontio ergo sum*. We are pushed to consider not only our 'roots,' which is the story of our particular clan or culture, but also the story of our particular self (though curiosity concerning each is commonly mingled). We are so pushed because, on some level, we come to feel that identifying our story and understanding it – getting it out (that is, inside-out) and getting it straight – is essential to our survival, and to our sanity; that, in the end, all we really have *is* our story; that we live our lives in and through this story and it is ultimately who we are. More specifically, we come to feel that 'to live without a story is to be disconnected from our past and our future. Without a story we are bound to the immediacy of the moment, and we are forever losing our grip on the reality of our own identity with the passage of discrete moments' (Winquist, 1974, 103).

Our response to the autobiographical imperative can issue in a number of forms. While private reminiscence is the most obvious, ordinary conversation is one as well. There is no such thing as idle chatter. Much of it, as we have seen, is a complicated, agenda-laden process of telling stories: about ourselves, our neighbours, our world. This brings us back to gossip. Though it has an evident negative or destructive side, when it becomes 'talking against,' it has a positive side as well, an informative side, when it becomes 'talking about': about what is going on in the neighbourhood or – in the case of men, in their need for 'news' – about what is going on in the wider world (Tannen, 1990, 96–122). Either way, gossip can fill a natural and necessary function, binding us together in a community of concern – a function that the alternative, silence, might be hard-pressed to carry out.

Building on the basic need to converse, Pennebaker (1990) argues
that, at work in us all, is a basic 'urge to confess' (13). The search for
someone to listen to us, he says, really listen, rarely ends – especially
when our experience of the average listener is that they are so busy
'storyotyping' us, so keen on transforming us into characters in their
own life-story, that they are of little help in getting out our own.
Hence the continuing popularity of professional listeners: pastors and
priests, therapists and analysts, whomever we set aside in our midst,
and gladly pay, to hear us out. Hence also the enduring appeal of
reading – not only of biography and autobiography, as we might
expect, but of fiction as well. One result of reading is the implicit
validation of our own otherwise unechoed experiences. Thus we read
books to find out who we are. Not only reading, but clearly any kind
of writing (short of an actual autobiography) is also a way of responding to the autobiographical imperative. Recording dreams, writing
letters, composing poems, compiling résumés, keeping scrapbooks,
even just making lists of thing we have done or hope to do, can constitute ways of getting our story straight – ways open to us all.

Among such activities, tracking our thoughts and feelings through
a journal is one of the richest ways to answer the urge to confess –
though one that, to date, seems favoured by women more than men.
Such a project can become 'a fundamental project of self-creation' (Van
Daele, 1990, 251), a way of 'shaping words into one's life story' (158),
a means of 'giving birth to [one]self as a character in [one's] own life
story' (256). The journal becomes a place to keep our story safe, what
Anaïs Nin considered 'a safe word-shop for self-creation' (Friedman,
1988, 44). Though it still operates on the level of expression, it is as
close as possible to that of experience, to our inside story. As avid
journalers will attest, responding to the autobiographical imperative
by such a means can be profoundly spiritual in nature. In the words
of autobiographer Alfred Kazin, it is 'directly an effort to find salvation, to make one's experience come out right' (1981, 35). It is thus, we
could say, 'religious' – at least according to the broad, embraceable
definition put forward by novelist John Updike. Religious, he says, 'is
our persistence in feeling that our life is a story, with a pattern and a
moral and an inevitability' (1989, 239). Religious also, I would add, is
our persistence in feeling that our *world* is a story too.

As we have seen, the search for a self-story and a world-story are
intertwined. To entertain a theory on how our world hangs together
– past, present, and future – is, by implication, to entertain a theory on
how our life hangs together within it. The larger stories swirling about

in the world around us shape our self stories in turn. We soak in their plot-lines through our pores – their points of view, their conflicts, their morality, their modes of self-characterization, their themes, their atmosphere. The more extensive and intensive our need to 'pull it all in' – our self, our world – then the more philosophical, the more scientific, the more 'religious,' we may be deemed, even when we accept that no 'sacred masterplots' can tell the whole story. In this way the personal becomes the philosophical for us and the philosophical, the cosmological. The stronger the autobiographical imperative within us, then the bigger the picture we try to see: not a Grand Unified Theory (GUT) but a Grand Unified Story (GUS).

What can we say, though, about that mysterious point at which we awaken (if we do) to such a 'religious' awareness? What can we call that moment in time when we come alive to our story – or at least to our need for a *sense* of our story – the moment at which 'the autobiographical imperative' begins to be felt? Perhaps, borrowing from Beckett, we can call it 'the threshold of story.' The threshold of story, I submit, is that curious line separating the otherwise arbitrary concepts of 'adulthood' and 'childhood' – a line deemed discernible enough to warrant an entire field to study it: adult education. It is that point in our development when 'dawning in earnest' upon us is 'the startling and novel idea that [we] have a story' (Johnston, 1993, 1). It is a point that will obviously vary with each individual – though we can suppose it to coincide with the emergence of a sense of our ending, of our mortality: a sense that can hit us as early as adolescence or as late as never at all. It is the point when we begin to feel the weight of our own past piling up behind us, and the need to digest it, sort it out, make sense of it, and find a framework big enough to fit it all together. It is the point when we begin to see that our success in manoeuvring the path of our life depends on coming to grips with the story of our life – its main events, its plot and subplots, its principal themes, and the characterization of our selves it assumes; both its content and its form. It is the point when we begin to get a feel for the several stories of our life (outside, inside, etc.), of the gaps between them, and of the relationship between the many stories of our life and the one.

Back to Data

Autobiographical memory, we are seeing, is really a peculiar brand of fiction, what one psychologist calls 'faction' (Steele, 1986, 260). Furthermore, the 'auto' of autobiography is not some given, some once and for all centre of reference, but something we are continually reinventing (Eakin, 1988). Thus, from one telling to the next, our story is not the same, and neither are we. This feature of personal story would bother Data, if Data were inclined to be bothered, for 'he' would be firm on the question of *what* he is. (Note my refusal to say 'who.') The 'story' he would tell would be accurate to a T, but it would not be an especially good or engaging story, for it would be the story of events, not experiences. If anything, it would be an accounting of the *outside* story alone, for Data, I submit, would have no ordinary *inside*, no soul. It would clearly be 'the facts,' 'the truth' (at least of sorts), which means it would not be 'the lie of fiction' that Plato found so unsettling. None the less, Data's technically perfect reporting of the history of both his outer and even inner workings, however 'soft' his programmers might make them, could not have the gaps and holes, the vagaries and embellishments, the feelings and failings that constitute personal story for the rest of us – so interesting to hear yet so difficult to tell the same way each time. Memory-wise, Data is a passivist *par excellence*. Thus, his story would be too true to be good, and thus too good (too correct) to be human – rather like the 'idiot savant' whose recall of the phenomena of his life, though accurate, is sadly lacking in a sense of his self in their midst (Treffert, 1989, 30ff).

Data, of course, is not the real problem. The real problem is that intimidating character reputedly on some drawing boards at present – perhaps even Schank's – that can feel; that can make friends, counsel them, and tell them jokes (which may be the same as counsel them); a computer that can tell stories and even – which is so reassuring – carry on a fight. I speak of Son-of-Data, or Data II. But even Data II's would be a rather lame tale. Until or unless he were able to *forget*, we could not consider him a 'person.' Why? Because it is forgetting that makes autobiographical memory what it is. But what is forgetting, and what is its place in remembering?

As Schank (1990) argues, we can 'remember' an event only when we attend to it; only when it catches our attention, when it stands out from our standard routines, and we can make it into some sort of story, primitive though that story be. However, most of the events in our lives are not storyable at all, either because they take place too far from the focus of our attention at a given moment or because they are simply too small. They may get filed away *somewhere* in the pathways of the brain, but if so, they are far from readily retrievable. I may be able to make myself conscious of my breathing, at least occasionally, but, try as I might, I cannot make myself (and remain) aware of the instant by instant chemical process whereby individual air molecules are broken down by my lungs each time I inhale. Such processes are too tiny for my clumsy consciousness to make much of. Without meaning to, I consign them to the status of non-importance in the scheme of my life. The same automatic prioritizing, and thus forgetting, that occurs on the micro level occurs on the macro as well.

This is not necessarily a bad thing. 'Without forgetting.' says Nietzsche, 'it is quite impossible to *live* at all' (Langer, 1991, 40). If every event on every level of my existence received the full focus of my consciousness, I would be unable to function. My experience would be too crowded. And so would my thinking: too encumbered by too many details and too few generalizations, by too little feel for the broad patterns of my life, my relationships, my world. Perhaps Glover's omniscient God could cope with such clutter, but I would be inundated, overwhelmed, lost. It is good that the vast portion of my existence *is* lost – lost to consciousness, to experience, to memory – for if, like the proverbial elephant, I never forgot, I would never last: just as the world would never last if there were no death – the continual passing away of each form of life, in its time, to make room for another. (It is calculated that a single *E. coli* bacterium, unhampered by death, would divide every twenty minutes, thus producing in a single day a supercolony equal in size and weight to the entire planet!) Forgetting is essential to life, and when it fails to happen on its own, we often force it, admonishing ourselves and others to 'forget it,' to 'forgive and forget,' to put the past behind. Without forgetting, our life would be terrifying, or at least odd – as odd as that of the mnemonist whose ways were painstakingly studied by the Russian psychologist A.R. Luria (1987). Not only did 'S' have 'no childhood amnesia' (xxiv) but also 'the capacity of his memory had no distinct limits ... no limit to either the capacity ... or to the durability of the traces he retained' (11). 'Such a person,' Luria concluded cautiously, 'cannot mature in the same way others do, nor will his inner world, his life history tend to be like others' (151).

Finally, as forgetting is essential to life, to thought, to experience, so it may be to art, to creativity. Without it, there is too little mulch from which can spring the shoots of new ideas. 'A novelist,' writes Graham Greene, 'has a greater ability to forget than most men.' Indeed, 'he has to forget or become sterile. What he forgets,' Greene says, 'becomes the compost of the imagination' (1973, 160). By forgetting, the artist can translate fact into truth (Wolfe, 1983, viii).

With Data, however, it is not forgetting as such that is the issue. The forgetting by which autobiographical memory is characterized, and which necessitates the fictionalization and fabrication familiar to us all, is more than the loss of an occasional detail about our past. Such random forgetting could easily be programmed. Say, every 4000 facts, SOD gets one wrong, even 'loses it' entirely. Or every 400, or every 40, or every 4. Take your pick. Perhaps a formula for forgetting too intricate to detail here. It matters not. The point is: the more, and the more random, the forgetfulness, the better the story. The falser it is, the truer to life – to 'human' life, to 'personal' life. For the great price of technical perfection, we get the pearl of poetic appeal.

But we are forgetting something. Remembering for us, the basis of personal story as we know it, is so hit and miss, so fuzzy an affair, that it is difficult to envision any program that could duplicate it precisely. ('I rather doubt that computers' memories can ever approximate people's remembering of personal events,' writes Tulving, which are 'heavily impregnated with a sense of self'; they 'would be talking about words, rather than original experiences organized in time in its personal past' (Campbell, 1986, 307–8).) The programmed random forgetfulness I have in mind is a logical and technical impossibility, since the circuitry is ragged through and through. It is not that every fourth fact is forgotten while the other three remain intact but that all four suffer a forgetfulness in part. Furthermore, everything mushes maddeningly together. Forgetfulness is an issue less of quantity, that is, than of quality. In our human remembering, everything is always a bit off, always a little hazy, and the rules followed in the process (if 'rules' there be) embarrassingly elusive. Thus, in remembering, so in living every day: something is always lost.

But so is something gained. The dilemma here is that if both Data and Data II could forget as we forget, they would be rather poor machines, perhaps no longer machines at all. However, they might possibly be rich persons. Rich, because they could see themselves with a peculiarly person-al perspective, with a unique twist of irony and inanity, with always (alas) a dash of delusion. Rich, because they could choose to live not merely in the present but in either the future or the past as well. Rich, because, driven by the autobiographical imperative, they would *have* to tell stories, to keep from forgetting, to keep their experience straight – which means they could relate to the rest of us, in the grips of much the same need. Rich, because they could not only tell jokes but often tell them poorly, and, more to the point, could see themselves and the story of their life as always just a bit of a joke – perhaps even, on darker days, as a tale told by an idiot ...

Long on existence (as long as any *person* of the same age), the Datas of the world are short on experience, light on life, low on soul. Good thinkers though they be, they are not nearly sloppy enough to think – to act, to feel, to be – like persons. Yet, that is. That they can suffer now from 'viruses,' just like us, raises the possibility that they may at last have reached the first rickety rung of the evolutionary ladder, at the top of which, supposedly, are we (Kelly, 1991, 16–17).

The Author-ity of Our Stories

Obviously, different *persons* respond to the autobiographical imperative in different ways: more or less intentionally, articulately, artfully, authentically, and, as it were, authoritatively. The variables at work are, as we would expect, their gender, class, culture, age, race, creed, and so on; as well as their level of literacy, introversion, interest, imagination, 'intelligence,' and self-esteem. Many of these variables I shall consider under 'The Range of Storying Styles.' For now, I want to focus on the concept of self-authorship.

As we have seen, the authorship of a story and its narration are two distinct functions. In the case of a life-story, however, author and narrator – and character – appear to be one. When I tell you some segment or summary of the story of my life, I am all three at once, in so far as I am the star of the story, I relate the story, and, in the process, I *construct* the events that the story contains. Unless I am lying or deluding myself, though, I do not construct them out of thin air. I merely *re*-construct them in memory, imagination, and language from events that have presumably actually occurred. I may 'make' them 'into' a story – and 'into' this story rather than that – but I do not 'make' them in any fundamental sense. They are given.

Be this as it may, there are still times when it is appropriate to say that I 'make things happen,' as in make decisions and thus take control of the direction my life unfolds. Once more, however, the 'making happen' involved is not *ex nihilo*; rather it is a rearranging of circumstances or forces already existing, so that things happen in this way rather than that. In other words, something will happen regardless. By making an appointment with the doctor, and thus initiating the process of getting certain tests taken, I seem to *make* things happen. More-over, depending on the results to which these tests lead, one course of action will unfold as opposed to another. However, if I fail to make the appointment at all, things – something, events of some sort – will still occur. Even if by not making the appointment I make less work for the medical system as a whole, the nurses will still go about their jobs, the doctor will see other patients besides me, the lab will con-tinue to be busy, and I shall remain at home scribbling vigorously away.

Strictly speaking, I do not author my life. I do not arbitrarily design its plot from beginning to end; I seldom consciously decide what sort of character to construct myself into. Yet neither do I merely narrate my life. My author-ity with respect to the story of my life lies some-where between the two. That is, I do 'make' the events of my life 'happen,' at least in the limited sense just explored. In this respect, I *co*-author them – just as do characters who, as 'creations inside a creation' (Forster, 1977, 72), take on lives of their own within a novel – in partnership with some other author-itative agent, whether society, nature, fate, God, ultimate reality, or whatever my philosophical propensities lead me to call it. Furthermore, even in just *narrating* the events of my life. I am involved in 'making them up'; events never speak for themselves. In transforming them into experiences I have much liberty to interpret them as I will, to plot them now one way and now another into larger stories still, and to make as much or as little of them as I wish, with all of the effects this restorying process has on the self-creation both of myself and others. What we have, then, is the choose-your-own-adventure situation seen in the previous chapter. 'While I may not write the story, I choose the story in which I am cast as a character' (Carr, 1986, 93–4). And this, it can be added, is nothing to ignore: stories are not innocent.

This gives us a glimpse of an intermediate sense in which we have 'author-ity' over our life-stories. Self-authorship takes place when my self-narration become sufficiently self-conscious that I can begin to critique the plot-lines by which my self-narration has previously been carried out, and can question the genre by which I have hitherto been transforming events into experiences (tragic, comic, etc.) and hence into the stuff of my soul (Hillman, 1975a, 67). It takes place when I am able to hear *how* I am telling myself, how I have been storying my life's events thus far; when I realize that my life is one thing and my story another, that there is an aesthetic gap between them. As this realization dawns, I am in a position to re-construct not so much the events of my life themselves (at first at least) as the plots whereby I make them into my story. A new plot means a new story, and a new story leads to a new life. Thus, as I critique the *old* plots by which my story has previously been lived and told, and experiment with *new* ones, then I am assuming the authority of my life.

Naturally, people vary in this respect. Some, from the very beginning perhaps, are passive in the matter of self-creation; others, active. Some are less inclined to compose their own life-plot than to adopt one of the prepackaged ones proffered them by their family or clan, profession or culture, religion or cult. Others eschew such patterns passionately, preferring to 'do it their way' instead. Some allow life in general to select the events that become the experiences of their life in particular; others select their own events, in accordance with whatever story or genre or plot or characterization they are striving to live out. On one end, that is, are those who adjust their stories to fit the events of their lives; on the other, those who change the events to fit their stories, with all manner of gradations in between. 'Sometimes we must change the story to accommodate the events,' says David Carr, 'sometimes we change the events ... to accommodate the story' (1986, 61).

More often, people 'squander their authorship' (Polster, 1987, 7). Usually unwittingly, we deflect responsibility for it onto others, and to other forces and factors in the world around us, beginning with our family of origin. 'Day after day for years, family members go to sleep with their family drama patterned in one way, a way that perhaps satisfies none – too close, too distant, boring, suffocating – and on awakening next morning, they reinvent the same roles, the same relationships, the same plot, the same scenery, the same victims' (Jourard, 1971, 104). Furthermore, they reinvent the same author-ity structure, often with the unfolding fortunes of one individual (usually a parent, sometimes an infant!) as the object of greatest attention, such that his/her personal story becomes synonymous with the family story, in both others' minds and those of family members themselves. It gets more air time and is thus more author-itative than anyone else's, than even the family story as a whole. Everyone else is but a supporting character within it, one of an admiring (or captive) audience before which it is played out, or a silent shrub on the sidelines of its setting. Just as citizens of a country can live within the life-story of their leader, so, as family members, we can live less within our own life-stories than within that of 'the head of the house.' Our life-story is not our own. Such, says one psychologist, is a sad situation, for if 'we are living someone else's story, we are not contributing our unique talents to our communities' (Napier, 1993, 146). One psychotherapist identifies this tragic yet common dilemma as being 'miscast in the family plot': 'Too often, as children, we are encouraged to try to be something other than ourselves. It is demanded that we assume a character not our own, live out a life story written by another. The plot line is given. Improvisations are unacceptable, and the direction is an oppressive form of close-quarters tyranny' (Kopp, 1987, 4).

As we approach the threshold of story, however, we are increasingly unsettled by this situation, until, by all the ways in which we can 'leave home,' we rebel against the author-ity of the family and commandeer our story for ourselves. In this struggle, the hero of the family, former-ly, becomes our principal *ant*-agonist. As our *prot*-agonism is sufficient-ly asserted, though, we become heroes in our own right – in a relation-ship less of author-authored than, like all relationships ideally, of co-authors with equal influence in each other's self-creation. Thus, we can conclude with Carr that even if 'the self does not author itself,' does not 'create itself *ex nihilo* out of the chaotic night of temporal incoherence,' 'the narrative coherence of a life-story is a struggle nonetheless, and a responsibility which no one else can finally lift entirely from the shoul-ders of the one who lives that life' (1986, 96).

Permissive though our age may be, we still have a tendency to tell the stories about ourselves that we are *told* to tell, whether by parents, priests, politicians, popular heroes, or any one of the powers that be – the more so the more author-itarian these are. As Bruner says, there are certain 'forms of self-telling' that 'reflect the prevailing theories about "possible lives" that are part of one's culture' (1987, 15). What he calls 'theories about possible lives' I call versions, in this case of the impersonal, institutional, or ideological variety. Assuming the author-ity of ourselves, then, means becoming aware and critical of how these versions have shaped the form of our self-telling, how they have authored our stories already and influenced the way in which we transform, digest, or 'make' events into experiences. As Bruner puts it, 'the ways of telling and the ways of conceptualizing that go with them become so habitual that they finally becomes recipes for structuring experience itself, for laying down routes into memory, for not only guiding the life narrative up to the present but directing it into the future' (1987, 31).

What pushes us to cease squandering our authorship? All manner of things, as we shall see in the next section: poverty, unemployment, demotion, divorce; any set of circumstances by which we are dis-eased or dis-illusioned; whatever impels us to critical awareness of the plot-lines of the larger stories along which our personal stories have been drawn, by which our actions and reactions, puppet-like, have been choreographed. Formal education can (though may not) accomplish this as well, unseating our cherished assumptions about the way the world is, showing us how 'society' has in fact author-ized our actions and beliefs. As we have seen, the gradual erosion of the authority over us once held by the world's great religions, with their accompanying myths of redemption, has also driven us to assume more self-author-ship.

Once upon a time, for example, a sizable portion of the world's population appeared convinced that Christianity could confer coher-ence on all aspects of human life. Central to Christianity's power were the Bible and the body of doctrine derived from it. As Don Cupitt says, 'the self, the Book and the universe were all of the same shape – and it was a narrative shape' (1991, 63). A protracted crisis of confi-dence in the soundness of this shape, however, has forced the world to rely increasingly on its own resources, to 'come of age' (Bonhoeffer, 1972, 326–9). But so has the unmasking of the great 'secular myths of redemption' as well. By this I mean those structures or systems that, by encouraging belief in the benevolence of science, the goodness of democracy, or the inevitability of progress, have 'taught much of the human race to believe that ... the future must be better than the past' (Cupitt, 1990, 172); and 'that world-history-as-a-whole is like a very large but tightly constructed narrative, in which all events have been designed by the author to make some contribution towards the resolu-tion of the whole plot.' In abiding by such myths, then 'to believe that my life has a meaning was to believe that my doings are scripted, essential parts of a vast ongoing narrative with a preordained happy ending' (172).

At present, however, there is no such consensus as to 'who tells the world's story?' (Hall, 1982), let alone what that story is our *whether* it is at all. Twenty years ago this lack of consensus was hailed as 'the death of God.' In so far as 'telling stories is functionally equivalent to belief in God,' wrote one source at the time, '"the death of God" is best understood as modern man's inability to believe that human life is rendered ultimately meaningful by being incorporated into a story'

(Keen, 1970, 86). As a consequence of this inability, 'the plotting of the individual or social or institutional life story takes on new urgency" (Brooks, 1985, 6). Why? Because, as veteran diarist Anaïs Nin says, 'there is not one big cosmic meaning for all.' Rather, 'there is only the meaning we each give to our life, an individual meaning, an individual plot, like an individual novel, a book for each person' (Rainer, 1978, 268). Thus, if 'we are all asking, "what stories can we live by,"' then 'one way to begin to answer that question is to start telling our own stories' (Keen, 1993, 30).

The current absence of consensus about how to plot our stories, both self- and world-, is of course not something everyone mourns. For many, it is welcomed, given their peculiarly post-modern paranoia 'that it is really someone else – rather than we ourselves – who is plotting, ordering, controlling our life for us' (Hutcheon, 1989, 63). Yet, even if we no longer need to squander our author-ity to such 'master narratives,' just how free are we to re-story ourselves, to choose-our-own-adventure? If, as Nin intimates, our life is an unfolding novel, one over which we have the modified author-ity we have been describing, then, ironically, it is a novel that is already half-written by the time most of us are aware of our existence in its midst and of our power to re-plot it. Generations of analysts and counsellors have attested, though, that this situation need not deter us. Naïvely or not, they have preached the good news that we are not doomed to live and tell the same old story; that the leopard can change its spots; that it is possible to re-story our souls without relinquishing our authorship, uncritically at least, to some 'sacred masterplot.' Carol Pearson (1989), for example, celebrates 'the power of making explicit the myths that govern our lives' (xx). 'When we name them,' she says, 'we have a choice about our response' and 'can extricate ourselves from undesirable myths ... and/or ... can respect the archetypal pattern that is exerting control over our lives and learn its lesson' (xx). Otherwise, 'we are hostages to them and can do nothing else but live out their plots to the end' (xx).

All of this leaves open a few questions, one of which is whether the autobiographical imperative is automatically good. Hitler clearly had a measure of it: he wrote *Mein Kampf*. The passion for expressing 'the story of my life' is not identical, that is, to a passion for self-knowledge, leastwise not for truth. This means we are faced by the question of 'truth' in autobiography, both in the specific work we might write and in the far grander but informal opus that lies unwritten within us. Another question concerns control again: Are there limits to the control we can have, can expect to have, or would want to have, over what we remember, what we imagine, what we forget; over the genres by which we transform events into experiences; over what sticks as the stuff of our life-story and what is discarded? Still another question concerns the unique feedback effect on our experience of each mode of expression – i.e., how keeping a journal for ourselves self-creates us differently than writing an intimate letter to a lover, or selling ourselves to an employer in an interview, or pouring out our life-story to a therapist or friend. A final question is a theological one. It concerns the composition of 'the universe story' (Swimme and Berry, 1992), a question that post-modern suspicion does not necessarily invalidate. I have alluded to this question already, and will return to it, for it cannot be ignored in probing the poetics of self-creation. If 'divine' author-ity is conceivable at all, then I submit it can be envisioned on the analogy of the author-ity of a novel, in which case we have two choices. Either it is the kind of authorship exercised by a composer of pulp, for whom all events and details are calculated carefully in advance, or it is that of a writer of literature 'properly so called' (Collingwood, 1958), for whom neither the direction of the plot nor the development of its characters is known in advance, but for whom both unfold according to a design that is not predestined but emergent, evolving, open.

Such questions aside, a book on the stories we are is implicitly empowering. Our life-story is not simply assigned; theoretically, we can compose it however we want. It can be as novel as we care to make it. But assuming author-ity over our self-creation is easier said than done. Much courage, and en-courage-*ment*, is required, as is much vigilance, much awareness. Awareness of the myths or plots 'that govern our lives' – awareness of the larger stories in which our life-plots and self-characterizations are often prefabricated and by which they are pre-scribed – is a critical part of this, as I shall show now in turning to the re-storying of our souls.

The Re-storying of Our Souls

People change. They change physically and they change psychologically. They change on the outside and they change on the inside. They change in others' eyes and they change in their own. In this section I want to consider the *poetics* of personal change.

We have seen how our 'self' is in many respects a fictional construction: a house of anecdotes, a tangle of tales, a web of stories that
we tell ourselves, and/or internalize from others, about our past,
present, and future. As these stories change, we change. How we
story our selves affects everything about us, from our most superficial
associations to our most intimate relationships, from our idlest interests to our most cherished beliefs, from our occasional moods to our
overriding temperament or disposition. It affects the manner and
direction our entire lives unfold. It affects our self-creation. To the
extent 'a life as lived is inseparable from a life as told' (Bruner, 1987,
31), then if we can compose a different story we can create a different
life.

My focus here is how we re-story our souls. I say 're-story our
souls' not out of a religious agenda (though the Twenty-third Psalm
does leap to mind) but because at some point – the point of self-creation, a *sacred* point really – the concerns of religion converge with
those of both psychology and poetics. Psychology is the study of the
psyche, the Greek world for 'soul': 'that unknown component that
makes meaning possible, turns events into experiences' (Hillman,
1975b, x). Poetics is the study of *poiesis*, Greek for 'making things by
imagination into words' (Hillman, 1975a, 124). My focus, then, is how
we make and remake our souls deep in our imagination – and thus
'make up' our lives – through the stories we entertain inside us as to
who we are, where we have come from, and where we are going.

There are several ways this re-storying occurs. Though they can be
variously combined, they can be broadly categorized according to
whether they are natural or intentional; that is, whether they happen
automatically as a normal part of living or we deliberately seek them
out. Each of these can be further categorized according to whether
they are gradual or dramatic; whether they come about 'day by day
in every way,' or overnight, traumatically, all at once.

Natural Re-storying: Gradual

Strictly speaking, there is no time when we are not living in 'the vale
of soul-making,' for we are continually re-storying our souls. Our
stories are never the same. Not only is my story different from your
story, but technically, it is different from the story it was a decade ago,
a day ago, or only an hour ago. Our stories change. They change, if for
no other reason than because with each passing year, day, or hour

they get longer, which means there are literally more events *in* them – or at least more events to be *made into* them potentially. There are more events in them at the level not only of existence or outside story but of experience as well, the level of the inside story. There are more events that we have digested, transformed, or 'made,' through some imaginative process, 'into' experiences.

We can image how our stories change naturally by thinking of what happens to the world of a novel as we follow it through. Not only are more events accommodated but also more characters are worked in, more subplots woven into the main one, new themes raised and old ones revisited, more layers of possible meaning accrued, and, for those with eyes to see, more symbolic interconnections to be made. Like a great river the nearer it reaches the ocean, the story-world widens, deepens, thickens, more complicated by cross-currents and more teeming with life. And all of this happens so gradually we scarcely notice it. But happen it must, for the river must flow; the story cannot stand still. It is the same story with life.

As we grow up, buffeted about by siblings and parents, our behaviour is goaded in certain directions, our values infused, our self-concept (and thus our point of view) tapped slowly into shape. Moreover, our lives become more complex. We take up and lay down a succession of interests and hobbies, each with its accompanying trajectory into the future. Playing with model trains, we dream of being an engineer; dressing up Barbie, we hope to become a model woman. Sent off to school, we are saddled for half of each week with a set of ways to see the world, where it has come from, where it is going, and who we are in its midst: consumers in economics class, citizens in civics, carnivores in biology, complexes of molecules in chemistry and physics. Committed without our consent to a particular creed, we are gradually grounded in another whole version of the world-story, and thus of a self-story, a peculiar, 'religious' one: positively as a child of God, negatively as an original sinner.

Then there are the thousands of daily events that force us, slowly but surely, to modify our picture of how the world works, to open our eyes to what people are really like. Through reading, conversing, asking questions, forming impressions, gathering information, this picture steadily expands, widening our horizons and broadening our scope. As well, through a particular job or career, our fortunes, our character, our world-view, our self-image are all subtly but surely shaped by the ethos of the system in which we work.

In intimacy or marriage, we become enmeshed in the life-story of one person in particular: our life-plot becomes a subplot in theirs, and theirs in ours; our themes become their themes; their conflicts become ours. With children, and thus more characters (more creations inside a creation) to accommodate, our common life-plot thickens all the more. Indeed, in getting to know anyone and letting them know us, a complex process is always entailed, a detective process really: guessing at each other's outside story and inside story, gauging the integrity of their inside-out story to us and the accuracy of our outside-in one of them. This intricate, intertextual exercise occurs not only in relationships of some duration and depth, though, but potentially in our most casual conversations. 'Talk,' says Glover, 'affects self-creation': 'When we talk together, I learn from your way of seeing things, which will often be different from mine. And, when I tell your about my way of seeing things, I am not just describing responses that are already complete. They may emerge clearly as I try to express them, and as I compare them with yours. In this way, we can share in the telling of each other's inner story, and so share in creating ourselves and each other' (1988, 153).

Thus, the entire sweep of our life, from infancy to senescence, consists of 'continuous modifications and adjustments in [our] biographical tableau' (Berger, 1963, 61). It is one long sequence of shifts in the ways we story our lives and our worlds, however little they have yet been studied (Bruner, 1987, 15).

Natural Re-storying: Dramatic

But the re-storying that happens at the hands of ordinary life, though natural, is not always smooth. A car crash, a heart attack, a test result, a betrayal: in the twinkling of an eye, the shape of our entire existence is twisted out of recognition. We have to start again – a new life, a new story. But the more normal means of natural re-storying just considered can mediate dramatic changes of their own.

Returning to school in mid-life, being exposed to new ideas, new opinions, new challenges to old beliefs, simply reading a particular book – of such activities we may say they literally, and suddenly, 'changed my life,' catapulting us out of one life-plot and into another. They 'de-familiarize' our usual rendering of reality (Greene, 1990). More sharply than the gradual course of growing up, they strip us of our picture of how things are. They 'dis-illusion' us, forcing 'the painful shedding of hidden childhood assumptions' (Gould, 1978, 335).

Entering a profession can effect a similar swift change, particularly if we have been under-aware beforehand of how deeply our perspective would be transformed by the training required to get in, the day-to-day duties of living it out, the circles we must move in, and the like.

Going from singleness to long-term intimacy can also re-story us, and with a passion. Overnight, our life-story is no longer our own. Throwing in our fortunes with those of a spouse – and thence of in-laws, children, grandchildren, neighbours – our story gets away on us, with or without our consent. Besides, there is the risk, which goes with being at close quarters with others' life-stories, of having to re-story our own when theirs are significantly changed. Someone falls chronically or terminally ill and the family story is inconveniently disrupted. One of its cast is either out of the story altogether (like Tom in *The Purple Rose of Cairo*) or, if in it, then no longer as the same 'character,' meaning no longer playing the accustomed role, speaking the familiar lines, contributing the usual subplot, conflict, and theme. The rest of us must rally and re-story – as a family and as individuals – reinventing our roles, rewriting our lines, recreating our own 'characters.' If grandmother, formerly the family villain whom everyone loved to hate, is now a frail, forgivable ghost in a nursing home or casket, then who are we? Or we learn new information about one of us and we are shocked immobile. Our lives have been built on a lie: He has a mistress; she was adopted; he is an alcoholic; she has MPD; he is HIV-positive; she was raped, or abused, or abducted by a UFO. If the family story is large enough, flexible enough, open enough, then everyone 'adjusts.' Otherwise, we fall apart, or else, while we appear to adjust, the energies required to re-story our whole system build quietly below the surface until the inevitable eruption occurs.

In addition to the upsets of illness and the inevitable shifts of intimate life are the unsettling changes of being suddenly demoted or laid off: we can no longer entertain the view of ourselves as an indispensable character in the company story. Whereas many of the roles we play in life are outgrown naturally, even willingly, here is one we are robbed of overnight, and with it the cherished version of the self-world-story we have carefully composed around it. Then there are the occasional grand upheavals in the even larger stories in which we live: a market crash, a revolution, an earthquake. Not just ours but everyone's role, everyone's place, life-plot, self-characterization, is up for question: Who are we? Whom can we trust? What is real? Who is in control? Such events can be so explosive that, before we realize what is happening, they have launched us out of one way of storying our lives and landed us in the middle of another. We never know. However stubbornly we cling to the old story by which we have made sense of our lives, they drag us kicking and screaming into a new one. As we are no longer quite the same person (experientially if not philosophically), our life proves to be 'a diary in which we mean to write one story but are forced to write another' (Allen, 1978, 79).

But, the sort of re-storying forced by events themselves is of an *un*-intentional variety. We do not normally seek for our souls to be re-made in such an abrupt, unmanageable manner. Yet unintentional re-storying can occur through positive events just as much as through negative ones. We can be pressed into a new mode of storying our lives by an engagement as much as a divorce, a birth as much as a death, success as much as failure, winning the lottery as much as losing a job.

Intentional Re-storying: Common Features

So far, I have been looking at the ways we re-story naturally. Most often, these are too gradual to see, but sometimes they are dramatic. Again, we never know. Re-storying can be prompted at any time, with or without our seeking it. What I want to consider now, though, are the ways we seek to re-story our souls intentionally.

To begin with, there are forms of intentional re-storying that are intentional for everyone but us. Being thrown into a refugee camp or onto the street, being hypnotized or brainwashed or imprisoned, or being kidnapped by a cult, foists on us a re-storying – indeed an outright *de*-storying – by persons or powers we might otherwise avoid, and whose efforts we must expend much energy trying later to undo. Similarly, even in intentionally entering certain professions – such as medicine, the military, or the ministry – we can find our self-world-story forced to transform in directions of which we might not previously have approved.

Even though these sudden, other-intentioned re-storyings can and do occur, they are hardly the norm, nor are they my focus here. Let me identify some of the clues, then, that signal we are about to set out on the road to intentional re-storying on our own, whether gradually or dramatically, consciously or not.

Our journey can begin in nothing more precise than a vague restlessness that hits us on waking up: a mild frustration with life as it is,

a nagging fatigue with the way things are, a quiet but rumbling hunger for something new, for a fresh way of being in the world, in our
relationships, in our skin. Tired of ourselves, we pine not just for a
change or rest, for a break from the routine, but for a real shaking up,
a breaking out of our character, our role in the relationship, our part
in the family, our place in the company, our script in society. Gradually, this restlessness grows into an ever sharper sense that something
is not working: that there is another way to see ourselves; that we
have 'defined [ourselves] too narrowly' (Crichton, 1988, 184); that our
picture of the world is neither broad enough nor detailed enough to
account for our actual activities within it.

It is a suspicion that our self-world-story is too small; furthermore,
that it is not our own. Someone else has author-ity over it – a parent,
a partner, the powers that be – and we must wrest it back. It is a cynical insight into how others' stories of us are simply that: stories –
impressions, arbitrary constructions as to who we are; 'fictions' not
truths, not even particularly accurate ones, that grate increasingly
against our own. It is a sense that the larger stories in which our
personal one has been nested – the family story, company story, etc.
– are less and less conducive to its unfolding. That is, their plot-lines
are too tight, the roles they prescribe for us too stock, the themes they
value not our themes, their conflicts (and morality) not ours. Thus, we
fail to fit in. It is also the realization that there are discomforting gaps
not only between how we are seen by others and how we see ourselves
but also between how we project ourselves and how we really 'are,'
so far as we have any clear reading of what that is: gaps ... between
our outside story, our inside story, and so on. Indeed, the very fact we
can say 'that's the story of my life' may mean we finally have sufficient distance on our life to see that re-storying it can be achieved.

So, the autobiographical imperative peaks within us and, story-wise,
we resolve to take matters out of life's hands and into our own.
Though others dismiss us as trying to 'find' ourselves, their barbs
affect us less and less the more passionately we approach the threshold of story.

Intentional Re-storying: Gradual

Motivated to re-story, the question is how conscious we are in seeking
ways to do so. There are many means of intentional re-storying to
which we submit ourselves unaware of our hidden agenda amid them

to re-compose our lives. Over time, they change us, yet we might not otherwise have sought them out.

As we have seen, 'leaving home,' when done with a vengeance, can be a way to re-authorize, one that happens all the time. Another is distancing ourselves from old friends. Where they have routinely elicited a particular side of us, evoked one version of our life-story, we may no longer wish it reinforced. The less we want to play the same character in their life-story, that is, and the less our lives let us share a common story anyway, then the more we drift apart. Thus, fast friends become former friends. We start moving in different circles, associating with different people with different bents. The new friendships we forge invite us to story ourselves afresh. Or we get ourselves divorced, oppressed by the need to burst out of the old story in which the marriage has locked us. Or we quit our job and embark on a world tour, living and working in a different culture, speaking a different language, breathing a different way of making sense of the world. In the words of sociologist Peter Berger, 'we change our world views (and thus our interpretations and reinter- pretations of our biography) as we move from one social world to another' (1963, 64).

Or we may take up a new hobby, build a new body, pick a new pastime, or turn to talents long since buried and so enter a new, more creative phase. But releasing our creativity in this manner does not merely open up a new chapter in the old story; it can overturn that story entirely. How we have storied ourselves so far, we discover, is not written in stone; it too can be re-created. Keeping a journal may be part of this shift. Swept up by the autobiographical imperative, we turn inward, not knowing exactly why.

Intentional Re-storying: Dramatic

The more conscious we become of what we are doing and why, how- ever, the more deliberately we may seek out resources to help us with the how.

There are at least four directions we can turn to: education, religion, therapy, and a specific extension of therapy known nowadays as 'personal mythology.' We have seen how the first two of these can re- story us gradually, without our resorting to them intentionally. It is with such resortings I thus begin. First, though, we need to be clear what sort of re-storying we are talking about.

As a story gets longer it does not necessarily become different, any more than it does as its plot gets thicker. It is simply more of the same. The same is true with life. People caught in recurring patterns of relationship go from one liaison to another, living the same story, repeating the same themes, playing the same plot. Only the settings and characters change. A different life-story, however, a *re*-storied life-story, is one in which the overriding plot whereby we make events into experiences partakes of a different genre: comedy as opposed to tragedy; the tale of a victor as opposed to a victim; of a winner as opposed to a loser; of an overcomer, a pilgrim, or a child of the universe as opposed to a fool. It is, if you will, a re-genre-ated life-story, profoundly and privately reframed in much the same way as can be our perception of separate events within it. The horror we endure on the highway today, for instance, gradually becomes tomorrow's tragedy, next week's thrilling adventure, next month's amusing anecdote, and old age's illustration of the irony of life.

The psychologist James Fowler calls these overriding plots, 'master stories,' though we should not confuse them with the broad cultural or creedal formulae that Cupitt calls 'master narratives' and Brooks calls 'sacred masterplots.' They are the stories by which, on the *individual* level, 'our characters and faith orientations are shaped' (Fowler, 1981, 277). Echoing Hillman, Fowler says they are what 'we tell ourselves and by which we interpret and respond to the events that impinge upon our lives.' They are 'the characterizations of the patterns of power-in-action that disclose the ultimate meanings of our lives' (277). Thus, 'when a playwright-lawyer tells me that the fundamental truth about us and the universe is that "everything runs down," he is sharing with me in highly condensed form, his master story. When Miss T. tells us in her interview that "there is that of God in every man" and that this has come to be the central premise of her sense of life's meaning, she is letting us in on her master story' (277).

If our overall life-genre, what Fowler calls our 'master story,' is fundamentally the same as it was last year, last day, or last hour, then though our story is different in thickness and length, it will be much the same in kind: much like a piece of jazz can end with the same simple melody with which it began, no matter how exotically it has wandered in the middle or how unrecognizable have been its improvisations upon the central tune. The re-storying I am concerned with here, then, involves a change not in the *events* of our lives themselves, but in the genre, the fictional mode, the dominant version, the master story, the life-plot, by which we *interpret* them, transform them into experiences, and lay them down as memories. When such change happens, it is a re-form-ation of our lives, for it changes less the content of our life-stories than their form, less the crystals themselves than the pattern that connects.

What I shall be looking at now, therefore, are the media to which we turn as part of 'a deliberate, fully conscious and intellectually integrated activity' (Berger, 1963, 61) to rework our story – self-, world-, past, present, and future. Before proceeding, though, there is one corollary to all of this.

The genre by which we interpret events, making them into the experiences that are part of our inner story, can be expected to vary from one version to another of the myriad versions swirling about inside us. What is made of one event within one version may not be the same as what is made within another. Potentially, I can make as many experiences out of any event as there are versions to incorporate it into, or levels to view it on. For example, falling and breaking my leg while running to catch a bus can be interpreted on a personal level, as an indication of how stupid I am or how out of shape; on a political level, as an illustration of the inefficiency of the transit system; on a religious level, as a sign of God's punishment for my living such a slothful life; on a cosmic level, as one more proof that the universe is a cruel joke; or, with an overactive imagination, on all such levels at once. Furthermore, when these levels and versions interact and combine in all the ways we have seen they can, there is theoretically no limit to what we can make out of or read into any or all of our life's events. The world of our inner story is a world without end, a universe unto itself, like the outer universe in which it is lived.

Education

Much of what passes for education effects not the *re*-storying of the soul, of course, but the *de*-storying. Indeed, the failures of our educational system have been much decried. When perceived and carried out as the transmission of a given body of knowledge into our passively waiting brains, whether we want it or not, it can curtail our curiosity, kill our creativity, and leave us immune to the love of learning. At the same time, rather than enable us to critique the author-ity of the many larger stories surrounding our lives, it can often confirm us all the more in our mindless commitment to the values they mediate: increasing, not unseating, our loyalty to the establishment whose interests they serve. In some circles, however, education is practised in such a way that radical re-formation, real re-genre-ation, is both expected and, supposedly, achieved. Such education goes by many names. One is associated with a term coined by the Brazilian educator Paulo Freire, 'conscientization.' Closely linked to it is the concept of 'perspective transformation.' The scholar most responsible for highlighting this concept is adult educator Jack Mezirow (1978; 1990).

Mezirow identifies four kinds of learning in which we are normally engaged. One, he says, is 'learning how to do something. Another is learning about the way something works, relates to something else, how the pieces fit together. A third has to do with learning what others expect of me, how to anticipate their reactions and how to cope with other people. A fourth kind of learning is to form an evolving concept of myself as a person with certain values which seem important to me' (1978, 100–1). Earlier I chose to speak not about a self-*concept*, since it can connote something static, but rather about a self-*story*, since our view of ourselves is always temporal in nature, with a beginning, middle, and end. That is, while it is 'based on past experience and on how that experience was interpreted and valued by the learner' (Brundage and MacKeracher, 1980, 97), it is also oriented to the future and to the range of possible ways in which the learner anticipates how his or her life will turn out. Mezirow's fifth kind of learning, then, builds on learning how to form such a self-story yet goes beyond it. He calls it 'transformative learning' (1990, 1). A type of meta-learning really, a sort of secular conversion, it involves 'learning how we are caught in our own history and are reliving it,' and 'becoming aware of hitherto unquestioned cultural myths which [we] have internalized' (102). The essence of such learning is that 'we learn to become critically aware of the cultural and psychological assumptions that have influenced the way we see ourselves and our relationships and the way we pattern our lives' (101).

For Mezirow, transformative learning means learning about our 'meaning perspectives.' As already hinted, a meaning perspective has two dimensions. It is both 'a personal paradigm for understanding ourselves and our relationships' and a 'structure of cultural assumptions within which new experience is assimilated to – and transformed by – one's past experience' (101). In terms of the poetics of self-creation, a meaning perspective is both a self-story and a world-story. At a certain point in certain learners' lives, however, the dominant meaning perspective undergoes a major change, a sort of 'paradigm shift,' to borrow a phrase first formulated by Thomas Kuhn (1970). 'When a meaning perspective can no longer comfortably deal with anomalies in a new situation,' that is, 'a transformation can occur' (Mezirow, 1978, 104). Specifically, 'transformation in meaning perspective is precipitated by life's dilemmas which cannot be resolved by simply acquiring more information, enhancing problem solving skills, or adding to one's competencies' (108).

What Mezirow calls a meaning perspective we can consider as the overriding narrative framework by which we plot our lives and transform their events into experiences, one we may have borrowed from the larger stories surrounding us but that has burrowed its way deep into our souls. To critique it is to employ 'critical reflection' (Mezirow, 1990; Brookfield, 1989) to appreciate the 'fictive' dimension to these structures of our everyday world (Rogers, 1991). More simply, it is to see that our self-stories are indeed that, stories, and then to consider how they have come to be storied the way they have and thus could be re-storied. Such critiquing does not need a formal educational program to stimulate it. Rather, it can go on quietly in that occasional, private rebellion against the powers that be that any of us can stage at any time, on our own. Or, still informally but more dramatically, it can come out in the sort of single, sweeping rejection of the entire set of assumptions by which our life is bound that Robert Pirsig registered against the whole structure of Western civilization. As he cries out in his cult classic, *Zen and the Art of Motorcycle Maintenance*, 'the mythos is insane' (1975, 346).

Religion

Related to perspective transformation is religious conversion (Welton, 1991, 6, 20), where 'religion' is viewed less as a system of doctrines than as a vehicle of change. Conversion takes on new meaning in light of our discussion of life-story. As an explicit set of stories about the world (Cupitt, 1991, 61), one presumed to possess divine sanction at that, religion, any religion, is a rich resource and powerful force for re-storying the soul. To submit ourselves to a religion is to commit ourselves to an overt program of reconstruction, not only of our past but of our present and future as well. Slowly or swiftly, everything shifts. What was forgotten is now remembered; what was foreground is now background; where once was despair now is hope. We emerge, it seems, with a new perspective, a new nature: re-storied, re-stored, re-born.

As caricatured in its conservative Christian form, conversion involves 'seeing the light.' There is a suddenness to it, an overnight turnaround, a dropping of the scales from our sightless eyes. Everything about us and in us is illumined afresh. It involves a conscious surrender of the control of our lives to a higher power, handing over the author-ity of our stories to a being beyond ourselves. The message of this being is mediated by a congregation or cult in which conformity is strictly enforced to a singular story of the entire world, replete with definite plot, main characters, and central conflict: 'the old, old story,' with a garden at the beginning, a cross in the middle, an apocalypse at the climax, and a reward at the end. In such a conservative context, conversion can be but one more way in which we squander our authorship – and urge others to do the same.

We see this in extreme forms of fundamentalism where the faithful are exhorted to relinquish their self-authorship and accept a particular plot-line for experiencing the events of their lives, as well as a guiding grid to interpret the unfolding of their lives as a whole. 'Thus the convert to a religious faith can now understand his entire previous life as a providential movement toward the moment when the mist lifted from before his eyes' (Berger, 1963, 61). Rather than 'hero-conquering-all' or 'self-made-wo/man,' etc., motifs common in secular contexts, such a plot-line is 'seeker-found-by-God,' 'sinner-saved-by-grace,' or, more harshly, 'wretch-redeemed-by-the-blood.' However harsh, these can all be seen, though, as variations on what Frye considers 'the framework of all literature': the story of 'the loss and regaining of identity' (1963, 21) – a story he links to Christianity. 'From a literary point of view,' he argues, the story of Christianity is 'a comedy' (1988, 122). As the familiar song says, 'I once was blind but now I see, / Was lost but now I'm found.' Indeed, says John Gardner (1985), the very form of story itself, 'with its orderly beginning, middle, and end, is likely to hint at a Christian metaphysic' (88).

The more powerfully this plot-line compels us to re-story – past, present, and future – then the more it might be expected to achieve the coming together, the *con*-version, of the many versions of our life-story into one. The dark side of this, however, is that the more airtight or authoritative it also is, then the more rigorously we shall be exhorted to suppress any contradictory, subversive versions. Moreover, the more we shall be taught (explicitly or otherwise) that our life-story *before* conversion must be discredited; that we must disparage our past genre of experiencing as of no consequence, indeed of negative conse-

quence, now that 'the truth' has set us free. Trust in God will thus be
accompanied by distrust of self – and paranoia toward the world
(Keen, 1986).

Where our overriding version of our past has been the source not
of inner richness but of inner chaos, it is possible that we will welcome
this process of suppression and discreditation. If the past as we have
composed it for ourselves has been sufficiently negative, a source of
guilt or disgust or ennui, then, like Hoffer's 'true believer' (1951), we
shall be glad to give it up and trade it on a better model, a better
story. Thus conservatives caught in a liberal context can be highly
frustrated when no neat, new story (both self- and world-) is laid out
for them; when they are not instructed clearly what to believe; when
too much – particularly about themselves – is left to their own interpretation. For them, the tightly told, ready-made story other sects offer
– *you are a sinner whose only hope is Christ* – will seem a great blessing,
one they are unwilling to critique once they convert. Relieved of the
burden of making sense of existence on their own, assured that they
are on the winning side in the war between Good and Evil, they will
be filled with a sense of peace: *At last, I am secure; I know who I am; I
have come home. Here lies truth.*

We pay a price, however, if we do not question the author-ity of such
a story, for our own subversive inner versions will gradually converge
beneath our keenly controlled surface into a counterstory in which, as
we shall see shortly, lie the seeds of yet another conversion later on. For
some, the realization that no story is thus the whole story – of either the
self or the world – will be gloriously liberating. They will celebrate the
fact that there are no limits to what they can be. For others, the same
fact will induce 'a metaphysical agoraphobia before the endlessly overlapping horizons of one's possible being' (Berger, 1963, 63), and produce an accompanying increase in defensiveness and zeal. In other
words, 'the dawning recognition that this or any other conversion is not
necessarily final, that one could be reconverted and re-reconverted, is
one of the most terrifying ideas the mind can have' (63).

Airtight or open, rigid or flexible, imposed or emergent, conservative or liberal, 'the reinterpretation of one's biography' (61) that religion requires or inspires has for centuries been a principal means for
intentionally re-storying our souls. Re-storying religion itself, though,
so that it can understand its own storied nature and storying style –
and can operate with less rigid conceptions of the authority of its
vision of life – is a task that the faithful of whatever stripe might try

increasingly to take up. In this way, we could continue to evolve forms of religion that are truly nurturing of our creativity and spirituality (which may be the same) because they would be less obsessed with truth and more open to trust.

Therapy

There is one form of intentional re-storying, however, to which many of us are eventually either driven or drawn – that is, when life's natural re-storying becomes too painful or our resistance to it too powerful; or when one or the other of our family story, couple story, or personal story is no longer working. It is called 'soul therapy,' or, more commonly, psychotherapy. In it, the broad visions of religion and psychology converge. As Carl Jung confessed, 'among all my patients in the second half of life ... there has not been one whose problem in the last resort was not that of finding a religious outlook on life' (Storr, 1988, 192). In short, 'psychoanalysis promises a form of salvation' (2).

Therapy, says Hillman, 'is a restorying of life' (1975a, 168). It is 'the re-storying of experience' (White and Epston, 1990, 14). It is concerned, then, less with truth (the bait that lures us in religion) than with interpretation, with how we story our lives. This makes it an exercise less in archaeology than in exegesis: in helping us 'construct a more contradiction-free and generative narrative' of our life (Bruner, 1986a, 9). It changes 'the meanings [we] attach to things and events' and so 'reconstrues [our] world' (Jourard, 1971, 99). Such a perspective implies that the patient is 'a victim not of her history but of the story in which she [has] put that history' (Hillman, 1989, 79) – a victim not of her existence but of her experience. It is not the person that needs doctoring, therefore, but the story. 'Successful therapy,' insists Hillman, is 'a re-visioning of the story into a more intelligent, more imaginative plot' (80). Its operative principle is encompassed by the quip that 'if you want to change history, then become a historian.' People reach out for therapy, that is, when their stories, more than their lives, are no longer functional for them; 'when the narratives in which they are "storying" their experience, and/or in which they are having their experience "storied" by others, do not sufficiently represent their lived experience, and ... significant aspects of their lived experience ... contradict these dominant narratives' (White and Epston, 1990, 14–15).

In therapy, we seek to understand the stories of our lives with an unusual profundity and focus – in particular, those stories at the centre of our sense of self. Not just the party stories by which we manage others' impressions of us, but our core stories, often those most difficult to tell. We endeavour to do so by learning to ask of our stories certain key questions. 'Personal analysis,' says Schafer, 'changes the leading questions that one addresses to the tale of one's life and the lives of important others' (1983, 219). As such, the allure of therapy lies in 'the sense of an answer' (Schafer, 1989): a sense that out there somewhere lies the prize – the whole story of our lives, the *true* story; a sense that someday we shall get our story straight. This self-questioning in fact 'alter[s] the context of memory' so that we 'then re-collect our individual stories under an enlarged horizon' (Winquist, 1980, 50–1).

As I see it, the therapeutic process proceeds in three overlapping stages, each with its accompanying key question and its corresponding role for the therapist. Admittedly, these stages represent a simplification of the intricate and often lengthy work that will be done by any given therapist and client. Yet they provide a valid if broad brush picture of the poetic dynamics involved in 'care of the soul' (Moore, 1992) – not just in therapy, note, but in any context where such care occurs, including a classroom, a support group, or even *self*-care, as in keeping a journal – certainly in either intimacy or friendship. Indeed, people in good friendships care for each other all the time, as can family members, colleagues, even total strangers – sometimes entire communities or cultures.

The first stage is that of *narrating* the story of my life, which means simply telling it, venting it, getting it out, with an intensity and honesty I may never have experienced before. Of course, it may not come out as a seamless whole; instead, as a series of anecdotes of specific events, still lifes of particular moments, outpourings of pain and bits of impressions from all across the years. But behind the many lurks the one: 'The many stories clients use are attempts to convey ... the story of their lives' (Kennedy, 1977, 105). 'First *stories*,' echoes Frederick Wyatt, 'later *the* more or less coherent *story* urging to be told' (1986, 205). By responding to this urge (which I have called the autobiographical imperative), and so getting my story out, I in a sense exorcise it: not unlike the novelist who, upon telling the tale with which he has been pregnant, says Somerset Maugham, is thus 'rid of it' (Allen, 1949, 233). As author Michael Crichton says of writing about important experiences, telling your life is how 'you make the experience your own, how you explore what it means to you, how you come to possess it, and ultimately to release it' (1988, x).

At this stage the guiding question is simply *What* is *my story*? However, such narrating does not mean that I am telling 'simply' the same old story. Narrating this intensively, and extensively, means that something new is being brought about in my life; a distinct degree of self-*creation* occurs. 'We are simply more than we were before,' insists one counsellor (Winquist, 1980, 60). At this phase of re-storying, the therapist is primarily a *listener* – though of an open, supportive, non-judging kind I may seldom have had in the past (Schafer, 1983, 3–4), one who finds me truly interesting and thus affirms my novelty (Polster, 1987, ix). Above all, she is someone who keeps my story safe. In addition, she is alert not only to the content of the stories she hears (and of the stories behind the stories, those left untold) but also to their form, to *how* they are told. It is listening to patients in this way that the young Robert Coles was admonished by his mentor during his residency as a psychiatrist. 'He urged me to be a good listener,' writes Coles, 'in the special way a story requires: note the manner of presentation; development of plot, character; the addition of new dramatic sequences; the emphasis accorded to one figure or another in the recital; and the degree of enthusiasm, of coherence, the narrator gives to his or her account' (1989, 23).

The second stage in the re-storying process is that of *reading* the story of my life, which means, having told it, then studying it, evaluating it, and critiquing it with an honesty I may never before have experienced. Here my key question is *What* kind *of story is my story? What* genre *of story has it been?* At this stage I might look closely at some of my central or 'signature stories,' assessing what themes they reveal, how I have plotted them and characterized myself in their midst (as what sort of 'hero'), and what they would be like if I told them from another point of view. This is a strategy used by literature teachers to stimulate fresh insights in students' minds: How would story X be different, for example, if told not from the narrator's perspective but from that of the main character, a minor character, or the reader?[1]

This stage is a distancing, a stepping back, from my life-story. It is a stage of deliberate *de*-storying, which means purposely entering a state of relative storylessness where everything about my life *as composed* is, in principle, up for review. Usually, it involves a close review of my family story, or more accurately perhaps, my 'family myth' (Napier, 1993; Keen, 1993; Moore, 1992, 25–6): its themes, conflicts, characters, author-ity, plot-line, genre, etc. But it can also mean inquiring into the themes, characters, and so forth of the other larger stories that envelop my life as well – the impersonal, institutional, ideological, etc. – in which case, as we have seen, the personal could lead to the political. In other words, there is much power in this stage: 'as persons become separated from their stories, they are able to experience a sense of personal agency' (White and Epston, 1990, 16). However, there is also much vulnerability, too, as I question my entire way of being in the world and peer into parts of my experience maybe long ago submerged – secret parts, sacred parts. The therapist's role is correspondingly delicate. It may still not be, though, 'to *change* [my] story, for this is to deny it; it is, rather, to *expand and deepen* the story, thus releasing the energy bound within it' (Houston, 1987, 99).

Through both the narrating and reading, then, another key question comes to motivate me. It is *How can I change my story – how can I re-genre-ate, re-author it – now that I have read it and am therefore clearer on what kind of story it really is.* Specifically, it is *How can I find a story big enough, that has a horizon broad enough, to account for, accommodate, and re-member the events of my life so that as much of my life as possible is available to me as a coherent whole?* As I begin to ask this question, I enter the third main stage of the therapeutic process, the stage of 're-writing the inner story so far' (Glover, 1988, 153). This is the stage at which *re-storying* my soul becomes particularly possible, as, coached by my counsellor, I experiment not only with new ways of acting and reacting in my relationships with others but also with a fresh way of framing my life's events – a more self-affirming vocabulary, for instance, with which to tell myself what is going on and who I am. As such, it is the stage of 'retelling' my life (Schafer, 1992).

Weaving from one to the other and back, we do not advance through these three stages in lockstep fashion, for they are tightly entwined. In the words of Charles Winquist, 'we tell a story in order to find a story' (1980, 43). But in all of this subtle process, what again is the therapist? She is, of course, the one person we expect and pay not to 'storyotype' us but to take us in context and listen, *really* listen: to be the fair witness we may seldom find in our other relationships. Looked at in story terms, she is an open and impartial audience in the first stage. In the second, she is a 'helpful editor' (Bruner, 1990, 113). In the third, she is a co-author (Schafer, 1992, xv), and in two senses: both co-authoring *us* and being co-authored *by* us in turn, as, in the course of caring, she, too, is 're-storied.'

Robert Kegan (1982) enriches our sense of what therapy entails by seeing the therapist as a 'holding environment' while the person intentionally re-storying puts a new life-story together. She is a culture for the person to grow in (276), what he calls a 'culture of embeddedness.' Such a culture performs three functions. The first is confirmation. As the re-storier discloses and vents, the therapist-as-holding-environment 'holds on' (121). She both upholds and stays around, refusing to be driven away by the force or content of the telling. The second function is contradiction. As the re-storier begins to critique, to distance from, his own life-story, the therapist, too, 'must let go' (121), must stand back and ask, with the patient, what *kind* of story it is. The third and final function is continuity. As the re-storier experiments with a new way of telling *and living*, the therapist 'sticks around so that it can be reintegrated' into the fabric of his everyday life (121).

   Naturally, each school of therapy will have its particular convictions regarding which diagnostic story is all-encompassing enough to be adequate to this interpretive task – that is, to 'sufficiently represent' a person's 'lived experience' (White and Epston, 14). Classical Freudians will be committed to the Oedipal myth; Jungians, Adlerians, etc., to the 'fictions' that fit their own theories (Hillman, 1975a). It is not my place here, though, to side with one school over another, since my focus is less the specific *content* of re-storying than the general *form*, the shape of the process as a whole. Thus I want to look now at a particular therapeutic strategy that empowers us to choose – or make – our *own* guiding stories rather than having them prescribed for us by others. This strategy is connected to a concept that is intriguingly popular in current counselling circles: personal mythology.

Personal Mythology

'Personal myths,' writes psychologist-theologian Sam Keen, 'become constricting and boring unless they're examined and revised from time to time.'[2] Therefore, 'we need to reinvent ourselves continually,' he says, 'weaving new themes into our life narratives, remembering our past, revising our future, *reauthorizing the myth by which we live* (1988, 45; emphasis mine).

   In contemporary culture, say researchers Feinstein, Krippner, and Granger (1988), both the need and the capacity to carve out a personal mythology for ourselves is greater 'than in any previous period of history' (1988, 24). Their reasons for saying this lie in their analysis, like Brooks, Cupitt, and others, of the demise of the world's 'sacred masterplots' and 'master narratives.' Against the background of the pioneering work of Joseph Campbell,[3] they define a personal myth as 'a constellation of ideas, images, and emotions' (27). Through it, they say, 'we interpret the experience of our senses, give order to new information, find inspiration and direction, and orient ourselves to powers in the universe that are beyond our understanding.' Myths are 'the way that human beings code and organize their inner lives' (27), the overriding narrative patterns according to which they transform the events of their lives into their experiences.

As I have been using the term here, 'myth' differs from 'genre' in that genre is the genus, so to speak, of which any given myth is but one species. For example, within the genre of tragedy – which, like all of the modes of fiction, is never found in pure form (Frye, 1966, 28) – *nothing-ever-works-out-for-me* is one mythic formulation that it might take in a specific person's life. *Nobody-loves-me-or-ever-will* is another. Accordingly, it is possible to change one's myth yet stay within the same genre.

The process of 'mythmaking,' Feinstein and company continue, 'is the primary, though often unperceived, psychological mechanism by which human beings navigate their way through life' (24). It goes on all the time, whether we are conscious of it or not. 'During the life of the individual,' they argue, 'the guiding myths that order personal reality are constantly being challenged as new experiences are encountered' (30). In other words, 'when people encounter experiences that do not correspond with existing myths, they generally handle these contradictions by distorting the input or by altering the myth' (31). When enough experiences are encountered that contradict our overriding myth, then a countermyth develops at some unconscious level where they are 'recognized and stored' until the mass of the countermyth 'breaks into consciousness, often in dreams, fantasies, new ideas, or the emergence of a fledgling "subpersonality"' (32). Each personal myth, they insist then, 'holds within itself the seeds of a countermyth that may eventually emerge and challenge it' (34).

On the basis of such insights, they articulate a five-stage strategy for changing our personal myths. The first is to identify our current myth and recognize the conflict within it: the countermyth that is taking shape (39). The second is to bring the two myths into focus (41). The third is to seek a resolution between them (41–2). The fourth is to identify a larger myth that contains the redeemable dimensions of both (42). The fifth and final stage is to weave this larger or renewed myth into our everyday life (43–4). Such a renewed myth, such a new self-world-story, will prove its worth, they say, to the extent that it can

- [be] in accord with the individual's actual needs, limitations, and abilities;
- capitalize on opportunities and strengths, alerting the person to both internal and external resources;
- affirm and support underdeveloped aspects of the personality;
- accommodate polarities, contradictions, and paradoxes;
- gain autonomy from the limiting effects of early personal experiences as well as the myths of the surrounding cultures;
- attain harmony with archetypal and transpersonal sources of knowledge. (47)

In effect, this five-stage model is merely an elaboration of the three-stage one we have just been considering. Their broad outlines, as I see it, are the same. In the tradition of Hegel, they look like this:

THE STAGES OF RE-STORYING

THESIS
Telling a life
Client gets story out
Client identifies current myth
Therapist's function: *Confirmation*

ANTITHESIS
Reading a Life
Client steps back from story
Client identifies conflicting myth
Therapist's function: *Contradiction*

SYNTHESIS
Retelling a Life
Client develops larger story
Client identifies and integrates new myth
Therapist's function: *Continuity*

The Resistance to Re-storying

Whether we speak in terms of a personal myth, a dominant version, or a guiding life-plot, the formal therapy needed to critique and re-create it intentionally costs both money and time. It is therefore for the few. However, informal therapy – natural re-storying – is for the

many. Fortunately, there are many forms of it. 'Fortunately,' says
Karen Horney, 'life itself remains a very effective therapist' (Kennedy,
1976, 124). As we have seen, what therapy tackles intentionally, life
has a wondrous way of attempting on its own – attempting, but not
always achieving. So then, lest we think that re-storying, whether
natural or intentional, is also easy, let us remind ourselves of the
resistance it commonly meets – though I use 'resistance' here in an
everyday sense, not in a classical psychoanalytic one.

First, there will be resistance from others. When Father goes off into
the forest to beat the drum and explore his masculine spirituality, not
everyone might think it such a great idea. Mother may resent the
excess of sensitivity he suddenly displays, glad he is more alert to her
needs but bothered by how smarmy he has become. Children may
welcome the decrease in his manly tantrums yet be disturbed that
'daddy's not the same person anymore.' When we re-story, that is, we
step out of line. We undermine the author-ity of the script in which
we have previously played our part, and we challenge the integrity of
our fellow characters. We tip over whatever apple cart we have been
riding in hitherto: the marriage, the family, the neighbourhood, the
network, the clique, the club, the company, the country. Our co-actors
and co-authors might not like this; they may consider *our* mythos
insane. Thus they may push away our attempts at self-disclosure,
refusing to listen to us as (wittingly or not) we enter the first phase of
re-storying. To do so would mean letting go of the 'storyotype' in
terms of which they have dealt with us so far, in the process releasing
a cherished version of their own character. As a creation inside a creation, then, our personal mutiny, our tearing to pieces of the plot of our
common larger story, might not be applauded.

Second, there will be resistance from ourselves. We know that we
cannot change our stories profoundly overnight: our partners perhaps,
our opinions, even our moods, but not our stories. Besides, we grow
accustomed to the stories we are. We feel cozy inside them; we wish
to keep them safe. They have served us well. With them, we have
propped up an image of ourselves that has gotten us many good
strokes. The familiar is, if nothing else, familiar. They are, after all,
self-contained worlds that resist contamination from other stories. Thus
they get in the way of their own re-storying, and we get stuck more
unstuckably within them. Indeed, says Jean Houston, this is what
defines the neurotic: 'Neurotics cannot seem to move beyond their
story to broader contexts and deeper formulations' (1987, 99). Even

when we can see clearly that their reconstruction is essential, we know what work will be required to carry it through, and what courage; we are not certain we can muster and maintain it. There will be much material to face up to, many dreams to ignore no more, memories of painful episodes no longer to suppress, entire chapters to recollect and reclaim – not to mention all the wandering through the wilderness of no-story-land that awaits us before putting a new story in place. Then there is the fear that the others in our life, sleeping peacefully with things as they are while we toss and turn in the dark night of our soul, will be forced to re-story themselves, as the ripple effect runs through our every relationship. We might prefer to spare them the pain, to keep our self-creation to ourselves – as if we could. Or we resist because we are 'just plain stubborn,' because we 'hate change,' or because we have 'led a sheltered life,' and so do not see that, unless we take steps on our own, our tidy Dick-and-Jane story-world could blow apart by itself, or implode under the weight of a wider world that, even on good days, can read like a tale told by an idiot.

The Limits of Re-storying

Easy or not, the concept of re-storying leaves certain questions outstanding.

Is re-storying automatically for the better? Is it possible, for example, to re-story too often, to be too protean in our approach to life (Lifton, 1970, 37ff)? Is it possible to seek a self-story, or a world-story, that is too big, that tries to take in too much, and so risks tottering under its own width and weight? How do we know when radical re-storying is the sign of maturity and when of instability or insanity? What leads some to engage in re-storying so frequently, so mindfully, and so fiercely, while others resist it 'like crazy'? Is there a stage in which regular re-workings of our sense of self are acceptable – adolescence, for instance – but after which radical re-storying should stop – adulthood, say, when we ought to have 'found' ourselves? When is enough enough?

Do some people have a higher threshold of re-storying than others, a greater tolerance for things as they are? Why do some survive life's own dramatic re-storying while others collapse in its face? Does it relate to having a self-world-story that is not just too little but too brittle as well? What makes some stick to their story through thick and thin while others can relinquish it with apparent ease, able to function without falling to pieces? Do some have a higher tolerance for being in-between stories than others do? Are they less threatened, internally and interpersonally, by not quite knowing what their story is? And what does such not-knowing have to do with 'basic trust' or 'faith'?

Is there a limit to how much re-storying we should encourage in others? Are we being unethical when we encourage someone to re-story when there is incredible pain at stake, for both themselves and others? Do we sometimes try to wrest people's stories from them before they have indicated a desire or readiness to disclose them, however convinced *we* are that those stories are in need of renewal? What is our role and responsibility in this most delicate process? Indeed, what makes one person 'open' to another's re-storying in the first place, while someone else resists it – that is, what relationship to our own life-story (loose? critical? accepting?) enables us to be effective listeners to that of another: to be competent therapists, good analysts, or caring friends? Moreover, is the push to re-story others' souls one we should be making at all, or is it up to them? How do we know when there is a genuine need for our intervention in their re-storying and when we, and they, can trust to life to do it on its own?

What are the legal implications of re-storying? the philosophical ones? the theological ones? And what about standards? In re-storying, will any story do, as long as it is new and seems bigger and better than the old? What makes a good life-story, a healthy one? How do we know radical re-storying has been achieved and when it only *looks* like it has – that is, when it is really just the same old story with a different face? Is re-storying automatically for the better, any more than the autobiographical imperative is automatically good?

Might a society, let alone a family, be too unstable to survive – or too healthy – if everyone is intentionally and interminably at work re-storying their souls, and thus continually questioning the larger story of the society or family itself? What does our belief in, commitment to, and abundant options for re-storying say about us as a society? That we are addicted to novelty (Ross, 1992, 91)? If so, is this bad or good? How do cultures differ in the re-storying they encourage or condone among their members, or how rigidly they schedule and reconstruct it (with rites of passage and the like)? Can entire cultures, can societies themselves, be re-storied? If so, then how: naturally (both gradually and dramatically) or intentionally, with the historians continually retelling our collective past and our future from each new take on what is the 'true' story, the 'real' story, the 'whole' story?

Such a litany testifies to the untested nature of a poetic perspective on personal change. This book, however, represents an attempt to articulate that perspective and consider its application to numerous subtle aspects of everyday life. In the next section, I want to look at one aspect that is frequently overlooked in our academic efforts to appreciate how much human beings are alike. It is our deep-seated sense that we are each, in the end, unique.

The Novel-ty of Our Lives

If we allow that life can be linked to story – that a life can be *likened* to a story – then the question becomes what form of story. A comic-strip story? A soap opera? A fairy tale? A three-act play? Will any old story do?

Earlier we saw how among the many story-forms, the full-length literary novel, if not the final answer, has much in its favour for fleshing out the life-story connection. Besides its length, there is its breadth, its wordiness, its multimedia, many-layeredness, and its ability to capture both the subjective and social sides of everyday life. Though future fictional forms may supersede it, it represents our most extensive means to date for storying both the wideness of the world and the mystery of the self. 'All novels, of every age, are concerned with the enigma of the self,' writes Kundera. 'As soon as you create an imaginary being, a character, you are automatically confronted by the question: What is the self? How can the self be grasped? It is one of those fundamental questions on which the novel, as novel, is based' (1988, 23).

In this section, I want to continue to stretch our metaphor from life-as-story to life-as-novel: the novel-ty of our lives. The notion of novel-ty brings together the storied aspect of our lives with both our (self-) creativity and our uniqueness. Every person, it is said, is like *every* other person in some ways, like *some* other person in some ways, and like *no* other person in some ways (Hunt, 1987, 37). 'Every person born into this world,' writes philosopher Martin Buber, 'represents something new, something that never existed before, something original and unique' (Moustakas, 1967, 27). Even if our life-story falls finally into one or another of a limited range of modes (Frye, 1988, 54) or life-plots (Booth, 1988, 289), it is still distinctive. Like each literary story, it is a world unto itself.

There are two sides to this situation. On the up side is pride, the gratifying sense of our own substance and depth, our originality, our uniqueness: *This is my life and no one else's; no one could have lived it but me.* With such self-esteem, our motivation (more or less intense from one of us to another) is not unlike the novelist's: 'to create out of the materials of the human spirit, something which did not exist before' (Faulkner, 1968, i). On the down side is loneliness, the loneliness of the artist, 'the infinite loneliness of the unique' (Moustakas, 1961). As filled with others as our lives may be, we must walk by ourselves through the vale of soul-making. Nobody else can walk it for us. Upside or down, though, what can we say about our lives from what we know about novels?

The World of the Novel

This is not a book about whether specific novels are 'truer to life' than others, nor about the history of the novel as a narrative form. It is about the narrative nature of human experience and human interaction, for which the novel provides a rich (if not exhaustive) analogy. One obvious aspect of any given novel is that it is a self-contained world – like the universe as a whole: finite yet unbounded. It also *creates* a world, or rather elicits one in our imagination as readers. It gives us a standpoint from which we can view or assume, by our identification with its characters and events, an entire world of possibilities radiating outward – one largely invisible except for a few verbal clues (an adjective here, an allusion there) that lead us to 'fill in the blanks' and round it out on our own. This is the 'totalizing' dimension of fiction (Hutcheon, 1989, 62–3).

Like novelists, we too create worlds. 'Each one of us,' observes de Maupassant, 'makes for himself an illusion of a world – poetic, sentimental, joyful, melancholy, ugly or gloomy according to his nature' (Allen, 1949, 126). 'Illusion' may be unfair, for until we re-story it, and so step back from it and see *through* it, then it *is* our world, the only one we know. Indeed, it must *take in* everything we know; what it does not, effectively does not interest us. Without it we are lost, adrift in space and time. De-storied, stripped, like a turtle without its shell, we have no home. But the story-*world* we each create around us differs from everyone else's – as does our story itself – in terms of at least three overlapping features: its atmosphere, its openness, and its integrity. These make convenient markers for exploring the common ground between stories and lives, and, later, for playing with the differences in storying styles.

Atmosphere

In the novel *Wolf Solent* by John Cowper Powys ([1929] 1964), the main character, Wolf, is visiting Christie, his unrequiting lover. Seeing her surrounded by a pile of half-read philosophy texts, he chides her for not dealing more diligently with their ideas. 'I don't understand half of what I read,' Christie confesses lightly. 'All I know is that every one of those old books has its own atmosphere for me.' Under questioning, she explains: 'I regard each philosophy, not as the "truth," but just as a peculiar country, in which I can go about – countries with their own peculiar light, their Gothic buildings, their pointed roofs, their avenues of trees' (90–1). Philosophy or fiction, the experience can be the same.

Lovers of novels by Graham Greene may be far less interested in their outcomes than in the atmosphere of the peculiar country into which each work escorts them – Greene-land – the peculiar 'feel' of which, the allure, the spirit, is so familiar that, to them, the saying is true: If you've read one, you've read them all. Such readers may be inclined to gorge themselves, work by work, on one author's world at a time, reluctant to move on to the next's until they have had their fill of that feel.

How authors – of whatever kind of story: novels, short stories, etc. – can create a characteristic atmosphere, or their words can elicit it in readers' minds, is the mystery of 'style.' It is a function of several factors at once, from the actual vocabulary they employ to the themes they explore; from the imagery they introduce to their sequencing of summaries and scenes, of dialogue and description. It is a function of course of the particular type of novel they compose – detective, horror, psychological, philosophical – and of the overall genre (satire, romance, etc.) of which it partakes. It is also a function of plot.

Plots, we say, thicken as they unfold, and with them, often, the atmosphere in which they are encased. The thicker the plot, the rounder the characters, the subtler the themes, then the more everything is enshrouded in cloud, the more meanings the story suggests. The more lies between the lines. The thinner the plot, the less complicated its web of subplots, and the more obvious or simple the conflicts it entails, then the clearer that atmosphere, the easier we can see through it and assert what the story is 'about.' The fashionably slim plot-line and flat-tummied characters of a novel by Danielle Steel conjure a correspondingly vaporous atmosphere – through which it is easy to make out where things are going and which quickly dissipates when the book is put down. Not that it has no allure at all, or casts no spell over its reader, but it is obviously a different atmosphere from that of a novel by Drabble or Durrell, where, like Venus, the cloud cover can be so heavy as to hide the solid ground. In fact, some novels have little such ground at all, only a swirl of hot gases.

It is the same with people. The atmosphere of Randall-land may not have the fog of Greene-land nor the storms of Bronte-land, but it will be every bit as distinctive – as will Smith-land, Wong-land, Khan-land, and the like. Besides having a unique story, indeed because of it, each person we encounter has a definite space, a discernible presence. We sense it in the way they dress, the words they speak, the gestures they use. We can hear it in their voices, watch it in their posture, see it in their eyes. Entering their space is like peeking into a 'peculiar country,' another world: a Gothic romance in one case, a Greek tragedy, a comic opera, a satire, or a tale of high adventure in another. People do not merely look or walk different; they 'feel' different too. Whatever they do or say, there is an air about them that sets them apart: troubled or calm, warm or cool, cloudy or clear. It is the subtle yet palpable quality that novelists take such pains to describe about their characters (defeated, excited, questioning, and so on) and that changes with – that *is* – their mood. Much of this air, or course, we impute to them outside-in, depending on our own story or the stubbornness of our 'storyotyping' of them, yet much they give off, since others sense it too. It is the *field* – the 'non-material region of influence extending in space and continuing in time' (Sheldrake, 1989, xviii) – that surrounds them, precedes them, follows them. It is the spell they cast over the rest of us. The better we are at 'reading' it, even with no knowledge of their circumstances, present or past, then the more we are sensitive to shifts in it and, in general, the further we are either pulled into their orbit or repelled away.

Often, it is this atmosphere that first triggers our curiosity to inquire about the story beneath it, or shuts it off. We sniff their air and guess their tale, though we sometimes get it wrong. Simply because a person smiles so much, we may say he has a 'friendly' air, yet the reason, it can turn out, is far less friendliness than poorly fitting teeth. 'Some of us, however, have thicker atmospheres than others, and a few of us have an atmosphere of such opacity that it hides us entirely from view – we seem to be nothing but our atmosphere' (Malcolm, 1993, 94). Moreover, in life no less than literature, atmosphere can often be faked. With a touch of suede, a cigarette, and a certain stony silence, the 'Malboro Man' is easily affected: mountain stamina, rugged individualism, feet-on-the-ground masculinity. But buyer beware: there may be no rock at all, only an iceberg upside down: one tenth substance, nine tenths appearance: hot air dressed up as 'cool.'

As a living story, an embodied novel – with its unique vocabulary (plain or fancy), plotting (thick or thin), characterization (flat or round), and point of view (past-, present-, or future-oriented) – each person exudes a distinct atmosphere. For some, it is so thick that we never know where the rabbit will pop out next; for others, so thin we can 'see right through them' – or see through to solid ground. Defenceless, guileless, the latter are delightfully 'there,' transparent yet present. No layers, no airs: what we see, and hear, is largely what we get. Such people we *might* call 'open.'

Openness

What helps create the unique atmosphere of a given novel is the degree of openness its world displays. Though openness is a more elusive factor than atmosphere, I see it as a function of at least two elements: first, of boundaries and, second, of issues raised – which, by implication, means of endings.

As a work of fiction, a novel is by definition a closed world. Realistic as it may be, autobiographical as it may be, it does not pretend to be accountable to the 'real world' or facts. Moreover, it has its boundaries, in the sense that these events get in while those get left out. Yet some novels are more closed than others, their boundaries more tightly sealed. Some are pure fantasy. We do not expect them to connect to anything in the real world, except allegorically. In that sense (though maybe that alone), they are closed books. However, it is not enough to say that other novels are therefore 'realistic' simply because they refer to microwaves and Manhattan – which would make a novel by Robert Ludlum more 'open' than one by Jane Austen.

The openness I am referring to is a function of the size of the world it tries to encompass in terms not of physical geography but of emotional terrain. In that sense, a novel that jet-sets from Manhattan to

Malawi may cover far less wide a world than does one that unfolds entirely in one town. Indeed, says Hermann Hesse, 'a novel can deal with the most splendid material of world history and be worthless, and it can deal with a nothing, a lost pin or burnt soup, and be a genuine work of literature' (1978, 203). Exploring the subtleties of souls and the relationships between them, the latter type of novel does not dash across the surface but dives deep below it, inviting us to experience more emotions more profoundly on more levels.

Openness is also a function of the number and nature of the issues the story raises for us as readers, and the direction it drives us to resolve them. If no real issues are raised, other than whodunit, when, and why, then the novel is a closed book. If many are raised – ethical, philosophical, theological – but all are neatly answered by a preachy narrator, then it is scarcely less so. If, however, many are raised but few are resolved, then we are driven *outside* the novel for answers. A novel of this type offers us lots to discuss; its 'meaning,' if one there be, is suitably elusive, interpretable on more than one level at once, and comparable to that of other novels by other novelists who play with similar themes. In this way, Greene-land overlaps with Woolf-land and Drabble-land and Dostoyevsky-land, and so on. The other type, however, shuts discussion down. The tidiness of the ending makes it redundant. We know how everything 'turns out.' All that remains is the boring business of living 'happily ever after.' There is little to figure out, little between the lines, little below the surface. There is no symbolism to unpack, no possibilities to play with, no mists to roll away, and no meaty comparisons to make: Ludlum-land with Steel-land with Harlequin-land, and the like. All answers to all questions are given *inside* the book; only the dimmest can miss them.

This brings me briefly to the element of closure. The closure question concerns the *kind* of ending a story has, not the *number*. Whether two or twenty-seven, multiple endings do not in themselves make a story more open: in a quantitative sense, yes, but qualitatively, no. The degree of openness a story-world possesses is a function of the kind of ending it has. If too neat, too predictable, then readers get bored; too fuzzy or too surprising, and they get uneasy. The expected coherence of the story is missing; reading requires more rigour than they reckoned. Somewhere in between, however, is the story that makes us think – neither so tidy that it insults our intelligence nor so unintelligible that it intimidates and throws us off.

As we shift from literary story-worlds to lived ones, I believe this consideration of openness gives a fresh focus for some of our everyday observations about differences in 'human nature.'

For one thing, a *life*-story has boundaries too. These events and not those have been transformed into experiences, and in this way, not that. Like a literary story, it is a 'framed world' (Aichele, 1985, 25). However, the frame is less distinct for some than for others. Where picture ends and wall begins is occasionally unclear. Her life 'an open book,' so she claims, one person tells us the story of her life at the drop of a hat, in all its gory detail, no matter how delicate her revelations or how little her knowledge of us. She is *too* open, we feel, embarrassed; her border is too unguarded. Her story flows out of her, fills the room, and drowns us both in her drive to self-disclose: the autobiographical imperative run amok. Keep some of it to yourself, we want to say. Retain a secret or two. Have some allure.

There is also the person who is too open in the sense of identifying too easily with others, whose boundaries to incoming traffic are too open. Where the first flows *out* too much, this one is too open to the *in*-flow of others, and in either of two senses. First, he takes on others' troubles, in the sense of getting too much wrapped up in their stories and too little in his own. Or, second, he takes on others' characteristics, in the sense of being so attuned to the people he is with that, unconsciously, he imitates their accents and mannerisms – even, it can seem, their self-characterizations, their points of view, and, with time, their whole mode of plotting the stories of their lives. Such a person is rather like the teenager who, in the normal course of firming up his sense of self, tries on a sequence of others' self-stories for size, or, in the extreme, like the super-Touretter described by Oliver Sacks who, 'becoming everybody, lost her own self, became nobody' (1985, 123).

These examples represent one end of the spectrum of openness. At the other, though, is the one whose soul – whose story – is a city-state fortressed about by a high stone wall. Few get in, little gets out. 'She lives in her own little world,' we might say of her, meaning many things: She is a megalomaniac, concerned with her own agenda. She feels she is a legend unto herself. Or she is over-identified with one particular interest. 'Her whole life is her cats,' we say, or her garden, her husband, her career, or her 'cause,' whatever it may be. Or we could mean that the story she lives her life in terms of (possibly a religious one) is, to her, *the* story; anyone else's is no story at all. Or she is painfully private, profoundly shy. Or she is living out some fantasy or horror that few can figure out. Either way, the gates of her story-world swing inward, not out.

Between these extremes are those who have somehow struck a balance between revelation and secrecy, between being too public and being too private. *I like him*, we think to ourselves. *He is very open*, by which we mean the barriers, though there, can be gotten around. He is easy to be with: hospitable, receptive, safe. We can move smoothly from our story-world to his and back: few border checks, few questions asked, few credentials to produce. Mutual self-disclosure comes naturally, and with the resulting intimacy, self-creation.

Also, like each literary story, each life-story raises issues to resolve. We all carry within us a collection of questions we ask, conflicts we wrestle with, themes to which we continually return. But some people are more aware of their collection than are others. Those blissfully unaware seem easy to read: their stories sound straightforward, with little between the lines. Out of innocence, they are closed to inquiry. Some, however, are not only aware but uneasy as well. Their threshold of uncertainty low, they are driven to find clear, immediate answers – possibly *inside* an author-itarian system, such as an aggressive ideology or religion that specializes in dispensing them. These are the true believers. Others, again, are aware of their collection but excited. Questions are more enticing than answers, mysteries than truths. They seem to trust that their questions will not kill them, only call them outward to an ever broadening sense of self and world. Where true believers are finders, these are seekers; where the other's world is narrow, theirs is wide.

It may seem that openness is a function of complexity: the more complex a person's life – and life-story – then the more compassionate they will surely be, the more understanding of the experience of others. Yet complexity is no more a guarantee of openness in a life-story than it is in the story of an orgy depicted in a pornographic film. With characters in abundance and action galore (though little plot), few issues are apt to be explored by the actors, and perhaps even fewer by viewers. A person caught up in multiple subplots unfolding at once, 'mired in relationships' (Gilligan, 1982, 156), has a complicated life, to be sure – if only on the *outside*. Yet he may be so busy with his immediate existence, so preoccupied with the intricacies of his inner experience (its themes, conflicts, subplots, etc.), or so in need of a listener for his expression, that he is overly self-focused, closed both to his own story and to the stories of others – like so many, a poor listener. At the same time, a solitary person, with few characters and little drama in her life-story, on the *outside* anyway, may be marvellously open. Her inner story-world wide as can be, she may be a compassionate listener to, and holder of, the stories of others, able to imagine, by virtue of her own digested experience, what others think and feel.

So, what do we have? We have a difficult term to define, in both literature and life. Someone who seems open to me may seem closed to someone else. Like many things, openness (as atmosphere) is in the eye of the beholder. Furthermore, the same person who is 'open' to playing Monopoly may be closed to discussing a poem, or to listening to my tale of woe. It is hard to be open to everything. One word we might substitute is 'open-mindedness,' yet it is hardly less difficult to define (Hare, 1979). It is related to openness but can connote other things. Not everyone we would call open-minded would we also call open. A person can be open-minded in philosophical debate yet tight-lipped in talking – and rigid in thinking – about his own life-story, and stingy or awkward in listening to mine.

Still, we cannot escape it. We can feel it: Some people are just more 'open' than others. We could say they are more 'intelligent' too. This is provided that we are open to defining their intelligence, with Schank, in terms less of IQ than of their ability to tell (and listen) to stories; than of how they hold their own stories inside them; than of their level of self-awareness about the complex system (outside, inside, inside-out, etc.) not only of their own life-story but also of others'. Ultimately, what openness is, is an open question, yet one that a contemplation of the model of life-as-story cannot ignore. In the meantime, we can propose at least this much. Our 'openness' is a function less of our complexity than of our *compassion*, meaning the span of our emotional geography; than of our *curiosity*, meaning our willingness to explore outside ourselves for answers and insights; and than of our – what? – *childlikeness*, meaning our ability to live with loose ends, unresolved questions, mystery.

Integrity

A novel is never the single story it may seem. Though it appears to have a central story-line, it has no 'centre' as such. It is always many stories swirling about in one – 'an interweaving of many strands' (Beardslee, 1990, 172). There are as many strands or stories in a given novel as there are points of view from which to tell it and interpret it. There is the story that is contained in each chapter, or conveyed by each sub-plot that threads its way through the work as a whole. There is the story – or stories – the author may have had in mind for it to turn into before, during, and after its actual composition, in which process it may well have 'got away' on him. There is the story of the narrator, or of each of the narrators, through whom it is told or could be told. There is the story that each of its characters would perceive it to be from one scene or chapter to the next, if ever they were in a position to talk about it; or the story each *combination* or characters might determine it to be if their interchanges were ever to turn to such a subject. In so far as, in some novels, individual characters double as narrators, yet another set of versions of the story emerges.

Finally, there is the story that is read into and out of the novel by each person into whose hands it falls, who in turn, as and when they read it or talk about it with other readers, will entertain one theory after another as to what sort of story it really is and what it 'means.' Such theories themselves will be ever-changing speculations on the untold yet intuitable stories (past, present, and future) of each character or combination of characters within it – traces of which can often linger with the reader long after the reading. The more literary the fare we feed on, the more there is to digest; the more open the story-world, the more to see the story as being 'about' and the more often we may need to reread it. In sum, 'each time a reader engages with a novel, it will change; she or he can neither exhaust nor completely realize it. But this is in tune with … the enticing incompleteness of the world' (Greene, 1990, 265).

Despite the many stories within it, however, a novel is still only one story. It is the one story within which, between its covers, the many are contained. It is a con-version of the one and the many, a living, open-ended integration of the infinity of possible stories that it might mediate and of which it might be made. Each novel, we may say, is a universe unto itself, and not a closed universe either, but an open one, not only because it opens out to the entire world that it sketches and assumes but also because the countless versions for which it is the vehicle interact with, originate in, and relate to the universe of all other possible stories. Within each novel, the inner universe of stories converges with the outer universe of stories. The appreciation of such an insight in relation to the mystery of the self may be a sign of our *maturity* as persons – about which more in a minute.

What then of us? Integrity is a strong word, in the same lofty league as character, wisdom, and maturity. In story terms, however, integrity is less an ethical concept than an aesthetic one. It means integration. 'The more complete the story, the more integrated the self' (Crites, 1986, 163).

We all have a lot going on in our lives, both inside and out, some more than others. Looking at openness, we saw how we all have our unique set of conflicts, questions, issues. Looking at 'The Stories of our Lives,' we saw how we all have our different 'sides' and our different versions of any segment or summary of what lies *in*-side. Looking at plot, we saw how we all have our different subplots and chapters. Looking at personal mythology, we saw how we all have our dominant myths and countermyths. Open or closed, thick or thin, single or related, we all have our complexity. How well we are aware of it and hold it 'together' is the measure of our integrity.

On one end of the spectrum of possibilities are once again those who, driven by the autobiographical imperative, hold their life close to their chests – preferring not to have more happening in their life than they can handle, more events than they can digest as experiences. They prefer one plot-line at a time, and as tightly laid out as possible, not loose and meandering; a minimum of distractions and digressions; one chapter at a time, closing off one venture clearly before embarking on another. On the other end is the person who is 'all over the map,' more going on, inner and outer, than is getting sorted out. Where the former's world is a tidy English garden, the latter's is a jungle, tangled yet teeming with life. Where the path followed by the first is straight and narrow – a whitewashed village sidewalk on a Sunday afternoon – that by the second is a six-lane freeway at rush hour in a blizzard: the wide avenue that could lead to destruction.

Each end surely has its weaknesses and strengths. In the middle somewhere, though, are people who can entertain diversion yet maintain direction. Somehow, they strike a balance between action and reflection, complexity and focus, the many and the one: 'The more integrated a life,' says Michael Novak, 'the more all things in it work toward a single (perhaps comprehensive) direction. The richer a life, the more subplots the story encompasses. Interesting people are full of contradictions ... To bring integration out of wildly disparate tendencies is the mark of a great soul ...' (1971, 49).

Novel-ty and Maturity

This is not the place to trace the history of 'maturity' as a concept. It is as grand a term today as was wisdom in the past. Yet one definition may get us started. Maturity, writes Mezirow, relates to 'a developmental process of movement through the adult years toward meaning perspectives that are progressively more inclusive, discriminating, and more integrative of experience' (1978, 106). Thus, 'maturity holds the promise that becoming older may indeed mean becoming wiser, because wisdom can mean interpreting reality from a higher perspective.' Mezirow's views reflect those I am pondering here about the poetics of self-creation and the novel-ty of our lives. Accordingly, whatever else it is, maturation is the process whereby we are forever straining toward an inside story that can account for as many as possible of the events of our lives – however painful or pointless (that is, unstoryable) at the time of their occurrence – and transform them into experiences. This means a story big enough to tie these experiences together in a way that reveals a 'symbolic interconnectedness' between – a coherence to – all the features and facts of our existence. Maturation is the continuing struggle to compose (and live) a story that is free from falsehood, from inconsistency and self-deception, and from un-critiqued compliance with, and authorization by, the stories of others: The struggle to tell our *story*, our *whole* story, and *nothing but* our story.

As a goal, then, matur-*ity* is unattainable. As a process, matur-*ation* is unending. We can never quite catch up on the task of storying our lives. We under-read continually. There are always more events than can be made into experiences and more versions than can be conveniently converged into one. The emplotment of our life never keeps pace with its development (Hillman, 1975a, 131; White and Epston 1990, 11–12), as the following example illustrates.

To understand the 'meaning' of a particularly puzzling or disturbing event, say in an intimate relationship (a quarrel, a betrayal, even just an offhand comment), I need time to brood on it, to stew over it, to digest the significance of the sequence of moods it apparently triggers. Each such mood corresponds to a particular way of plotting the event: *She loves me, she loves me not, she loves me.* Eventually, I see it – that is, experience it – from enough different angles that its power to confuse me is diffused; its power to distract or destroy me is decreased. I re-story it in enough different ways that I can finally, if not forget it, then at least let it go – for now. Naturally, the length of time required to do so will depend on how *potentially* significant it was in the first place. 'The deeper the experience,' writes May Sarton somewhat cryptically, 'the more time is required to sort it out' (1986, 1973). I say 'cryptically' because the 'depth' of an experienced event is determined by the scope of the story in terms of which it is interpreted. In the end, I assign it an 'official version,' however provisional, by fitting it into a story of the relationship as a whole, and of my life as a whole, whose scope is broad enough to let me get on with my life without staying stuck in my anger, guilt, or grief.

This is only one event. When our lives are filled with events, many equally poignant, the task is never-ending to digest them all 'maturely' and so integrate them within a common and coherent story structure. Yet the yearning for such a structure is central to our development as persons. It is the autobiographical imperative, the quasi-religious 'faith which many people practice,' as psychotherapist Erving Polster puts it, 'that there is an underlying intelligence which they bring to all events that will ultimately bend these events toward a recognizable whole' (1987, 55). This returns us to the view of Jonathan Glover. Self-creation, he says, using the term as his equivalent for maturation, 'tends to make a life like a novel by a single author' (1988, 152).

The tendency to make a life like a novel by a single author is demonstrated by a tendency common to people of perhaps all walks of life, all levels of intelligence, and all types of philosophical orientation, however sceptical. It is the tendency to *read things into* the events of our lives and ferret out hidden meanings within them, what Viktor Frankl calls 'man's search for meaning.' In the previous chapter, we saw that the plot of a novel stimulates us to seek out the novel's 'symbolic interconnectedness.' The intensity of our desire to see such meanings and interconnections in our own lives indicates, then, the degree our relationship to them is literary – that is, poetic – in nature: the degree we think of them as constituting one vast, unfolding novel that, somehow at some time, must come together as an aesthetically coherent whole. 'Until you die,' says writer Alice Munro, 'you try to make a comprehensible story of your life' (Marchand, 1991, 2).

There are at least three contexts in which this meaning-making tendency is consciously encouraged: a therapeutic context, a spiritual or psychic context, and, as we have seen already, an explicitly religious context. Often, sensitivity to all three is mingled in the soul-making of any one person. However, each deserves its fair share of attention. To begin, I return to therapy.

A Therapeutic Perspective

As a re-storying of life, therapy is 'an exegetical discipline and not an observational science' (Winquist, 1980, 51). Like religious conversion or other processes involving 'a drastic reassessment of one's past life,' it provides us with a 'method of ordering the discrepant fragments of [our] biography in a meaningful scheme' (Berger, 1963, 62). As we have seen, this method involves at least three stages: telling, reading, and re-telling. Corresponding to these stages are at least three roles for the therapist, as auditor/listener, editor/critic, and co-author. For Erving Polster, these roles merge into one. The therapist, he argues, functions like a novelist and 'the novelist's perspective may be transformed into therapeutic method' (1987, x).

A key aspect of the therapist's work, Polster insists, is to help people 'to recognize the drama in their own lives,' to see their own story potential, to realize that 'no one can escape being interesting' (1, 3). Being able to appreciate how interesting we really are, how novel, is a critical step toward self-acceptance, self-esteem, wholeness. This is how therapists and novelists join forces: 'Novelists are foremost among artists in transforming the ordinary into the remarkable,' in 'delineating those experiences that many people omit from their personal awareness' (9). However, 'the extraordinary,' says Polster, 'is just waiting in the background of the ordinary for an inspirational force to release it' (8). In a well-written novel, 'everything that happens matters,' every word counts, and every detail 'contributes to the scene, our understanding, and the moment's suspense' (10). In a therapy session, 'everything that happens ... has similar potential.' That is, 'using the same creative selection process as the novelist, the therapist accentuates key experiences and provides leverage for the emerging dramas' (10). Thus, 'the therapist joins the novelist in making a big deal out of small selections from all that is actually happening, taking each event not only for its own sake but also for its meaning in an enlarged perspective' (10, 14).

In this respect the therapist functions not only as a novelist, trying 'to understand the deeper hidden meanings of events,' as Guy de Maupassant says (Allen, 1949, 124), but as an educator as well, where education is defined 'as intelligently directed development of the possibilities inherent in ordinary experience' (Dewey, [1938] 1969, 89). Many people need little help to see the possibilities, and the drama, in the details of their lives. Indeed, some see far too much, and through wrong-coloured glasses at that. The paranoiac tends to read something into everything, refusing to leave one stone unturned, making life miserable for others and a scrupulous hell for himself. Such self-reading Polster is neither *de*-scribing nor *pre*-scribing. Although in a novel 'everything counts' (14), 'in daily living there is no such likelihood':

'Chance meetings with old friends, trips to the hardware store, lost car keys, and forgotten appointments may or may not slip right through the ordinary person's consciousness' (14). None the less, he insists, 'in the hands of the expert novelist or psychotherapist any of these events might be the focal point of a spellbinding story or a successful therapy' (14).

Of course therapy never proceeds in a theoretical vacuum. As we have noted already, Freudian therapists encourage their clients to read the stories of their lives in different ways than do Jungian ones, and so on. Each school of therapy seeks to re-story a life in a unique manner, to re-plot it according to a particular framework. Moreover, within each school, there is more than one framework. 'There are Freudian versions of the Freudian perspective,' says Roy Schafer, 'that differ from mine' (1989, 200). In the same way, the analysand himself comes to analysis equipped not with one story alone but with many, a variety of versions of part or all of his life. We have a situation then where 'the analyst approaches the analysand as *sets of stories* to be retold in terms of the *storylines* provided by preferred analytic theories' (193). In so far as within any framework the analyst's stories are pitted against the analysand's, therapy is thus always 'a battle of stories' (Hillman, 1975a, 139).

My purpose here is not to debate the meaning-reading strategies advocated by particular schools. It is merely to draw attention to the fact that the therapeutic movement in general constitutes one key medium of the meaning-reading drive, one whose influence we can detect in the lives of many adults. Indeed, as members or descendants of 'the age of analysis,' we have all been invited to become detectives into the secrets of our souls: co-editors and co-authors – with therapists or without – of the ever wider novels into which these souls could be re-storied.

A Spiritual Perspective

The need to read meaning into the events of our lives is natural within a second general context as well, what can be considered a spiritual or psychic context, or the context of what has been called 'depth psychology.' Characteristic of such a context is the quasi-religious belief in 'fate,' in an overriding 'plan,' in a cosmic blueprint according to which our fortunes are mapped in advance, our story-lines already laid out. It is the belief, as Etty Hillesum expresses it, though certain she would

soon be sent to a concentration camp, 'that I have a destiny, in which
the events are strung significantly together' (1985, 91). It is the belief,
as novelist Henry Miller words it, that 'every man has his own destiny' and that 'the only imperative is to follow it, to accept it, no
matter where it lead him' (1955, 180; 1977, 179). It is the belief, as
depth-psychologist and master-journaler Ira Progoff (1975) puts it, that
it is 'possible for all the events and relationships of our life to show us
what they were *for*, what their purpose was in our lives, and what
they wish to tell us for our future. Thus we gradually discover that
our life has been going somewhere, however blind we have been to its
direction and however unhelpful to it we ourselves may have been'
(11).

The presence of such a belief may be more widespread than we
think, even in our presumably advanced, modern society. On one
level, a particularly 'superstitious' level, it is in evidence whenever we
are drawn (secretly or not) to the 'paranormal,' to the notion of
unknown forces behind the scenes of our everyday world, or to one
form or another of divination, whether tea leaves or tarot cards, palm-
istry or astrology, Ouija boards or crystal balls. On another and more
general level, however, it is in evidence whenever we have the vague
but persistent feeling that a certain sequence of events is a 'sign' of
something, was 'meant to be,' has happened 'for a reason.'

One writer to bring this belief to the fore is psychiatrist Jean Shinoda Bolen. In *The Tao of Psychology*, Bolen highlights the thought of
Carl Jung on the controversial concept of 'synchronicity.' Synchronicity, Jung believed, is 'an acausal connecting principle that manifests
itself through meaningful coincidences' (1979, 6). Such coincidences are
'events, dreams, and meetings that seem to contain meanings deeper
than themselves' (xi). Developments in the outer world seem symbolic
of those in the inner one. Synchronistic events of this sort convey 'a
meant-to-be feeling' (53). In the midst of them, we have the sense of
being involved in 'a waking dream' (37–8) and we experience the
feeling, 'which grows with each new addition, that "something is
trying to tell (us) something"' (30), the feeling that 'we are not alone'
(95). The 'something' is The Self – the same as we considered in chapter 1.

One of the more alluring notions to which belief in synchronicity
leads, says Bolen, is expressed by writer Richard Bach: 'Every person,
all the events of your life, are there because you have drawn them
there' (Bolen, 60). If we are 'open' to them, then, things happen to us,

and people come into our lives, at just the right time: *When the student is ready the teacher arrives.* In effect, this means the end of the accidental. 'If the people and events of our lives are here because we have drawn them here,' says Bolen, 'then what happens in our lives apparently by chance or fortune is not really accidental' (61). Our way seems strangely blessed.

In general, believes Bolen, the concept of synchronicity bridges the gap between a number of realms at once: Eastern and Western philosophy, science and religion, physics and psychology, matter and mind, the conscious and the unconscious. For her, it is 'the Tao of psychology, relating the individual to the totality' (7). To the extent that we are attuned to it, she would say, we hold the key to the art of living: 'If we personally realize that synchronicity is at work in our lives, we feel connected, rather than isolated and estranged from others; we feel ourselves part of a divine, dynamic, interrelated universe. Synchronistic events offer us perceptions that may be useful in our psychological and spiritual growth and may reveal to us, through intuitive knowledge, that our lives have meaning' (7).

A Religious Perspective

Bolen's identification with the philosophy of Taoism points to the third main context in which meaning-making is encouraged: explicitly religious spirituality – leastwise in its softer, non-fundamentalist varieties, where unquestioning doctrinal conformity is neither enforced nor encouraged. Again, I am not trying to argue the merits of one tradition over another, but to identify some of the dynamics at work in the ways people in any tradition plot the events of their lives into the stories of their lives. Since the background I come from is Christian, I shall be limiting myself to that particular tradition, though parallels to others can conceivably be drawn.

A term that surfaces sooner or later in discussions of Christian spirituality is 'providence.' Belief in providence is of two kinds: general and special. Belief in general providence is belief that the world as a whole has been created by and is cared for by a divine Creator – 'a cosmic artist or storyteller,' as it were, 'by whom the significance of every event and every life is guaranteed' (Haught, 1984, 104). Belief in special providence builds on belief in general providence and holds that the Creator somehow 'leads' or 'guides' the affairs of those individuals who are faithful in devotion, prayer, and trust. Belief in special providence, which is my focus here, assures such individuals not only that 'all things work together for good,' or that 'every cloud has its silver lining,' but also that none of the events of their lives are entirely accidental. It assures them that each event is significant because it is ultimately part of an overriding 'plan' for their long-range material and spiritual welfare.

For many, such a belief is the source of much comfort and strength. Amid life's sudden and often senseless upheavals, they derive great peace of mind from the conviction that 'the will of God' is busy transforming their bane into blessing and their pain into potential for growth, however mysterious its ways of doing so. But it is not only in the tragedies of life that such people discern the divine will at work. In the most ordinary of its details as well, they sense the hand of providence 'working that which is well-pleasing in God's sight.' The following prayer by theologian John Powell captures what is for many the heart of this belief:

When you chose to create this world, you knew the blueprint and the design of my life: the moment of my conception, the day and hour when I would be born. You saw from all eternity the color of my eyes and you heard the sound of my voice. You knew what gifts I would have and those that I would be without. You knew also the moment and the circumstance of my dying. These choices are all a part of your will for me. I will try lovingly to build an edifice of love and praise with these materials which you have given me. What I am is your gift to me. What I become will be my gift to you. (1984, 153)

The belief in providence is not always expressed in such benign phrases, however, nor embodied in innocent deeds. Indeed, its abuses are widely documented. In fundamentalist circles, for example, whether Protestant or Catholic, every kind of moralism and militarism, racism and authoritarianism, has been justified in its name; the oppression of women tolerated; and the misfortunes of countless individuals' lives interpreted in terms of divine punishment or the work of the devil, with the debilitating guilt and self-deprecation such interpretations inspire. By the same token, not all expressions of the belief are necessarily so destructive – or so demonic. Indeed, there is a spectrum of expressions in spiritual circles, each more or less healthy, depending on how deeply the details of our existence are honoured, how sincerely our ordinariness is valued, and how compassionately the divine reality is deemed to view the faults and failures of our human one.

In *Spirituality and the Gentle Life*, priest-psychotherapist Adrian Van Kaam (1974) counsels his readers to develop the quality of gentleness. 'Gentleness,' says Father Van Kaam, 'is a special way of listening to myself and others and all that happens in my life' (35). It 'helps me to hear in each new situation subtle nuances that merge because of slight changes in the people and circumstances connected with it' (33–4). Such gentleness, however, is more than mere passivity. It is 'more than relaxation and giving in; it is more than the opposite of fight, work, and ambition' (33). It is a special kind of activity, even of assertiveness, though one characterized by peacefulness, acceptance, and trust. It is an active gentleness to 'everything that touches significantly upon what I am doing' (33). 'When gentle,' says Van Kaam, 'I listen to the situation as God allows it to be. I flow with it obediently. I quietly give myself over to it' (34). In the process, I see far more in each detail of my life than its 'work-a-day meaning': 'A gentle listening to the world gives me the opportunity to hear its revelation anew ... People, events, and things begin to nourish my spiritual life. They lift my heart to God' (34).

Another author to consider the experience of providence is the late Trappist monk, Thomas Merton. Celebrated for his anti-war, activist writings in the fifties and sixties, as well as for exploring the links between Eastern and Western spiritual traditions, Merton writes in a similar vein as Van Kaam. In *Seeds of Contemplation* (1972), he articulates his conviction about the inherent holiness of each detail of our daily lives. 'Every moment and every event of every man's life on earth,' he says, 'plant something in his soul ... grains of [God's] life that would spring up one day in a tremendous harvest' (12, 14). Everything is thus grist to the spiritual mill, just as it can be for the fictional one: 'from the glimpse of a face in the street,' says Somerset Maugham, 'to a war that convulses the civilized world, from the scent of a rose to the death of a friend' (Allen, 1949, 233).

To Merton, one kind of learning is essential: 'We must learn to realize that the love of God seeks us in every situation,' he says, 'and seeks our good. His inscrutable love seeks our awakening' (13). The kind of awakening Merton believes the love of God is seeking, though, is not an awakening to some essential self that is already there in nascent form, merely waiting to be actualized, as the vision of Powell can imply. Though essentialism has a long history in Christian circles, there have been many challenges to it during the past century under the influence of existentialists such as Kierkegaard, Heidegger, or Sartre (Macquarrie, 1973). Like the theologian Moltmann with his insight that a human being's 'essence is not handed to him as a finished product but assigned to him as a task' (1975, 20), Merton operates with his own form of existentialism, one that leads him to have a self-process in mind that is decidedly creative. Hence he says, 'our vocation is not simply to be, but to work together with God in the creation of our own life, our own identity, our own destiny' (25). This creation of our own lives – or this co-creation of our lives with God – requires, as Van Kaam saw too, not a passive submission to the world but an active engagement with it. Nor are its consequences predestined in a hard and fast sense; rather, they are open-ended, unpredictable, free. In his view, 'to work out our own identity in God, which the Bible calls "working out our salvation," is a labour that requires sacrifice and anguish, risk and many tears. It demands close attention to reality at every moment, and great fidelity to God as He reveals Himself, obscurely, in the mystery of each new situation. We do not know clearly beforehand what the result of this work will be' (26).

A further twist to the belief is provided by theologian John Haught (1984). Writing out of the perspective of process philosophy (see 'The Concept of Self-Creativity'), and thus employing aesthetic more than theological categories, Haught sets the individual's struggle to read meaning into the events of his life in the context of the creative unfolding of the universe as a whole: 'As the creative advance of the universe brings more and more novelty into the picture,' he says, 'the events of the past are continually given a new and unanticipated significance. As the sea of events that make up the cosmos broadens and deepens, the meaning of each individual happening is itself intensified and widened. *Its final meaning, therefore, cannot be determined from its own limited perspective any more than we can determine the meaning of the early episodes of a novel without reading it to the end*' (104; emphasis mine).

Unlike more conservative formulators of the belief in providence such as Powell, Van Kaam, Merton, and Haught all advocate a view of the divine intention, then, that is immanental as opposed to transcendental, natural as opposed to supernatural, emergent as opposed to predestined, and personal as opposed to paternal. In Merton's words, 'in all the situations of life the "will of God" comes to us not merely as an external dictate of impersonal law but above all as an interior invitation of personal love' (12).

Whether in an immanentalist or transcendentalist form, belief in the intelligent involvement of a divine will in the intimate affairs of individual lives has been tenaciously attractive throughout the course of Western history. Moreover, it is being continually revised with each new generation of theologians who set themselves to ponder the relationship between God and the world. As educators in the broad sense, and as students of the poetics of self-creation, we have two choices. On the one hand, we can dismiss such a belief as groundless superstition or religious escapism, and, with it, dismiss what it can tell us about the process of meaning-making in many people's lives. On the other, we can accept it at face value as at least some indication of the origin and nature of the need to read the unfolding events of our lives as comprising a coherent, aesthetic whole.

I have been concentrating here only on Christian forms of providence, and ironically on Catholic versions at that – Catholicism being the tradition most commonly criticized for its author-itarian structure. Within Christianity generally, though, Protestant expressions of the belief differ from Catholic ones, liberal ones from conservative ones, and those of one denomination from those of another. Beyond Christianity, comparable beliefs take a comparable range of forms in each of the world's other major religions. My intention here, however, is not to detail the meaning-reading strategies of particular traditions or to decide which ones are 'better,' for that is an issue of content more than of form. I am simply drawing attention to the fact that one source of the meaning-reading drive is formal religious spirituality, as interpreted and fortified by official doctrines, and that, for many of the adults with whose self-creation we are concerned, such a source is stubbornly at work behind the scenes of their actions and ideas. That is, their life-stories continue to be profoundly if uncritically composed (plotted, etc.) in terms of the larger stories of the creeds into which they have been pushed or pulled from their earliest years, with no adult conversion or no conscious decision for or against one over another.

Novel-ty: Further Thoughts

Common to all three of these contexts in which self-reading is encouraged is the conviction that none of our life's events is entirely accidental – that is, pointless, meaningless, unredeemable, wasted. In the therapeutic context, this conviction takes the form of a sense that the details of our daily lives, properly read, reveal a particular psychological thread linking them meaningfully together. If we can follow that thread, we discern the underlying, dynamic pattern whereby our relationships and fortunes have hitherto tended to unfold. We see what diarist Tristine Rainer (1978) calls 'the plot of [our] life created by [our] subconscious slowly through time' (265). We see our personal myth, become more able to critique it, and, if we choose, move beyond it.

In both the psychic or spiritual context and the explicitly religious one, the thread does not end within ourselves. Rather, it is tied to powers that may operate through us but are effectively beyond us. The goal of life in these contexts is to discern this thread whenever possible in our everyday lives: the sort of thread that Hillesum exclaims 'run[s] through my life, through my reality, like a continuous line' (1985, 113), or that Progoff believes 'has been forming beneath the surface of our lives, carrying the meaning that has been trying to establish itself in our existence' (1975, 11). It is to see this thread and honour it as 'the secret signature of each soul' (Lewis, 1970, 146). To do so requires the development of a particular kind of discipline. Like the one called for in reading a novel, such a discipline is alert to the role of each event in the working out of the plot of the story as a whole, whatever that plot may be, alert to how it adds to the unfolding of that plot a significant dimension and contributes toward its denouement, its 'chief glory,' its destiny. In such contexts, we develop the sense that if only we have 'eyes to see' we can read each of our life's events as a unique revelation of the movement of a larger, more 'author-itative' reality within which it finds its ultimate source, whatever that reality be called: the Tao, the Transpersonal, the Unconscious, the Higher Self, Providence, or God.

In so far as this common conviction about the meaning-potential of our life's every event raises the question of free will and determinism – not to mention the problem of evil, and indeed, again, the definition of 'event' itself! – then with Fingarette (Kegan, 1982, 11) I believe we are faced with an important realization: A thorough exploration of the relationship between self-creation and self-storying is ultimately impossible in the realm of psychology and/or literary theory alone. At some stage, it must extend into territory traditionally held by metaphysics and theology. It must ask about the implications for our understanding of the learning process of at least *some* people's belief that the successful unfolding of their personal stories depends on the cooperative relationship they maintain (through prayer, meditation, etc.) with the one they see as the final author-ity of their lives, the master narra-tor, 'the cosmic storyteller,' within whose story they believe they live and move and have their being.

So some people believe, of course, yet maybe not many. For many – the majority of us possibly – the situation is less clear. Only a faint trace of such a belief remains, yet the question to which it is the answer refuses to die. 'What kind of story are we in?' writes theolo-gian John Dunne (1973): that is the question. The question, he says, 'we might ask if we were characters in a story and the storyteller would let us ask it' (2) – a question that has been put with perhaps no greater poignancy than in our own century by storytellers like Samuel Beckett, with his *Waiting for Godot*, and Luigi Pirandello, with his *Six Characters in Search of an Author*. In the end, though, it may matter less whether we read the stories of our lives through religious lenses primarily, through psychological or spiritual ones, or through some combination of the three, than simply that some sort of deliberate self-reading is integral to how many of us manoeuvre through our lives and search for meaning in their midst.

There are two postscripts to this notion of life-as-novel. The first concerns an assumption that may be detected in what I have been saying so far, which is that the story of our lives can be radically re-storied – in the sense of undergoing a change in the genre whereby events become experiences, etc. – and yet somehow remain the same story. Common sense tells us that any novel re-genre-ated this radi-cally partway through would be a rather broken-up book. I am not talking here about a final product, however; I am talking about an unfolding process, one of which we may only recently have taken conscious authorship. In reality, the product is never completed, the final lines never written. We are the writers, so to speak, and we are *in* the writing still. As such, our ongoing task, as we waken to it, is to take the events of our life thus far, or rather the experiences we have composed them into, and fashion a life-story that succeeds in pulling them ever more integrally together, revealing ever more fully the symbolic interconnectedness between them. In the process, therefore, we continually re-*read* them, which means *de*-construct earlier readings and construct new ones (Rubin, 1986, 69), so that our inside story is less and less a mere 'collage of reminiscences' (editor's note for Bruner, 1988, 574) and more and more a coherent, fictional whole.

The second postscript is related to the first, as well as to the matter of integrity. It concerns the relationship between the one and the many in personal identity. On the one hand, we have the peculiar fixation of much psychology with 'tell[ing] a single story, construct[ing] a consistent character, fix[ing] an identity' (Keen and Fox, 1974, 9). On the other, we have the post-modern awareness of the inherent multiplicity of selfhood, according to which 'the self does not stand apart from a narration, but is constituted, even at the unconscious level, by the narrative conventions of the society in which it comes to be' (Beardslee, 1990, 170). Thus, 'although usually consciously relating to only one or a few,' the self 'always participates in a bundle of stories' (172). Between these two perspectives lies a great chasm. Moreover, knowledge of even the *possibility* of the latter prevents us from going home again to naïve belief in the former.

The notion of the *novel* of our lives, however, while appearing to be one more form of the need for a singular identity, enables us to have our cake and eat it too. It provides us with an image of diversity-as-unity and of the many-as-one, complicated though that image may be: a novel of which we are at once author, narrator, and reader; in which we have not one 'character' but several; which is poly-plottable; and which can be variously versioned and endlessly re-storied. The oneness involved here, though, is a oneness that is less *within* us than we ourselves are within – just as the countless stories that constitute a novel are *within* the novel. 'Our tales are spun,' Dennis Dennett reminds us, 'but for the most part we don't spin them; they spin us' (1991, 418). Our life-story lives less inside of us than we live inside of it.

This is a significant shift in understanding, 'a new way of defining personality and psychology' (Keen and Fox, 1974, 9). Rather than being concerned with *identity*, which can be seen as a kind of 'repetition compulsion, a conspiracy to put a consistent face before the world,' we can be concerned with helping 'an individual *lose* identity' and thus reverse the usual approach, which leads to our being 'defined more by *neglected* possibilities than by realized ones' (9–10). Such a perspective leads us, naturally, to consider the stories we leave untold.

The Stories We Leave Untold

In her far-reaching study *Secrets*, Sissela Bok likens 'the death of an individual ... to a universe going extinct' (1984, 21n). Human beings, she says, 'can never be entirely understood, simultaneously exposed from every perspective, completely transparent either to themselves or to other persons. They are not only unique but unfathomable' (21).

Bok's view accords with mine. Inside each of us lies not only a library of stories (both the many of our lives and the one) but a clearing-house for all other stories as well, the universe of stories, for there are few stories to which we cannot in some way relate. Yet of the countless stories we could tell of *ourselves*, there are comparatively few we do. 'Much of our stock of lived experience goes unstoried ... it remains amorphous, without organization and without shape' (White and Epston, 1990, 12). We make nothing of it. There is a quiet tragedy in this. As Polster says, 'The raw material for stories is always being formed. Each moment in a person's life hosts an endless number of events. Considering the abundance of this treasure, relatively few stories emerge' (21).

The purpose of this section is to consider the how, what, and why – as well as the *so what?* – of the stories we leave untold. I can express the value of doing so in simple terms: The story untold is the life unlived. The more un-storied existence we can transform into experience, that is, and the more untold experience we are able to express, then the more powerfully and profoundly can our self-creation proceed: the more author-ity we have over the storying and re-storying of our own lives. Such an insight is hinted at by a variety of sources.

'If human life is the *experience* of life,' as Sidney Jourard argues, then 'he who experiences more, with greater intensity, lives more' (1971, 93). If 'self-creation tends to make a life like a novel by a single author,' as Jonathan Glover claims, then the wider the world of that novel becomes, then the richer will be our experience of ourselves: the more our life will be 'deeply lived' (Nin, 1981). If 'a life as lived is inseparable from a life as told,' as Jerome Bruner maintains, then the more we can tell the more alive we can be: the more substantial and centred, the more 'fierce with reality,' we can become (Scott-Maxwell, 1968, 42). Finally, if 'I am the story I can tell about my own life,' as Don Cupitt proposes, then 'the more artistically coherent and ethically satisfying the story I can tell the more emotionally fulfilled I shall feel' (1991, 67).

All this need not mean, however, that we have to tell our story to *others*. We may decide to keep it to ourselves. Yet, having storied it, it is at least ours to keep. In other words, the wider our awareness of the stories we are, then the more power we have in relation to others. By this I mean: the better we are able to cope with their tendency to 'storyotype' us; the more confidently we can critique the several larger stories in which the forms of our self-telling originate; and the wider is the circle of our compassion, our capacity to comprehend others, and our ability to identify imaginatively and sensitively with the world of stories in general – both literary and lived.

In reading a novel, our sense of the untold stories is crucial to our understanding of the told (Connelly and Clandinin, 1990, 10). Although most of us 'underread,' our playing with what lies *between* the lines – what Kermode calls 'narrative secrets' (1980, 79ff) – is essential to our feeling the full range of possibilities pointed to *by* the lines. It enhances the story's allure, enriches its atmosphere, thickens its world. It is the same with us.

We all have – and need – our secrets. They define us, give us substance, atmosphere, allure. If our hearts were always on our sleeves, if our stories were continually on our lips, if we took no tales to our graves, we would be like pictures that are all foreground and no background. As it is, even the simplest of us is fraught with background. The very lines in our faces attest to it, poignant with our untold experience: like a tightly coiled spring behind our eyes, waiting for some trustable soul on which to be released. This story potential is what renders us the energized, interesting species we surely are. Ultimately and fortunately, of course, telling *all* is as impossible as it is undesirable. The more we learn to tell, to both ourselves and others, the more we find there is to tell, a discovery that awaits all beginning journal-keepers. The deeper we dip into the well, the more water we find.

What we are considering here is the question of balance – between discretion and disclosure. Just as discretion is a big (if not the better) part of intimacy, so our own untold stories play an unsung yet undeniable part in the poetics of our self-creation. Appreciating the broad vista of the story of our life is impossible apart from an occasional peek at what Margaret Atwood calls 'that submerged landscape of the things that are never said, which lies beneath ordinary speech like hills under water' (1988, 341). Before peeking at that landscape here, let me make three points by way of clarification.

Clarifications

First, in discussing the stories we leave untold, I am not talking about all the jokes we have listened to, laughed at, and promptly forgotten.

Nor am I talking about all the bits of gossip we have heard about others but that have quietly slipped our mind (though such bits have remarkably adhesive qualities). Nor am I talking about the countless stories we have read or seen or heard each day through the news, but that no human memory could possibly retain. I am talking about stories that concern *us*: the stories of all the individual episodes and experiences, subplots and periods, situations and scenes that make up the one ever-unfolding creation we point to or imply when we speak of 'the story of *my* life.'

Second, in so far as I am talking about memory, I am talking about autobiographical memory. However, given that the stories we tell about ourselves (or could tell) are not just reflections on the past but also projections into the future, rehearsals of what might be, then I am not talking about memory alone. I am talking about hopes and fears, wonderings and worries, dreadings and dreams. It is not just the annals of past experience that are pertinent to the poetics of learning, that is; it is the anticipations of future experience as well. As White and Epston explain in their discussion of the storying of experience, 'since all stories have a beginning (or a history), a middle (or a present), and an ending (or a future), then the interpretation of current events is as much future-shaped as it is past-determined' (1990, 10).

Third, I am concerned here with at least two levels of untold stories. On the one hand are the stories we leave untold on the level of experience, which means stories we leave untold to ourselves. Not all of our existence can be experienced; relatively speaking, little of it *is* experienced. 'Many things happen to me,' says Stephen Crites, 'that I am not able to integrate into any story, and to that extent such things are not experienced' (1986, 160). On the other hand are the stories we leave untold on the level of expression, which means stories we can tell ourselves but leave untold to others. Granted, the stories we conceal with our lips we may reveal with our looks, and may scream with our eyes, yet ultimately not all of our experience can be expressed. Relatively speaking, little of it *is* expressed. We all have more existence than we can possibly experience and more experience than we can possibly express. As our unstoried existence lies all *around* us, so our untold experience lies locked up *inside* us.

Yet the line between these two levels is not distinct. Where one begins and the other ends, and which comes first in which situation, is never crystal clear. Stories on one level merge with stories on the other. There can be stories we find ourselves telling someone else (whether a therapist, confessor, or friend) before we are able to tell them to ourselves. Fashioning our inside story from our outside one and our inside-out stories from our inside one – these two processes are in continual interaction. This interaction is at the heart of the poetic enterprise through which we continually make our souls.

The Natural Limits to Self-Storying

This last clarification brings out the point that there are a number of natural reasons for the stories we leave untold. To save confusion later, I shall spell a few of these out.

First of all, most of us are oblivious to the story potential of our own infancy – at least, at the time. Few of us remember our birth. Nor can we recall and recount the lion's share of our existence for some time thereafter, at least not until we have acquired the necessary mental skills, the ability to differentiate between self and other, and certainly the vocabulary to do so – as well as the culturally derived forms of self-telling on which any self-storying relies. Though the timing will vary at which we each emerge as self-conscious creatures from this early blissful ignorance, such 'childhood amnesia' is unavoidable. But it is not automatically a negative thing, any more than is forgetting itself.

Second, we are hard-pressed to story what we failed to notice the first time around. 'This means that in any situation, with its near-infinite number of things that could be noticed, we notice only those things that are important for our immediate purposes. The rest we ignore' (Berger, 1963, 56–7). Our immediate purposes vary according to any number of factors. If we are primarily 'visual learners,' then, effectively, what we see is what we story – leastwise more so than if some other sense where uppermost in our engagement with the world. In the telling, sights will stick but sounds will fade, while smells will scarcely have been noticed in the first place. Similarly, if according to the theory of 'multiple intelligences' (Gardner, 1990) our dominant frame of mind makes us zero in on the logical-mathematical, the musical, the linguistic, or the spatial possibilities in our existence, then those are what we shall make more of. In our telling of our life-story, this frame will colour – will construct – our life events. The intellectual autobiographer will highlight the history of her involvement with ideas; the musical one, with tunes; and so on. The same pattern can be expected in relation to our dominant 'learning style,' 'personality type,' etc., each of which will influence our point of view, our self-characterization, and our self-plotting: what, unconsciously, we select for experiences and what we reject.

Third, our self-storying is limited because of the fact that, just as life involves a regular re-storying, it involves a regular de-storying as well: a dis-illusioning with respect to the future, that is. At every stage, we are like readers who must give up theory A on how the story will turn out in favour of theory B, as the plot takes this twist and not that. When the hoped-for job is not offered to us after all, we have to let go of the idea of drawing that salary and living in that city. When the engagement is broken, we are released, regrettably, from the dream of the picket fence around that particular house with that particular spouse. Furthermore, being burdened with raising a family, with pouring out our lives for others, can, if not de-*story* us, then quietly de-*value* us – in our own eyes. We can lose touch with our own story, in terms of its merits and contents alike.

Fourth, at the other end of the lifeline from infancy is old age. If our blindness to our birth limits our self-storying, no less so does our decline toward our death. Death is the great de-storyer. The thickening of our life-plot that accompanied our earlier years turns gradually into the narrowing that leads unwaveringly to our end. 'The closure of the end of a narrative effectively excludes meanings that have not participated in the story' (Beardslee, 1990, 171). As Forster reminds us, 'nearly all novels are feeble at the end. This is because the plot requires to be wound up' (1962, 93–4). Their very drawing to conclusion – thus losing the interest of the reader – is in a sense their undoing, their denouement, their decomposition. In life, this feebleness, this undoing, can go hand in hand with frustration: frustration for the aged themselves as they find the autobiographical imperative intensifying at the same time as they are running out of time and energy to respond to it – to make sense of, to possess, their lives. Frustration for their families as well, who can only look on helplessly as their lives so often outlast their stories. As the novelist Kurt Vonnegut puts it, 'If a person survives an ordinary span of sixty years or more, there is every chance that his or her life as a shapely story has ended and all that remains to be experienced is epilogue. Life is not over, but the story is' (Schiebe, 1986, 143).

Keeping Our Stories to Ourselves

Much of what we *do* story we none the less leave untold. I see the reasons for this falling into two broad categories: things we *fear* and things we *lack*.

In the first category, there is the general fear of losing our personal power. As we know from our sense of suspense in following any story, there is great power in that part of it that lies before us yet untold. As the story unfolds, however, and our 'sheer narrative lust' (Lewis, 1966, 103) is satiated, then the allure of the story as whole – its power over us – diminishes. The fear of losing our power as we go public with our *personal* story can motivate us to keep it to ourselves. 'Better to keep your mouth shut and be thought a fool,' our motto runs, 'than to open it and dispel all doubt.' Deep within us all, then, may be a Don Juan. 'It is best to erase all personal history,' he said, 'because that would make us free from the encumbering thoughts of other people' (Castaneda, 1975, 30). Other people's thoughts encumber us of course because of the fierce realities of ignorance, gossip, and prejudice. Any segment or summary of our story, once expressed, becomes subject immediately to the 'storyotyping' of others, to being ground up and spat out by the rumour mill, to being distorted, misin- terpreted, read the wrong way – thus to the loss of the prestige or reputation we would like to impress them as having. To keep our story safe, therefore, many of us deem it wise to move to a new town or travel to a new culture and start a new life, or story our old one afresh. Or, as I say, we keep silent.

Traditionally, the 'strong, silent type' has been seen as a person of power. Usually a man, he is someone who reveals sufficiently little of the story of his life that he is considered not just difficult to make out but also 'deep' – and therefore desirable: a man of mystery and allure. Not all silent types are seen as strong, however, which is why the erasure of personal history, the keeping safe of our story, can some- times backfire. The silent type of *woman* may be seen by society not as deep at all, not as a 'cold and lonely lovely work of art,' but as 'dumb,' not only without a voice but without value as well.

Then there is the fear of reprisal. To tell our story or some portion or version thereof, we can fear, is to risk punishment by someone else, whether divine or human. For the victim of abuse, the haunting spectre of her abuser and of what he will do if his 'cover is blown' makes it mandatory that she keep her story safe. For people who are secretly lesbian or gay, there is the fear not only of reprisal from society at large but also of ridicule and rejection by individuals who have been close to them all along, once the story of their orientation exits the closet. Such people have learned throughout life – have *had* to learn – to keep their stories safe: often so safe, so deeply buried, that they become self-deceived. Similarly, for the illiterate person in a literate society, the sufferer of some stigma or disease, the illegal alien, the fugitive, the impostor, the bigamist, the slippery politician, the uncaught criminal or the ex-con – for any who have anything to hide, who lead 'a double life' – there will be acute awareness of the imperative to keep their stories to themselves.

There is also the fear that the stories we let slip out might get used against us, perhaps not in a court of law but in our everyday relationships. We have seen how delicate is the development of intimacy, story-wise: how much is riding on the stories we reveal to each other, withhold from each other, and read into each other – characterizing, even caricaturing, each other not as we are but as we project each other to be. The same projection is no less involved in our more casual encounters. Hence our need to be careful not to 'cast our pearls before swine' lest our listeners form the wrong impression and so push us subtly but surely away. This is impression management. Rather than release them immediately into the conversation with each new person I meet, for example, I may keep my minister stories to myself – funny things that happened to me on the way to the funeral, and so forth. I do this not because I am ashamed of these anecdotes but because of how quickly they can trigger people's 'storyotypes' of ministers as a group. On the basis of little or no knowledge of me personally, they rush to unfair assumptions about who I am, where I have come from, and where I am going. In the process, they thrust on me their unexpiated guilt, their unresolved anger at the pain in their world, or their unrequited yearning for union with the divine. With few are these stories safe.

For some of us, there is the fear not so much of reprisal from others, or of rejection or betrayal by them, or of angering them, but of hurting them. We withhold certain stories about ourselves, even lie, because we do not want to disempower them – by 'topping' *their* stories, for instance. Or because we want to protect them, prevent them from suffering needless confusion or doubt, about either us or themselves. So we shield them from the whole story, not because we believe it unimportant for them to know but because we know it would disillusion them, strip them of their current cherished version of not only us but also of themselves, their family, their world. Moreover, we feel unwilling or unqualified to be the culture of embeddedness that they need to stick around until they can re-story. Where their author-ity stands in the way of our own, we may also fear the repercussions that our disclosure could unleash on *us*, since our story clearly contradicts theirs. All the while, of course, we may defend our silence in such matters not as dishonesty but as discretion, not as cunning (or coward-ice) but as compassion.

Finally, for some of us the fear involved is the fear of being engulfed by memories – by entire chapters perhaps – so awful that they must be vigorously repressed. There are stories that we are not only not yet ready to tell – because we lack the words or because we cannot make up our mind as to their 'meaning' – but also may never be ready to tell. 'I would lose my mind if I remembered everything,' says Holocaust survivor Elie Wiesel (1988, 254). Besides memories of things we did or endured in the war, this category includes specific memories of humili-ation, of horror, of abduction, of abuse – of that skeleton in our closet, that one unmentionable event that sits like a black hole at the heart of our history, that silent centre round which all our self-storyings must skirt. Or it could include memories of nothing in particular: of whole, cold decades sometimes, to which we allude to others with only a word or sigh, or dismiss with a single label like 'tough times' – as did the hero of Evelyn Waugh's *Brideshead Revisited*, sweeping across half the life of himself and his long-lost lover with the simple sentence: 'She, too, had had her dead years' (1962, 293). Of whatever type, some mem-ories can be repressed so profoundly that not only is self-deception a possibility but so is insanity, given the untolled potential of our untold stories to sabotage our souls. Essential as our secrets are, that is, the darker ones may be our undoing – until and unless they are brought to the light, where we can deal with them by defusing their undue power within our life-plot to limit the scope and skew the direction of our self-creation.

The Lack of Listening

In the second broad category, things we *lack*, is another range of rea-sons our stories get left untold. One of the most obvious is simply the lack of opportunities to engage in story-telling to, and with, others – particularly others who can appreciate them, who come from a com-parable context. We need to 'find an audience for the untold tales ... permission to tell the stories that are our own birthright.' Otherwise our situation is like that of the tree falling in the forest. That is, 'you can't tell who you are unless someone is listening' (Keen and Fox, 1974, 9). This is the dilemma of the prisoner, the refugee, or the ill – and often the elderly as well. Poor Aunt Mary, her only company a TV, a teapot, and a cat, is seldom in a situation of having someone to tell her story to. And even when she is, fewer and fewer people – or less and less of a variety of people – may have the patience to listen to her, especially when her speech or hearing is in any way diminished. Thus the countless stories she *could* tell die quietly of attrition. Sadly, then, many of 'the greatest stories have never been told: they lie under cemetery stones or have turned to dust or sand' (Surmelian, 1969, 92).

In so far as the stories of others stimulate the telling of our own, being starved for ordinary conversation also leads to our stories being left untold. Simply put, nobody *asks* us to tell them. But it is not that we lack a listener as such, for a listener who gets us to tell – or lets us tell – the same old stories over and over may be doing us no favours. When, for example, our social circle is limited to people whose lives are much like ours, their life-stories similar in content and form, these may be the only stories ever elicited or allowed, in which case we need new contexts. We need listeners, supportive yet impartial, who invite or challenge us to tell more of our stories than those we are most accustomed or encouraged to tell – the ones about the war or the divorce or the time the bull chased us down the lane: listeners, moreover, who offer us the space to 'read' any or all of our stories with the critical awareness required to re-story our soul as a whole.

Tragically, even when surrounded by people who otherwise care for us deeply, we may still not receive this kind of listening, the kind required to tell our untold stories without fear of ridicule, reprisal, or misrepresentation. Often, parents fail to provide it because, as we have seen, how we tell ourselves to them tends to be distorted by *our* version of *their* version of what our story is. Moreover, their version may not be terribly up-to-date, may be frozen in the past. For a while, lovers or friends can suffice in this regard, but eventually, with them too, the common story we construct between us can cloud our own story out; and the desire to break free and start telling our story to someone new, and in a new way, becomes overwhelming. Either that or, as with parents, the version of our story with which the other person operates becomes so familiar or so dominates their perception of us that it prevents us from telling not only new stories but old, untold ones as well.

Looking at this from another perspective, the people we most trust are the people we believe will keep our stories *in* trust, will keep our stories safe. Often these are intimate partners, though not always. While it is true that partners keep many of our stories (Pennebaker, 1990, 109), they sometimes do so unsafely, or at least inaccurately. That is, they can be as subject to false memory syndrome of us as we can be of ourselves. They can tell us that event X in our lives happened in one way when in fact it happened in quite another. In so far as we defer to their author-ity, we may accept their version as true. None the less, they know things about us – past, present, and future – that others do not, the correct recall of which we ourselves might otherwise lose. This can easily occur if, for example, we are unattached for much of our lives and so have no one to story our lives with us, no one to check our tendency to embellish or omit. However distorted, then, their stories of us may be better than a stock of patently untrue ones, or none at all.

Furthermore, with our partners we also share unique 'couple stories,' subtle references to which can pepper our every conversation. Such anecdotes are often our social stock-in-trade: *Dear, why don't you tell them about the time we went camping in Colorado. You tell that story so well!* Besides carrying many of our most delicate confidences, then, these people share in some of the most pivotal events of our adult lives – although what they make of them inside themselves, and how they express them inside-out to others, can be drastically different than they are for us. All the same, when for one reason or another they leave us, they take with them a chunk – a chapter – of the story of our life. In some way, great or small, their departure de-stories us.

To come back again to the very old, such de-storying can be a hard fact of life. With fewer friends visiting them who know their story (if only outside-in) and fewer loved ones outliving them in whose life-stories they have been characters in turn, they can become increasingly disoriented. This disorientation increases, of course, when the larger stories in which they have been embedded – the family, the neigh-bourhood, the culture – are unfolding at a speed or in a direction with which they cannot keep pace. But it is not just other people who keep their stories safe; so also do their routines, their surroundings, and their possessions. Like people, these things constitute a 'holding envi-ronment' for them, confirming them and continuing for them through-out the many changes of their lives. Thus, when we must institutional-ize them – confining them to little rooms with strangers for companions and a box of knick-knacks and photographs to remind them who they are – we must acknowledge what it is we are doing. We are stripping them of their story. Though it may be impossible to care for them by any other means, and though their advancing senility may be taking a toll of its own, we must realize what, story-wise, is at stake.

So, apart from encounters with strangers-on-trains to whom our story can come out in ways that are wonderfully new, perhaps the only situation in which we can tell it as freely as we wish and as fully as we need is the therapeutic one. By this, of course, I really mean the *ideal* therapeutic situation – one in which no particular plot-line is projected onto us (Schafer, 1983, 5–13), in which someone is open to our story in a non-judgmental manner and is willing to be the culture of embeddedness that confirms us, contradicts us, and continues for us along the lonely road of re-storying. Sadly, though, such ideal listening is rare. In the minds of people who strongly identify with a religious storying of the world, however, it is not only possible but, they would say, real. It is focused in the concept of a personal God, someone to whom they believe no story is too dark to be confessed or too dense to be understood. Their conviction that someone thus knows the outside story of their lives, comprehends the inside story, and sees through both the inside-out stories and the outside-in stories – that they are listened to on all four levels at once – provides them a sense of centredness and stability. It enables them to accept the bewildering, ever-changing multiplicity of the stories of their lives comforted by the notion that within the omniscient authority of God they are not finally many but one.

Events and Experiences

A further lack is the lack of experiences. Our lives lack experiences because they contain either too many events or too few.

People who have too many events lead lives that are filled with events yet comparatively empty of experiences. Lacking either the time or the talent to examine their lives, or the opportunity to talk about them with others, they cannot adequately digest those events into experiences. In turn, this may increase their *appetite* for events – for enough events, that is, to make up for the lack of experiences in their diet. Thus their eyes become bigger than their stomach. They become the kind of people to whom the celebrated biographer James Boswell was referring when he ventured 'that a man should not live more than he can record, as a farmer should not have a larger crop than he can gather in' (Clifford, 1962, 32). Characteristic of such folk can be a restlessness, a shallowness, and – no matter how busy they may be, no matter how many activities they may be 'into' or trips they may take or products they may consume – a chronic boredom. All existence and no experience, that is, makes Jack a dull boy. 'Had we more experiencing,' says Hillman though, 'there would be need for fewer events,' because 'experience coagulates events ... digestion tames appetite' (1975a, 150).

Having too few events befalls not only the senior or the shut-in, of course, but also people whose diet of events, though full, is restricted in variety. This situation arises for a range of reasons: the monotonous routine (chosen or imposed) of their daily lives, the crushing repetition of menial or unchallenging work, or the narrow round of ritual that defines their daily existence due to unemployment, poverty, or simply an impoverished imagination.

Related to lack of experiences is simply lack of time. For whatever reasons, the lives of many of us are so fast-paced and so filled with events that it is possible for us to tell stories about only a tiny fraction of all that we suffer or do. As noted already, the examination of life requires time. To make its events into experiences, a period of digestion is mandatory. Too little time to transform too many events into experiences in our inside story is a recipe for poetic indigestion, for constipation ... perhaps even nausea. Paradoxically, it is a recipe for spiritual malnutrition as well, for hunger of the soul, which results in an increase in the speed of the human race. With more experiences, though, we would have need of fewer events 'and the quick passage of time would find a stop' (Hillman, 1975a, 150).

Vocabulary and Voice

Two related lacks involved in leaving our stories untold are the lack of vocabulary and the lack of voice. The former is the focus of those concerned with the spread of literacy. Without language, as we have seen, self-creation on the hermeneutical level is automatically limited. Language is the principal tool with which we name and claim our existence, rendering it experienceable and hence expressible. 'The limits of my language,' says the philosopher Wittgenstein, 'are the limits of my world.' Decades of studying the ties between language, thought, and life have made us open to such an insight, able to accept that, in many respects, the 'self' itself is a linguistic construction. 'We are made of words all the way down' (Cupitt, 1990, 163, 166). Thus, the lack of words to reflect on the realities of our life can only curtail the poetic process whereby outer is transformed into inner, event into experience, and the stuff of our existence into the stories of our lives. We cannot tell what we cannot story, and we cannot story what we lack the *words* to story. As Edward Bruner argues, 'some experiences are inchoate, in that we simply do not understand what we are experiencing, either because the experiences are not storyable, or because we lack the performative and narrative resources, or because vocabulary is lacking' (White and Epston, 1990, 13).

The mere possession of a language is not enough, however, for there are degrees of competence within any given language. Competence relates, for example, to the actual *number* of words in my working vocabulary. More words mean more of my existence can be rendered tellable – though it need not mean this. Hemingway managed to tell us a great deal about the human story with a rather limited vocabulary. Competence also relates to the kind, complexity, and subtlety of my words: the more complex, more subtle, my words can (though need not) mean the more complex and subtle aspects of my experience I can express. Growing up in a family in which my behaviour or ideas are routinely labelled 'stupid' or 'silly' or 'dumb' limits my linguistic resources for making sense of my life. More diplomatic terms like 'challenged' or 'free-spirited' or 'creative' can help me frame my self-concept quite differently.

Competence relates, too, to the stock of clichés and slang expressions that I pick up from the circles I move in and employ in my everyday speech. Yet, lively and colourful though these be, employing them mindlessly may mean that I have less rather than more of my experience available to express. I can talk the talk all right, but my acceptability to others is bought at the price of incomprehensibility to myself. Wealth of acquaintances is matched by poverty of soul. Competence can also relate to my familiarity with words and expressions from languages besides my own. Being confined to English does not allow me to capture – to experience and express – the same range of nuances that I could if I had access to a language with fifteen words for friendship or twenty-five for snow.

Linked to lack of vocabulary is lack of voice. Addressing it is the focus of those concerned with the plight of people who may have lots of access to language but little to power. These include members of

minority groups or people marginalized from the mainstream by
virtue of class or race, as well as individual women and men trapped
in abusive relationships whose stories are so severely and systematically silenced that, essentially, they cease to be (Belenky et al, 1986,
21–34). For many women, for instance, the convergence of the two
lacks, voice and vocabulary, is the direct result of living amid a language that is in many ways man-made. Writing equally of biography,
autobiography, and fiction, Carolyn Heilbrun asks 'how can women
create stories of women's lives with only male language?' (1988, 40).
In the same vein, Carolyn Burke argues that 'when a woman writes or
speaks herself into existence, she is forced to speak in something like
a foreign tongue, a language with which she may be personally un-
comfortable' (Smith, 1987, 57). The female composing her life in some
form of the autobiographical act, whether formal or informal, is thus
pushed into a kind of 'cultural ventriloquism': 'a gesture of impersona-
tion that requires [her] to speak like a man' (57). I shall return to this
theme in a moment.

A Poverty of Plots

A related lack, possibly the most profound, is the lack of plot-lines
with which to story the events of our lives in the first place – to em-
plot our development, that is – even when, technically, we are in
possession of the requisite vocabulary and voice. Plot, Ricoeur reminds
us, is what 'makes events into a story' (1980, 167). How we both
fabricate our inside stories and communicate our inside-out ones may
thus be seen as dependent on the range of plot-lines available to us to
do so. Since plot-lines are by definition selective, the events that one
leaves out another will include.

By the same token, if all the stories of the world converge within us,
then presumably all possible plot-lines converge within us as well.
Witness the ease with which any story, no matter how unusual we
find it, can engage us on at least some level. However, some of these
plot-lines are more deeply ingrained in us than others, so that no
matter what segment or summary we recount of our life-story it is
expressed in one or another of a predictable range of ways. The largest
factor in deciding which will be the most deeply ingrained is our
childhood conditioning. By this I mean the patterns of interpreting
relationships and events that were laid down in the critical first years
of our lives in a particular family system – or family story.

'Early in life ... we learn how to talk about our lives ... We learn in the circle of the family ... We learn the family genre: the thematics, the stylistic requirements, the lexicon ... procedures for offering justifications and making excuses, and the rest of it' (Bruner and Weisser, 1991, 141). These become so habitual that they become 'recipes for structuring experience itself, for laying down routes into memory, for not only guiding the life narrative up to the present but directing it into the future' (Bruner, 1987, 31). Thus, the family genre powerfully affects the individual genre – 'the genre through which events become experiences' (Hillman, 1975a, 146). This is, of course, no more startling a notion than we have been considering all along, which is that our personal stories are strongly shaped by the larger stories in which our lives have been rooted. Yet, even if the effect of the larger genre on the lesser is normal enough when we think about it, it can be quite problematic as far as the poetics of self-creation is concerned. The family genre can conceivably so overwhelm us, for example, that vast portions of our existence that at the time may have had adventurous or even comic possibilities for us personally were either cast in our minds in a tragic vein or else left unstoried altogether.

In the same breath as the family genre, we need to talk again about the *couple* genre. For many in our culture, life in a family of origin leads to life in an intimate relationship with one other person (or series thereof) and eventually also with children. In this couple context, as in the family context, each person's life gets storied by the other in particular ways. As I grow into relationship with my partner, not only does she become a character in my life-story but I become a character in hers. Accordingly, the genre according to which she stories my life – though she may seldom spell it out to me – is one that implicitly pre-scribes a set of plot-lines according to which the events of my life, both in relationship with her and on my own, can and cannot be storied. As White and Epston put it, 'we prune, from our experience, those events that do not fit with the dominant evolving stories that we and others have about us' (1990, 11–12). In other words, she sees me in a certain way, or entertains a certain outside-in story of me, and this invariably influences the way I both see *and do not see* myself. When my way of seeing myself corresponds more or less comfortably to hers (and the very concept of intimacy suggests such a correspondence), then being in the relationship means that I am probably not leaving any *more* of my stories untold than I would be if I were on my own. In fact, I may be leaving far fewer untold than if I were in relationship with someone else less compatible with me from a story perspective. When this correspondence is lacking, that is, the relationship can come seriously undone. When *my* story of me turns out to be significantly at variance with *her* story of me (and vice versa), then misinterpretations may abound, mistrust grow profound, and the integrity of our couple story itself eventually break down.

All of us suffer from a lack of plot-lines for storying our lives due to the dearth of stories that surround us on a day-to-day basis in our American-European culture – of *different* stories, that is. While the quantity of such stories is overwhelming, the kind is not. Putting it generously, the kind of stories that are our daily bread makes for a sadly narrow menu: Harlequin romances, spy thrillers, shoot-em-ups, sitcoms, soaps ... and, in so far as a game is a story too, baseball, football, hockey, and golf (Cawelti, 1989, 115–16; Eco, 1989, 128–9; Frye, 1988, 110). If 'our character ... changes, grows, and diminishes, largely as a result of our imaginative diet' (Booth, 1988, 257), then we feast on meagre fare. Most of these are the same old story, reflecting a limited range of ways to move from a beginning through a middle to an end. The long-term effects on our self-creation of feeding on the crude diet they provide us are depressing to contemplate, however little they have as yet been studied from a poetic (as opposed to ethical) perspective.

Most commonly, they are stories with Hollywoodized plots 'where everything works out in the end' (Connelly and Clandinin, 1990, 10). They are stories that, in the case of the average situation comedy, simplify the complexity of everyday life so grossly that 'in thirty-minute episodes (which end up as eighteen to twenty-two minutes of action between commercials), familial problems are recognized, defined, and solved' (Brookfield, 1990, 236). In its guidelines to prospective authors, Harlequin Enterprises stipulates, for example, that in composing the plot of a book in its popular 'Romance' series, 'a legitimate, sustained and resolvable conflict is essential. The plot should not be too grounded in harsh realities; traditional romances need an edge of fantasy, of dream fulfillment, yet they must be plausible.' Such a plot usually has a limited morality as well, featuring a set array of ways to construct and resolve conflict and a predictable arrangement of good guys and bad guys, winners and losers. In addition to being a limited morality, though, it may also be seen as a male morality.

Where women are continually exposed to such stories, many of their own stories may get left untold because the plot-lines mediated by popular culture allow them to make little of many of their lives' events. In her analysis of the dilemma facing women autobiographers, for instance, Sidonie Smith (1987) says that 'the typical and model script of a woman's life is very much a convention of patriarchal culture, one that women autobiographers must and do attend to' (10). Tracing the historical development of women's self-storying, she identifies 'four predominant life scripts available to women' during the late medieval and Renaissance periods. These were 'the nun, the queen, the wife, and the witch' (31), all of which are amply evident in the media-ted stories of our own time. Heilbrun extends the spirit of Smith's work in *Writing a Woman's Life*, where she explores the links between gender, power, and story. Her thesis is that 'women have been deprived of the narratives, or the texts, plots, or examples, by which they might assume power over – take control of – their own lives' (1988, 17).

In the past, but even in the supposedly more enlightened present, says Heilbrun, 'women's lives have been contrived' (18). Prior to about 1970, 'only the female life of prime devotion to male destiny had been told' (26). But woman, she insists, has 'the right to her own story' (17). Otherwise, she goes 'mad,' which means she is confined to 'her ultimate anonymity – to be storyless' (12). Like the 'silent' women whom Belenky et al have studied, she fails to develop 'a narrative sense of the self – past and future' (1986, 136). It is thus to 'the woman's quest for her own story,' to the search for 'new ways of writing the lives of women,' that Heilbrun believes women must be committing their energies (18). The aim of Heilbrun and Smith is to underscore the connection between having a story and being a person. Without their own stories, lived and told in their own terms, women, they argue, can neither have their own lives, possess their own voices, nor be their own persons. This they would see as a direct result of the historical dominance of men in the telling and shaping of the stories that fill our world. As one source puts it, 'Men have told the stories and framed the cultural precepts; women, reading those stories and bound by those precepts, have too often found themselves living men's stories rather than telling and living their own' (Frye, 1986, i).[4]

This lack of one's own story, they insist, has generally been the lot of women more than of men. Witness the scarceness of women's autobiographies and biographies both – until recently, that is. In her study of diary-keeping in women's lives, Krista Van Daele suggests that this situation may be changing. 'At the present time,' she says, 'the culture is full of creatively told stories that support a woman's growth and development' (1990, 281). It is worth asking, though, if the patterns and plots available to men are necessarily any truer to life for them than patriarchally patterned ones have been for women – however privileged men's stories have been within the 'master story' of Western society as a whole. In other words, are the plot-lines open to men – the male stories – even if more numerous, any less stock and stultifying than those open to women? This is a powerful question, one that the current barrage of books – by men – debunking the 'macho myth' and championing men's liberation suggests may not soon go away.

The importance of the untold stories in the life of an individual is paralleled by their importance in the world as a whole. There too the principle prevails that self-creation is linked to self-story. As the inside story of a given civilization – that is, the history of it written (inside-out) by its own interpreters – is able to accommodate, account for, and consider more and more of its own outside story, then the self-concept of that civilizaton must change, however gradual the process and great the cost. Specifically, as the overall self-story of Western society is opened to include the previously untold stories of the poor, of various minority groups, or of women – told of course from their respective points of view (and there will be many within each group) – then that same society self-creates in new ways. Old prejudices are opposed, new policies put in place, and new attitudes practised, thus changing the direction in which it unfolds. Furthermore, with my society's story so expanding, my own story receives implicit permission to expand as well. In this way, the political becomes the personal. As an individual woman or black, for example, I find my personal story is increasingly sanctioned and accepted. As I come to identify it with the now no-longer-*un*told story of women or blacks in general, that is, it grows within me in importance and power.

An obvious corollary to these observations is that the wider the variety of stories to which we expose ourselves – authored by both men and women – the greater the range of plot-lines (as of characterizations and points of view) available to us for storying and re-storying our souls. Thus, potentially, the more events of our lives we can take in and transform into experiences, the more nuances in such experiences we can notice and honour, and the broader the range of experiences we can therefore express. This makes an enquiry into the poetics of self-creation an implicit plea not only for greater literacy but for greater *literary* literacy as well (Bogdan, 1990b). In the words of Northrop Frye, 'only literature gives us the whole sweep and range of human imagination as it sees itself' (1963, 42). That is, 'we can't speak or think or comprehend even our own experience except within the limits of our own power over words, and those limits have been established for us by our great writers' (43). As such, 'literature is a human apocalypse, man's revelation to man' (44).

Forgetting Again

Accepting this corollary leads us to reflect once more on the role of ordinary forgetting in the stories we leave untold. The reasons behind forgetting ought to be the object of interest for all educators, particularly educators of adults. It may be enough to say that a learner has no head for remembering history and to leave the matter at that. However, to say he has no head for remembering the history that happens to be his own: this is not enough. To the extent that a learner's sense of his past and future influences his apprehensions about, participation in, and evaluation of a given educational experience, affecting what he both brings to it and takes from it, then we must grapple in earnest with the issue of remembering and forgetting.

At some point we have all been curious why some of the events of our lives stand out and others recede, why some float freely to the surface of our consciousness and others sink to the bottom. We have all been befuddled why we forget some events, which at the time we assumed we would *never* forget, yet remember others; conversely, why events that at the time did not seem memorable at all turn out to be precisely the ones that stick in our minds thereafter. Though some events may both stand out at the time and stick with us ever after, it is generally difficult to know in advance which ones will stick and which ones will not, difficult to predict beforehand what we shall remember and what we shall forget. We may suppose it has something to do with what we 'make' of them.

Theoretically, there is no limit to what we can make of a given event, which helps explain why we often require considerable time to fathom the 'meaning' of the more important of life's events. Of course, that some events are more 'important' than others, if true, is not straightforward. They are not inherently so. The importance attributed to a given event depends on what we do with it. If we do nothing with it, if we make nothing of it, then it is an event and little more. It does not make it into our inside story; it does not become an experience; it cannot be remembered. Two people may be present in the same place at the same time for the same basic occurrence. In that sense, it is an 'event' in each of their lives. Each can experience it, however, in decidedly different ways. Where, for one, it drops from memory almost immediately into the great inner well of generalized event memory (Schank, 1990), for the other, it is transformed into something around which a thousand delicious nuances come subsequently to accrue. C.S. Lewis alludes to such a situation in *The Problem of Pain*: 'you have stood before some landscape which seems to embody what you have been looking for all your life; and then turned to the friend at your side who appears to be seeing what you saw – but at the first words a gulf yawns between you, and you realize that this landscape means something totally different to him, that he is pursuing an alien vision and cares nothing for the ineffable suggestion by which you are transported' (1970, 145–6).

Roger Schank says that 'a good theory of mind ... must contain a model of how and why we create new stories and of what happens to experiences that do not get encoded as stories' (1990, 16–17). There are of course varying degrees according to which events (Schank's 'experiences') do or do not get encoded as stories, as well as various levels on which they may or may not get interpreted. There are events I may have succeeded in making into a story on one level, that is, but have failed to do so on another: events made into experiences that remain island episodes – story-ettes – that stand more or less by themselves because they cannot be incorporated into, or nested within, a larger story still. These are the stories I leave untold not because I have lost them from memory forever but because I currently lack the story-line to link them with other episodes into a fuller-length story, though I may have had such a story-line in the past. They are there within the total 'repository of stories' that constitutes my soul, yet they are part of 'the detritus of my history' (Truitt, 1987, 209). They become the compost heap from which fresh life may later sprout, like a writer's rich store of story material that is left over after one novel yet used in the next. 'Those aspects of lived experience that fall outside of the dominant story,' say psychologists White and Epston, 'provide a rich and fertile source of the generation, or re-generation, of alternative stories' (1990, 15).

Until then, however, such stories can be occasionally resurrected if the right trigger is pulled or the correct question asked, as we saw in considering mood in the previous chapter. For example, I may suddenly be able to remember a particular long-lost episode when, out of the blue, I am asked to recall a situation in my life in which I was the object of a practical joke, or was violently angry, or was hopelessly in love, etc. Asked the right question, countless episodes, seemingly gone from memory for good, can come racing back to mind.[5] Though temporarily forgotten, they are not technically gone. They are 'there,' awaiting only the necessary trigger to catapult them into consciousness. Seen more seriously, however, the inability to remember certain episodes may be an example either of self-deception, which I shall shortly consider, or of a significant impairment of our autobiographical memory.

There are often, of course, very understandable reasons why we forget many of the things that have happened to us throughout our lives, however vividly they may have stood out for us at the time: a concussion, a blackout, or the loss of too many brain cells after too much drinking or drugs. All of these situations lead to an impoverishment of autobiographical memory, but not necessarily to its impairment *per se*. They lead to changes in it in terms of quantity, but not necessarily of quality. As we have already noted, two features of autobiographical memory are essential: it is memory 'for a whole lifetime' and memory 'for the self' (Rubin, 1986, 69). Any impairment of either our sense of self or our sense of time therefore leads to the impairment of our autobiographical memory – though which impairment is the chicken and which the egg is open to debate.

In certain memory disorders both such disruptions combine. Victims of a concussion or stroke, or of an illness such as Alzheimer's disease or Korsakov's Syndrome, experience significant amnesic symptoms. One of the most bizarre forms of amnesia, however, is associated with multiple personality disorder (MPD). For people who suffer such an extreme impairment of their autobiographical memory, it seems there is no central 'life-plot' (Booth, 1988, 268, 289) because there is no central, singular 'self,' or sequence of selves, which holds the memories for the whole of their lifetime, only a number of isolated, multiple selves. Before diagnosis as having MPD, for instance, Truddi Chase (1987) was described simply as having 'trouble with time' (3). In *When Rabbit Howls*, her autobiographical account of the therapy she eventually underwent, she says that at one point she had no more than 'five memories of an entire lifetime and confetti shreds of the rest' (201). Known throughout the book simply as 'the woman' – the name given to the central presenting personality by the other ninety-two selves, or 'The Troops' – Chase writes that 'for various Troop members the concept of time may be very different. The woman and each of the others have significant periods of time missing from their awareness, periods lasting from a few minutes to days. For those times when a particular self is not present, it is difficult to know how much time has passed or when specific events took place. For the absent selves, that time did not exist' (xxii).

Though this kind of forgetting is far from the norm, there may be mild forms of dissociation to which we are all at times subject. As Roberto Assagioli expresses it, elaborating on the 'sub-personalities' he believes are at work within us, 'ordinary people shift from one to the other without clear awareness, and only a thin thread of memory connects them; but for all practical purposes they are different beings – they act differently, they show very different traits' (1987, 75). A common name for such dissociation is self-deception.

Self-Deception

Self-deception is not an abstract metaphysical concept, nor an issue of concern for philosophers alone. It is a topic of interest to us all. It concerns 'the imaginative resources [we] use in giving experience its aesthetic coherence' (Crites, 1979, 107). If we are to appreciate the poetics of learning, it cannot be ignored. Self-deception affects self-creation.

As commonly construed, self-deception is a 'mismatch' of stories about the self and its involvements (Polonoff, 1987, 45). It is a discrepancy between the story I tell myself and the story others see me to live. In relation to our discussion here, it is a gap – a particularly troublesome gap, that is, since there can never be *no* gap – between the inside story of my life and either the outside story or the inside-out story, or both. The nature and extent of such gaps are of course the focus for discussion in a variety of forums: the courtroom, the confessional, the counselling office, and the coffee shop on Gossip Row. In all of these settings, however – and, at times, in the privacy of my own heart – what tends to happen, says David Polonoff, is that 'the story I tell myself of my life is put next to the true story of my life, the life I have in fact lived. Inequalities and differences are noted on a tally sheet of correspondences. In this accounting of false propositions, omissions, and missed connections, some are then judged innocent, others guilty. The guilty ones are the self-deceptive ones' (45).

Unfortunately, determining self-deception in this way is easier said than done. As we have seen, 'the true story of my life, the life I have in fact lived,' is not accessible to me, certainly not in its entirety nor in an undigested, uninterpreted form. It is available to me only through the countless stories I have made up about it and that constitute my inside story as a whole. In trying to ascertain the extent of my self-deception, therefore, I am faced with a seemingly impossible question: 'If all we can know about ourselves is a story, what is to say that one story is superior to another? How do we establish the rightness of a story if there are no independently available facts to which it must correspond or, rather, if the same set of facts can correspond to any number of stories?' (47). Establishing the rightness of a given version of any segment or summary of the story of my life, says Polonoff, though difficult due to the absence of a 'true story,' may none the less be carried out in terms of three main criteria: coherence, believability, and empirical adequacy.

As far as coherence is concerned, the story must hold together within itself. If, on the inside level, I believe myself with equal fervency to be both a history instructor and the late king of Siam, then I am probably insane. The two stories are incompatible within me; they indicate my consciousness is split. But coherence, says Polonoff, is not a sufficient criterion. It is possible that my inside story is wonderfully coherent within itself (that I am a *reincarnation* of the king merely *disguised* as an instructor), yet when I tell it inside-out it is quite *in*coherent to the ears of those trying to make sense of me outside-in. Because of my daily meditation on what I believe is my real identity, that is, every detail of my inside story may square perfectly in my own mind with that of his royal highness, and yet, day after day, my students see only an absent-minded professor wandering the hallways muttering to himself in a string of odd-sounding phrases. My story may be good, to me at least, but woefully far from true – rather like that of Ross Perot, spoiler candidate in the 1992 American election. Perot was described as having a 'carefully tended story' – a rags-to-riches 'myth' that endeared him to many an American heart. Some parts of his myth, it was accused however, 'appear to be self-created'; indeed, 'much of the story is open to dispute' (Church, 1992, 17–18). Bringing this point closer to home, 'the good story' I tell myself on a given 'good day' might well be an utterly false story. To those who know me, I am deluding myself. I am glossing over gross mistakes rather than acknowledging them, forgetting things I have done and seen and been (or not) in the past in order to convince myself and others that the 'good story' is the 'true story' and nothing but – in the process, making everyone else's day a bad one.

The second criterion for determining whether I am self-deceived, therefore, is the believability of my story. 'To be believable,' says Polonoff, 'a self-narrative must be not only internally coherent but externally coherent as well. That is, an individual's story of his life must conform in some degree both with the version that others in the culture form of themselves and with the versions that others form of him' (50). A critical aspect of believability, says Polonoff, is thus liveability. If I do not wish to be labelled self-deceived, then I must demonstrate that, even with the secret self-image of a deceased Oriental monarch, I can compose and lead a liveable life, a life that goes somewhere, or, in Polster's terms, is 'directed' (1987, 32). If I am unable to do so, then I can fairly be categorized as self-deceived. If I *am* able to do so, however, while still sticking to my story inside, then I am technically not self-deceived, at least according to these criteria. Consequently, a further criterion must be invoked, that of empirical adequacy – not accuracy, we note, but adequacy.

Even if the facts of what I have undergone or done are unavailable in an uninterpreted form, Polonoff says, 'there remains a set of "primitive" experiences, obstinate and intractable, which must be assimilated to any narrative version' (52). These 'primitive' experiences – which Booth calls 'primary experiences' (1988, 15) – form 'the atomic units of narration, ' and 'though they do not dictate one particular ordering, they set boundaries to what can count as right orderings' (Polonoff, 52). In short, 'right versions must be compatible with this set; better versions are those able to organize the entire set with greater coherence' (52). Such a perspective accords with the object of much modern psychoanalysis, which is 'not so much to reconstruct the patient's life archaeologically as to help him construct a more contradiction-free narrative of it' (Campbell, 1989, 369). In terms of the levels of life-story, the inside story, as well as the inside-out story by which it is expressed, is ultimately responsible to the outside story. Though it can never accommodate the whole of that story – though it can only ever be but a version of it, seen 'through a glass darkly' – it is perpetually accountable to it. I may be free to compose myself, that is, but not entirely to *make myself up* (Polonoff, 53). Not any old story will do.

Coherence, believability/liveability, empirical adequacy – with such criteria, says Polonoff, we have 'a clearcut basis for rejecting certain versions of the self as wrong' (53). Although they still do not determine the 'right' version, they give us 'a range of rightness and a way of evaluating alternatives.' The effect of Polonoff's argument, I believe, is to underline the need to seek versions of my life-story that will enable me to coordinate and accommodate as many 'atomic units of narration' as I can, or will maximize the amount of my unstoried existence I transform into experience, thus widening and deepening the world of the novel I am. The search for such versions is the focus of ethicist Stanley Hauerwas.

'Each of us needs to establish some sense of identity,' Hauerwas insists, 'in order to give coherence to the multifariousness of our history as uniquely ours and as constitutive of the self' (1977, 87). Self-deception is thus the inevitable companion of the autobiographical imperative: of our need for unity, for integrity. It is the systematic delusion of ourselves, Hauerwas says, 'in order to maintain the story that has hitherto assured our identity.' Hence, 'the extent of our self-deception correlates with the type of story we hold about who and what we are' (88). Self-deception occurs, for example, when particular episodes in my life fail to fit with the overriding story I am telling myself about who I am, where I have come from, and where I am going. Let us suppose that story is the story of a 'good-old-boy-with-family-values-who-is-hard-working-and-honest-and-rises-above-all-odds-to-make-good-in-the-big-city.' Thus, the story of the creditor breathing down my neck about an overdue account, or of the shady deal two years ago to try to cut a few tax corners, or of the torrid, extramarital affair with my secretary last month, or of my emotionally intense relationship with a colleague, a man – these may become difficult for me to tell, not only to others, but also to myself. They contradict my official version of who I am. They may need to be edited out, 'forgotten,' repressed. However, if enough such stories accumulate, then they may come together as a kind of countermyth and overthrow that version altogether. Should this happen, I shall be in search, consciously or not, of a new guiding story by which to understand myself, past, present, and future – even if I have to undergo considerable inner turmoil until I find one.

The more open I am to finding such a new guiding story, however, one large enough to account for engagements that contradict my old one, then the more I can be called mature. Maturation, says Mezirow, is the movement toward 'meaning perspectives that are progressively more inclusive, discriminating, and more integrative of experience' (1978, 106). If for 'meaning perspective' we substitute 'story,' then maturation is the more or less conscious movement from story unto story, in the direction of one that can account for those aspects of my life, those episodes and engagements within it, that undermine the authority of whatever overriding story I have been operating with hitherto. In Hauerwas' words, 'through our experience we constantly learn new lessons, we gain new insights, about the limit of our life story' (95). It is possible for me to resist this movement, of course, and to insist on staying with a story that cannot possibly accommodate certain episodes, is unable to plot them or fit them in, can 'make nothing' of them. Meanwhile, however, these episodes will pile up and up, putting progressively more pressure on my dominant myth, rendering it ever more fragile and requiring ever more exotic rationalizations and more rigid defenses. Even if it does not actually break down, it is apt to become so brittle, so in need of buttressing, that life for both me and those around me will become increasingly impossible to bear.

This analysis of self-deception might lead us to the mistaken notion that it is always a dramatic phenomenon. It is not. There is a garden variety of self-deception at work with respect neither to the story of my life as a whole nor to any particular episode or chapter within it but rather to the manner in which I go about telling *any* of my story. Such self-deception involves less what I tell than how I tell it. It involves the artful telling, to myself and others, of a story that manages to be neither true, strictly speaking, nor false. It involves simply plotting the story a bit differently, placing the emphasis on different syllables, without necessarily either dropping or changing any of them. 'Without necessarily falsifying any of the "facts" that are subject to empirical test,' says Stephen Crites, 'I can weave a story or a scenario or an image that systematically distorts my underlying sense of how a course of events adds up, and also the real motives of my own course of action' (1979, 125).

In this respect, self-deception is not an exotic, isolated phenomenon but 'the normal pathology of everyday life' (110). Every time I relate some summary or segment of my life to myself or others, I am involved in it, inevitably. Inherent in narrating any event is a straying away from 'what actually happened,' however slightly or innocently: a quiet but discernible progression from fact to fiction. Indeed, without such fictionalization, consciousness as we know it might well be impossible. As Bruner and Weisser put it, 'lying is the origin of consciousness'; that is, 'the consciousness that emerges when one recognizes the distinction between what has "happened," how one has reported it, and how else it might have been interpreted' (1991, 132).

It is upon such lying that our lives are built, for 'once one commits oneself to a particular "version," the past becomes that version or becomes inflected toward that version' (132). In the words of Carolyn Heilbrun, 'we tell ourselves stories of our past, make fictions or stories of it, and these narrations *become* the past, the only part of our lives that is not submerged' (1988, 51). In short, 'we define and construct out sense of self through our fictions' (Brooks, 1985, 36).

None of us, it appears then, can avoid deceiving ourselves. 'To be is to be rooted in self-deception' (Hauerwas, 95). It is a 'permanent possibility implicit in the very dynamics of experience' (Crites, 1979, 128). Our involvement in self-deception is guaranteed by the very fact that we are simultaneously performer and audience in our own drama (Goffman, 1959, 80–1) – or narrator, protagonist, and reader of our own story (Sarbin, 1986, xvii, 16–19). However, our determination to minimize that involvement is the measure of our maturity, and our courage. Since, from this perspective, the overcoming of self-deception requires a continual critique of the dominant version – a stepping back from the guiding story – by which we live our lives and make events into experiences, then at every stage of the re-storying process we shall be forced to live, in a sense, without a story. For a time, we shall be storyless.

Storylessness is not an easy burden to bear; for some it means insanity. Most of us, however, live in a state of storylessness – 'in-between stories' (Berry, 1987, 187) – more than we think, in so far as at any given time any given guiding story will be unable to make complete sense of all of our life's events. That is, the emplotment of our life always lags behind its development – though for most of us this lag will be manageable, and the gap between life and life-story not so glaring as to force us to re-story in a radical way. The point is that storylessness in itself is not bad, not automatically the sign of madness. Indeed, as Alfred Adler reminds us, only 'neurotics and psychotic individuals ... live totally within their fictions, creating more and more elaborate delusional systems' (Frick, 1982, 45). Healthy individuals are not so easily taken in by their own self-stories. Instead, they 'employ their fictions in order to live more fully, more creatively, and to bring themselves out more completely as they transform reality' (45). As Erving Polster notes, 'we all live at the transition point between now and next. It is through this movement that people stay fresh and through it that the stories of our lives grow' (1987, 67). Without some element of storylessness, that is, we have little incentive to continue our search for a life-story that is 'bigger and better.'

In sum, a measure of self-deception is a fact of our lives – as is a measure of secrecy, irony, forgetfulness, confusion, or indeed any feature of our self-experience that arises from the inevitable gaps between the levels of stories we are: outside, inside, etc.[6] The task of closing such gaps by monitoring our hearts for self-deception, however, is one we must consciously assume the more we would take on the author-ity of our selves and the re-storying of our souls – the more we would achieve a life-story that is both 'artistically coherent and ethically satisfying' (Cupitt, 1991, 67). As most of us can attest, this is no small task, since resistance to re-storying is strong. Our old story, with its 'built-in immune system' (Bridges, 1980, 71), strives stubbornly to stay the same. However destructive it may be, it does not relish being de-storied itself. Nevertheless, our health and growth depend on it happening, as does our maturation. Identifying, analysing, and integrating the countless versions of part or all of the story of our lives is an indispensable component of the unending work – the poetic work – that is central to self-creation.

The Range of Storying Styles

People are different from one another. Some are female, some male; some tall, some short; some lean, some stout. Some are athletic, others artistic; some are quick and loud, others slow and quiet; some are buoyant and light, others burdened and dark; and, of course, some say to-may-to, while others say to-mah-to. But we demonstrate our differences not only in these comparatively obvious ways – in the ways we walk or talk or stir our tea – but in less discernible ways as well: in the opinions we hold, the presence we exude, and the patterns and propensities that characterize our emotions and relationships. Each of these differences, obvious or not, contributes to – indeed constitutes – the unique individuals we are.

In this book, I have been formulating a further difference in which our uniqueness is based. It is a difference in how we compose a life for ourselves out of the raw material of our genes, our environment, and the ever-rolling stream of influences, events, and encounters that comprise our existence on a day-to-day basis. It is a difference in the way we interpret these influences and digest these events and fashion from them a more or less integrated whole. It is a difference in the way we are present in the midst of our own lives, as of our relationships and our world. It is a difference in our personal 'style' – that certain unsayable something that, over and above and running through everything else, distinguishes a Degas from a Monet, a Vivaldi from a Bach, an Atwood from a Greene, and a you from a me. Specifically, it is a difference in our *storying* style.

The Concept of Storying Style

My purpose in this section is to highlight a few of the factors we might consider in appreciating how storying styles vary from one of us to another. A host of these I have already detailed, and I have hinted at still more; it would be redundant to belabour them here. By way of a quick summary, however, what I intend by the concept of storying style involves the peculiar ways in which we plot our experiences (thickly or thinly, etc.), characterize ourselves (flatly or roundly, etc.), and view our lives (*vis-à-vis* the past, present, or future, etc.). It involves the particular genres in terms of which we digest the events of our existence, transform them into our experiences, and compose them into the story of our life overall; as well as the set of myths that dominates our sense of who we are, where we have come from, and where we are going. It involves the sorts of versions of part or all of our story that come out of us most frequently in conversation: the motivations behind them, the origin of them, and the combinations among them. In addition, it involves the intensity with which we feel and respond to the autobiographical imperative; the balance we work out between the many stories of our lives and the one, between the told and the untold; the degree to which we assume the author-ity of our lives; and our level of awareness and intentionality in their re-storying. It involves furthermore the configuration of weightings we give to the various levels of our lives (outside, inside, inside-out, and outside-in) and to the various modes of our self-consciousness (author/narrator, protagonist, and reader). Finally, it involves the special quality of atmosphere, openness, and integrity that sets our story-world apart from that of everyone else.

The road to understanding similarities and differences in human nature has of course been paved with one worthy system after another, from an array of psychoanalytic theories to theories of multiple intelligences, personality types, learning styles, and the like. Layering it over with one more system still will scarcely make our ride any less bumpy, nor bring our destination any better into view. If anything, it may confirm us all the more in our cynicism about systems in general. But the business of thinking, as I perceive it, has as much to do with being interesting as it does with being definitive, and the idea of storying styles is nothing if not interesting. At the same time, it is not *merely* interesting. Once we accept the possibility that there is an *aesthetic* dimension to our relationship with both others and ourselves, that our lives and our worlds are more composed than received ready-made, and that they are so composed in large part because of the stories we tell ourselves about them, then the idea of storying styles becomes not only intriguing but entertainable in a serious fashion.

Besides the aesthetic dimension of our lives, it enables us to appreciate the *temporal* dimension as well. Our storying style concerns not just our static pictures of ourselves (our self-concept), not just our general potentials or measurable capacities (our personality type, learning style, and so forth), but how we go about situating ourselves *as ourselves* in relation to the three principal dimensions of our life in time: our remembered past, our lived-through present, and our anticipated future. Because it can allow for the ways we compose ourselves *in time*, therefore, the concept of storying style is able to appreciate the real novel-ty of our lives. 'Biologically, physiologically,' says Oliver Sacks, 'we are not so different from each other; historically, as narratives – we are each of us unique' (1985, 111).

At the same time, if no two of us ever live the same life-novel, if our individuality is rooted ultimately, as Dewey has reminded us, in our personal history, then to try to typologize storying styles may represent merely one more respect in which we depersonalize and disempower ourselves – something that in our technologized, scientized age has robbed us of our humanness too much as it is. Yet as literary theorists have tried to categorize the range of literary stories, surely there is some merit in anticipating the range of lived ones. Furthermore, if the way we story our lives has a direct effect on how we create our selves and relate to others, then it is clearly not an academic exercise alone but a very practical one. It is an inquiry into matters not just of aesthetics but of ethics, and not just of poetics but of politics.

Researching Storying Styles

What factors should we take into account to appreciate the ways we story our lives? In the light of foregoing sections, we can expect certain obvious ones to play a part. Besides gender, age, and life-stage (or -phase), they include the level of our development – morally, cognitively, and psychosexually; the level and kind of our education, both formal and informal; and the level of our 'intelligence,' something that, as Schank proposes, may be measurable less in terms of IQ than of the sophistication of our skills in composing and exchanging stories. Included as well is the level of literacy we have acquired, and of literary literacy at that. Undoubtedly, there is also our family of origin, our birth order within it, the set of myths surrounding it, and the plot into which it cast us at birth. Furthermore, there is our native culture (whether urban, suburban, or rural), as well as our class, creed, and race, and the storying patterns that accompany both. There is also the overall stability of our current life-context, political and physical, and thus our susceptibility to the dramatic re-storying it can suddenly thrust us into. Necessary as it is, then, a complete cross-referencing of all such factors and their effects on the content and form of our self-storying is clearly beyond the scope of this essay. Given their inevitable impact, though, let me suggest the shape of a research strategy with which we might obtain 'data' on the differences, story-wise, in our individual temperaments.

Along lines laid out by Bruner and associates (1987; 1990), I envision a confidential interview format in two stages. In the first, interviewees would be invited to take a limited amount of time – say, an hour – to tell 'the story' of their lives however they wished. During this time the interviewer would try to listen as much to *how* the stories are told as to *what* they contain, to the form as much as to the content, to the style as much as to the stuff. In the second stage, specific questions – crafted, say, from the following clusters – would be asked in such a way and such an order for interviewees to reflect on their lives with a degree of sophistication that increases gradually from beginning to end. Many of the questions are admittedly loaded, assuming the very thing after which they are inquiring … as in much research, where the act of observing determines what is observed and what we look for is often what we get. Yet, in so far as most of us have at least a mild interest in the nature and direction of our life-story *as* a story, such questions would probably be welcomed, in the process yielding material that – suitably 'coded' and interpreted – can only enrich our understanding of the poetics of the soul.

1. Would you like to say something now about what *kind* of story your story is, or what kind it might sound like to others? A love story, sob story, adventure story, horror story, soap opera, comedy, tragedy, fairy

tale, 'a tale told by an idiot,' a full-length novel, a series of short stories,
or 'just one damned thing after another'? Do you have some sense of
what is the central theme of your story, of what it is 'about'? How do
you think your story is like other people's stories? How does it differ?
How do you think it fits into the story of your family? your country?
your world? What sorts of things help to clarify your sense of the story
of your life? For example, leafing through photo albums, talking with
your parents, children, or friends about old times? Facing a life-wrench-
ing challenge? Therapy? Religion?

2. How often would you say you tell the story of your life, at least in
summary form? Each time, is it the same old story or are there markedly
different versions of it? Why? How would you compare the way you
have just recounted it to me with how you have told it to other people
in other situations at other times? In general, how enjoyable is telling
your story to you? How interesting do you think it is for others? From
one telling to another, do you tend to emphasize some aspects or episodes while downplaying others? If so, what do you make of this? Do
you think there is anyone who knows the whole story of your life, the
true story, the unexpurgated version? How do you feel about this? Who,
if anyone, would you like to have as your official biographer? Why?
What would they need to know about you to do their job properly? If
you were suddenly in the middle of a life-or-death situation and had a
vision of your whole life story laid out in front of you, what version of
that story do you think you would see? What events or images would it
contain?

3. As you heard yourself speak, what sort of 'character' do you think you
have cast yourself as in the midst of your story? What other characters,
if any, have figured in your story as well? Do you feel you have indeed
always been the main character – the hero/ine of your own story? Are
there certain kinds of hero/ines in movies or books upon whose character
you have ever secretly tried to model your own? Why? Can you think of
any situation, relationship, or challenge in your life in which you behaved
or acted or decided in a way that was 'out of character' for you? What
was happening within you at the time? Do you think it affected the way
in which you understood the story of your life thereafter? Can you recall
a situation in which you were aware of someone mis-representing you,
i.e., of having or telling what your considered the 'wrong' story of you?
How did you feel at the time? How do you think it affected your life?

How much control would you say you have over your story and how it
unfolds? Who do you think is its principal author?

4. If you were to write a full-length autobiography, how would you structure it? What title would you assign it? Would you be inclined to emphasize outer events or inner ones? If you were to divide it into different
episodes or 'chapters,' what would these be? If you were to think of it as
having a main plot and various subplots, what might each of these be?
What have been the central or recurring conflicts in your life? Can you
point to any part of your story that, thus far in your life at least, seems
like a critical turning-point – say, a 'climax' or a 'denouement'? Which
parts do you find to be most interesting to tell, to hear about? Can you
imagine plotting the same basic events of your life in some other manner?
To what sort of story might that different plotting lead? What tone would
you try to strike? What sort of audience would you gear your autobiography toward? Which episodes would you concentrate upon; which
would you omit? What would be your criteria for this selection? What
message would you hope to get across, and for whose benefit? How well
do you think your story would hang together? How much would the
story differ from the story of your life as it might be told someday by
your biographer?

5. Assuming you will live a number of years yet, how do you think your
story will change? How would you like it to change? How do you think
it will end? How would you like it to end? If you could rewrite the story
of your life in any way, from beginning to end, how would you do so?
Why? It has been said that every time a person dies it is as if a library had
burned down. What do you make of such a statement? What sorts of
stories might you yourself leave untold? How would you feel about this?
If your story were somehow 'to be continued' – as a sequel, so to speak,
in some other life – what direction do you think or hope it might take?

Numerous as these questions are, no doubt additional ones could be
asked to determine how differently people story their lives. I believe
this collection suffices, however, to indicate the range and interrelation
of the more critical variables at stake. Besides providing interviewees
with an opportunity to celebrate the richness of their experience and
an implicit invitation to assume greater author-ity over their lives, to
enter into some intentional re-storying, it offers us the opportunity to
appreciate the complexity of a number of theoretical issues. It opens

the way for further research into, among other issues, the link between fact and fiction in personal story; the connection between self-plotting, self-characterization, and self-deception; and the relationship, generally, between self-storying and self-creation. It also ushers into the arena of official discussion the (ethical) issue of the function interviewers themselves play in the interview process – that is, not just as 'objective' researchers but as co-authors of the interviewee's life-story, eliciting versions of it that may never have emerged before, and, for the duration of the encounter, acting as cultures of embeddedness that confirm, contradict, and continue as the interviewee, perhaps unconsciously, tests out a new one.

One intriguing issue to which we are led by all this concerns the kind of categorization that could be done when life-as-story is seen through the lenses of *point of view* – that is, in terms of three main perspectives at work in the telling of any literary story: that of the narrator, the protagonist, and the reader. It is on this trio that I now want to focus in the central portions of this section. In doing so, I am aware that the point of view issue is only one of many planks in the platform of a storying style system. It is a rough one at that, though what usually first impresses us about the people we meet (whether or not it can be put into words) is in fact their point of view – not their opinions (on politics, etc.) but their viewpoint or standpoint on their own lives.

Protagonists, Narrators, and Readers

Given the complexity of self-consciousness, we of course all relate to our life-stories in terms of all three perspectives. Yet, in general, some of us may relate primarily as narrators, some as protagonists, and some as readers. Though this observation has as yet no 'data' to support it, let me play with the possibilities it can suggest, beginning with the mode conceivably most basic to our self-relationship, that of the protagonist.

In the protagonist mode, people are most involved in just being and doing, in getting on with their lives on a day-to-day basis. Protagonists are doers. They act, therefore they are. Everyone of us spends at least some time in the protagonist mode in so far as we have at some point been a baby. A baby is basically all action and no talk. Such sounds as a baby makes, we assume, are not 'talk' in the usual sense – though they may function as such by attracting the attention of the adults on whom they so totally depend. They are actions more than speech. Such reflections as babies may have are, because of their lack of language (both inner and outer), either too cloudy or too vague, we suppose, to conclude they occur at all. Grown-ups who relate to the story of their life primarily in this protagonist mode, then, will generally act first and talk later – and reflect last of all. In the extreme variety, they will throw themselves into life so thoroughly and so busily, whatever they do, that they will have little sense that that life might be, or might be imaginable as, a story. They will be far from the threshold of story, low on the autobiographical imperative, unlikely to seek re-storying. They are so thoroughly *in* their story, so to speak, that *being* a story and *having* a story are one. To the extent that they are aware of their story, however, they may tend to associate it with the outside story only, with the level of existence alone, with the annal of the actual events of their life only minimally digested.

In the narrator mode, though people are possibly no less active in their lives than their protagonist counterparts, they are perhaps most naturally inclined to talk about their lives. Narrators are talkers. They tell, therefore they are. In the extreme variety, they are most active in their lives when they are talking about them, when they are telling stories about them. They talk first and act second. Narrators are extroverts. They need an audience to tell their stories to. If in therapy, they may have difficulty getting past the first phase. Some narrators can tell their stories so attractively in fact, can have 'the chronicling gift' so remarkably (Edel, 1973, ix), that their audience will listen to them ad nauseam: in awe at how dramatic they are able to make their lives sound, impressed at how much air time they can command, amazed at their talent for making so much of so little, intrigued by the detailed episodes (as opposed to *re*pisodes) they are able to recount. Indeed, they can seem to be full of stories, seldom at a loss to contribute a fresh one to the conversation at hand, whether to delight or instruct. Narrators can lead us to believe Henry James's observation that stories happen to people who know how to tell them. Indeed, they can seem to lead storied lives – certainly to see stories everywhere, and not only in their own lives but in others' as well. Narrators make good gossips. Adept at storying others' lives *for* them, though, they often fail to see that their outside-in versions of their subjects correspond only vaguely, if at all, to what goes on inside. Because they can be wrapped up in their own stock of stories (however limited in number or depth), they may not make good listeners to the stories of others – especially of other narrators.

The more highly developed their talents for telling, and the more intense their egotism, the more likely narrators may be to keep a log of the events of their lives, or to write a memoir of the exploits and adventures by which they perceive those lives to be defined. Compared with the protagonist, the narrator, because less immersed in doing and being, has a greater sense of the story – or at least the stories – of his life. He would associate 'the story of this life,' however, primarily with the many different inside-out stories of his life, that is, with the level of expression. The danger for narrators, of course, is that they may be too easily taken in by their own stories, becoming to that extent 'unreliable,' mistaking the inside-out story of their lives for the inside one, even the outside one: the whole story.

Some talkers, however much they talk, may talk about their lives on a level of self-awareness scarcely removed from that of their protagonist counterparts. Although they talk a great deal about themselves, they talk from the level of existence more than of experience. They talk more about the events of their lives than about the experiences. Granted that no event we can talk about has not already been processed poetically to some degree and thus experienced, some events are more experienced than others. The sort of narrator I am talking about here recounts the events of his life virtually raw, that is, with a minimum of reflection. He regurgitates them barely digested. In talking, he relays his life play-by-play, like the ten-year-old who tediously retells a story event by detailed event, with lots of action but little plot: *Yesterday I did that, today I am doing this, tomorrow I will do this and that both*. In effect, he is missing a step, skipping a stage, jumping a level. He seems not to think before he speaks, but to express the events of his existence without first having experienced them. Thoughts and nuances seem absent; little lies between the lines. Instead of talking it out – as a way of sorting it out – he simply … talks. Hence, he can seem to have little of substance to say. What may be happening, of course, is that his way of transforming events into experiences is essentially external in nature. Rather than talking it up within himself, he talks it out with others. None the less, there may be narrators who ruminate on the events of their lives hardly at all, making them excellent candidates for psychological indigestion.

Finally, people who operate primarily in the reader mode, though possibly no less active in or talkative about their lives, are most naturally inclined to be reflective about them. Readers are thinkers. They reflect, therefore they are. Where narrators hold forth, readers hold back, more inclined to keep their stories to themselves. They think first and talk later, and in certain cases scarcely act at all – somewhat like some writers who, says Annie Dillard, 'do little else but sit in small rooms recalling the real world' (1989, 44). In the extreme variety, they are most active in their lives when they are thinking about them, mulling them over, brooding upon them – to the point perhaps where their unlived lives become not worth examining. (All experience and no existence also makes Jack a dull boy.) If in therapy, readers may have difficulty getting past the second phase of the re-storying process and getting on to a new life-narrative.

Where narrators are extroverts, readers are introverts. Most advanced of the three in the realm of inner speech, their audience is internalized. Like the keener readers of novels, they constantly (again, in the extreme) read between the lines of their own lives, processing and re-processing what happens in them, seeking out their own narrative secrets. They analyse what each incident in their lives might mean, how it might figure in the flow of their story as a whole, and, between one part and another, what connections can be seen, what patterns can be discerned, and what plot can be made out. When readers are in the narrative mode, they may tell more sophisticated, more nuanced self-stories, reflective of a less direct, more mediated or meditated, involvement with events.

Compared with narrators, readers have a greater sense of, concern about, even obsession with, the meaning of their story as a whole – its point: as one, at least potentially, and not merely many. They are more alert to discrepancies between the many, more concerned to make the many into one, and more keen to perceive the novel-ty of their lives overall. In this respect, where protagonists are most involved in their lives, readers are most detached from them – outside them, as it were, in the same way as a real reader is, in the end, outside a novel. They are prime candidates, perhaps even more seriously than narrators, for Sartrean bad faith. As Robert Kegan might express it, readers are not entirely embedded 'in' their story; instead, they 'have' it (1982). In *having* more than *being* their stories, readers are therefore more able, even than narrators (who straddle the strange line between their stories and their lives), to critique their stories and to ask what kinds of stories they are. They may also be more able to read the life-stories of others. That is to say, they may make better listeners – and better readers or critics of the larger stories around them. They may also, though, be more easily taken in by, caught up in the spell of, and entwined into others' life-stories, instead of sustaining a sense of respect for the uniqueness of their own. Rather than becoming co-authors of others' stories, they become co-opted by them. In other words, as we hinted earlier in talking about openness, readers may have problems with boundaries.

The more finely tuned their talents for self-reading, and the more concentrated their desire to grasp the meaning of their story as a whole, the more likely readers may be to keep not so much a log of events as a journal of experiences, and to write not so much a memoir of their outer life as an autobiography of their inner one. (As one scholar suggests, emphasis is placed in the former on 'the world of events,' while in the latter on 'character, personality, self-conception' (Weintraub, 1975, 823–4).) In terms then of the levels of life-story, readers more readily relate to themselves on the level of inside story, may seem indeed to have 'more going on' inside them, and may be inclined – or try – to relate to others on the same level, inside-to-inside. However, they may often be disappointed in their attempts, given the more prevalent pattern of interacting at the level of inside-out and outside-in. Moreover, they are apt to be more sensitive than are narrators to the outside-in stories others have of them, and more sceptical of the integrity and authenticity of the various inside-out stories of themselves that they are required, by convention, to convey.

Cautionary Comments

Protagonist, narrator, reader – such distinctions are admittedly blunt, for in everyday life these modes are never as neat as I have carica-tured them here. Indeed, we are all protagonists, narrators, and readers of our lives in various proportions in various situations in various life-stages or chapters. A schema like this can seem little more, therefore, than parlour-game speculation on the broad classes of people into which we might light-heartedly divide the world – that is, doers, talkers, and thinkers. None the less, it opens the way to ponder aspects of being human that are routinely overlooked in analyses of a more scientific nature. 'Opens the way' is a positive expression of its value; 'opens a Pandora's box' may be a more realis-tic one. To accommodate the full range of variations, of permutations and combinations, to which it leads us, much fine-tuning is obviously required.

Some people, for example, seem to be all talk and no action, yet they engage in considerable reflection when no one is listening. Conversely, others seem to be all action and no talk, yet they engage in considerable reflection when no one is looking. It depends in part on how they are trying to characterize themselves. In an era when, for men at least, action and talk are the more highly rewarded modes, many may hide or deny their otherwise natural propensities for introspection. By the same token, with men traditionally accustomed and encouraged to be both the principal actors and the prime talkers on the world stage, with a disproportionate share of stage time and air time and a language tilted in their favour to begin with, women down through the ages may be pushed from the start to be less livers and tellers of their own stories than readers – listeners, viewers, witnesses, critics – of men's. Many women are readers, that is, not by nature or choice but by circumstance: by an imbalance of power that overrides, though sometimes underwrites, their inherent orientation. Furthermore, being in situations where they are routinely and systemically dominated by others, women (or indeed members of any marginalized group) can be forced to become so attuned to the question of 'what next?' in the stories of their oppressors, and such wily anticipators of the latters' every move and mood, that the time and energy they have to ask 'why?' of their own story is significantly diminished. Related to this is the possibility that some individuals, whether female *or* male – therapists and social workers, for instance – are more proficient at and more open to reading others' stories than they are their own. This in turn raises the question of how people of one dominant mode tend to interact – in conversation, intimacy, or therapy – both with one another and with people of a different mode: talkers with talkers, for example, or talkers with readers, reader with doers, doers with doers, and so forth.

Similarly, the schema I am proposing points to the subtle range of ways in which, as narrators, we relate to the story we narrate, that is, in terms of degree of omniscience, self-consciousness, reliability, irony, detachment, etc. (Booth, 1966); or in terms of whether, like narrators in novels, we have a preference for dialogue over action, summary over scene, and so forth. In other words, it hints at the complex possibilities at work in the *rhetoric* of our self-telling: our vocabulary and tone, our characteristic gestures, our relative flair for the dramatic, and the ways we tend to use our stories: to instruct, delight, entice, distance, etc. Moreover, it invites us to ask the question of how we learn or absorb or imitate all of this from others, how (as well as why and whether) it varies from one narration to the next, and how these variations effect corresponding changes in the atmosphere around us in the eyes and ears of others. It also opens the way for us to clarify the correlations between each of these three modes and the four principal orientations to time to which Mann et al (1972) have pointed. It tempts us to propose, for example, that protagonists are 'sensing' types, oriented toward the present, while readers are either 'feeling' types, oriented toward the past, or 'intuiting' types, who need to have a sense of all three tenses at once. In addition, it leads us to consider the different ways in which protagonists operate within their own life-story in terms of their power *vis-à-vis* both the other characters who figure within it and the environment they perceive to surround them (Frye, 1966, 23–4).

Another thing this schema pushes us to play with is the complexity of the connection between reader and story in general, as well as the indispensability of the reader to the story's very existence. It lures us to entertain the implications of the differences that critics have identified between the reasons readers read in the first place – whether they are 'point-driven,' 'information-driven,' or 'story-driven' (Beach, 1990, 217); or plot-driven, character-driven, theme-driven, atmosphere-driven, etc. For example, might people who read themselves in a primarily plot-driven manner be concerned with the significance of the *events* of their lives more than of the *characters* or relationships within them, and so put the stress on events in any instance of self-telling? Furthermore, we are forced to reckon with the ramifications for self-reading of the relationship between 'real readers,' 'implied readers,' and 'narratees' (Rimmon-Kenan, 1983, 80) – as well as of the range of roles that readers *per se* play in relation to any text: whether they are 'planners,' 'composers,' 'editors,' or 'monitors' (Tierney and Gee, 1990, 198). It also helps us appreciate the plethora of variations in the scope and depth at which self-reading occurs. In other words, some of us may read our lives intensely but not necessarily broadly, keenly but not critically; while others of us may read not just critically but hyper-critically – or *under*-read them in some ways and *over*-read them in others.

Finally, the schema raises the question of whether people who are avid fiction readers (in a culture whose members are generally little-read) necessarily make good 'readers' in the sense intended here, simply because they like to read. It poses the possibility that such people can become so entranced by 'the vivid and continuous fictional dream' (Gardner, 1985, 97) that they find the real world less deserving of their energy and imagination, which may mean, in turn, that they abandon the challenge of realizing their *own* dreams. If literature is 'man's revelation to man,' that is, then such readers run the risk of getting more caught up in the revelation than in the reality it supposedly illuminates for them, just as some religionists can get carried away by religion for religion's sake and lose sight of the world it would purportedly have them love. It also raises the question, which lurks unasked behind bibliotherapy (Gold, 1990; Coles, 1989), of whether avid readers of fiction necessarily make 'better' story-ers of their own lives than do readers of non-fiction, or than do non-readers altogether – or indeed than do those who consume their fictions not through the book but through the television or the movie screen.

A Cycle of Self-Storying?

Tentative as it is, this schema shows that an approach rooted in the poetics more than the psychologics of human development can provide an enticing take on the subtleties at work in the stories we are. Yet the relationship between these three modes is not only more complicated than portrayed here but probably also more cumulative than cut-and-dried, more continuous than discrete, and more cyclical than linear. The model I propose for conceiving it, therefore, is that of a spiral. Accordingly, we would move from a primarily protagonist mode, where we are immersed 'in the middest' of our life-story; to a primarily narrator mode, where we possess a voice to relate the story of our life to others and ourselves; to a primarily reader mode, where we can ask what kind of story it is and can critique the larger stories around us that have helped construct us in the particular way they have. We can imagine it possible, then, to reenter the protagonist mode all over again in a new and more self-aware way, on a level where we are back in the midst of the story, as principal character (indeed hero/ine) therein, yet no longer as unmindfully so. We both *have* our story, as it were, and *are* our story; the gap between the two has been bridged. We have also read our story so well and questioned its composition so critically that we have in effect *re*-storied it. Thus, we have come out on the other side of it, ready not only to live it in a new and more author-itative manner, but also to talk it and read it at a whole new level: one on which we might be open to re-storying our souls all over again. The cycle I envision can be diagrammed as in the figure below.

Storying Style Cycle

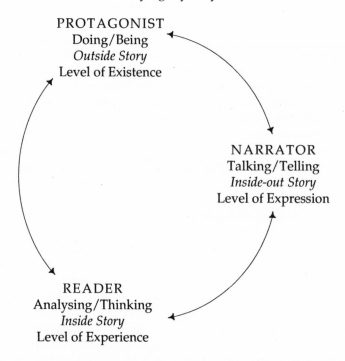

PROTAGONIST
Doing/Being
Outside Story
Level of Existence

NARRATOR
Talking/Telling
Inside-out Story
Level of Expression

READER
Analysing/Thinking
Inside Story
Level of Experience

This is clearly but one of many schemas that a poetics of self-creation tempts us to formulate. In a sense, it is the most basic. To account for other broad differences between storying styles, additional schemas would need to be designed and coordinated, each with its accompanying collection of questions. One such difference, which I have referred to throughout, relates to the fundamental genre by which we transform the events of our life into experiences and interpret the unfolding of the story of our life from beginning to end.

Questions about Genre

Though Frye's 'modes' tend not to appear in pure form, is it possible that some of us experience our lives and our world primarily in terms of the tragic one, routinely crying the blues, accentuating the negative, seeing only the hopeless possibilities in everyday events? In his study of the paranoid personality, for instance, Ernest Keen (1986) points out

that 'the comic, ironic, and romantic (and other) possibilities for interpreting my life and experience disappear' (178). My sense of my life-
plot becomes 'singularly tragic.' Certain larger stories we live within,
he goes on to suggest, can be infused by the same tragic paranoic, or
'cataclysmic' (188) genre – whether these be cultural stories or religious ones – such as some forms of fundamentalism reflect in their
obsession with hell and the end of the world. On the other hand, we
may ask, is it possible that others of us construct our lives in an essentially comic way instead, regularly seeing events in them as confirma-
tions of the silly but endearing side of life, the redeemable side –
turning even the most terrible of them (of the operation, the divorce,
the Depression, the war) into the stuff of a knowing smile or a good
laugh? Do others of us again compose our lives largely in terms of the
romantic, ironic, or even mythic genre? Moreover, what is the influence on our preferred personal genre of our family genre, or of the
dominant author-ity figure in that family? If she or he has always
viewed the world tragically, and has urged or argued that view upon
us at every opportunity, what chance has an adventurous orientation
had to survive in our soul? Furthermore, what is involved in changing
from one genre to another, to 'one of the better genres,' as Booth
somewhat cryptically calls it (1988, 268)?

Another set of questions has to do with whether the way we genre-
lize the events of our lives is a constant feature of our 'temperament'
or 'disposition' or changes automatically (if gradually) as we move
from one 'season' of life to another? Levinson et al (1978) suggest, for
example, that in the midlife season of a man's life, particularly as he
wrestles with the polarity of Destruction/Creation (208), there is the
possibility of arriving at a 'tragic sense of life.' Such a sense derives,
they say, 'from the realization that great misfortunes and failures are
not merely imposed upon us from without, but are largely the result
of our own tragic flaws' (225). There is also the question of whether
as children, apart from the overriding genres operative within our
family of origin, we are most naturally inclined to view life through
comic lenses; while, as adolescents and young adults, through roman-
tic-adventurous lenses, as middle-aged adults through ironic lenses,
and as seniors, through tragic ones? (Here we are reminded of Rubin's
question about the change in self-storying that is manifested when 'a
college sophomore [is] asked to recall an event encoded by a 6-year
old' (1986, 69).) And what about the link between life-stage and life-
genre that might relate to the evolution of our skills in constructing,

telling, following, and exchanging stories generally, and in our master-
ing and being critically aware of basic story conventions (see Gardner,
1981; Mancusco, 1986; Tompkins, 1982)?

In the same vein, it is tempting to enquire how the way we genre-
lize our lives might vary not just by person or family or life-stage but
also by culture, where unique configurations of larger stories are in
place (institutionally, ideologically, religiously, politically, etc.), each
with its peculiar complex of plots and subplots, conflicts and morali-
ties, major and minor characters, points of view, themes, and genres.
Are some cultures essentially tragic cultures, that is, while others are
romantic, comic, or ironic? Naïve though it sounds, this is a valid
question, and I am by no means the first to consider it.

In his contribution to the study of self-narratives, Karl Scheibe
writes of the 'U.S. thirst for adventure' (1986, 142) that is evident in
the kinds of literary stories Americans commonly consume, and of
the effects of this thirst on how they envision the purpose of life.
Surmelian, for example, says 'there is more action in modern American writing. Scene, drama, seem natural to this country. The American is a man of action. European fiction,' on the other hand, 'tends
more to the essay form' (1969, 37). As Annie Dillard has pointed out,
we will 'search the novels of Virginia Woolf in vain for so much as
a single horse' (1982, 46). In a similar vein, Elie Wiesel (1988) insists
that as a post-Holocaust Jew 'life is not a happy event in the absolute
sense of the word. It's always a tragedy, by definition. It's short. We
come from nowhere; we go nowhere' (259). Or, as psychotherapist
Sheldon Kopp echoes, 'the Children of Israel are historically committed to a heroic tragic vision of themselves and their sufferings'
(1987, 5).

Of course, merely considering this question of cultural genre – as
of national 'character' – steers us into treacherous intellectual waters,
where we can easily go aground on the craggy generalizations it
tempts us to construct. Yet a poetics of self-creation cannot ignore it.
Throwing caution to the wind, there is the related question of how
our personal stories are re-genre-ated: for example, as our post-Viet-
nam American culture shifts, however slightly, from a predominantly
victor (adventurous) mentality to more of a *victim* (tragic) one, or, as
European cultures have been for some time perhaps, to a more
world-weary, *ironic* mentality. Or, say, as Christianity (in its liberal
forms at least) shifts from a triumphalist perspective to a trench-war
one: from siding with the rich and powerful to struggling with the

poor and powerless. Furthermore, besides a genre-preference and a characteristic temporal orientation (Hall, 1984), might different cultures, as *cultures*, with their unique histories and native languages, lean toward a distinctive point of view? Are some cultures – like some individuals, families, cliques, religions even – primarily protagonist-types (action-oriented), while others are reader-types (analysis-oriented), and others again narrator-types (talk-oriented) – that is, storytelling cultures in which members are immersed from birth in a lively oral tradition, whatever the style of stories they are trained to tell?

Finally, as I have been wondering throughout, how is our genre of self-storying tied to our gender? Are women conditioned, for instance, to transform the events of their lives in terms of one set of genres, often foisted on them by default, while men, as would-be conquering heroes riding solo into the sunset, are taught to do so in terms of another? Carol Pearson (1989) suggests as much in her mapping of human development in terms of the 'six archetypes we live by' that I referred to earlier: the Innocent, the Orphan, the Wanderer, the Warrior, the Martyr, and the Magician. The life of the Warrior, she argues, is the typical male pattern of development. 'Men,' she writes, 'are pushed into having control over their lives and power over others, into being Warriors, before they know who they are. They get to the Warrior stage quickly but then get stuck there' (7). In so far as 'it is the end of the story that traditionally determines whether the plot is comic or tragic,' the life of the Warrior is therefore 'lonely and ultimately tragic' (9). The lives of women, on the other hand, 'tend to be overly dominated by the Martyr archetype' (7).

Outstanding Issues

Clearly, any consideration of the range of storying styles needs to incorporate the gendered perspective that Pearson and others propose, a need I have sought to acknowledge in everything said so far. Yet a host of additional differences have been lying unfocused either on or just below the surface throughout. To conclude, let me pull some of these together in point form by reminding us that we also differ in terms of:

• the overall temporal orientation we have within our stories, whether primarily toward the beginning, middle, or end (i.e., the past, pres-

ent, or future), and how this orientation varies with our culture,
class, personality type, or life stage, etc. – e.g., do the elderly automatically become more past-oriented simply because they are elderly?

- the sense we have of *endings* in general, not only those of the stories
  we read, watch, and hear, but those of the story of our life as a
  whole – i.e., whether we are primarily accepters, disdainers, postponers, waiters, resisters, peekers, etc., and whether we prefer tidy
  endings or can live with loose ones
- the way our storying styles may change from stage to stage – or
  chapter to chapter – and the pace and extent of the re-storying (re-
  genre-ation) that we may either seek or endure along the way
- the sense we have that our life-stories might be continued in, or
  from, another life again, and the degree to which this influences the
  way we read events in our lives now – e.g., as not real compared
  with what is to come, as 'but a dream,' or as merely 'a faint tracing
  on the surface of mystery' (Dillard, 1975, 9)
- the kind of author-ity we exercise in relation to our life-stories (passive or active); how conscious we are of that authorship and how
  much of it we forfeit (as well as why and to whom); and the interaction that occurs between those aspects of ourselves that represent,
  respectively, the 'real author,' 'implied author,' and 'narrator'
  (Booth, 1966, 277–8)
- the artfulness of our ability to tell stories in the first place, specifically our own – that is, to story the events of our lives into experiences – in light of James's observation that 'stories happen to people
  who can tell them' (Bruner, 1987, 14); and the ways we 'use' our
  stories (the range of motives behind those uses), the types of themes
  our stories contain, and the characterizations of ourselves and others
  that they reflect
- the nature and extent of our 'storyotyping' of others, how we characterize them, genre-lize about them, plot their lives for them, etc.:
  whether de-storyingly, out of prejudice, or generously, seeing more
  virtue or value in their lives than they might see themselves; and
  how these tendencies have been influenced by the family or culture
  in which we have been brought up
- the number and variety of 'characters' besides ourselves – for example, children, colleagues, partners, etc. (as well as subpersonalities) – that we acknowledge, accept, or try or need to accommodate
  into the cast of our own life-story

- the kinds of stories generally to which we are attracted (i.e., roman-tic, tragic, comic, ironic, or picaresque, as well as 'good news' or 'bad news'), and the plot-lines toward which we are overtly or covertly most drawn, not only in novels and films but also in biog-raphies, autobiographies, acquaintances, institutions, and ideologies
- the extent to which we intentionally try to, or think we ought to, plot (as in plan) the unfolding of the incidents of our lives
- the number of 'subplots' we are able to incorporate into the 'main plot' of our lives, and the nature and degree of the change in the relationship between them
- the level of our avoidance, tolerance, or need, of tension or trouble, struggle or suspense, complexity or crisis, 'agon' or conflict, in our lives: whether external conflict or internal, whether on the level of outside story or inside story, whether situational or psychological, inter- or intra-personal
- the degree of our susceptibility to the allure – to being mesmerized by the spell – of the various stories we see and read, of our own inside story and inside-out stories, of our outside-in stories of others and theirs of us
- the number of levels on which we are able (or try) to 'read' the events of our lives, to ask not only 'what next?' but also 'why?' con-cerning them, and to see the symbolic interconnectedness among them, as well as the variables affecting this ability
- the extent we perceive there to be compatibility – or gaps – between our inside story, our outside story, and our various inside-out stories, and the degree of secrecy, self-deception, self-deprecation, and irony to which this perception leads us
- the strength of our need to keep our story as a whole 'safe,' and the effect this has on the company we keep – for instance, leading us to let into our lives only those who confirm us (or at least a certain version of us) or, on the other hand, those who contradict us and thus challenge us 'at the deepest level' (Sarton, 1977, 131); and finally
- the relative power of plot *vis-à-vis* character in determining how our story unfolds, and the degree to which the latter renders us accept-ing of or rebellious against the construction of the former.

This section has been a kind of concession to the scientific impera-tive, which, wherever possible, would make out patterns in the work-ings of nature. Focusing on *human* nature, that is, I have tried to sketch the outlines of a schema that could account for the plethora of patterns whereby we compose our lives. This is only a beginning obviously. The task of coordinating the countless variables involved, however fascinating it would be to take on, is massive. By making such a beginning here, however, I believe we have travelled a sizeable distance toward appreciating the importance and implications of the life-as-story metaphor, and the pivotal part it plays in our understanding of self-concept and self-creation. In the final section, I shall capsulize our journey so far and reflect on what it leads us to add to a consideration of 'the art of living.'

The Art of Living Reconsidered

A final section bears a big burden simply because it comes so near to the end. Readers expect it to bring the book to a 'resonant close,' to pronounce the final, crowning word upon everything said so far. Writers hope it comes out with sufficient flourish to hide from readers' eyes the multitude of conceptual sins that may have been committed in secret throughout. For *this* final section, I have humbler hopes in mind, two in particular: first, to make a little clearer the thrust of our enquiry up to now, and, second, to point out a few – though only a few – of its broad implications for how we look at the nature and purpose of our lives. I shall tackle the first task by laying out not a comprehensive summary of the poetics of self-creation but simply a highlighting of certain basic propositions around which it revolves. For the second, I shall offer three open-ended reflections on the links between novels *per se* and the stories of our lives.

Basic Propositions

1. If any one idea should by now stand out, it is this: There is a peculiar but unavoidable *gap* between our selves and our lives. I have conceived this gap in terms of a variety of oppositions. It is a gap between our existence and our experience, and between our experience and our expression. It is a gap between the facts of life and the artifacts we form from them in memory and imagination. It is a gap between living and telling, between biology and biography, between development and emplotment, between nature and character, and

between life and life-story. It is a gap that ultimately divides us from all the un-languaged life-forms with which we share the planet.

Many phrases might encompass what happens within us and because of us as we invariably try to deal with this gap – to bridge it, close it, exploit it, ignore it, or be nauseated by. Those I have been focusing on here are self-creation, self-culture, self-deception, the autobiographical imperative, and 'the story of my life' – as well as the homespun expression 'the art of living,' a term whose time, I submit, has returned. Each of these phrases underlines the basic point that living is never a straightforward enterprise; it is always an *aesthetic* one. For even the most limited among us, to live a life is not to let it unfold willy-nilly but, consciously or otherwise, to try to do something with it: to construct it into one shape, according to one style, as one type of artwork, and not some other. Our lives do not just 'turn out' a certain way; we help turn them out that way ourselves. We do not live them in a purely passive manner but take an active role in their unfolding. We do not merely accept or discover or actualize our selves; we also create them, where 'create' is understood in the basic sense of 'make.' We make decisions, make choices, make plans, make mistakes, make sense, and, if we are lucky, we make 'it' – whatever 'it' may be taken to mean. In the end, none of us escapes the imperative to make 'something' of our lives as a whole. But we make ourselves in more subtle, more interior, and perhaps more significant ways as well – hermeneutical ways, we may say. That is, we make ourselves in our own hearts and minds in the way we make sense of the events of our lives: that is, the way we interpret these events to ourselves and make them into experiences that constitute the inner world of our unique 'self.'

2. It can be argued though – and I have been tracing the shape of such an argument here – that this 'self' is inseparable from a collection of countless stories: How we transform events into experiences, in other words, is conceivably by weaving tellable stories out of them. 'Through the telling of events,' says Hillman, 'the soul takes random images and happenings and makes them into particular lived experiences' (1975a, 143). This story-telling tendency – this autobiographical act – is a form of fictionalizing really, one that effectively 'turns life into text, however implicit or explicit the text may be' (Bruner and Weisser, 1991, 136). Indeed, 'it is only by textualization that one can "know" one's life' (136), which means that 'there is no such thing psychologically as "life itself"' (Bruner, 1987, 13). As Sartre would say, we live

our lives *through* our stories and we understand ourselves, others, and our world in terms of them.

For instance, I have short stories and long stories, precise stories and fuzzy stories, public stories and private stories. I have stories about myself, about others, and about my world; stories of my past, my present, and my future. I have stories within stories, stories of isolated incidents, and stories of entire subplots or chapters. Some of my stories are naturally more memorable than others, some are memorable only for a limited period, and some, while memorable in principle, are seldom if ever told – or, if told, then only in a general form, such as 'the sort of thing I *used* to do.' However, the total of these innumerable stories – more or less memorable, specific, or frequently told – comprises what I refer to as 'the story of my life.'

3. 'The story of my life' in the singular, though, is not a clearcut concept. It can be understood in one or more of at least four ways: first, as the outside story, the whole story of the 'facts' of my existence, of my 'life itself' – undigested and uninterpreted. Second, as the inside story, which is what I *make* of the outside story inside of me and is therefore known to me alone, though which I draw from whenever I disclose myself to others: It is the total of my 'personal, practical knowledge' or my 'experience.' Third, then, as the inside-out story, my inside story as I express some segment or summary of it to others (whether verbally or non-verbally, consciously or not) and whose construction and conveyance in any interaction will depend on my mood, my motive, my audience, etc. Fourth, as the outside-in story, the crude version of my life-story that others *com*pose about me and *im*pose upon me, one that, alas, I may have little control over, yet that can profoundly affect the scope and shape of my self-creation. About such a schema, however, I need to add four brief points.

First, the outside story, inside story, etc. are commonly intertwined in my mind. When I think of the 'story' of my life, I think of a mixture of things at once: the facts of my life, my interpretation of those facts to myself and others, and others' interpretation of them to me. However, where exactly 'the story of my life' lies for me along the spectrum of inside-outside, with which levels I identify most, and the degree of my awareness of the gaps between them, determines how in my everyday life I manifest those aspects of being human that, academically, are often overlooked, such as my humour, irony, honesty, cynicism, and compassion.

Second, there are as many versions of my inside-out story as there are people or situations that elicit it from me. Furthermore, there are as many versions of the outside-in story as there are people and powers around me who have a perspective (personal or impersonal) on who I am, where I have come from, and where I am going. Some of these versions (for example, those of therapists, parents, partners) can be so clear, authoritative, and regularly reinforced that, for all intents and purposes, I may accept them as 'true' and try to act out my 'character' as they require.

Third, each version of each segment or summary is not a story of the past alone. On some level, it is always a projection into the future – if only in the sense that in telling or entertaining it I am conscious of and curious about *what might happen when* or *what might have happened if*. I live always 'in the middest,' poised between what has gone before and what lies ahead. If I am in the midst of an event or situation that is still unfolding, that has not yet 'ended,' then in my interpreting and telling it I am never unmindful of the ever-changing relationship between its beginning and its yet undetermined end.

Fourth, and very important, I do not story my life in a vacuum. The forms of my self-telling are necessarily influenced by the stories and plot-lines I consume from the world around me, through reading, listening, and watching. They are also influenced, and profoundly so, by the shape and style of the several *larger* stories within which I have lived because of being rooted in a specific family, in specific relationships, in a specific sequence of communities, cultures, classes, and creeds – and indeed in a specific race and gender. These larger stories have supplied me with the forms of self-telling on which I have been obliged to draw in composing my personal one, inside and out.

4. With respect to my inside story in particular – my 'experience' or 'soul' – the total number of individual stories by which it is constituted is constantly growing. So too is the number of versions or points of view by means of which I can understand them, or the number of ways I can plot them together into a larger, more all-embracing story. However, the drive to make them into such a story – the desire to discern the integrity and interconnectedness of my inner world over time – can be seen as central to my nature: the source and the sign of my 'sanity.' It is the autobiographical imperative. The larger, unified story toward which this imperative impels me can be thought of as the *novel* of my life. In this novel, the many stories of my life find unity

in the one – though this unity usually eludes me, for I am constantly in its midst.

Like its literary counterpart, the novel of our lives can be critiqued in terms of typical story categories, such as plot, character, and point of view. Using these categories to analyse life-stories is a reversal of the more common approach of using psychological categories to analyse literary ones, yet it illuminates aspects of self-creation that psychological perspectives may overlook. For example, through the category of plot, it illuminates the selectivity that goes on in constructing the stories we are: our choice (conscious or not) of these events and not those, these stimuli and not those, for incorporation into and as our experience. It illuminates the peculiar features of our sense of ourselves in time: our sense of an ending, our anticipation of retrospection, our inclination to live our lives forward yet understand them backward. It also illuminates the inescapable yet potentially positive role of conflict in life, of *agon* – what Michael Novak calls 'the law of life' (1971, 73) – without some element of which our story, like any story, has nowhere to go and no way of getting there. It has no energy, no engine, and no goal. Through the category of character, it illuminates the fine line between fiction and reality, and opens up for examination the peculiar dynamics at work in fashioning 'the fictional side of human nature' (Hillman, 1975a, 128). Through the category of point of view, it illuminates the subtle and ever-changing complexity of our self-consciousness by introducing the seductive yet complicated notion that we are simultaneously the co-author/narrator, protagonist, and reader of our own unfolding novel. Finally, it illuminates the range of possible styles whereby, in general, we each go about storying our lives.

5. Whether through sudden crisis or the ordinary events of 'life itself,' however, the many stories of my life are being continually reworked within me, continually recombined with each other, and continually retold, both to myself and others, by means of one or another or come combination of numberless viewpoints or versions. My story is not cast in stone. And as it changes, I change, as do my perceptions and opinions, beliefs and behaviours, routines and relationships. Thus, the way I story my life influences how I live it; it affects the scope and direction of my self-creation. Furthermore, in so far as I am always a character in the life-stories of others (as they are in mine), it affects their self-creation as well. The contemplation of self-creation is a task in the realm not only of aesthetics, then, but of ethics as well. This

close link between my life and my story means that, practically speaking, *having* and *being* a story are impossible to distinguish.

Sometimes, however, we deliberately set out to rework our life-story, past and future. Therapy, religion, and education are three media in society whose stated agenda is – or can be – to help us do that. Each prescribes particular strategies and story-lines for us to re-genre-ate our stories, to re-story our souls, and, in some cases, to assume more author-ity over such re-storying ourselves. At least in North American society, the influence of these media is pervasive. Few of us escape the sense that, somewhere and somehow, there is 'a better way' to live our lives, a 'better genre' on which to build our 'life-plot' (Booth, 1988, 268), a better myth by which to move through the world, and that one or the other, or some combination, of these three media holds the key to finding it.

In general, of course, each medium has its favoured approach for helping us attain a story large enough to account for the many and varied engagements of our lives. Each has its formulae for constructing one overriding story within which we can weave together – can achieve the con-version of – the several stories that we are. For instance, the range of master stories therapists advocate may not harmonize easily at all with that advocated by religionists or educators. None the less, aided by these media or not, the degree of our openness to (and success at) re-storying our lives in a more all-encompassing manner is the measure, on the negative side, of our insanity and self-deception and, on the positive side, of our wisdom and maturity.

Overall, this openness is a function of our willingness to examine our lives, to reflect on the many meanings and possible interpretations of particular events within them, and to critique the influence upon these interpretations of the various larger stories in which we are embedded. It is a function of our willingness to *read* the stories we are. Each time we do so, we hold our lives differently within our consciousness and widen the horizon of – thicken and enrich – the novel within which those various stories may find a common focus and direction. A poetics of self-creation is therefore an implicit plea for us to take a more meditative approach to everyday life. It is an implicit plea for integrity and openness; for an improved digestion of the events of our existence; for making more of our lives, period; and for assuming more author-ity over their composition. It is also a plea for expanding our souls and thus, I believe, a prescription for greater (self)-creativity.

Self-as-Novelist: The Question of Art or Craft

My first reflection concerns how novels vary in relation to two main elements: convention and invention. 'Conventions,' writes critic John Cawelti (1989), 'are elements which are known to both the creator and his audience beforehand – they consist of things like favorite plots, stereotyped characters, accepted ideas, commonly known metaphors, and other linguistic devices, etc.' (89). 'Inventions,' on the other hand, 'are elements which are uniquely imagined by the creator such as new kinds of characters, ideas, or linguistic forms' (87). 'Most works of art,' Cawelti admits, 'contain a mixture of convention and invention' (88). This means that no novel, however literary, is devoid of conventions. No novel is *entirely* novel, is not in some way genre-lizable, not on some level 'the same old story.' Likewise, no dime-store romance, however predictable it may be, fails to introduce at least some element of invention, some slightly different twist in the development (if much there be) of its characters. None the less, any given novel will incline toward one end or the other of the convention-invention scale.

As with novels, so with novelists: There are novelists who undertake writing at the convention end of the spectrum and see it primarily in terms of *career* (Rogers, 1991, 29ff) – and as craft. Other novelists undertake it on the invention end of the spectrum and see it in terms of vocation (22ff) – and as art. The former is less imaginative, ultimately, because more controlling of both the process of their writing – for example, cranking out a quota of words per day and best-sellers per year – and the product. The reason their product 'cannot be great art,' though, is 'because it is too predictable and too much committed to its own conventions. It is written to a formula, a market. When we buy it, there is an implicit understanding that we are not going to have our expectations confounded. We'll get the conclusion we want' (Cupitt, 1991, 25).

The latter novelists, on the other hand, are the kind I have been considering repeatedly thus far: the kind whose characters, as Joyce Carol Oates says of hers, 'dictate themselves' (Rogers, 27); the kind who, like D.H. Lawrence, 'must write to live' (24). Unlike their more conventional counterparts, their work – as art – 'is always a little difficult, a little transgressive. It does not conform to our expectations, but challenges our very notion of form, and thereby enhances life' (Cupitt, 1991, 25). For such novelists, 'more than the drive for money, fame, and security is at work' (25). For them, writing is a calling.

Indeed it is the main medium of their self-expression. This makes them committed to the 'esthetic axiom' whereby 'the more of yourself you're able to give your art the stronger your art will be' (Huddle, 1990, 31). (Or as novelist Thomas Wolfe puts it, 'all serious creative work must be at bottom autobiographical,' must 'use the material and experience of (the novelist's) own life' if anything is to be created 'that has substantial value' (1983, 19).) Consequently, they may find that writing entails 'securing solitude, risking madness' (Huddle, 24), that it 'increases one's prospects for anguish, self-doubt, and related sorts of suffering' (26), and that it makes them 'obsessive, driven people' – the kind of people John Gardner equates with 'true artists' (1985, xx). Curiously, they may also find that they are often overshadowed by their own creations; that their novels become bigger than their own lives – to others and even to themselves. 'Great novels,' says Milan Kundera, 'are always a little more intelligent than their authors' (1988, 158).

As with literature, so with life: there is no sharp line between convention and invention. Indeed, both elements are necessary: 'If the individual does not encounter a large number of conventionalized experiences and situations, the strain on his sense of continuity and identity will lead to great tensions and even to neurotic breakdowns. On the other hand, without new information about his world, the individual will be increasingly unable to cope with it and will withdraw behind a barrier of conventions as some people withdraw from life to compulsive reading of detective stories' (Cawelti, 1989, 87). None the less, as novels, peoples's lives will vary according to which end of this spectrum they are inclined, convention or invention. And, as novelists, people themselves will vary according to whether they view the construction of their lives as career or vocation, craft or art. So then, convention-career-craft vs. invention-vocation-art: thin ice though they make, might these categories not constitute a set of crude criteria for assessing the 'artfulness' of an actual life?

Just as for some novelists writing is essentially a craft, so it can be for some individuals in living their lives. At every turn, they seem to take the unimaginative route, the low road, the path of least resistance. They seem to question little the stereotypical roles they are assigned by society, the clichés of speech and thought and behaviour that they can buy for a song, the assumptions about the nature and purpose of life they have inherited from parents or picked up from others, the forms of self-telling implicit in the larger stories in which they live. For one good reason or another, they squander their authorship, thereby diminishing the novel contribution they might make to their own self-creation, and to the world. This is not to say their lives lack integrity at all or that in certain situations they lack courage. But it may signify something about their lack of the larger, more embracing courage Paul Tillich calls 'the courage to be.'

By the same token, just as for other novelists writing is largely an art (improvisatory at that), an uncertain reaching out in which characters wrestle with and change their plots and so create themselves, so can living be for some individuals. Unlike their more conventional counter-parts, they see the path of life as that: a path, a journey, an adventure. They see it as a life-long response to the call to break new ground, to pose new possibilities, to raise new questions, to 'grope for the new forms that will carry their experience' (Jourard, 1971, 63), to make out of the raw material of their lives 'something which did not exist before' (Faulkner, 1968) – or, in James Joyce's phrase, 'to forge in the smithy of [their] souls the uncreated conscience of [their] race.' In short, the more a person approaches living as an exercise in self-invention (or at least in more consciously choosing between the conventions of self-invention to which she conforms); the more she sees being true to that exercise as the purpose of her life; and the more she sees her goal as the achieve-ment of a life that is artistically coherent and ethically satisfactory, then might her life not merit the label 'work of art'?

Life-as-Novel: The Question of Truth

My second reflection picks up on one implication of my first: that a person's life-story is an artwork to the extent that, in living it out, she is being 'true' to herself. This is a familiar line of thinking, but, as we should now be seeing, it is not without its problems. The concept of a singular 'true self' somewhere inside us waiting to be discovered or e-duced, accepted or actualized – the concept of a person who we 'really are' yet, paradoxically, are called to become – this concept, however frequently espoused in psychology and religion and everyday life, reflects an essentialism that, if not wrong, can at least be critiqued. In fact, critiquing it is in part what I have been about in this book, devoted as it has been to the poetics of self-*creation* – that is, to the composing more than the receiving of a self.

In his own questioning of the true self concept, Wayne Booth (1988)[7] insists that 'we build what becomes our character' by means of 'a kind of play-acting with characters or characteristics,' of 'a kind of faking of characters' (252). Through our exposure to fiction and 'the company we keep' with fictional characters, we are therefore involved in a special but positive kind of 'hypocrisy,' Booth says, without which the development of our character is limited: 'authors play roles by creating characters, and readers and spectators play roles by re-creating them, hypo-critically' (252). Accordingly, we must move from the notion of a 'true self' to that of a 'social psyche' (246). In other words, 'there are no clear boundaries between the others who are somehow both outside and inside me and the "me" that the others are "in"' (239). From my musing here on the link between inside-out and outside-in, on the confusion of fiction and reality, and on how we are 'storyotypical' characters in each other's life-stories, I find myself in sympathy with Booth. If the notion of our 'true self' can be so easily challenged, though, what about the notion of our 'true story'?

We have seen how our lives are made up of many stories, not one alone. The inside story of our lives is in fact a whole collection of stories, while the specific tales we spin for others out of them are countless, varying endlessly in terms of the plotting, characterization, and point of view with which we compose them. Moreover, for any one event, though it presumably 'happened' in only one way, there are many ways it can be interpreted and told, many 'experiences' into which it can be made, many stories to which it can lead. Thus 'anyone can reel off multiple autobiographies of his own life,' write Bruner and Weisser (1991), 'can include different materials, organize it around different themes (within limits), make it match different moods, slant it for different audiences, and so on' (135). Besides the vast number of stories we can and do tell about ourselves, however, there are vastly more we leave untold, for reasons I have already reviewed. These include the plethora of possible stories that fall by the wayside because there are simply too many events, on too many levels, coming too fast to be attended to and transmuted by our imagination into story-able form. The better portion of our existence goes unstoried altogether. So, to speak convincingly about the 'true story' of my life may demand an even greater leap of faith than to speak about my 'true self.'

Furthermore, the very combination of the two terms, adjective and noun, is peculiar. What truly is a 'true story'? How can a story be 'true' and yet still be a 'story'? And how can it be a 'story' and yet still be 'true'?

A story can be true in either of two respects. First, as a record of the way things really happened in the realm of the 'facts': This is the truth intended by a history text or a biography, truth that is determined and told outside-in. Second, as a reflection of the way things really are – emotionally, ethically, spiritually – in the realm of the human soul: This is the truth intended by a painting or a poem, truth that is determined and told inside-out.

Concerning the latter, truth is not a technical concept but an aesthetic one. As such, a great novel about a fictional hero can be truer and more 'telling' than an official biography of a real one. Fiction can be far truer (though far stranger) than fact. In fact, if no story is formed from it at all (by reporters or historians or ourselves), then fact has no such truth to tell. It is *mere* fact. So it is that a good story, though fabricated, can claim us and shake us and affect our self-creation in incredible ways; witness the enduring power of the plays of Shakespeare or the parables of Christ.

Concerning the former, a record of the way things 'actually happened' would be, if true, then tedious: a listing, one after the other, of all possible 'events' or 'facts' on all levels with no interpretation. If history (or rather the philosophy of history) has taught us anything, though, it is that no such 'facts' exist. Such a record is not just tedious but technically impossible. Beyond the supposedly 'true' story of a given event lurks another story still waiting to be told. Thus, the work of historians, scientists, theologians – as of detectives, jurists, and journalists – is never done. It is impossible to tell *the* truth, as in the one account of events behind which lies no other version. As Cupitt puts it, truth is simply 'the story on top at present' (1991, 20). Or, in Berger's words, 'the "true" understanding of our past is a matter of our viewpoint ... Today's "insight" becomes tomorrow's "rationalization," and the other way around' (1963, 59).

Considering 'the story of my life,' then, the concept of the *true* story is problematic through and through, in so far as I am not merely the reporter of the raw events I relate but the chief interpreter of them too (which frequently means chief distorter and embellisher) – not to mention the primary reader, critic, editor, and reviser of these same interpretations. My point though is that, in terms of life-story, the two kinds of truth are not entirely separate. Indeed, they converge in every autobiography that has ever been written as the fictionalizing of the writer affects the facts of the life. The 'truth' of a given autobiography is neither purely factual/technical nor purely fictional/aesthetic, though it usually strives to be both, and is judged worthy by critics if it succeeds: if it tells us both 'the truth' and 'truth'; if it is not just the same old story, like what we find in the true confessions of the rich and famous (or the famous for *being* famous), but is novel; if the life-story outlasts the life; if the soul behind it has something to say to us beyond the bare listing of events and achievements: some message, some pearl, some parable to live by. The two truths also converge, I believe, in every small, informal, unwritten autobiographical act that everyone of us engages in every day – every time we undertake to express our experience of our existence.

What meaning can we preserve then in the notion of 'truth' as it relates to life-story? Are we to despair even of *telling* the truth about our lives, or about any one event within them, let alone of *knowing* that truth? Many, of course, have long since given up asking the question: whether consciously, through reasoning about the textual complexity of self-consciousness, or unconsciously, through either disinterest or despair, having resigned themselves to the duplicity of the everyday world. But despair of the issue of truth is not necessarily an answer. An answer lies, I believe, in the distinction between truth and truthfulness, though the two are commonly confused. Where truth is elusive, truth*fulness* lies within reach.

Sissela Bok (1989) underlines this distinction in the course of considering the nature and implications of lying from a variety of angles: ethical, legal, and epistemological. 'The whole truth *is* out of reach. But this fact has very little to do with our choices about whether to lie or to speak honestly, about what to say and what to hold back' (4). Therefore, she says, 'we must single out … from the countless ways in which we blunder misinformed through life, that which is done with the *intention to mislead*; and from the countless partial stabs at truth, those which are intended to be truthful' (8). I relate Bok's distinction between truth and truthfulness to that between product and process. *The* true story of my life is unattainable, but a *truer* story is not. Accordingly, we must ask the question of truth in terms less of the product of our life-story, which we never finish weaving anyway, than, once again, of the process. Put this way, if in the continuous process of storying our lives we keep alert to the possibility of self-deception, if we remain open to reading and critiquing the stories of our lives internalized from others or constructed out of those in the culture around us, and if we strive to accommodate and account for more of the actual events of our lives, then, at least in terms of our at-

tention and *in*-tention, are we not being 'true' – if not to our 'true self'
then to (what?) the autobiographical imperative, the call to self-create,
the lure of life at large?

Self-Creativity: The Question of Control

Self-as-novelist and life-as-novel: these are enticing extensions of the
life-as-story metaphor. My final reflection carries on from them, then,
and concerns how in the end each novel *has*, or *is*, a life of its own.

In strict terms, no one has control over a novel. Once composed and
circulated, it is the property of no one, accessible to all. It is 'in the
air,' like a symphony of Beethoven or a poem of Blake. No one, so to
speak, is minding the story. The author, however much she has initiated its composition, soon surrenders control of it not merely to the
muses nor, eventually, to her readers and critics, but also, *during* the
composition, to her characters themselves, and to the largely unpredictable interaction between them and the plot in which she places
them. In turn, such control as the narrator (or narrators) might have,
though tighter than that of the author, as in closer to the story, is none
the less limited to the author's overall plan, however emergent it be.
Though the main character, as a creator within a creation, a storyteller
within a story, may be said to have some control over how the story
turns out – as we saw with Tom Baxter's defection from *The Purple
Rose of Cairo* – it is control, technically speaking, not *over* the story but
within the story. Even then, it is restricted by the other characters, as
well as by the contingencies of the plot in which all of them are
embedded.

Perhaps it is the plot, then, that has control over the story? However, in so far as the plot is dependent upon the characters – not to
mention the narrator and author – then neither does it as well. What
about the reader then? Recent trends in literary criticism show us how
the reader's control over the story is far greater than it was ever
deemed in the past, when an older and more author-centred (more
authoritarian) paradigm held sway; they show us how readers are
always co-authors of any story they read. None the less, though free
to make of the novel whatever story they will, readers are eventually
bound by the words on the page. Every reader and every reading are
sooner or later accountable to the text itself. Good readings attend to
it with care; poor ones do not. Perhaps this means the text itself has
control over the story, in the sense of being the final arbiter of its

meaning and vitality. We soon see how fragile such a notion is too, however, for without a reader and his or her story-making imagination, surely the text is ... dead.

Einstein said once that analysing the atom was child's play compared with analysing child's play. The same could be said of analysing story – not its content so much as its very form. A story is a funny thing. Even the simplest story is far from simple. In so far as each of us *is* a story, of which we are variously co-author/narrator, protagonist, and reader, and in so far as that story is still unfolding and is constituted of countless other stories besides – stories swirling around within us and about us, stories that are growing in number by the hour, and stories that can be combined with each other in an infinity of ways – then each of us is a rather funny thing too. We are novel, that is: unique and unfathomable. Ultimately, no one has control over our story – not even ourselves perhaps, inasmuch as we live *within* that story, much of which has been composed for us by others. 'Our tales are spun,' Dennett reminds us, 'but for the most part we don't spin them; they spin us' (1991, 418). As great novels can be to those who compose them, our stories are often larger than our lives, if only in our own minds, and may even last longer than them too, at least in the minds of others. In light of this point – and with James's notion of the 'germ' of a story (Allen, 1949, 155) and Aristotle's of the *energeia* of a story and its initial organic 'form' buzzing in the background – it is perhaps difficult to deny that our life-novel does have a life of its own: that we have a unique 'destiny' to work out (Merton, 1972, 12), 'bliss' to follow (Campbell and Moyers, 1988, 155), 'message' to discover (Van Kaam, 1972, 92), or 'soul' to nurture (Moore, 1992). If so, then it means we must admit a measure of essentialism into our thinking after all, if only by the back door – or the trapdoor of the unconscious. Despite the fatalistic flavour of this very real possibility, how our stories are told and how they unfold still depends, more than we may have realized hitherto, on our own agency. It depends on our own imagination, on our capacity to create ourselves.

In the first chapter, we saw how treatments of creativity have characteristically revolved around three general categories: persons, processes, and products. In *self*-creation, these categories find a strange convergence: The self is simultaneously the agent, the action, and the achievement of its own creation. The self that creates itself is both the self that is doing the creating and the process of creating itself. This convergence of person, process, and product can be seen even more

clearly, I believe, as we become comfortable relating the self – the soul
– to the notion of a complex, ever-thickening novel of which we are
curiously poised in the midst. In relation to this novel, besides being
its co-author/narrator, protagonist, and reader, we are simultaneously
its teller, its telling, and its tale.

These convergences within each of us may represent, on the one
hand, a happy way to overcome the subject-object split that has
plagued the Cartesian metaphysics we have inherited concerning the
self and that is currently so widely critiqued. On the other hand, they
may represent the kiss of death upon all of our supposedly scientific
attempts to decipher the dynamics whereby we become the people we
are – if for no other reason than because in our efforts to adjudicate
the aesthetic coherence of another's self-process we ourselves are part
of the cipher. 'Since narrative is universal,' says Booth, 'there can be
no "control group" consisting of untouched souls who have lived life-
times without narrative so that they might study unscathed the effects
on others' (1988, 41). To such a dilemma, however, perhaps we need
to say *so be it*. If ever the 'uncertainty principle' applied, surely it is
here. Perhaps the self, its creation, and its learning constitute a problem too defiant to be solved, a story too intricate to be untangled, and
a mystery too elusive to be expressed. Perhaps, in the end, we are
faced with a conundrum of the kind the poet alone can see:

> O chestnut tree, great-rooted blossomer,
> Are you the leaf, the blossom or the bole?
> O body swayed to music, O brightening glance,
> How can we know the dancer from the dance?

Summary

In so far as self-creation is a synonym for learning, what I have been
doing throughout this book is exploring the *poetics* of learning, in the
process going down numerous unusual paths. In this final chapter, I
have been considering how these paths converge into certain implications for those whose work is the counsel, care, or education of adults.

Some of these implications are practical in nature. They concern, for
example, the links between learning and literature, the allure of literature generally, and the personal value in being literarily literate as a

means of increasing the stock of story forms with which to make sense of the events of our lives. They concern the nature and importance of storytelling in general, both in everyday life and in specific contexts, such as support groups, consciousness raising, and qualitative research. They concern the definition by which to distinguish adulthood from childhood in the first place. Accordingly, adults are persons who stand on, or seek to cross, 'the threshold of story,' whose central concern on some level is with understanding what sorts of stories their lives are, where they have come from, where they are going. In general, however, the principal implications are theoretical more than practical. They concern less how we do adult education than how we understand adult development; less the external construction of the learning environment than the internal complexity of the learner; less the design of specific curricula than the dynamics of self-creation.

Practical or theoretical, to the extent we take them seriously, we put ourselves in a frame of mind that sees living not as a craft ultimately but as an art, and a peculiarly literary art at that, because it has to do with the never-ending process of storying and re-storying the stuff of our lives. As an art, it is an 'uncertain reaching out,' an enterprise of interpretation, improvisation, and invention. It involves the continual and unpredictable process of trying to maintain a dynamic balance between order and chaos, form and content; between ambition and ambiguity, action and reflection, integrity and openness; between convention and invention, intention and interruption, continuity and change; between the old and the new, the told and the untold, the familiar and the unforeseen; between the outer and the inner, the forest and the trees, the one and the many.

Managing such a balancing act is a delicate affair. It requires attention to detail at every turn. It requires meditating on the many meanings of the events of our lives with something of the imagination of the novelist, the concern of the critic, the care of the therapist, and the devotion of the saint – and, occasionally, the lucidity of the fool. It requires a conviction and a curiosity, even a sense of celebration, concerning the unfathomable uniqueness – the novel-ty – of each individual soul, above all our own. It requires a sense that each of us 'embodies an adventure of existence,' and that 'the art of life is the guidance of this adventure' (Whitehead [1929]/1967, 39). The more we master that art, no matter how poor our lives might otherwise be, the more they may partake of the rich diversity-yet-integrity, the openness and the truth, of a full-length novel, and the more they may add to the wealth of the world. As Annie Dillard writes, so encouragingly, 'a completed novel in a trunk in the attic is an order added to the sum of the universe's order. It remakes its share of undoing' (1982, 174).

EPILOGUE

There were three men went down the road
As down the road went he:
The man he was,
The man folks saw,
The man he wished to be.

Source unknown[1]

As the poem points out, our awareness of ourselves is at best problematic. In fact, it is a thoroughly complicated affair: many-levelled,
multi-faceted, and ever-changing. What I have been attempting to do
in this book is to examine this complexity by playing with the extraordinary implications of a rather ordinary metaphor: 'the story of my
life.' I have chosen to do so because when it comes to the mystery of
learning, the mystery of self-creation, metaphor may be our last resort.
Yet in the house of metaphor are many fine rooms: life-as-battle, life-
as-puzzle, life-as-journey (Kenyon, 1991). Life-as-story can claim no
special status. Moreover, like *any* metaphor, it has its limitations, as I
trust we have seen. By probing it, however, I believe we set off a
shower of alluring possibilities for understanding the meaning-making
mechanisms that are central to being human.

My examination is obviously far from complete. The foregoing is but
the first stage, a beginning only, the scaffolding for some future, more
careful project. In so far as it has itself been a story – the story of my
thinking to date – it has been a rather meandering tale, one that raises
more questions than it resolves and, like the average novel, carries
with it a whole 'ragbag of concerns' (Polster, 1987, 1). Accordingly, I
find myself reluctant to lay out clearly what it has been 'about,' hesi-
tant to spell out in neat, unambiguous terms the agenda it sets for
continuing research. A story does not work that way. To engage our
imagination from beginning to end, it must rely on nuances and hints,

subplots un-wrapped-up, loose ends left untied. The better or more artistic the story, then the more open it remains, the more loose-ended it is left. Any listing of recommendations or conclusions would seem out of place, beside the point, aesthetically uncouth. Having said this, perhaps I can make a few 'concluding' comments none the less. I make them in the form not of conclusions as such, however, but (continuing in the pragmatic vein of the previous chapter) of a few further issues that professionals in a variety of fields might wish to ponder – within the framework, that is, of a poetics of self-creation, for they are issues that other frameworks may be less able to frame, let alone to settle.

Further Issues

Law

If 'the truth' is as elusive as we have seen, then what are we to understand as the purpose of that whole, costly, complex apparatus whereby, case after case, it is supposedly sought? Given the fictionalizing of memory and the battle of stories the average trial becomes, what is it – apart from the truth*fulness* of its participants – that can be determined 'beyond a reasonable doubt' when there are so many occasions 'for refraction of the original incident': in the transaction between initial occurrence and witness, witness and counsel, counsel and judge, judge and jury, and jurors themselves (Marshall, 1969, 103)?

Moreover, given the inescapably fictive dimension to all testimony, what are these various players to make of pleas of 'insanity,' or of the mystery of 'motive'? And what about the concept of personal responsibility before the law, according to which each individual is presumably the 'hero' of his or her own life-story? Indeed, what of the very establishment of 'the law' itself, arising as it inevitably does out of the political and economic interests, the assumptions about truth and human nature, that are embedded in a particular configuration of larger stories – that is, culture and class, country and civilization?

Finally, what alternative methods might there be for pursuing justice? In the native Indian one described by Rupert Ross (1992), for example, one side's story is never pitted adversarially against another's, as it is in our 'Western' one. Rather, counsel is given and sentences are assigned by means of a subtle system of storytelling that participants engage in, parable-like, not so much to nail down 'the truth' – to determine who did it and why – as to heal the community that has been rent by the deed. What shift in our thinking and interrelating might be effected if, as a society, we were to inch closer to such a model?

Religion

If, like science, a given religion tells us what is really only a particular *story* of the world – of where it has come from, where it is going, who we are in its midst; of the main conflicts at stake in it and the themes woven through it – then what about the belief, in fundamentalist circles at least, that 'the truth' must be defended and disseminated at all costs, that spiritual survival lies in seeing the light in one way alone? If 'the truth' is ultimately a story, then will any old story do? By what criteria, that is, do we determine that one world-story (and thus the self-story it prescribes) is 'better' than another? In what measure does it depend on the genre in which it is cast and proclaimed?

Given that the Christian story, for example, can be variously packaged as a tragedy (Henn, 1956, 282), a comedy (Frye, 1988), or an adventure (Haught, 1984; Tournier, 1965; Kelsey, 1980) – a variation that makes it adaptable to different cultures yet makes interfaith 'dialogue' truly a battle of stories – which of these is necessarily a 'better genre' and why? Is the evaluation of 'better' a matter of the success of a given genre – in a given context and for a given personality type – at capturing the imaginations or igniting the hopes of potential converts? And what becomes of the concept of conversion itself, with its implicit de-valuing, its de-storying, of the prior life-story (if not the life) of the convert?

With such grand questions in the background, how are pastors and rabbis and priests to see their role in the search for 'meaning' that they help people to tackle? in the re-storying they facilitate? in the counselling and confessoring they dispense? in the safekeeping of secrets they provide? Moreover, what is their responsibility as custodians and communicators of 'the' story for a congregation whose members will have their respective, often widely divergent, readings of it; who, in addition, will be living through their own personal and communal stories; and who, like the members of any community, will be bound problematically together not just by story-*telling* but by story-*typing* too – not just by compassion, that is, but also by gossip?

What is the effect on these same members' sense of their *human* agency when they conceive the divine agency less in terms of the invention and maintenance of a clock than of the composition of a novel, meaning that they are not cogs in a wheel but creations inside a creation – free to create themselves and their world much as they will, for better or worse: either kicking the story to pieces or ushering it to its resonant close?

Gerontology

Granted that 'story' is only one of many metaphors for capturing the complexity of life (Kenyon, Birren, and Schroots, 1991), what use can be made of it by those who study the ageing process and the shifts in self-concept it invariably prompts? How can the story metaphor help those who try to formulate working definitions of 'health' or 'competency' or 'maturity'; or those who consider the conundrums created when life outlasts life-story – like the book that is returned to the shelf once the novel within it is read? How can it illuminate the role of those who work with the aged directly, listening and encouraging, as they use their stories to 'negotiate status' (Tarman, 1988), as they attempt to make sense of their existence, to come to grips – good memory or not – with their own ending, their denouement, their de-storying? As they try, in a flurry of last-minute response to the auto-biographical imperative, to get their story out or down or straight, whether for posterity or themselves?

Do the elderly generally become more detached from their own life stories *as stories*, able to tell about themselves as if 'they' – the person they were back when – were a distant character in the life of someone else? In other words, does the length of life itself, or the decrease in physical activity that goes with the aging process, tend to push a person – with or without the assistance of their preferred storying style – out of the protagonist mode and more and more into the narrator and/or reader modes? Furthermore, what use can be made of the story model in counselling the families and friends of the dying or deceased: those left behind, that is, who have lost a central character in their own life-stories and who must thus re-story their system and themselves?

Finally, by shifting from a psychological paradigm of life-span development to a poetic one, what respect can we recover as a society for the elderly in our midst – for the maturity or coherence they may achieve; for the fierceness with reality, the 'truth,' they may have to impart? According to such a paradigm, none of us receives a life-story ready-made. Rather, we compose one, living and telling and spinning one that is more or less novel, and that thickens as it unfolds. Toward its end, however, a certain *de*-composing or 'narrowing' must eventually occur. But need this denouement be seen as automatically a diminishment? With it, is there not the potential, as there is in story *per se*, for an aesthetic integrity to the course of our life as a whole – an integrity for which one word might be 'wisdom'? 'When at last age has assembled you together,' asks Florida Scott-Maxwell, 'will it not be easy to let it all go, lived, balanced, over?' (1968, 42).

Counselling

If therapy of whatever variety is essentially 'a restorying of life' (Hillman, 1975a, 168), then what is the role of the therapist (analyst, social worker, counsellor) in the life of a couple or a family, where obviously more than one story is at stake? In terms of relationships generally, what understanding of the origin, function, and dysfunction of interpersonal attraction might counsellors acquire once they take 'the allure of story' into account?

How ought counsellors to assess the merits, story-wise, of the several therapeutic plot-lines that they have to choose from in 'the battle of stories' involved in working with a given client? What, for example, makes one plot-line work better than another with a given client? Is it because, for that person at least, it has more of a 'salvational tone,' as do many modern psychologies and therapies (Moore, 1992, xii); or because it promises an 'answer' (Schafer, 1989); or simply because it is more inspiring or encouraging – as can be the case with certain life-span development theories, for instance, in which 'the underlying narrative structure [is] romance, where the hero engages in adventures of self-discovery filled with hope' (Sarbin, 1986, xviii)? What injustice is done to the novelty of individual clients, however, when counsellors tacitly force them to re-story in, for example, a romantic manner, whereas, poetically speaking, their lives might represent and deserve acceptance (even celebration) as tragic, ironic, or even picaresque compositions, with a coherence and integrity all their own?

What are the effects of journal-keeping (even of computer-assisted self-therapy) in the process of re-storying, as contrasted to those of the 'talking cure' that is central to the traditional therapeutic process? From the perspective of self-creation, what is it about such self-directed therapy that is different from, perhaps even better than, what goes in the more conventional, dialogical setting – where the potential is greater for the 'storyotyping' tendencies, the 'encumbering thoughts,' of the therapist to skew the client's self-disclosure? In other words, how is self-author-ity influenced differently through the literal medium than it is through the oral and visual (face-to-face) one? As well, what assistance to self-creation is provided by using fiction in therapy – bibliotherapy, that is – or by encouraging the client to be, in general, more literarily literate?

Against a story background, what are the implications for the work that therapists do of current research into things like false memory syndrome, neurolinguistic programming, autobiographical memory, and language acquisition? Moreover, what are the challenges that confront counsellors from a poetic perspective given the unusual problems of personal identity presented by conditions such as amnesia, Alzheimer's disease, transsexuality, or by the more severe types of dissociation like schizophrenia and multiple personality disorder?

What happens to counsellors themselves in their role as auditors, editors, and co-authors of – as novelists eliciting – the stories of others? What is or ought to be their relationship to their own life-story material – open, flexible, critical? Furthermore, how critical ought they to be of the larger stories in which both they and their clients live?

In the same vein, given the problems attending the notion of 'truth,' what is the overall *goal* of counselling anyway? What definitions of, for example, 'functioning' or 'sane' or 'adjusted' should it assume? Finally, what about the ethics of what is, effectively, *interfering* in clients' self-creation – though presumably with greater insight and sensitivity than is the case in their 'ordinary' interactions with others every day? What are the ethics, that is, of 'meddling' in the most sacred of realms: that mysterious inner region where events are transformed into experiences and existence is made into soul?

Adult Education

If 'self-concept' and 'past experience' play the pivotal role commonly claimed for them in how and what we learn (Brundage and MacKeracher, 1980), then what spin is put on our *theories* of learning when neither notion can be conceived apart from its *storied* complexity; apart from the idea that we see ourselves and interpret our world *through* our stories, without which we can scarcely say who we are or relate to what we are learning? If 'making meaning' is understood in terms less of prosaic notions like 'information processing' than of poetic ones like 'world-making,' 'story-telling,' and 'novel-composing,' then what reworking is entailed in our sense of – and research on – the subtleties of personal growth? And what of the 'care' component to adult education (Daloz, 1986, 3, 237), whereby teachers and students, themselves so often 'in transition,' have the opportunity to function less as competitors of each other than as co-authors *with* each other, or 'cultures of embeddedness' *for* each other, as they mutually recompose their selves and their worlds?

What about the thrust within adult education circles in the direction of mentoring programs, or of 'prior learning assessment,' when these approaches are analysed and evaluated against the background of the autobiographical imperative? Also, what happens to our understanding of such processes as 'empowerment' or 'conscientization,' of 'perspective transformation' or 'critical reflection' – as of such concepts as intelligence, maturity, or wisdom – if we view them through poetic lenses as much as through psychological ones, therefore invoking alternative terms like re-storying, author-ity, or re-genre-ation with which to understand them? Given the possibility that 'some metaphors *create* something new' (Kenyon, Birren, and Schroots, 1991, 7), then how creative, and how helpful, do such reformulations actually prove? What insights do they reveal? What do they obscure? What, from an educational perspective, are the actual strengths and limitations of the story metaphor, the story model, the story method?

Finally, assuming there *is* a method in the metaphor – that is, the facilitation of transformative learning or re-storying – then what part might be played in that method by

- exposing learners to texts of fiction, biography, or autobiography with 'emancipatory potential' (Greene, 1990), in order to stimulate a perspective transformation?
- urging learners to trace a life-line, analyse their 'signature stories,' or keep a journal, so that they can see not only that they *have* a story (or stories) but that they have in large part composed it themselves, and can thus recompose it, both inside and inside-out?
- inviting learners to map the arrangement of the various larger stories in which their personal ones have been situated; to assess the influence of these stories on their own self-creation; and to critique them in terms of their poetic structure – that is, their themes, heroes, conflicts, genre, morality, authority, atmosphere, and style, as well

as their prescriptions for plotting (evaluating or prioritizing) events and for characterizing people?

This is but a quick catalogue of the kinds of questions we put into orbit around us once we move in the direction of a poetic approach to everyday life. It may suffice to show, though, just how much hard thinking there is ahead of us to be done – as much as has surely been done already. Having concluded it with adult education, a field in which I frequently labour, I want now to offer a few final reflections on the nature of the educational 'call.'

Poetics and the Calling of Education

None of us is an island. To talk of the novel-ty of our lives is not to lapse into individualism. Our personal stories can only ever be recounted with reference to some combination of larger stories in which we live and move and have our being. These are the stories of the families and communities, the cultures and creeds, the gender and class, in which we are always characters in turn: stories in which our individual self-creation plays some small part (though ideally a responsible and creative one) in how their plots unfold. In this sense, the story of our lives connects ultimately with every other story, both within us and without. Thus the fiction-friendliness that most of us feel, and the unfailing allure of the world of stories in general, fiction or not. In that world, no one story ever stands on its own: all belong to 'one big interlocking family'; all together comprise 'the order of words' (Frye, 1963, 18, 38). Furthermore, within any single story there is no 'single story' anyway, only a more or less intricately woven web of stories. As in the physical universe, so in the poetic one: everything is connected to everything else.

So, if our life *is* a story, it is at bottom not one story but many. But it is many in the way the average novel is many. In other words, having many stories at work within us is not evidence – as a pure postmodernist might think – of the impossibility of any sort of centred self (Beardslee, 1990, 172). Nor need it suggest a pathological split in our self-consciousness (though such pathologies exist), any more than having many subplots and chapters, episodes and events, conflicts and characters, within one novel signifies its destruction. On the contrary, the more stories at work in the novel, the richer, more engaging, and indeed 'truer to life' we shall probably deem it. That is, of course,

provided the many stories do not pull so strongly in opposite directions that they pull the one story to bits – as in certain lower-grade
novels or movies in which the writers seem unable to decide from one
scene to the next whether to make it a tragedy, a comedy, or an adventure, so clumsily are the genres confused. The novel, in order to
accommodate the many, must therefore also be one. To the extent that
it is not, we may say that it fails *as* novel.

Not all novels, of course, will achieve this balance between the one
and the many, and neither will all souls. Just as there are bad novels,
so there are broken souls: souls that fail to hold the many stories of
their lives in healthy tension with the one; souls that are fragmented,
uncentred, unfocused; souls that are filled with contradictions that
continually undermine the integrity of their engagements with others;
souls that, like some novels, fail to go anywhere, or to hang together,
or to ring true; souls that, in the extreme, are – literally – split. The
measure of this failure can be seen as the degree such souls are self-
deceived; the degree their stories as a whole are not just artistically
incoherent but ethically unsatisfying; the degree the stories they tell,
both to themselves and others, fail to fit even marginally (for they
never fit entirely) with the stories that others both hear them tell and
see them live.

Based on all that we have considered so far, therefore, I propose that
our calling as 'educators' – liberally defined, as people interested in the
e-ducing (the drawing out) and the edu-*care* (the nurturing) of our
fellow human beings – is to do and to be whatever we can to turn this
failure around. But in a mutual manner, for as we elicit and host the
stories of others – as we audit, edit, and (co)author them – we are
invariably re-storied ourselves. Our vocation, then, is to do and to be
whatever we can to help each other to both tell and live '*our* story, our
whole story, and *nothing but* our story.' If, as we sometimes hear, within
us lies at least one novel, then our calling is to midwife one another as
we give that story birth: as we get it out and get it straight, its unique
'message' embodied in the life that we alone can compose. It is to encounter each other 'at the edge of experience' where 'story and anti-
story meet' (Dornisch, 1979, 61). It is to help each other expand our
inside story to more faithfully accommodate the outside one, and so
transform more of our actual existence into available experience. Moreover, it is to understand more critically the gaps between that inside
story and the stories told inside-out by ourselves and read outside-in
by others. It is to provide each other a safe, hospitable space in which

we can tell ourselves and read ourselves as much as we need. It is to help us re-story ourselves in such a way that the one story will more integrally embrace the many; that we will be able to tell, at least to ourselves, more of the stories we have hitherto left untold (especially those of the self-sabotaging kind); that we will be able to identify, to critique, and to discern between the many master-stories that vie for our allegiance in the world at large; and that we will be allowed a more self-conscious defence against the 'storyotyping' of both others and ourselves.

In the natural re-storying that goes on every day, the story of our life need not of course be discontinuous with any or all of its previous versions, any more than with the addition of each subplot and chapter a novel is different from what it was before. Though thicker, it may still be the same old story. There are degrees of re-storying. Some re-storyings are more radical than others, so much so that through them we find our lives literally re-genre-ated. We find ourselves living a markedly different myth, telling a decidedly different story, possessing a fresh future and a refurbished past. Whatever such re-storying is called – whether perspective transformation or conversion, reprogramming or rebirth – by acting as agents of its occurrence in each other's lives perhaps we can keep ourselves closer to whatever awesome energy it is that assists us, simultaneously, in re-storying our souls and recreating our world.

In the end, to adopt a poetic approach to education is to be drawn increasingly into the company of dramatists, novelists, and raconteurs. Their insights into the art of storying lead us to a renewed appreciation of 'the art of living' – of the one, grand, aesthetic project that all of us face: that of composing our own lives. In consequence, we are obliged to grapple with a thousand beguiling questions concerning 'the fictional side of human nature.' As many of the sources I have cited make clear, however, we have at last raised the lid of the box in which, until lately, such questions have lain. What choice have we, I ask, but to open it all the way?

NOTES

Prologue

1 Perhaps especially *adult* educators, argues Barry Bright (1989), as he critiques their field roundly for its 'cafeteria approach to psychology' (48), its '"bad" eclecticism' (50), its 'bastardizing' of 'its derived knowledge content' (34), and its 'epistemological vandalism' (34).

I The Aesthetics of Living

1 Self-direction, though also common, can be excluded from this list because it usually appears in its adjectival form – self-direct*ed* – and is used more to modify a word like 'learning' than to describe a model of the self.

2 Michael Daniels (1988), though critical of Maslow and of the conceptual foundations of self-actualization, acknowledges the positive place this concept can play in our lives: 'a theory of self-actualization should ... be understood as providing a *myth* of human development, a symbolic language that enables people to make sense of their existence, to plan their route through life, to conjure elusive experiences, and to facilitate subtle metamorphoses' (13).

3 In *Self-Creation*, billed as 'the national bestselling classic of self-improvement,' George Weinberg (1978) articulates the flip-side of this notion. Introducing it as 'the basic principle at work every day of your life behind the creation of your personality,' he insists that 'EVERY TIME YOU ACT, YOU ADD STRENGTH TO THE MOTIVATING IDEA BEHIND WHAT YOU'VE DONE' (131; emphasis Weinberg's).

4 Going one step further, we might move here from the image of an iceberg to that of an island. Following Carl Jung, we are all islands in a common sea (Roy, 1984, 33) – where the sea (or sea bottom) corresponds to the 'collective unconscious' by means of which all of us are ultimately connected. Taking a still more scientific step, all of us, all life forms, all things period, may be seen as united in the 'implicate order' – a concept

with which more than a few in the world of physics are currently playing. These are enticing directions to pursue, especially since they suggest
the possibility that just as our experience can shape our existence, so can
consciousness shape the concrete world, so can psychology affect physics,
and so can 'mind' influence 'matter' (Peat, 1987; Bohm and Peat, 1987).

II Life and Literature

1 Unfortunately, the term *genre* defies precise definition. If it is taken to
refer to groupings of literary works with respect to their overall form,
technique, and purpose, then, on a grand scale, the main genres are lyric
poetry, essays, and fiction. Within fiction, however, the question of genre
reappears, in so far as fiction includes any kind of narrative writing that
is 'drawn from the imagination of the author rather than from history or
fact' (Thrall et al, 1960, 201). Thus we have such subgenres as parables,
fables, fairy tales, epic poetry, drama, short stories, and novels. Within
the world of the novel, however, the question of genre emerges yet again,
in so far as novels can in turn be categorized according to form, technique, and purpose.

2 'Most of the stories straining to shape under my hand,' writes James,
'have sprung from a single small seed ... the stray suggestion, the wandering word, the vague echo, at the touch of which the novelist's imagination winces as at the prick of some sharp point' (Allen, 1949, 156).

3 Instead of referring to such concerns as 'theological' it would be more
accurate to use the term 'theodical' since theodicy, strictly speaking, is the
study of the problem of evil. However, the heading 'theological,' in addition to matters theodical, includes matters of meaning as well, such as are
under discussion here.

4 Or from a person or persons whom the novelist knows within her own
self. Novelists can be novelists, it could be said, because they have developed to an art form (literally) the capacity we all have to transform the
events of our lives into experiences that can thus be fed on or lived off of
in memory and imagination. For this reason, says Annie Dillard, 'many
writers do little else but sit in small rooms recalling the real world. This
explains why so many books describe the author's childhood. A writer's
childhood may well have been the occasion of his only firsthand experience' (1989, 44).

5 Another interesting study of differences in cultural conceptions of time is
Anthony Aveni's *Empires of Time* (1989), in which he compares modern

AE cultures with those of the ancient Aztecs, Mayans, Incas, and Chinese. For a discussion of how conceptions of time may be changing within AE culture itself – as we shift, for example, from face clocks to digital ones – see Jeremy Rifkin's provocative *Time Wars* (1989).

6 To Martha Nussbaum (1989), 'emotion is the acceptance of, the assent to live according to, a certain sort of story' (218) – about ourselves, our relationships, our world. One corollary of this is that to make sense of (and so not be dominated by) a given feeling – be it anger or anxiety, sadness or elation – is to ask ourselves *what is the story here?* The next question is whether we might have got the story wrong, in which case we can engage in 'an unwriting of stories' (226).

7 The American humorist Garrison Keillor (1986) adds an insightful twist to this notion of living within a leader's story. In his analysis of the unique leadership style of fellow Midwesterner, Ronald Reagan, he says that, compared with other presidents under whom he grew up, 'Reagan was the best storyteller.' That is, 'he saw America as a fabulous land, a small town of sixty million Christian families who work hard, play ball, and handle their own problems. He truly believed in his story and was disinterested in other, gloomier visions ... [H]is enemies ... were serious men, who trusted scholarship and experience and competence, but he revealed their crucial flaw: *they had no story, and a man who has no story is a man with no truth to offer*' (xvii – xviii; emphasis mine). For a perspective on the influence of Reaganism on the storytelling done through television news, see Daniel Haillin (1988, 34–41).

III The Poetics of Learning

1 In her story 'Kew Gardens,' Virginia Woolf goes one better. Rather than telling her story from the perspective of a minor character, she tells it from that of the natural setting in which the story takes place. Indeed, she seems bent on pondering how unusual and inconclusive our human affairs might appear to a snail crawling across the garden floor, whose careful progress is essentially the story's plot!

2 Because of its present popularity, it is tempting to use 'myth' too casually in discussing the poetics of self-creation, and to assume that myth and story can be interchanged with impunity. This assumption needs to be critiqued. Besides Bruner's point in contrasting a myth to a novel (1965, 52–3), there is the point made by Frank Kermode in comparing myth with fictions generally. 'Myths,' he says, 'are the agents of stability; fictions are the agents of change' (Crossan, 1975, 56).

3 Besides Campbell's considerable contribution to our sense of the nature and function of personal mythology (1973; Campbell and Moyers, 1988), numerous other scholars have been pushing in the same direction. These include Carol Pearson (1989), Stephen Larsen (1990), Jean Shinoda Bolen (1984; 1989), Sam Keen (1991), and most recently, Clarissa Pinkola Estés (1992).

4 While men have traditionally been the most numerous as writers of stories, women, says one report, have been the most numerous as readers. 'If we had to put together a portrait of a typical reader of literature in the United States today,' Zill and Winglee (1990) tell us, 'the person would be a middle-aged white female living in the suburbs of a Western or Midwestern city. She would have a college education, and a middle- to upper-middle class income that was not derived from her literary activities' (ix).

5 This is the genius of a simple book by David Fisher and Patty Brown, *The Book of Memories* (1990), the purpose of which is to help us 'use [our] recollections of the past to bring pleasure to the present.' It consists of a list of questions that prompt us to reminisce: 'Whose house did you and your friends usually go to to play?' or 'What was the angriest you ever made your parents?' The book's premiss is that 'we are the sum total of our experiences and that every experience we've had in life is stored forever in our mind' (5).

6 Included in this list may be the kind of confusion that can characterize those we would describe as 'well-read.' I refer to readers who feed on a diet of plot-lines that is, in effect, too rich for them; readers who have insuffient time, opportunity, or perhaps intelligence to digest them – that is, to reflect on their application to their own lives.

7 Says Booth, 'since the Enlightenment people have increasingly thought of their own essential natures ... as something – a "true self" – to be found by probing within. For complex reasons, much modern thought about the "individual," the un-dividable center, has stressed the search inward for the core of the real "me," the authentic self. In that search, one tends to peel off the inauthentic, insincere, alien influences that might deflect the self from its unique, individual destiny' (237).

Epilogue

1 Apparently anonymous, although psychologist Raymond Cattell attributes it to the poet John Masefield (from conversation with John Gillis, Cattell's biographer).

References

Abrams, P. 1982. *Historical sociology*. Ithaca, NY: Cornell University Press.

Aichele, G. 1985. *The limits of story*. Philadelphia: Fortress Press.

Allen, C.L. 1978. *All things are possible through prayer*. New York: Jove.

Allen, W. 1949. *Writers on writing*. London: E.P. Dutton.

Arieti, S. 1976. *Creativity: The magic synthesis*. New York: Basic.

Assagioli, R. 1987. *Psychosynthesis: A collection of basic writings*. London: Penguin.

Atwood, M. 1988. *Cat's eye*. London: Penguin.

Augros, R.M. and G.N. Stanciu, 1986. *The new story of science*. Toronto: Bantam.

Augustine. 1961. *Confessions*. London: Penguin.

Aveni, A. 1989. *Empires of time: Calendars, clocks, and cultures*. New York: Basic.

Bailin, S. 1985. On originality. *Interchange* 16(1), 6–13.

– 1988. *Achieving extraordinary ends: An essay on creativity*. Boston: Kluwer Academic Publishers.

Barbour, I. 1990. *Religion in an age of science: The Gifford lectures 1989–1991*, vol. 1. San Francisco: Harper & Row.

Bartoli, J.S. 1985. Metaphor, mind, and meaning: The narrative mind in action. *Language Arts*, 62(4), 332–42.

Bateson, M.C. 1989. *Composing a life*. New York: Atlantic Monthly Press.

Beach, R. 1990. The creative development of meaning: Using autobiographical experiences to interpret literature. In D. Bogdan & S.B. Straw (Eds.), *Beyond communication: Reading comprehension and criticism*, 211–35. Portsmouth, NH: Boynton/Cook Heinemann.

Beardslee, W.A. 1990. Stories in the postmodern world: Orienting and disorienting. In D.R. Griffin (Ed.), *Sacred interconnections: Postmodern spirituality, political economy, and art*, 163–75. Albany, NY: SUNY Press.

Beck, C. 1989. Is there really development? An alternative interpretation. *Journal of Moral Education*, 18(3), 174–85.

Belenky, M.F., B.M. Clinchy, N.R. Goldberger, and J.M. Tarule, 1986. *Women's ways of knowing: The development of self, voice, and mind*. New York: Basic.

Benjamin, B.S. 1964. Remembering. In D.F. Gustafson (Ed.), *Essays in philosophical psychology*, 171–94. New York: Anchor.

Benjamin, W. 1969. *Illuminations*. New York: Schocken.

Bennett, J. 1964. *Virgina Woolf: Her art as a novelist*. Cambridge: Cambridge University Press.

Berger, P.L. 1963. *Invitation to sociology: A humanistic perspective*. Garden City, NY: Anchor.

Berger, P.L. and T. Luckmann, 1967. *The social construction of reality: A treatise on the sociology of knowledge*. Garden City, NY: Anchor.

Berghorn, F.J. and D.E. Schafer, 1986–7. Reminiscence intervention in nursing homes: What and who changes? *International Journal of Aging and Human Development*, 24(2), 113–27.

Berman, M. 1991. The body of history. In J. Brockman (Ed.), *Ways of knowing: The reality club 3*, 247–82. New York: Prentice-Hall.

Berne, E. 1964. *Games people play*. New York: Grove.

Berry, T. 1987. The new story: Comments on the origin, identification, and transmission of values. *Cross Currents*, 37(2–3), 187–215.

Birren, J. 1964. *The psychology of aging*. Englewood Cliffs, NJ: Prentice-Hall.

– 1987, May. The best of all stories. *Psychology Today*, 91–2.

Blythe, R. 1980. *The view in winter: Reflections on old age*. London: Penguin.

Bogdan, D. 1983. Censorship of literature texts and Plato's banishment of the poets. *Interchange*, 14(3), 1–16.

– 1990a. Reading and 'The Fate of Beauty': Reclaiming total form. In D. Bogdan & S.B. Straw (Eds.), *Beyond communication: Reading comprehension and criticism*, 167–95. Portsmouth, NH: Boynton/Cook Heinemann.

– 1990b. Toward a rationale for literary literacy. *Journal of Philosophy of Education*, 24(2), 211–24.

Bohm, D. 1980. *Wholeness and the implicate order*. London: Ark.

Bohm, D. and F.D. Peat, 1987. *Science, order, and creativity*. New York: Bantam.

Bok, S. 1984. *Secrets: On the ethics of concealment and revelation*. New York: Vintage.

– 1989. *Lying: Moral choice in public and private life*. New York: Vintage.

Bolen, J.S. 1979. *The Tao of psychology: Synchronicity and the self*. San Francisco: Harper & Row.

– 1984. *Goddesses in every woman*. New York: Harper & Row.

– 1989. *Gods in every man*. New York: Harper & Row.

Bonhoeffer, D. 1971. *Letters and papers from prison*. New York: Macmillan.

Booth, W.C. 1961. *The rhetoric of fiction*. Chicago: University of Chicago Press.

- 1966. Types of narration. In R. Scholes (Ed.), *Approaches to the novel*, 273–90. San Francisco: Chandler.
- 1988. *The company we keep: An ethics of fiction*. Berkeley: University of California Press.
Bridges, W. 1980. *Transitions: Making sense of life's changes*. Toronto: Addison-Wesley.
Briggs, J. 1988. *Fire in the crucible: The alchemy of creative genius*. New York: St Martin's.
Bright, B.P. 1989. Epistemological vandalism: Psychology in the study of adult education. In B.P. Bright (Ed.), *Theory and practice in the study of adult education: The epistemological debate*, 34–64. London: Routledge.
Brookfield, S.D. 1989. *Developing critical thinkers: Challenging adults to explore alternative ways of thinking and acting*. San Francisco: Jossey-Bass.
- 1990. Analyzing the influence of media on learners' perspectives. In J. Mezirow (Ed.), *Fostering critical reflection in adulthood*, 235–50. San Francisco: Jossey-Bass.
Brooks, P. 1985. *Reading for the plot: Design and intention in narrative*. New York: Vintage.
- 1988. The tale vs. the novel. *Novel*, 21(2, 3), 285–92.
Brundage, D.H. and D. MacKeracher, 1980. *Adult learning principles and their application to program planning*. Ontario Ministry of Education.
Bruner, J.S. 1965. *On knowing: Essays for the left hand*. New York: Atheneum.
- 1986a. *Actual minds, possible worlds*. Cambridge, MA: Harvard University Press.
- 1986b. Narrative and paradigmatic modes of thought. In E. Eisner (Ed.), *Modes of knowing*, 97–115.
- 1987. Life as narrative. *Social Research*, 54(1), 11–32.
- 1988. Research currents: Life as narrative. *Language Arts*, 65(6), 574–83.
- 1990. *Acts of meaning*. Cambridge, MA: Harvard University Press.
Bruner, J.S. and S. Weisser, 1991. The invention of self: Autobiography and its forms. In D.R. Olson and N. Torrance (Eds.), *Literacy and orality*, 129–48. Cambridge: Cambridge University Press.
Butler, R. 1964. The life review: An interpretation of reminiscence in the aged. In R. Kastenbaum (Ed.), *New thoughts on aging*. New York: Springer.
Campbell, Jeremy, 1989. *Winston Churchill's afternoon nap: A wide-awake inquiry into the human nature of time*. London: Paladin.
Campbell, Joseph, 1973. *Myths to live by*. New York: Bantam.
- and B. Moyers, 1988. *The power of myth*. New York: Doubleday.
Carey, J. 1987. *Eyewitness to history*. New York: Avon.

Carey, J.W. (1969). Harold Adams Innis and Marshall McLuhan. In R. Rosenthal (Ed.), *McLuhan: Pro and con*, 270–308. London: Penguin.

Carr, D. 1986. *Time, narrative, and history*. Bloomington: Indiana University Press.

Casey, E.S. 1987. *Remembering: A phenomenological study*. Bloomington: Indiana University Press.

Castaneda, C. 1975. *Journey to Ixtlan: The lessons of Don Juan*. London: Penguin.

Castle, E.B. 1961. *Ancient education and today*. London: Penguin.

Cawelti, J.G. 1989. The concept of formula in the study of popular literature. In B. Ashley (Ed.), *The study of popular fiction: A source book*, 87–92. Philadelphia: University of Pennsylvania Press.

Chafe, W. 1990. Some things that narratives tell us about the mind. In B. Britton and A. Pellegrini (Eds.), *Narrative thought and narrative language*, 79–98. Hillsdale, NJ: Lawrence Erlbaum Associates.

Chase, T. 1987. *When Rabbit howls*. New York: Jove.

Chatman, S. 1978. *Story and discourse*. Ithaca, NY: Cornell University Press.

Church, G.J. 1992, June 29. The other side of Perot. *Time*, 16–22.

Clifford, J.L. (Ed.), 1962. *Biography as an art: Selected criticism 1560–1960*. New York: Oxford University Press.

Coles, R. 1989. *The call of stories: Teaching and the moral imagination*. Boston: Houghton Mifflin.

Collingwood, R.G. 1958. *The principles of art*. New York: Oxford University Press.

Connelly, E.M., and D.J. Clandinin, 1988. *Teachers as curriculum planners: Narratives of experience*. New York: Teachers College Press.

– 1990. Stories of experience and narrative inquiry. *Educational Researcher*, 19(5), 2–14.

Cowley, M. (Ed.). 1977. *Writers at work: The 'Paris Review' interviews*. First series. London: Penguin.

Crichton, M. 1988. *Travels*. New York: Ballantine.

Crites, S. 1971. The narrative quality of experience. *Journal of the American Academy of Religion*, 39(3), 291-311.

– 1979. The aesthetics of self-deception. *Soundings*, 6(Q), 107–29.

– 1986. Storytime: Recollecting the past and projecting the future. In T.R. Sarbin (Ed.), *Narrative psychology: The storied nature of human conduct*, 152–73. New York: Praeger.

Cross, K.P. 1988. *Adults as learners: Increasing participation and facilitating learning*. San Francisco: Jossey-Bass.

Crossan, D. 1975. *The dark interval: Towards a theology of story*. Niles, IL: Argus Communications.

Csikszentimihalyi, M., and O.V. Beattie. 1979. Life themes: A theoretical and empirical exploration of their origins and effects. *Journal of Humanistic Psychology*, 19(1), 45–63.

Cupitt, D. 1990. *Creation out of nothing*. London: SCM Press.

– 1991. *What is a story?* London: SCM Press.

Daloz, L.A. 1986. *Effective teaching and mentoring: Realizing the transformational power of adult learning experiences*. San Francisco: Jossey-Bass.

Daniels, M. 1988. The myth of self-actualization. *Journal of Humanistic Psychology*, 28(1), 7–38.

Danto, A.C. 1985. *Narration and knowledge*. New York: Columbia University Press.

Davies, P. 1988. What are the laws of nature? In J. Brockman (Ed.), *Doing science: The reality club*, 47–71. New York: Prentice-Hall.

Dawson, S.W. 1970. *Drama and the dramatic*. London: Methuen.

Dennett, D. 1991. *Consciousness explained*. Boston: Little, Brown.

Dewey, J. [1916] 1966. *Democracy and education: An introduction to the philosophy of education*. New York: Free Press.

– [1938] 1969. *Experience and education*. New York: Collier.

– [1940] 1962. Time and individuality. In H. Shapley (Ed.), *Time and its mysteries*, 141–59. New York: Collier.

Dillard, A. 1975. *Pilgrim at Tinker Creek*. New York: Bantam.

– 1982. *Living by fiction*. New York: Harper & Row.

– 1989. *The writing life*. New York: Harper Perennial.

Dittes, J.E. 1985. *The male predicament*. San Franciso: Harper & Row.

Dixon, J., and L. Stratta, 1986. Textures of narrative. *Educational Review*, 38(2), 103–11.

Dornisch, L. 1979. Experience as life's story. *New Catholic World*, 45–61.

Drabble, M. 1989. *A natural curiosity*. New York: Penguin.

Dunne, J.S. 1973. *Time and myth: A meditation on storytelling as an exploration of life and death*. Notre Dame, IL: University of Notre Dame Press.

Durrell, L. 1977. Interview. In G. Plimpton (Ed.), *Writers at work: The 'Paris Review' interviews*. Second series, 257–82. London: Penguin.

Eakin, P.J. 1985. *Fictions in autobiography: Studies in the art of self-invention*. Princeton, NJ: Princeton University Press.

Eco, U. 1989. The narrative structure in Fleming. In B. Ashley (Ed.), *The study of popular fiction: A source book*, 124–34. Philadelphia: University of Pennsylvania Press.

Edel, L. 1959. *Literary biography*. New York: Anchor.

– 1973. Introduction. In J. Glassco, *Memoirs of Montparnasse*. Toronto: Oxford University Press.

- 1988. Interview. In G. Plimpton (Ed.), *Writers at work: The 'Paris Review' interviews*. Eighth series, 24–72. London: Penguin.

Edman, I. 1928. *Arts and the man: A short introduction to aesthetics*. New York: Norton.

Eisenstein, H. 1983. *Contemporary feminist thought*. Boston: G.K. Hall.

Ellul, J. 1965. *Propaganda*. New York: Random House.

Ermath, E. 1983. Fictional consensus and female casualties. In C. Heilbrun and M. Higonnet (Eds.), *The representation of women in fiction*, 1–18. Baltimore: Johns Hopkins University Press.

Estés, C.P. 1992. *Women who run with the wolves: Myths and stories of the wild woman archetype*. New York: Ballantine.

Estess, T.L. 1974. The Inenarrable contraption: Reflections on the metaphor of story. *Journal of the American Academy of Religion*, 42(3), 415–34.

Even, M.J. 1987. Why adults learn in different ways. *Lifelong learning: An omnibus of practice and research*, 10(8), 22–7.

Faulkner, W. 1968. *The wild palms*. New York: New American Library.

- 1977. Interview. In M. Cowley (Ed.), *Writers at work: The 'Paris Review' interviews*. First series, 119–41. London: Penguin.

Feinstein, D., S. Krippner, and D. Granger, 1988. Mythmaking and human development. *Journal of Humanistic Psychology*, 28(3), 23–50.

Fergusson, F. 1961. Introductory essay to *Aristotle's Poetics*. Trans. S.H. Butcher. New York: Hill and Wang.

Field, J. 1952. *A life of one's own*. London: Penguin.

Firman, J., and J. Vargiu, 1978. Dimensions of growth. In *Synthesis*, 3–4.

Fisher, D. and P. Brown, 1990. *The book of memories*. New York: Perigree.

Fisher, J. 1989. Teaching 'time': Women's responses to adult development. In F.J. Forman (Ed.), *Taking our time: Feminist perspectives on temporality*, 136–49. Toronto: Pergamon.

Flynn, D. 1991, Spring. Community as story: A comparative study of community in Canada, England, and the Netherlands. *The Rural Sociologist*, 24–35.

Forman, F.J. 1989. Feminizing time: An introduction. In F.J. Forman (Ed.), *Taking our time: Feminist perspectives on temporality*, 1–9. Toronto: Pergamon.

Forster, E.M. 1962. *Aspects of the novel*. London: Penguin.

- 1977. Interview. In M. Cowley (Ed.), *Writers at work: The 'Paris Review' interviews*. First series, 23–35. London: Penguin.

Foucault, M. 1988. *Politics, philosophy, culture: Interviews and other writings, 1977–1984*. New York: Routledge.

Fowler, J.W. 1981. *Stages of faith: The psychology of human development and the quest for meaning*. San Francisco: Harper & Row.

Frick, W.B. 1982. Conceptual foundations of self-actualization: A contribution to motivation theory. *Journal of Humanistic Psychology*, 22(4), 33–52.

Friedman, S.S. 1988. Women's autobiographical selves: Theory and practice. In S. Benstock (Ed.), *The private self: Theory and practice of women's autobiographical writings*, 34–62. Chapel Hill: University of North Carolina Press.

Fritz, R. 1989. *The path of least resistance: Learning to become the creative force in your own life*. New York: Fawcett Columbine.

Frye, J.S. 1986. *Living stories, telling lives: Women and the novel in contemporary experience*. Ann Arbor: University of Michigan Press.

Frye, N. 1963. *The educated imagination*. Toronto: CBC.

– 1966. Fictional modes and forms. In R. Scholes (Ed.), *Approaches to the novel*, 23–42. San Francisco: Chandler.

– 1988. *On education*. Toronto: Fitzhenry & Whiteside.

Gardner, H. 1982, March. The making of a storyteller. In *Psychology Today*, 49–63.

– 1988. Creative lives and creative works: A synthetic scientific approach. In R.J. Sternberg (Ed.), *The nature of creativity: Contemporary psychological perspectives*, 298–321. Cambridge: Cambridge University Press.

– 1990. *Frames of mind: The theory of multiple intelligences*. San Francisco: Basic.

Gardner, J. 1978. *On moral fiction*. New York: Basic.

– 1985. *The art of fiction: Notes on craft for young writers*. New York: Vintage.

Gawain, S. 1982. *Creative visualization*. New York: Bantam.

Gergen, K.J. 1977. The social construction of self-knowledge. In T. Mischel (Ed.), *The self: Psychological and philosophical issues*, 139–69. Oxford: Basil Blackwell.

Gergen, K.J., and M.M. Gergen, 1986. Narrative form and the construction of psychological science. In T.R. Sarbin (Ed.), *Narrative psychology: The storied nature of human conduct*, 22–44. New York: Praeger.

Getzels, J.W. 1985. Creativity and human development. *International encyclopedia of education*, vol. 2, 1093–1100. New York: Pergamon.

Gilkey, L. 1965. *Maker of heaven and earth: The Christian doctrine of creation in the light of modern knowledge*. New York: Doubleday.

Gilligan, C. 1982. *In a different voice*. Cambridge, MA: Harvard University Press.

Glover, J. 1988. *I: The philosophy and psychology of personal identity*. London: Penguin.

Goffman, E. 1959. *The presentation of self in everyday life*. New York: Doubleday Anchor.

Gold, J. 1988. The function of fiction: A biological model. *Novel*, 21(2–3), 252–61.

- 1990. *Read for your life: Literature as a life support system.* Markham, ON: Fitzhenry & Whiteside.

Goodman, N. 1986. *Ways of worldmaking.* Indianapolis, IN: Hackett.

Gould, R. 1978. *Transformations: Growth and change in adult life.* New York: Simon & Schuster.

Greene, M. 1990. The emancipatory power of literature. In J. Mezirow (Ed.), *Fostering critical reflection in adulthood,* 251–68. San Francisco: Jossey-Bass.

Griffin, D.R. 1989. *God and religion in the postmodern world: Essays in postmodern theology.* Albany, NY: SUNY Press.

Groen, R. 1990, October 9. Cross Current. *Globe and Mail,* C1.

Gunn, J.V. 1982. *Autobiography: Towards a poetics of experience.* Philadelphia: University of Pennsylvania Press.

Hall, C. and V.J. Nordby, 1973. *A primer of Jungian psychology.* New York: New American Library.

Hall, D. 1982. Who tells the world's story?: Theology's quest for a partner in dialogue. *Interpretation,* 36(1), 47–53.

Hall, E.T. 1984. *The dance of life: The other dimension of time.* New York: Doubleday.

Hallin, D.C. 1986. We keep America on top of the world. In T. Gitlin (Ed.), *Watching television,* 9–41. New York: Pantheon.

Hamilton, A.C. 1990. *Northrop Frye: Anatomy of his criticism.* Toronto: University of Toronto Press.

Hardy, B. 1968. Towards a poetics of fiction. *Novel,* 2(1), 5–14.

Hare, W. 1979. *Openmindedness and education.* Montreal: McGill-Queen's.

Harman, W. and H. Rheingold. 1984. *Higher creativity: Liberating the unconscious for breakthrough insights.* Los Angeles: Jeremy P. Tarcher.

Harré, R. 1993. Foreword. In J. Shotter, *Cultural politics of everyday life,* vii–viii. Toronto: University of Toronto Press.

Hartshorne, C. 1971. The development of process philosophy. In E.H. Cousins (Ed.), *Process theology: Basic writings,* 47–66. New York: Newman Press.

Hauerwas, S. 1977. *Truthfulness and tragedy: Further investigations into Christian ethics.* Notre Dame: University of Notre Dame Press.

Haught, J.F. 1984. *The cosmic adventure: Science, religion and the quest for purpose.* New York: Paulist Press.

Heilbrun, C. 1988. *Writing a woman's life.* New York: Ballantine.

Henn, T.R. 1956. *The harvest of tragedy.* London: Methuen.

Hesse, H. 1978. *My belief.* London: Triad Panther.

Hillesum, E. 1985. *An interrupted life: The diaries of Etty Hillesum 1941–43.* New York: Washington Square.

Hillman, J. 1975a. The fiction of case history: A round. In J.B. Wiggins (Ed.), *Religion as story*, 123–73. New York: Harper & Row.
– 1975b. *Re-visioning psychology*. New York: Harper & Row.
– 1989. *A blue fire*. New York: Harper & Row.
Hoffer, E. 1951. *The true believer*. New York: Harper & Row.
Hook, S. 1943. *The hero in history: A study in limitation and possibility*. Boston: Beacon.
Houston, J. 1987. *The search for the beloved: Journeys in sacred psychology*. Los Angeles: Jeremy P. Tarcher.
Howe, I. 1989, May 8. The human factor: Are characters like people? *New Republic*, 30–4.
Huddle, D. 1990, October 7. How much of my story is true? *New York Times Book Review*, 15–17, 31.
Hunt, D. 1987. *Beginning with ourselves: In practice, theory, and human affairs*. Cambridge, MA: Brookline Books.
Hutcheon, L. 1989. *The politics of postmodernism*. London: Routledge.
Jackson, P.W., and S. Messick, 1967. The person, the product, and the response: Conceptual problems in the assessment of creativity. In J. Kagan (Ed.), *Creativity and learning*, 1–19. Boston: Beacon.
Jenkins, P. 1989. *Close friends*. New York: Fawcett Crest.
Johnson, B. 1981. Introduction. In J. Derrida, *Dissemination*, vii–xxxiii. Chicago: University of Chicago Press.
Johnston, J. 1993, April 25. Fictions of the self in the making. *New York Times Book Review*, 3, 29, 31, 33.
Jourard, S. 1971. *The transparent self*. New York: Litton Educational Publishing.
Kaplan, J. 1986. The 'real life.' In S.B. Oates (Ed.), *Biography as high adventure: Life-writers speak on their art*, 70–6. Amherst: University of Massachusetts Press.
Kaufman, S.R. 1987. *The ageless self: Sources of meaning in late life*. New York: New American Library.
Kazin, A. 1981. The self as history: Reflections on autobiography. In A.E. Stone (Ed.), *The American autobiography: A collection of critical essays*, 31–43. Englewood Cliffs, NJ: Prentice-Hall.
Keen, E. 1986. Paranoia and cataclysmic narratives. In T.R. Sarbin (Ed.), *Narrative psychology: The storied nature of human conduct*, 174–90. New York: Praeger.
Keen, S. 1970. *To a dancing god*. New York: Harper & Row.
– 1988, December. The stories we live by. *Psychology Today*, 42–7.
– 1991. *Fire in the belly: On being a man*. New York: Bantam.

- 1993. On mythic stories. In C. Simpkinson and A. Simpkinson (Eds.), *Sacred stories: A celebration of the power of stories to transform and heal*, 27–37. San Francisco: HarperCollins.

Keen, S., and A.V. Fox, 1974. *Telling your story: A guide to who you are and who you can be*. Toronto: New American Library.

Kegan, R. 1982. *The evolving self*. Cambridge, MA: Harvard University Press.

Keillor, G. 1986. *We are still married*. London: Penguin.

Kelly, K. 1991. 'Designing perpetual novelty: Selected notes from the Second Artificial Life Conference.' In J. Brockman (Ed.), *Doing science: The reality club*, 1–44. New York: Prentice-Hall.

Kelsey, M.T. 1980. *Adventure inward: Christian growth through personal journal writing*. Minneapolis, MN: Augsburg Publishing House.

Kennedy, E. 1976. *The joy of being human*. New York: Image.

- 1977. *On becoming a counselor: A basic guide for non-professional counselors*. New York: Continuum.

Kenyon, G. 1991. *Homo viator*: Metaphors of aging, authenticity, and meaning. In G. Kenyon, J. Birren, and J. Schroot (Eds.), *Metaphors of aging in science and the humanities*, 17–35. New York: Springer.

Kenyon, G., J. Birren, and J. Schroots (Eds.), 1991. *Metaphors of aging in science and the humanities*. New York: Springer.

Kermode, F. 1966. *The sense of an ending: Studies in the theory of fiction*. New York: Oxford University Press.

- 1980. Secrets and narrative sequence. In W.J.T. Mitchell, (Ed.), *On narrative*, 79–97. Chicago: University of Chicago Press.

Kidd, J.R. 1973. *How adults learn*. New York: Cambridge, Adult Education Company.

Kliever, L.D. 1981. *The shattered spectrum: A survey of contemporary theology*. Atlanta: John Knox Press.

Kopp, S. 1987. *Who am I ... really?: An autobiographical exploration on becoming who you are*. Los Angeles: Jeremy P. Tarcher.

Kuhn, T. 1970. *The structure of scientific revolutions*. Chicago: University of Chicago Press.

Kundera, M. 1988. *The art of the novel*. New York: Harper & Row.

Laing, R.D. 1967. *The politics of experience*. New York: Ballantine.

L'Amour, L. 1989. *Education of a wandering man*. New York: Bantam.

Langer, L.L. 1991. *Holocaust testimonies: The ruins of memory*. New Haven, CT: Yale University Press.

Langs, R. 1988. *Decoding your dreams*. New York: Ballantine.

Larsen, S. 1990. *The mythic imagination: Your quest for meaning through personal mythology*. New York: Bantam.

Lasch, C. 1978. *The culture of narcissism: American life in an age of diminishing expectations.* New York: Norton.

Le Guin, Ursula. 1989a. *Dancing at the edge of the world: Thoughts on words, women, places.* New York: Harper & Row.

– 1989b. *The language of the night.* New York: HarperPerennial.

Leitch, T. 1986. *What stories are: Narrative theory and interpretation.* University Park: Pennsylvania State University Press.

Lessing, D. 1973. *The summer before the dark.* London: Penguin.

Levinson, D.J., C. Darrow, E.B. Klein, M.H. Levinson, and B. McKee, 1978. *The seasons of a man's life.* New York: Ballantine.

Lewis, C.S. 1964. *The last battle.* London: Puffin.

– 1966. On stories. In *Essays presented to Charles Williams*, 90–105. Grand Rapids, MI: Eerdmans.

– 1970. *The problem of pain.* New York: Macmillan.

Lifton, R.J. 1970. *Boundaries: Psychological man in revolution.* New York: Vintage.

Lindaman, E. (Speaker). 1976. Images of the future. *Thesis theological cassettes.* 4(8). Toronto: United Church of Canada.

Lindbergh, A.M. 1955. *Gift from the sea.* New York: Vintage.

Lodge, D. 1988. The novel now: Theories and practices. *Novel*, 21(2–3), 125–38.

Luria, A.R. 1987. *The mind of a mnemonist.* Cambridge, MA: Harvard University Press.

Lynch, G., and D. Rampton (Eds.). 1992. *Short fiction: An introductory anthology.* Toronto: Harcourt Brace Jovanovich.

MacIntyre, A. 1981. *After virtue: A study in moral theory.* London: Duckworth.

MacLean, R., and A. Veniot. 1990. *Terror: Murder and panic in New Brunswick, May–November 1989.* Toronto: McClelland & Stewart.

Macquarrie, J. 1973. *An existentialist theology.* London: Penguin.

Malcolm, J. 1993, August 23 and 30. The silent woman – I. *New Yorker*, 84–159.

Mancusco, J.C. 1986. The acquisition and use of narrative grammar structure. In T.R. Sarbin (Ed.), *Narrative psychology: The storied nature of human conduct*, 91–110. New York: Praeger.

Mann, H., M. Siegler, and H. Osmond, 1972. The psychotypology of time. In H. Yaker, H. Osmond, and F. Cheek (Eds.), *The future of time: Man's temporal environment*, 142–78. Garden City, NY: Anchor.

Mansfield, R.S., and T.V. Busse. 1982. Creativity. *Encyclopedia of educational research*, vol. 2, 385–94. New York: Free Press.

Marchand, P. 1991, April 21. Telling stories. *Saturday Magazine: Toronto Star.*

Margulis, L. 1988. Big trouble in biology: Physiological autopoiesis versus Mechanistic Neo-Darwinism. In J. Brockman (Ed.), *Doing science: The reality club*, 211–35. New York: Prentice-Hall.

Marshall, J. 1969. *Law and psychology in conflict*. Garden City, NY: Anchor.

Maslow, A.H. 1964. *Religions, values, and peak-experiences*. London: Penguin.

– 1968. *Toward a psychology of being*. New York: Van Nostrand.

Maurois, A. 1956. *Aspects of biography*. New York: Appleton-Century-Crofts.

– 1986. Biography as a work of art. In S.B. Oates (Ed.), *Biography as high adventure: Life-writers speak on their art*, 3–17. Amherst: University of Massachusetts Press.

May, R. 1976. *The courage to create*. New York: Bantam.

McGuire, M. 1990. The rhetoric of narrative: A hermeneutic critical theory. In B. Britton and A. Pellegrini (Eds.), *Narrative thought and narrative language*, 219–36. Hillsdale, NJ: Lawrence Erlbaum Associates.

Merton, T. 1972. *Seeds of contemplation*. Wheathampstead, Herts, UK: Anthony Clarke Books.

Mezirow, J. 1978. Perspective transformation. *Adult Education*, 28(2), 100–10.

– 1990. How critical reflection triggers transformative learning. In J. Mezirow (Ed.), *Fostering critical reflection in adulthood*, 1–20. San Francisco: Jossey-Bass.

Miller, H. 1955. Reflections on writing. In B. Ghiselin (Ed.), *The creative process*, 178–85. New York: New American Library.

– 1977. Interview. In G. Plimpton (Ed.), *Writers at work: The 'Paris Review' interviews*. Second series, 165–91. London: Penguin.

Miller, J.B. 1976. *Toward a new psychology of women*. Boston: Beacon.

Mishler, E.G. 1986. *Research interviewing: Context and narrative*. Cambridge, MA: Harvard University Press.

Molinari, V. and R.E. Reichlin, 1984–5. Life review reminiscence in the elderly: A review of the literature. *International Journal of Aging and Human Development*, 20(2), 81–92.

Moltmann, J. 1975. *The experiment hope*. London: SCM Press.

Moore, T. 1992. *Care of the soul: A guide for cultivating depth and sacredness in everyday life*. New York: HarperCollins.

Moustakas, C.E. 1961. *Loneliness*. New York: Prentice-Hall.

– 1967. *Creativity and conformity*. New York: Van Nostrand Reinhold.

Mozart, W.A. [N.d.] 1955. Letter. In B. Ghiselin (Ed.), *The creative process*, 44–5. New York: New American Library.

Mumford, L. 1951. *The conduct of life*. New York: Harcourt Brace Jovanovich.

Murdoch, I. 1967. *Sartre: Romantic rationalist*. London: Fontana.

Napier, N.J. 1993. Living our stories: Discovering and replacing limiting family myths. In C. Simpkinson and A. Simpkinson (Eds.), *Sacred stories:*

A celebration of the power of stories to transform and heal, 143–56. San Francisco: HarperCollins.

Neisser, U. 1986. Nested structure in autobiographical memory. In D. Rubin (Ed.), *Autobiographical memory,* 71–81. New York: Cambridge University Press.

Nierenberg, G.I., and H.H. Calero, 1973. *How to read a person like a book.* Richmond Hill, ON: Simon & Schuster.

Nin, A. 1981. The personal life deeply lived. In A.E. Stone (Ed.), *The American autobiography: A collection of critical essays,* 157–65. Englewood Cliffs, NJ: Prentice-Hall.

Novak, M. 1971. *Ascent of the mountain, flight of the dove.* New York: Harper & Row.

Nussbaum, M. 1989. Narrative emotions: Beckett's genealogy of love. In S. Hauerwas and L.G. Jones (Eds.), *Why narrative?: Readings in narrative theology,* 216–48. Grand Rapids, MI: Eerdmans.

Olney, J. 1972. *Metaphors of self: The meaning of autobiography* Princeton, NJ: Princeton University Press.

– 1980. Autobiography and the cultural moment: A thematic, historical, and bibliographical introduction. In J. Olney (Ed.), *Autobiography: Essays theoretical and critical,* 3–27. Princeton, NJ: Princeton University Press.

Olson, D. R., and N. Torrance (Eds.), 1991. *Literacy and orality.* Cambridge: Cambridge University Press.

Owen, H. 1987. *Spirit: Transformation and development in organizations.* Potomac, MD: Abbott Publishing.

Packard, E. 1982. *The Forbidden Castle.* New York: Bantam.

Palmer, P. 1983. *To know as we are known: A spirituality of education.* San Francisco: Harper & Row.

Pascal, R. 1960. *Design and truth in autobiography.* London: Routledge & Kegan Paul.

Pearson, C.S. 1989. *The hero within: Six archetypes we live by.* San Francisco: Harper & Row.

Peat, F.D. 1987. *Synchronicity: The bridge between matter and mind.* New York: Bantam.

Penelhum, T. 1967. Personal identity. In *The encyclopedia of philosophy,* vol. 6, 95–107. New York: Macmillan.

Pennebaker, J.W. 1990. *Opening up: The healing power of confiding in others.* New York: Avon.

Pirsig, R.M. 1975. *Zen and the art of motorcycle maintenance: An inquiry into values.* New York: Bantam.

Plantinga, T. 1992. *How memory shapes narratives: A philosophical essay on redeeming the past.* Lewiston, NY: Edwin Mellen Press.

Platiel, R. 1990, July 31. Mohawks locked in power struggle. Toronto. *Globe and Mail*, A7.

Poetics. 1987. *Encyclopedia Britannica, Micropedia*, vol. 9, 523.

Polkinghorne, D. 1988. *Narrative knowing and the human sciences*. Albany, NY: SUNY Press.

Polonoff, D. 1987. Self-deception. *Social Research* 54(1), 45–53.

Polster, E. 1987. *Every person's life is worth a novel*. New York: Norton.

Poulet, G. 1956. *Studies in human nature*. Baltimore, MD: Johns Hopkins University Press.

Powell, J. 1984. *The Christian vision: The truth that sets us free*. Allen, TX: Argus Communications.

Powys, J.C. [1929] 1964. *Wolf Solent*. London: Penguin.

Prigogine, I. 1984. Wizard of time. In P. Weintraub (Ed.), *The Omni interviews*, 333–50. New York: Omni Press.

Prince, G. 1987. *A dictionary of narratology*. Lincoln: University of Nebraska Press.

Progoff, I. 1975. *At a journal workshop: The basic text and guide for using the intensive journal*. New York: Dialogue House Library.

– 1985. *The dynamics of hope*. New York: Dialogue House Library.

Rainer, T. 1978. *The new diary*. Los Angeles: Jeremy P. Tarcher.

Rappoport, H. 1990. *Marking time*. New York: Simon & Schuster.

Renza, L.A. 1980. The veto of the imagination: A theory of autobiography. In J. Olney (Ed.), *Autobiography: Essays theoretical and critical*, 268–95. Princeton, NJ: Princeton University Press.

Ricoeur, P. 1980. Narrative time. In W.J.T. Mitchell (Ed.), *On narrative*, 165–86. Chicago: University of Chicago Press.

Rifkin, J. 1987. *Time wars: The primary conflict in human history*. New York: Simon & Schuster.

– 1989. *Entropy: Into the greenhouse world*. New York: Bantam.

Rimmon-Kenan, S. 1983. *Narrative fiction: Contemporary poetics*. London: Routledge.

Rogers, M.F. 1991. *Novels, novelists, and readers: Toward a phenomenological sociology of literature*. Albany, NY: SUNY Press.

Rorty, A.O. 1988. *Mind in action: Essays in the philosophy of mind*. Boston: Beacon.

Rosen, H. 1986. The importance of story. *Language Arts*, 63(3), 226–37.

Ross, R. 1992. *Dancing with a ghost: Exploring Indian reality*. Markham, ON: Octopus Publishing Group.

Rothenberg, A., and C.R. Hausman (Eds.), 1976. *The creativity question*. Durham, NC: Duke University Press.

Roy, A. 1984. Physics and PSI. In P. Brookesmith (Ed.), *The enigma of time*, 21–36. London: Orbis Publishing.

Rubin, D. (Ed.), 1986. *Autobiographical memory*. New York: Cambridge University Press.

Runyan, W.M. 1984. *Life histories and psychobiography: Explorations in theory and method*. New York: Oxford University Press.

Sacks, O. 1985. *The man who mistook his wife for a hat, and other clinical tales*. New York: Summit.

Sagan F. 1977. Interview. In M. Cowley (Ed.), *Writers at work: The 'Paris Review' interviews*. First series, 301–9. London: Penguin.

Sampson, E. 1989. The deconstruction of the self. In J. Shotter and K. Gergen (Eds.), *Texts of identity*, 1–19. London: SAGE Publications.

Sarbin, T.R. 1986a. Introduction and overview. In T.R. Sarbin (Ed.), *Narrative psychology: The storied nature of human conduct*, ix–xviii. New York: Praeger.

Sarbin, T.R. 1986b. The narrative as a root metaphor for psychology. In T.R. Sarbin (Ed.), *Narrative psychology: The storied nature of human conduct*, 3–21. New York: Praeger.

Sarton, M. 1977. *Journal of a solitude*. New York: Norton.

– 1981. *The house by the sea*. New York: Norton.

– 1986. *Recovering: A journal*. New York: Norton.

Sartre, J.-P. [1938] 1965. *Nausea*. Trans. Robert Baldick. London: Penguin.

– 1968. In E. Fromm and R. Xirau (Eds.), *The nature of man*, 313–19. New York: Macmillan.

Schafer, R. 1980. Narration in the psychoanalytic dialogue. In W.J.T. Mitchell (Ed.), *On narrative*, 25–49. Chicago: University of Chicago Press.

– 1983. *The analytic attitude*. New York: Basic.

– 1989. The sense of an answer. In R. Cohen (Ed.), *Future literary theory*, 188–207. New York: Routledge.

– 1992. *Retelling a life*. New York: Basic.

Schank, R.C. 1983, April. A conversation with Roger Schank. *Psychology Today*, 28–36.

– 1990. *Tell me a story: A new look at real and artificial memory*. New York: Scribner's.

Schank, R.C. and R.P. Abelson, 1977. *Scripts, plans, goals, and understanding: An inquiry into human knowledge structures*. Hillsdale, NJ: Lawrence Erlbaum Associates.

Scheibe, K.E. 1986. Self-narratives and adventure. In T.R. Sarbin (Ed.), *Narrative psychology: The storied nature of human conduct*, 129–51. New York: Praeger.

Scholes, R. and R. Kellogg, 1966. *The nature of narrative*. New York: Oxford
  University Press.
Scott-Maxwell, F. 1968. *The measure of my days*. London: Penguin.
Selden, R. 1989. *A reader's guide to contemporary literary theory*. Lexington:
  University Press of Kentucky.
Sheldrake, R. 1989. *The presence of the past: Morphic resonance and the habits of
  nature*. New York: Vintage.
Shiff, R. 1979. Art and life: A metaphoric relationship. In S. Sacks (Ed.), *On
  metaphor*, 105–20. Chicago: University of Chicago Press.
Shoemaker, S. 1967. Memory. *The encyclopedia of philosophy*, vol. 5, 265– 74.
  New York: Macmillan.
– 1975. Personal identity and memory. In J. Perry (Ed.), *Personal identity*,
  119–34. Los Angeles: University of California Press.
Shotter, J. 1975. *Images of man in psychological research*. London: Methuen.
– 1993. *Cultural politics of everyday life*. Toronto: University of Toronto Press.
Shotter, J. and K.J. Gergen (Eds.). 1989. *Texts of identity*. London: SAGE
  Publications.
Shumaker, W. 1966. *Literature and the irrational: A study in anthropological
  backgrounds*. New York: Washington Square.
Smith, S. 1987. *A poetics of women's autobiography: Marginality and the fictions
  of self-representation*. Bloomington: Indiana University Press.
Spence, D. 1986. Narrative smoothing and clinical wisdom. In T.R. Sarbin
  (Ed.), *Narrative psychology: The storied nature of human conduct*, 211–32.
  New York: Praeger.
Spender, D. 1980. *Man made language*. London: Routledge & Kegan Paul.
Stainton Rogers, R. and W. Stainton Rogers, 1992. *Stories of childhood:
  Shifting agendas of child concern*. Toronto: University of Toronto Press.
Steele, R.S. 1986. Deconstructing history: Toward a systematic criticism of
  psychological narratives. In T.R. Sarbin (Ed.), *Narrative psychology: The
  storied nature of human conduct*, 256–75. New York: Praeger.
Steinbeck, J. 1970. *Journal of a novel: The East of Eden letters*. London: Pan.
– 1972. *Travels with Charley*. Toronto: Bantam.
Steiner, C.M. 1979. *Scripts people live: Transactional analysis of life scripts*. New
  York: Bantam.
Storr, A. 1988. *Solitude: A return to the self*. New York: Ballantine.
Stroup, G.W. 1981. *The promise of narrative theology*. Atlanta: John Knox Press.
Surmelian, L. 1969. *Techniques of fiction writing: Measure and madness*. Garden
  City, NY: Anchor.
Swimme, B. and T. Berry, 1992. *The universe story: From the primordial flaring*

forth to the ecozoic era – a celebration of the unfolding of the cosmos. San Francisco: HarperCollins.

Talbot, M. 1992. *The holographic universe.* New York: Bantam.

Tannen, D. 1990. *You just don't understand: Women and men in conversation.* New York: Ballantine.

Tannenbaum, A.J. 1985. Creativity: Educational programs. *International encyclopedia of education,* vol. 2, 1100–3. New York: Pergamon.

Tappan, M.B., and L.M. Brown, 1989. Stories told and lessons learned: Toward a narrative approach to moral development and moral education. *Harvard Educational Review,* 59(2), 182–205.

Tarman, V.I. 1988. Autobiography: The negotiation of a lifetime. *International Journal of Aging and Human Development,* 27(3), 171–91.

Taylor, M.C. 1984. *Erring: A postmodern a/theology.* Chicago: University of Chicago Press.

Teselle, S.M. 1975a. *Speaking in parables: A study in metaphor and theology.* Philadelphia: Fortress Press.

– 1975b. The experience of coming to belief. *Theology Today,* 32(2), 159–65.

Thomas, A. 1985. Learning and time. *Canadian Journal of University Continuing Education,* 89–98.

– 1992. *Beyond education.* San Francisco: Jossey-Bass.

Thomas, L. 1987. A long line of cells. In W. Zinsser (Ed.), *Inventing the truth: The art and craft of memoir,* 127–48. Boston: Houghton Mifflin.

Thrall, W.F., A. Hibbard, and C.H. Holman, 1960. *A handbook to literature.* New York: Odyssey Press.

Thurber, J. 1977. Interview. In M. Cowley (Ed.), *Writers at work: The 'Paris Review' interviews.* First series, 83–98. London: Penguin.

Tierney, R.J. and M. Gee, 1990. Reading comprehension: Readers, authors, and the world of the text. In D. Bogdan and S.B. Straw (Eds.), *Beyond communication: Reading comprehension and criticism,* 197–209. Portsmouth, NH: Boynton/Cook Heinemann.

Tompkins, G.E. 1982. Seven reasons why children should write stories. *Language Arts,* 59(7), 718–21.

Torrance, E.P. 1967. Scientific views of creativity and factors affecting its growth. In J. Kagan (Ed.), *Creativity and learning,* 73–91. Boston: Beacon.

Tough, A. 1971. *The adult's learning projects: A fresh approach to theory and practice in adult learning.* Toronto: OISE Press.

Toulmin, S.E. 1977. Self-knowledge and knowledge of the 'self.' In T. Mischel (Ed.), *The self: Psychological and philosophical issues,* 291–317. Oxford: Basil Blackwell.

Tournier, P. 1965. *The adventure of living*. Trans. E. Hudson. San Francisco: Harper & Row.

Treffert, D.A. 1989. *Extraordinary people: Understanding savant syndrome*. New York: Harper & Row.

Truitt, A. 1987. *Turn: The journal of an artist*. London: Penguin.

Updike, J. 1989. *Self-consciousness: Memoirs*. New York: Fawcett Crest.

Van Daele, C. 1990. *Making words count: The experience and meaning of the diary in women's lives*. Unpublished doctoral dissertation, University of Toronto.

Van Kaam, A. 1972. *On being yourself: Reflections on spirituality and originality*. Denville, NJ: Dimension Books.

- 1974. *Spirituality and the gentle life*. Denville, NJ: Dimension Books.

Vargiu, J. 1978. Subpersonalities. *Synthesis*, 1, 60–3, 73–89.

Von Franz, M.-L. and F. Boa. 1988. *The way of the dream*. Toronto: Windrose Films.

Watts, A. 1957. *The way of zen*. New York: Vintage.

Waugh, E. 1962. *Brideshead revisited*. London: Penguin.

Weinberg, G. 1978. *Self-creation*. New York: St Martin's.

Weintraub, K.J. 1975, June. Autobiography and historical consciousness. *Critical Inquiry*, 821–48.

Weisberg, R.W. 1986. *Creativity: Genius and other myths*. New York: Freeman.

Welton, M. 1991. *Seeing the light: Christian conversion and conscientization*. Unpublished manuscript.

White, H. 1980. The value of narrativity in the representation of reality. In W.J.T. Mitchell (Ed.), *On narrative*, 1–23. Chicago: University of Chicago Press.

White, M., and D. Epston, 1990. *Narrative means to therapeutic ends*. New York: Norton.

Whitehead, A.N. [1929] 1967. *The aims of education and other essays*. New York: Free Press.

Wiebe, R. (Ed.), 1970. *The story-makers*. Toronto: Macmillan.

Wiesel, E. 1988. Interview. In G. Plimpton (Ed.), *Writers at work: The 'Paris Review' interviews*. Eighth series, 225–64. London: Penguin.

Wiggins, J.B. (Ed.), 1975. *Religion as story*. New York: Harper and Row.

Winchester, I. 1983. Creation and creativity in art and science. *Interchange*, 16(1), 70–6.

Winquist, C.E. 1974. The act of storytelling and the self's homecoming. *Journal of the American Academy of Religion*, 42(1), 101–13.

- 1980. *Practical hermeneutics: A revised agenda for the ministry*. Chico, CA: Scholars Press.

Witherell, C. 1991. The self in narrative: A journey into paradox. In C. Witherell and N. Noddings (Eds.), *Stories lives tell: Narrative and dialogue in education*, 83–95. New York: Teachers College Press.

Wolfe, T. 1983. *The autobiography of an American novelist*. Cambridge, MA: Harvard University Press.

Woolf, V. 1966. Mr. Bennett and Mrs. Brown. In R. Scholes (Ed.), *Approaches to the novel: Materials for a poetics*, 187–206. San Francisco: Chandler.

– [1929] 1977. *A room of one's own*. London: Grafton.

Wright, W. 1989. Sixguns and society: A structural study of the Western. In B. Ashley (Ed.), *The study of popular fiction: A source book*, 105–7. Philadelphia: University of Pennsylvania Press.

Wyatt, F. 1986. The narrative in psychoanalysis: Psychoanalytic notes on storytelling, listening, and interpreting. In T.R. Sarbin (Ed.), *Narrative psychology: The storied nature of human conduct*, 193–210. New York: Praeger.

Young, L.B. 1986. *The unfinished universe*. New York: Simon & Schuster.

Zahn, J.C. 1966. Creativity research and its implications for adult education. For *U.S. Department of Health, Education, and Welfare*.

Zemke, R. 1990, March. Storytelling: Back to a basic. *Training*, 44–50.

Zill, N. and M. Winglee, 1990. *Who reads literature?: The future of the United States as a nation of readers*. Washington, DC: Seven Locks Press.

Zinsser, W. (Ed.), 1987. *Inventing the truth: The art and craft of memoir*. Boston: Houghton Mifflin.

Index

Because of the interdisciplinary dimension of this book, key terms like 'plot' and 'story,' and freshly coined ones like 're-storying' and 'novel-ty,' have been used throughout it to refer to both the specific realm of literature and the general one of everyday life. In the determining of many headings and subheadings in this index, it has been impossible to separate these two frames of reference. To reduce the duplication to which this usage leads, I have included cross-references for as many entries as possible and cast a handful of headings in both singular and plural form – for instance, 'dream(s),' 'hero(es),' and 'story(ies).'

Adler, Alfred, 307

adult development: bias toward improvement in, 147–9; as disillusionment, 236, 285; and emplotment, 137; phases vs. stages vs. chapters in, 147–9; self-actualization as myth for, 355; and storied dimensions of meaning-making, 350–1. *See also* adult education; adulthood; maturity.

adult education, 5–6, 350–2; care dimension of, 351; and critical reflection, 244; criticisms of, 355; and critique of larger stories, 351–2; and forgetting, 299; issues raised by story model, 350–2; and perspective transformation, 150–1, 243–4, 351; and re-storying, 242–4, 351. *See also* education; learning.

adulthood, 4; vs. childhood, 223; and episodic memory, 213; and threshold of story, 152, 220–3, 343

adventure, 21, 97, 133, 336; and *adventus*, 34; and *agon*, 97; American thirst for, 324; and art of living, 75–6, 343; 'Choose-Your-Own,' 183–4; Christian story as, 347; discerning the nature of our story as, 206; in dreams, 63; each life as, 11, 75–6; and education, 75; Sartre on, 92. *See also* genre(s); therapy.

ageing: and changes in self-storying, 152; and de-composing a life-story, 349; and desire for sequel, 150; and de-storying, 290–1; and identification with fictional heroes, 169; and life outlasting life-story, 348; and maturity, 268; and memory loss, 211; and old person as library, 184–5; thickening of memory during, 216; and untold stories, 289–91. *See also* death; gerontology; storytelling; wisdom.

in, 140; and narration, 89–90; 'plotting' in writing of, 131; and re-storying, 256–7; and secular redemption myths, 231; and storytelling, 131; written by victors, 100. *See also* outside-in story; personal history; story(ies).
Hoffer, Eric, 180
Homo fictus, 155–6
Hopi Indians, 181
Horney, Karen, 254
Houston, Jean, 207, 250, 254
Howe, Irving, 70
human nature: fictional side of, 4, 12, 263, 332, 354; and need for news, 97–8; and self-culture, 71; and storying style, 327–8
Hutcheon, Linda, 139, 143, 232, 258
Huxley, Aldous, 51

ideology: defined, 199; and personhood, 199
impression(s): management, 190, 248, 287; fictional characters as of real persons, 153; as outside-in story, 56–7; and storyotyping, 133–4
improvisation: and art of living, 76–7; and women's lives, 76–7
individuality: and creativity, 28; Dewey on, 35; and experience, 51; and novel-ty, 35, 257–8; and temporality, 35
inside story: defined, 49–52; as expectation, 53; as experience, 49–54; and future, 53; and past, 52–3; as personal, practical knowledge, 51; as semi-conscious monologue, 52; as 'story,' 52. *See also* experience(s); self; soul.

inside-out story, 58–60; and auto-biography, 60; as life-story, 58. *See also* expression; life-story.
intelligence: and art, 70; as ability to tell (and listen to) stories, 66, 265, 311
intimacy: and couple story, 106–7; and discretion vs. disclosure in, 108, 282; and re-storying, 236–7; and storying, 103–8; and untold stories, 287
irony: and differences between people, 182–3, 330; as mode of fiction, 163; and point of view, 182–4; and self-reading, 182–3. *See also* genre(s).

James, Henry, 122, 124, 160, 315, 341, 356
James, William, 27
Jenkins, Peter, 133
Jesus (the historical), 186
jokes, 100, 130, 282
Jourard, Sidney, 51, 60, 229, 247, 281, 336
journal-keeping: in education, 351; and intentional re-storying, 240; as self-care, 248; and self-creation, 222; in therapy, 349; and untold stories, 282; and versions of self-story, 189; women vs. men and, 297–8. *See also* expression; inside-out story.
Joyce, James, 336
Jung, Carl, 31, 142, 177, 207, 247, 272, 355

Kant, Immanuel, 209
Kaufman, Sharon, 54, 56, 187
Kazin, Alfred, 222